The Female Consumer

THE FEMALE CONSUMER

Rosemary Scott

Associated Business Programmes
London

*English language edition, except USA and Canada
published by*
Associated Business Programmes Ltd
17 Buckingham Gate, London SW1

Published in the USA and Canada by
Halsted Press, a Division of
John Wiley & Sons Inc
New York

First published 1976

Printed and bound in Great Britain by R. J. Acford Ltd.
Industrial Estate, Chichester, Sussex

ISBN 0 85227 044 5

TO MY MOTHER, IRENE, AND MY FATHER, WILLIAM

WITH LOVE

Contents

Introduction

Women are not economically powerless. They own wealth in their own right, some £30,000 million; they are important investors, share-holders, trust and capital holders. They contribute directly to the work-force and two-thirds of the archetypal female consumers work in and out of the home*. Yet, in these areas men still predominate, and the female contribution while considerable is still subordinate to that of man, and will be for a little while yet.

In the woman's function as consumer, however, she is indomitable and it is indisputable that the phenomenon of female consumption in Western society is marked by two overriding principles: first, that it is massive and second, that it is both frequent and extensive.

In the first case, we must note that expenditures which she controls directly make up the largest sectors in consumer expenditure indices. In 1973, consumer expenditure on all sectors was £44,759 million, just over 70% of the gross national product at factor cost. Of this expenditure two of the largest categories carrying 28% of the total, food, and clothing and footwear, goods valued at £12,230 million, were bought almost entirely by women.

Apart from these sectors women were also responsible for the purchase of most household and chemist goods, and were largely responsible for the actual decision to buy most goods in the consumer durable section, adding further control over expenditure of £6,000 million per annum. In fact, taking the first five categories of consumer expenditure by value, we can estimate that the balance of expenditure and influences on expenditure by sex would be, female to male, at least 54–45%†.

All these estimates of expenditure are, however, in money/value terms and in order to do justice to the second principle of female consumption, its frequency and extent, it is important to note the number of individual purchasing decisions quite apart from simple value. One durable item, for example, which may represent a male or female purchase represents one

---

* *See* Table 68, *Social Trends*, HMSO (1974); *Woman, Wife and Worker*, HMSO (1969) and Census of Population 1972.
† *See* Table 159 in *Facts and Focus*, Central Statistical Office (1974).

purchase decision. Yet, several thousand food purchase decisions would be required to make up the same financial value of a durable item and in these decisions, women predominate.

In fact, taking this angle rather than purchase value, it is estimated that women in Britain and America decide 75–90% of consumer sales. Yet, in addition to the two principles underlying female consumption which we have just observed, there is one other factor which must be noted. Parallel to these two principles but, in a sense, more pervasive, there is the fact that female consumption, for all that it is massive, rhythmic and essential and despite the fact that without it the consumer marketing industry would disintegrate with startling rapidity, is a phenomenon which is so taken for granted that it is, in effect, denied.

This denial is demonstrated by the myriad marketing text books, manuals and reports which forbear to make one mention of the woman buyer, although the entire thesis of their work may revolve around her.

It is demonstrated by all advertisers and marketers who persist in observing the female consumer through their, usually male, eyes and often smug and ignorant preconceptions; who insist on portraying her and communicating to her in their terms, instead of hers.

It is denied by the politicians and retailers who continue to make patronising references to the 'housewife' as a goddess of anti-inflationary measures yet who, at the same time, refuse her simple legal rights such as being responsible for her own hire purchase agreements.

It is denied by the lecturers, the business consultants, the trade magazines, the researchers, the managing directors and the data clerks, who play around with the mechanics of the marketing organisation and forget that the starting handle does not lie with them but in a shopping basket held firmly and capably by a woman; the female consumer of whom they really know little and of whose real welfare they care less, if at all.

If this book has any purpose, then, it is to act principally as counter-balance to this vast tradition of denial.

Yet, because this is a sortie into what could be termed an institution it does not, by any means, suggest a bland reiteration of the obvious. This study is not just a reformulation of the old, old story, a dusting round the edges of the standard stereotype. It is a description of the female consumer with a difference in that it sees her function through the emphasis of her vantage point and *en route,* it is to a large extent a criticism and reformulation of many of the assumptions and principles which the advertising and marketing industry has held about the woman buyer for far too long. These conventions will be challenged, evidence shaken out and reformulated, new principles contended, old information re-presented *in toto* and some basic criticisms made.

The seven sections of this book will each take differing approaches to the female consumer. In a sense they are integrative; in a sense, they are separable. In no way are they homogeneous.

The first four sections are largely descriptive and establish the extent, the nature and the variety of female consumer response and the influences working on that response. They will look at how the woman buys, both as housewife and as an individual woman in her own right; how she dominates some markets and how she is encroaching on others.

The last three sections will still be descriptive to an extent but also more critical of the approach by marketers and advertisers to the female consumer and their attitude towards her. These chapters will show how the female consumer, the marketer and the advertiser relate within the concepts of mass media, mass culture, prescriptive imagery and social responsibility. They will also suggest to the marketer and advertiser where weakness rather than strength can be found in the mechanics of the consumer market, particularly within the research processes.

In total, it is hoped that the book will leave the reader with an impression of the complexity, the multi-faceted nature of female consumer behaviour and that it will demonstrate the ingenuity, the strength and intelligence of the woman in the buying function*.

It is hoped, in particular, that it will render obsolete any book, attitude or research which seeks to deny her importance, her contribution or her vitality and, in particular, any study which sees her as incidental rather than central to the thesis of consumer marketing.

In a sense, the book is a challenge to everyone connected with the consumer marketing industry to have the courage to take another look and think again. After all, without the female consumer they would be out of a job tomorrow. It is time they not only accepted this fact, but started to look at some of its implications.

---

* In addition to the data given in this book, a supplement has been especially compiled bringing together from a wide variety of sources all the relevant statistics on the female consumer and her markets. Copies of *The Female Consumer Statistical Supplement* are available from the publisher only (£20).

PART I

Shops and Products

This first section of *The Female Consumer* is largely a descriptive one. It seeks to draw together the main trends and factors which characterise the housewife's shopping environment, her use of it and some mechanical variables associated with certain important, if selected, markets and products. To some extent, it will represent a swift sortie through the self-evident although there have been few occasions when the data have been filtrated in such a way. This will provide a base for the analyses and criticisms which will follow.

For the sake of clarity, an arbitrary division is made between food and non-food markets—although there is some evidence that the housewife divides her shopping in a similar way (*see* Part II). Two chapters devoted to each market will examine shopping methods and shops, and certain important products respectively.

Generally, it is important to see the shops as the female consumer's workshops, the shopping methods, habits and routines as her tools. In Part II we shall see the skill and behavioural variables which circumscribe this environment.

1. Shopping and Shops—the Food Market

SHOPPING

Food shopping for the female consumer has a contradictory function. On the one hand survey evidence seems to concur on its functional, chore-like and menial characteristics—an unavoidable housewifely duty*—while other evidence also stresses the provider-role characteristics tied up with its base in nurturance and life-sustenance. Within this unbalanced framework (which has really been grossly neglected as a problem by marketing research in favour of the juicier morsels assumed to be found in psychographic shopper variables) there are nevertheless certain clear, predictable shopping rhythms to be discerned.

Approaching these rhythms from the more mechanical angles (behavioural aspects are examined in Part II) certain observations can be noted on the housewife's food and grocery shopping.

Time Spent on Food Preparation

Of all the time that they spend on food preparation during the week, housewives spend 1·7 hours in shopping for it compared to 0·9 hours planning it and 0·5 hours putting away what they buy. The longest activities involved with food are the washing and tidying (7·1 hours) the cooking (9·0 hours) and the eating of it (6·5 hours)[1].

Pattern of Food Shopping

Shopping for food takes place most often on Thursday, Friday and Saturday, with 55% of housewives choosing Friday and Saturday for their major purchases. If small household goods are included then this proportion increases to 64% (see Table 1:1). In addition, the following have been observed:

1. Those housewives with children aged 5–15 years are slightly more likely to shop on Fridays than those with children of other ages.
2. Women with husbands of 29 years or less but no children, are more likely to do shopping on a Saturday than other age groups with children,

---

* See Part II, chapter 5.

3

probably reflecting a greater tendency for both partners in this sector to work during the week.

3. Women in Class C2 are more likely to do shopping on a Friday than other class groups.

4. Women in Scotland are more likely to divide their time relatively equally between the two days, Friday and Saturday, than in any other region.

In general, however, Friday is consistently the most important day for food purchases when these are combined with other small, household goods although, if food is purchased alone, (*see* Table 1:1) which is an unlikely

Table 1:1 Consumers' Expenditure— the Importance of Different Shopping Days

A. No. of days a week household is shopped for:	6 or 7 days	4 or 5 days	3 days		2 days	1 day		Av. Amt.	
All households (100%)	40	14	17		20	11		Week £	Main day £

B. Days any shopping done (%)	Mon 54	Tue 69	Wed 58	Thu 61	Fri 80	Sat 68	Sun 5	8·27	

C. Main shopping day (%)	2	5	3	12	40	24	(n)	3·93	

	(%)	(%)	(%)	(%)	(%)	(%)	(%)		(%)
Married with children*									
Age of eldest: 4 or less	1	6	2	13	47	23	–	8·81	51
5–15	1	4	4	13	50	23	–	10·52	50
16–20	1	4	5	13	44	27	–	11·95	48
Married w/o children									
Age of husband: 29 or less	–	2	2	9	36	37	–	7·54	50
30–64	1	5	4	11	41	26	(n)	8·32	49
65 & over	3	10	5	17	36	13	–	6·43	43
No married couple	3	5	2	9	28	24	(n)	5·15	41

Social class: AB	1	8	4	12	39	15	–	9·81	45
C_1	1	6	3	12	39	24	–	8·39	50
C_2	1	3	3	12	44	26	–	9·10	49
DE	3	5	3	11	37	25	(n)	6·96	46

Region: London and SE	1	8	4	12	38	21	(n)	8·44	47
SW and Wales	3	4	4	10	39	19	–	8·05	44
Midlands	1	4	3	8	42	29	–	8·28	52
N. West	2	6	3	15	42	21	–	8·38	47
NE and North	2	3	2	14	41	27	(n)	7·87	49
Scotland	2	1	1	10	35	30	–	8·36	45
% Weekly Expenditure on all Food	8	11	10	14	26	28	3	–	–

*Children in this analysis are aged 20 or under.

Source: *Daily Mirror* Readership, Income and Consumption Study (1971).

situation, then Saturday would become the major day. It is also interesting to note that this shopping pattern has remained relatively unchanged since 1962 when 85% of shopping purchases were made on Thursday, Friday and Saturday compared to 79% in 1966 and 76% in 1971. The biggest change has occurred in the importance of the Thursday which has declined over the period; otherwise, Friday has maintained the same level of purchase and Saturday has increased its rate*.

Nevertheless, given this general pattern of food shopping, there are more specific patterns in days of purchase for different food items.
For example:

1. Frozen foods are more often bought on a Thursday, compared to a Saturday for jellies.
2. Bread is purchased fairly consistently throughout the week with a peaking on Saturday, which is a similar pattern for packet-crisps and chips.
3. Snack meals are more often bought on a Tuesday than any other day except Saturday, while margarine and butter follow the common pattern of highest purchase on Friday and Saturday †.

Times of Food Purchase

Within any one day the most common time for food purchase is 9–12 a.m. and 2–4 p.m. for non- and part-time working housewives, while those who work full-time prefer to shop between 9–12 a.m., 12–2 p.m. and 4–6 p.m. † †

Shopping Trips

During an average week, the housewife will make at least three grocery trips. Four out of ten housewives shop daily for necessities and five out of ten shop more than four times a week. Only 30% of housewives have managed to restrict their shopping to once or twice a week (*see* Table 1:1).

Of these trips at least one will be a major trip, usually to a supermarket and two-thirds of housewives will use a supermarket regularly for food purchases. The other smaller trips are usually concentrated in various food independents. Only 2% of households, biased towards ABs and Southern England, do infrequent bulk-buying.

The *IPC* survey for the *Daily Mirror* in 1973 says:

It remains to be seen whether out-of-town shopping areas with parking facilities can significantly increase the trend towards bulk buying. It could be argued that 11% of households usually shopping only one day per week is, in fact, indicative of such a trend, but if so, the conclusion would seem to be that this is an area where change is coming about quite slowly, compared with North America.

---

* *IPC Consumer Marketing Manual* (1973).
  † *IPC Consumer Marketing Manual* (1974); 'Odhams Branded Food Survey', (1968).
  † † Watford Survey (1973)[2].

Two other observations which can be made on shopping frequency are that:

1. The regularity of shopping trips indicates that more than half of households are 'available' to the retail trade *on every day of the week except Sunday.* 80% of shoppers were about on Fridays but 54% said they did some shopping on Mondays.
2. The rate at which women shop has actually increased since 1962: 54% of women made more than four shopping trips and 11% only one in 1971 compared to 21% and 27% respectively in 1962. This is despite the meteoric rises in frozen food purchases and convenience foods for long shelf storage. Any trends toward fewer trips and bulk storage must, correspondingly, be viewed as still in their infancy*.

Shopping Trips

In terms of area, most housewives will shop locally for minor shopping trips but often consider a shopping trip to another area a necessity for the major expedition. This major trip will often involve use of the family car, and attract several family members, including the husband. A *Daily Mirror* Survey in 1974, for example, found that husbands, particularly in the over-65 and under-35 age group, were frequently prepared to help their wives with the main shopping trip. 63% did some major household and food shopping with their wives and 17% shopped for food on their own at least once a week.

When the major trip is to a super- or hyper-market retail outlet then women will often travel by car. Where the journey is shorter, then she will prefer foot or bus*.

Nevertheless, according to a survey by Hillier 1971[3] on 'out-of-town' shopping centres more women are travelling further to shop. He found in his survey that 53% of shoppers travelled for 10 minutes, 48% of whom travelled 2–3 miles. Women who owned car licences (20% at the time of the survey) were particularly well-favoured towards 'one-stop' centres. In addition, a survey on a 'Woolco' store found that 32% of women who lived less than half mile from the store still travelled there by car†.

That distance travelled is an important factor in store management was noted by a survey for Fine Fare which showed that as much trade (42%) came from customers living less than a mile from the store, as those who travelled 1–10 miles (49%)[14].

Certainly, for the woman, shopping expeditions represent the main reason for all journeys that she makes, with those associated with work, lying

---

* *IPC Consumer Marketing Manual* (1973).
† Woolco, Thornaby, 'A Study of an Out of Town Shopping Centre' (1973), Retail Outlets Research Unit, Manchester Business School.

second. These trips associated with shopping vary from 18–37% of journeys —depending on the age of the woman*.

Once in the supermarket (comparable figures are not available for other shops), the housewife has been found to display certain 'average' behaviour characteristics. For example, she tends to buy at least 30 product units and spends about 22 minutes passing through the store. Of the total shopping trip, 70% of the time is spent actually in the store, shopping[1].

Shop Loyalty

Despite the relatively high frequency of shopping trips the housewife will still tend to visit very few different shops. One estimate suggested that 70% of weekly food shopping trips were 'one-shop' trips with the housewife mainly returning to the same shop each time (1966)[4]. Another estimate suggested that 80% of housewives do their shopping in an average week at only one or two shops (1966)[5]. Bucklin (1966)[6] in a study of American housewives found a similar pattern in that the housewife was found to average three shop visits per week which included two different shops in one week and just over three in three weeks. Seggev (1970)[7] in a study of nine different product groups found that usually only three different shops were used by the housewife *over a 20-week period.* Where there was variation it was product-based.

Nevertheless, this high level of shop loyalty may, to some extent, depend on what shops are available in an area and the awareness by the housewife of other outlets in her district.

In a survey quoted by Simmons (1972)[8] it was found that while 82% of housewives knew of a Co-op in their district only 41% knew of a Tesco and 22% a Sainsbury. Within one group of shops, the Co-ops, there were even regional variations of awareness levels so that those housewives in the East Midlands were more likely to know of a Co-op in their district than those in Wales.

Shop loyalty will, however, also relate to factors which the housewife associates with a particular shop and examples of these were noted in surveys in 1962 and 1966 [9,5].

A comparison of the results of these two surveys indicated the increasing importance of 'a wide range of cut-prices' and 'self-service' although there was also a marked increase in awareness of the advantage of delivery as supermarkets (with no delivery service) became more common.

Another comparison between different types of stores shows that housewives value the nearness to home in the case of independents, the range of goods in the case of multiples, the range of cut-prices in the supermarkets and the dividend in the Co-op. Particularly low on the list come cleanliness

---

* National Travel Survey (1973).

in the case of supermarkets, friendliness in the case of Co-ops, the range of goods in the independents and the range of cut-prices in the multiples[5].

Finally, two important factors should be noted about food shopping which will be examined in more detail in Part II. First, despite more help by her husband and family, it is still the job of the housewife to do the shopping. It is she who ultimately plans and takes responsibility for food and household purchases. In the *Daily Mirror* survey of 1973[10] it was found that in 9 out of 10 households, food and household stores were bought by the woman of the house regardless of whether she worked or not. Second, food shopping is a necessity rather than a pleasure. Compared to shopping for certain non-food goods such as clothing and larger items such as consumer durables, which we shall describe later, food shopping is often seen as a chore to be accomplished as efficiently and painlessly as possible.

THE SHOPS

In the *Annual Review of Retailing*[13] food shops' sales were estimated for 1973 at about £8,200 million, an increase of £900 million and about a 12·6% increase on 1972. This is in value terms. In volume terms the effects of inflation and general cutbacks had started to show an effect in a slight reduction in volume sales as opposed to the steady maintenance of volume over the previous few years.

Food shops did better than in 1972 but the increase was just below average so that their share of total retail sales was down from 41·0% to about 40·8%. Nevertheless, household spending in the UK averaged £39·43 a week in 1973 according to Family Expenditure Survey figures and food accounted for the biggest slice of this at 24·4%. Regionally, the South-East household spent the most but the smallest amount of its budget: 23·1% compared to Northern Ireland at 28·5%. This is in line with Engels law which predicts that the more affluent a region then the less as a proportion it spends on food. In the case of the South East the average spent per household on all family expenditure is over £40 while Northern Ireland is the lowest but one, at £31·66.

Highest individual expenditures in the food category are for beef* and veal*, poultry*, milk*, biscuits/cakes*, bread*, and alcoholic drink*.

Over time, there has, however, been a decrease in the proportion of food spent in total household spending as households have had available increasing amounts of discretionary income. The proportion of 24·4% in 1973 compares with 27·8% as recently as 1965–7. In contrast, the spending on alcoholic drink has increased steadily over the years as a proportion of household expenditure, which emphasises a shift towards 'luxury' goods*.

---

* Family Expenditure Survey, HMSO (1973).

Specialist Food Shops

Shops which sold nothing but food recorded total sales of £2,825 million in 1972 and of these off-licences took £390 million, bakers and fishmongers, £362 million and £97 million respectively, butchers, £974 million, green-grocers £374 million and dairies, £630 million. The total number of outlets in this category is, however, declining in face of the onslaught by grocers and supermarkets. In 1971 there were just over 94,000 specialist food shops, some 10,000 less than in 1966 and of these dairies, for example, lost 4·7%, bakers 4·0% and off-licences 9·5%. Turnover per outlet, as one would expect, rose in certain of the independent categories. Off-licences, for example, raised their average turnover per outlet by 80% between 1966 and 1971 to £133,000 while dairies increased theirs by 34% to £133,000 per outlet, butchers 37% to nearly £26,000 and greengrocers 35% to £15,000. Bakers and fishmongers both recorded below average turnover per outlet during the same time period (up 19·5% and 17·5% respectively). Neverthe-less, despite these seemingly optimistic figures there is no doubt that, over time, specialist shops will continue to decline and only retain their market hold where their specialisms are of minimal importance to the grocers and supermarkets: that is, greengrocers, butchers and fishmongers. As we shall see later these types of outlets will retain their independence largely because of housewife reluctance to shop for fruit and vegetables, meat and fish in the supermarket environment[11].

Grocers and Supermarkets

Sales through grocery and supermarket outlets have increased at the expense of certain independent stores and in 1972 notched up a sales income of £4,315 million. They account for 60% of food-shop turnover and numbered 108,000 outlets in 1971, a figure which included the big multiples such as Sainsbury and the smaller independent grocer groups such as VG.

Multiples in this sector, after their huge expansionary strides of the last decade, have now reached near-saturation (in volume terms) for food and are diverting their attention to non-food goods, a factor which will be discussed in more detail later. Nevertheless, although their share of retail outlets is considerably smaller than that for independent food stores, they still manage to pull in turnover figures far healthier than the smaller shops. In 1971 multiple grocers accounted for 11·4% of all retail sales although their share of retail outlets was just 1·8% in the 1966 Census of Distribution[12].

Generally, estimates from the Economic Intelligence Unit for 1974 put overall food shops as heading for an average annual growth rate of 12% (independents 6%) which represents a 3·6% improvement over 'all retailers'[13].

Shop Usage among Housewives

Within the gross division of food shop types that have just been noted, housewives can show considerable variability of response. For example, as far as grocery shopping is concerned, surveys have shown that:

1. 19% of housewives use Co-operatives for most of their purchases (14% self-service).
2. 40% use Multiples for most of their purchases (44% self-service).
3. 29% use independents for most of their purchases (11% self-service).
4. Usage of Co-operatives is highest among OAPs and lowest among class A (26%, 10%).
5. Multiples are used most among Class A/B and least among OAPs (52/53%, 40%).
6. Independents are used most among Class A (32%).
7. These divisions are further variable between fresh meat, fresh fruit and vegetable shopping although independents are consistent favourites for these product groups*.

Furthermore, when asked to name the grocer which they 'used most often', another preference pattern has been found to emerge among housewives favouring the Co-op (28%) followed by Tesco, Marks and Spencer and Sainsbury (16% each). Fine Fare and Woolworth came 13% and 10% respectively†.

While 64% of housewives say that they use supermarkets regularly, this varies as follows:

1. From 89% for married couples without children to 47% where there is a 'no-married' shopper† †.
2. From 70% for class C2 to 57% for class DE† †.
3. From 69% for London/SE to 48% for Scotland.

When asked to name their top four supermarkets the results were:

1. The Co-op (13%) which came highest in the North West (20%) and lowest in London/SE (10%) and class AB.
2. Sainsbury (12%) which came highest in London/SE and class AB.
3. Tesco which came highest in London/SE and the North West and lowest in Scotland. It was also highest in class C2 and where there were young children.
4. Fine Fare which came highest in the South West, Wales and the Midlands and lowest in the South-East*.

To conclude, it is certainly within the environment of the food shop that we find the highest level of female consumer activity and obviously the highest rate of purchaser to consumer (such as housewife to family) purchase decisions. In addition, food shops are the most profitable and expansive

---

* National Food Survey (1969).
† British Market Research Bureau Target Group Index (1972).
† † 'No-married' and DE groups probably contain a high proportion of OAPs.

sector of the national retailing trade, and even within the fluctuations of economic climate tenaciously hold their own. Food shops, food purchase and the female consumer are mutually supportive institutions and if they are characterised by anything then it is predictability, reliability and sheer economic enormity.

REFERENCES

1. 'The Food Industry', a *Better Homes and Gardens* Report, Vol. 42 (1) (February 1970), p. 43, (Woman and Food Survey).
2. 'Watford Survey', noted in 'The Future of Pedestrianised Shopping Precincts', *Retail Business*, 190 (December 1973), p. 25.
3. Terry J. Hillier, 'Out-of-Town Regional Shopping Centres—a reality by 1980?', *British Journal of Marketing*, Vol. 5 (1) (spring 1971), pp. 34–41.
4. 'Mrs Housewife and her Grocer', Alfred Bird and Sons (1966).
5. 'The Southern Shopper Revisited', Southern Television (1966).
6. L. P. Bucklin, 'Testing Propensities to Shop', *Journal of Marketing*, Vol. 30 (January 1966), pp. 22–7.
7. E. Seggev, 'Brand Assortment and Consumer Brand Choice', *Journal of Marketing* (October 1970), pp. 18–24.
8. Martin Simmons, 'Market research as an aid to the Corporate Marketing Decisions of Retailers', *Journal of The Market Research Society*, Vol. 14 (3) (1972), pp. 152–70.
9. 'The Southern Shopper', Southern Television (1962).
10. *Daily Mirror* Household Readership Income and Consumption Study Report (1973), IPC Surveys Division.
11. 'Specialist Food Shops', *Retail Business* (December 1973).
12. 'Grocers and Supermarkets', *Retail Business* (1972).
13. 'Annual Review of Retailing', *Retail Business* (March 1974).
14. Fine Fare 1973 in 'The Future of Superstores', *Retail Business*, 187 (March 1973).

2. The Food Market—Markets and Sales of Selected Products

The housewife maintains infinite positions of response to the myriad edible odds and ends which choke up the 'food market'. From liquorice allsorts to powdered rice, cornflakes to oranges, kippers to olives, the housewife must represent and translate the consumer response of several people—let alone her own—and discriminate this response to each product and brand within each product field, and each product field within each store.

The permutations of such actions are mind-blowing and thus there is a tendency to view the food market in terms of more simplified general product response—which is what we must do here. Granted this simplifying of housewife response we shall, as will be attempted with non-food goods in chapter 4, note some of the variables which float more or less cohesively around certain food products as a means to credit the variability rather than homogeneity of the female consumer shopping decision.

SELECTED MARKETS AND SALES OF GENERAL FOODS

Bread

In the £450 million bread market the housewife buys mainly white bread (85%) and the wrapped variety because she believes that 'the softest is the freshest'. Mothers Pride and Sunblest are the two largest single manufacturers dividing 27% of the market equally between them and 'others', mainly local firms, take up all the remainder.

£1,336,000 was spent on promoting bread to the housewife in 1971 but over the last five years she has been gradually buying less so that consumption of bread has fallen by over 10%. In the UK bread accounts for about 5% of consumer expenditure on food[1].

Crisps

In the market valued at £85 million in 1973, estimates put crisp consumption at about 3 lbs per head per annum. This is an important sector for child

12

purchase but it is women who buy the largest quantity at 60% of all sales, and predominantly in the C2 category which accounts for 40% of the market by social group. Nevertheless, they are obviously buying as much for their family as themselves since they only consume marginally more than men[2].

Cheese

The market, worth £105·9 million in 1969, is dominated by English cheese at 80% of consumption with cheddar taking two-thirds of this. In terms of family use, it is those housewives with the least time who buy the most cheese; 87% of housewives with children buy cheese regularly compared to 78% without. It is a relatively classless market with only marginal differences in consumption between housewives in the AB and DE category, but there are still 20% or more housewives who do not buy cheese regularly and in 1969 the Cheese Bureau started a £430,000 campaign to boost cheese sales[3].

Biscuits

The trend among women is to buy more expensive biscuits in smaller quantities so that the average family receives just over three packets per week. In 1973 total sales through grocery outlets were valued at £171 million but they continue to absorb a reducing share of the household food budget. In terms of taste, digestives, crackers and Rich Tea biscuits are still the favourites[4].

Cereals

This market at £50·2 million in late 1969 and estimated to be growing at 5% per annum, recently attracted the attention of the Monopolies Commission in June 1971 largely because of the domination of the market by Kelloggs who at that time took 40%, with its Cornflakes alone taking a third of the total breakfast cereal market.

Major brands tend to have inherent housewife regional strengths so that the Weetabix cereal is strongest in the Midlands while Shredded Wheat finds its fans in and around London. Generally, however, cereal consumption tends to decline up to the North-Eastern corner of England.

Housewives with young children buy greater quantities of cereals than those without (75% compared to 38% respectively in the seven days prior to the IPC Food Survey in 1968) while in class terms, cereal consumption is highest in the C2 category and lowest in the DE group[5].

One factor which explains the increased importance of cereals over the last decade is the decline of the traditional English breakfast. It seems that we are following the continental trend of eating less food (a BMRB study in 1968 found that only 28% of households are now starting the day with a cooked breakfast compared to nearly all families in 1958) and the American habit of eating in shifts (an American survey of 1965 found that three-quarters of American families do not eat breakfast together and in one-third of families at least one person is asleep when the first person eats). Housewives, of course, now feel that it is also less of a reflection on their role to let the family help themselves (in America a third of the husbands and children serve themselves to breakfast) while with up to 60% of married women working there is obviously less time to prepare elaborate breakfasts. In fact, to many women, breakfast cereals are really an extension of the convenience food market[5].

Cakes

Over £200 million worth of cakes are consumed in Great Britain every year and about 70% of British housewives buy cakes and pastries regularly. Nevertheless, overall sales decline at over 5% per annum which is as much a function of the declining British tea as the increase in cereals is due to the decline of the British breakfast[6].

Salt

In 1969 this £4½ million market was dominated by expenditure variables on class bases rather than age or presence of children. Housewives in the C2 group buy the most while consumption in the AB group is the lowest. Pensioners and DE members also buy more than average while all housewives buy significantly more in winter[7].

Fruit and Vegetables

In 1971 household expenditure on all fruit and vegetables rose in real terms by 9% in 1969 to £1,200 million and most of this was spent in the traditional greengrocer. In 1973 greengrocers took 58% of expenditure compared to the 22% of supermarkets and in 1970 48% of housewives stated a preference for shopping at greengrocers compared to other store types. It seems that supermarkets which only attracted a 12% preference are distrusted in terms of quality and the advantages of prepacking are still not enough to outweigh the absence of personal confrontation over the goods*. In fact pre-packing is not seen as adding value through cleanliness and convenience so much as adding cost for its own sake. One recent consumer-survey quoted by the *Retail Business Report* (1973)[8] on groceries notes that while housewives bought pre-packed mushrooms they in fact would have preferred to have bought them loose if they had been available.

Meat and Vegetables Extracts

This market is led by OXO which took 58% by value in 1970 with Bovril

---

* Prices Profits and Costs in Food Distribution, Report No 105 of the National Board for Prices and Incomes (1970).

second at 18% and Marmite third at 13%. The market is worth just under £2 million and is dominated by women with children at school age, while young families and pensioners consume less. In the 65-plus group only 26% of housewives regularly purchase meat extracts and convenience and time-saving factors are the main reasons for high consumption in the age groups 25–54[9].

Fish

In 1968 the domestic consumption of fish was worth £78·4 million but tended to be linked with age. Generally, the older the housewife the more she tended to buy so that those in the over-55 group bought the most. Otherwise, most is eaten in the highest and lowest income groups and least by those with young children.

All-in-all, however, this has become a very unfashionable and unpopular market. A study by *Retail Business* on fish[10] notes that the product has a negative image in the eyes of the housewife and for this reason is a 'marketing failure'. It is also bought less and less by the working housewife who, if she buys it at all, will go for the frozen or preserved variety.

Jams, Marmalades, Syrups and Treacles

Strawberry jam is still the most popular flavour with housewives and it accounts for 28% of all jam sales with raspberry and blackcurrant next in popularity. Younger housewives consume more than average and, not surprisingly, those with children. To some extent it is viewed still as a semi-luxury and attracts most users in the C2 group. Consumption is below average in the AB and C1 categories.

Marmalade sales are dominated by the 'thick-cut' variety which takes 60% of all marmalade sales but housewives' purchases have stayed stable over time so that average expenditure on marmalade has not changed for ten years, staying at around £0·05 a week and taking 0·2% of average household expenditure.

In the total jam and marmalade market, marmalade accounted for 40% at £15·1 million in 1969 with jam taking up the 60% at £23·1 million. Robertson's still dominate the market, selling 1 in 3 jars of jam and over 40% of all marmalade.

Syrups and treacles are really very traditional products and are used more, as one would expect, by older housewives (the 35-54 age group) than any other group, so that the market remains static and may even be declining as old habits and treacle puddings die the death with less housewife time for elaborate cooking[11].

Flour

This is another product which depends on the older housewife with her more traditional 'provider' ways. In 1970 this £34 million market was dominated by the housewife in the 35–55 year age group. The younger housewife, it seems, is more prepared to try convenience foods, cake mixes and canned puddings (see later section on convenience desserts) although there is more home baking, and thus higher flour consumption among those housewives with children who do not go out to work. This category uses 6·93 ozs per week and is viewed by flour marketers as the most hopeful group for future trends [12].

Sugar

The value of the sugar market has dropped by £17 million from £119 million in 1963 to £103 million in 1968 while sugar consumption per person dropped to 16 ozs per week in 1968 from 17 ozs in 1963.

Just under half of all sugar purchases per week are made by the housewife for the home although those in the older age groups and especially old-age pensioners buy the largest proportion. With the market now affected by international supply and pricing problems there could well emerge a new consumption pattern as purchases are reduced or supplemented by sugar substitutes.

Peak consumption is during the colder months—the first and last quarters of the year—when more hot drinks are consumed, so changes in sugar consumption could well reverberate throughout the whole beverage sector [13].

Butter and Margarine

The 'average housewife' spends about 5p a week on margarine although those over 55, and especially over 65, consume considerably less than average. These latter groups prefer butter.

Margarine and butter markets complement each other in that while butter sales peak in the AB and D/OAP ends of the social scale, margarine finds its main market in the C/D1 groups. Big eaters of margarine are in the North West and Scotland where the average purchase is $2\frac{1}{2}$ times that of those in the West. Nevertheless, margarine manufacturers spent over £3 million in 1968 convincing the housewife that margarine was as good as butter, fighting, no doubt, a consumption situation where of the $\frac{1}{2}$lb of butter or margarine which is consumed per person per week, over two-thirds is taken up by butter [14].

Meat

As with fruit and vegetables, the housewife still likes to purchase her meat at the traditional independent, although there are some signs that the younger and less experienced housewives are turning to the supermarkets. This retreat by the younger housewife is largely a function of 'butcher nervousness' noted by a motivational research survey [15] to be related to ignorance of names and types of meat 'cuts'. It seems that knowing what meat to buy for which occasions is heavily tied up with certain traditional areas of housewife skill. The older housewife takes a pride in knowing the names of chops and joints and cuts and what they are used for and indulges a process rather like haggling in the butcher shop. This, the survey notes, terrifies the less knowledgeable and inexperienced young housewives who turn to the anonymity of the supermarket, higher prices notwithstanding. One of the reasons that butchers have started to cover their walls with lurid pictures of parts of cows and pigs and sheep, all labelled and described in terms of cooking usage, is to attract this young housewife's custom back to the shop.

Of all the types of meat, beef is still the most popular purchase for the traditional roast beef dinner. Sales of bacon have declined with the rout of the 'English' breakfast, while those of ham have increased as 'bacon and eggs' for breakfast give way to 'ham and eggs' for tea. Mutton and lamb maintain their position intermediate between beef and pork. Estimates in 1973 [16] put the average consumption of beef for all households per annum at 25 lbs per head, mutton and lamb at 17·4 lbs, pork at 9 lbs, poultry at 23 lbs and offal and canned meats at 8 lbs each. London, the South East and the South West eat more meat than any other region.

Tea and Coffee

Since 1960, consumption of tea in the UK has dropped by just under a pound a head although the UK still consumes more tea than any other country except Eire (8·8 and 8·9 lbs per head respectively). Over the same period coffee has trebled in popularity so that, while in 1960 18% of the National Food Survey had purchased instant coffee over the previous 7 days, in 1970 this had increased to 30% [17].

Much of the popularity of instant coffee has been achieved with the reduction in its associated image of 'laziness' and 'bad housewifery' and this is illustrated by a replication by Webster and Pechmann in 1970 [18] of the famous Haire coffee study [19] of 1950. In the Haire study housewives had been presented with two identical shopping lists which had differed only to the extent that one included 'real' coffee among its list of purchases and the other 'instant' coffee. The purchaser of instant coffee had been described by a variety of negative characteristics such as 'lazy', 'a bad mother' and a 'slovenly housewife'.

When Webster and Pechmann retested this phenomenon in 1968 they discovered some startling changes. In the later study it was the user of the 'real' coffee who came in for the negative characteristics on the grounds that she was over-traditional in her attitudes to housewifery and was 'dull, phlegmatic, with no elegance and no imagination'. The instant coffee user had become 'quick', 'energetic', 'out-going', 'friendly', 'physically active' and 'busy'.

If anything is testimony to the dynamism of definitions of 'good housewifery' then this is and it demonstrates how changing priorities on the part of women will correspondingly affect their perceptions of product image.

The product groups noted briefly above are those which most women at some time, given some highly variable market patterns, will purchase for themselves and their families. It is not an exhaustive study and the illustrated products were chosen randomly but it does show how product perceptions and purchase patterns by women cannot be generalised. Merely because most women will buy margarine and jam does not mean, for example, that those who buy most jam will be the ones who buy most margarine. Looking at the female consumer market is rather like looking at something through a telescope; from a distance there is a marked homogeneity about the activity but a closer look will reveal smaller activities and patterns which follow quite different channels and routes.

Before moving onto the non-food market, however, there are two food areas which are deserving of a little more study than those we have remarked above. These two areas, frozen foods and convenience foods, are worthy of added attention mainly because they represent two highly significant trends in female consumer behaviour which are in turn a function of the new social behaviour of women:

1. Women no longer feel to the extent that their mothers and grandmothers did that their role is bound up in onerous and time-consuming food preparation. The changing attitudes towards a 'correct' provider role that Webster and Pechmann [18] noted in their replication of Haire's study on coffee can be extended to other aspects of housewife behaviour.
2. More women—married women in particular—are working, so that their time for household work is restricted. On the other hand, another income means that bulk buying becomes more financially viable and the higher cost of convenience foods becomes an opportunity cost in relation to time saved.

FROZEN FOODS

The UK frozen food market increased by over 250% in the period 1963–73 from £62 million in 1963 to £220 million in 1973. In 1973 frozen food sales were 23% above the corresponding level for 1972.

Frozen foods are now sold in about 60% of food shops, mainly grocery and greengrocery outlets. The sales vary, however, with each outlet so that the Co-op frozen food sector represents 2·2% of its sales, while that for the independents represents 4·1%. Multiples fall in between at 2·9%. Independents account, in fact, for 43% of frozen food sales through all grocery outlets [20].

The 'home freezer' centres are the newest form of shopping and 49% of freezer owners purchase their goods at these centres with the next on the list, butchers, taking 21%. There are about 800 of these centres in the UK, selling mostly in bulk packs, and they can be divided into two main types—retail trading (such as Bejam) and home deliveries (such as Alpine Eversedt). Bejam have increased their outlets already from 5 to 65 from 1969 to 1973 and sales from £268,000 in 1969 to £16·9 million in 1973. Some supermarkets are now considering opening up their own freezer centres and the Co-op already operate some [20] while Sainsbury plan to open 40 freezer centres under their name in 1975–6. Home delivery, on the other hand, is still a relatively minor sector accounting for only 7% of all frozen food sales.

In comparison with other countries, the UK consumption of frozen food per head compares favourably with that in Denmark, Switzerland and Norway, but it is Sweden and the USA who lead the field in this market. Nevertheless, UK frozen food consumption has more than doubled since 1964 from 8·2 lbs per head to 18·6 in 1972.

It is interesting to note that over the period 1962–72 frozen food sales in the UK have moved in the opposite direction to total food expenditure as a proportion of the total household budget. Over this period, family expenditure on food items has fallen in relation to total spending from 25% to 20% while the expenditure on frozen foods has increased from 1·3% to 2·4% and the increase is expected to continue [20].

Predictions put the market at around £400 million by 1978 with the industry growing at about 11% per annum. Of this, £350 million will be attributed to retail sales and the rest to catering. Furthermore, it will not remain an upper class phenomenon to enjoy the fruits of bulk purchase and out-of-season produce. Originally, freezer purchase was dominated by AB households but now it is the C2DE households who account for 46% of home freezer ownership.

In terms of the goods themselves, vegetables, fish and fish products now account for 74% of housewife purchases and the trend is one toward whole frozen meals. Women in the USA who are further into this market than those in the UK now buy a smaller proportionate amount of commodity goods, and buy prepared dishes which now make up 30% of all American frozen food consumed. New products in America, such as pizza, lasagna, curry, 'gourmet' dishes, prawn cocktails and trout, account for about two-thirds of the growth of frozen foods. Future trends also indicate frozen breakfast meals and more snacks. The 'art' of housewifery, it seems, is on its way out.

CONVENIENCE FOODS

Along with the increase in frozen foods which are, after all, only a form of convenience shopping, go increases in certain sectors of the convenience food market. Although their rise has not been as meteoric as the frozen sector, convenience foods have still maintained a steady increase since the early 1960s.

The HMSO *Household Food Consumption and Expenditure*, 1969–70 and the Family Expenditure Surveys isolate this group as the biggest single factor in food purchase increases. Between 1953 and 1969 average food expenditure per head rose by about $23\frac{1}{2}$% while food prices rose by about $20\frac{1}{2}$% leaving an overall gain of $2\frac{1}{2}$% in the real value of food purchase per head. 'Practically all this gain was in convenience foods for which the total value of purchase rose by over $18\frac{1}{2}$% between 1963 and 1969.'

Results of a J. Walter Thompson Survey (1970)[21] and a Nielsen survey (1970)[21] also support this trend. They show between them that convenience foods grew more than canned foods but in turnover terms exceeded total grocery turnover rates of +69% between 1960 and 1970 by a further 47% (+116%). In addition, four new convenience food categories, instant milk, instant potato, instant puddings and tea bags were, by 1970, already worth at least 20% of the value of five convenience categories which had been established for up to 15 years.

Nevertheless, given the steady increase in product sales in this category, what features are associated with convenience foods that housewives find so attractive?

A survey on American housewives in 1968 found that over half the respondents gave 'time' as the most important reason to buy convenience foods, while 'work-saving' followed well below at a quarter of replies. The survey suggested that 'time' was something to spend on the family or other purposeful pursuits whereas spending extra money simply to lessen effort collided with the traditional ethic. Time-saving was considered more important in the 35–44 age group but this perceived advantage declined with age.

In households where the wife was employed, respondents were more likely to mention as the important characteristic of convenience foods—'time-saving'—than did respondents who were not employed*.

Examples of some Convenience Foods

Meals. This market, which is now thirteen years old, was started from scratch by Batchelors and is now worth around £7 million. In a survey on convenience meals[22] *Retail Business* quotes Dr. E. H. Hoblyn of the Food Machinery Association who notes that the British housewife spends on average $1\frac{1}{2}$–2 hours per day preparing and cooking food for her family. Thirty years ago she spent double this amount of time. Dishpan hands are no longer regarded as either necessary or desirable badges of office and the growth areas of the £3,590 million grocery market in the UK are now clearly identified as 'convenience foods'.

Nevertheless, one of the trip-ups in this market is that many sections of the

---

* 'The Food Industry', a *Better Homes and Gardens* Report (1970).

British housewife and working mother market that forms an ideal target for convenience meals have a strong streak of conservatism. For instance, fish and chips is still Britain's most consumed dish (curry is third) and a recent *Evening Standard* survey by Opinion Research Centre in October 1969 (quoted in *Retail Business*) showed roast beef still the most popular meat dish in Britain. Mass Observation Limited, in a study on how many Britons in a 2,000 sample had visited a foreign restaurant, found that the number who had never been totalled 65%, despite the 30,000–50,000 Chinese restaurants in the UK. Heavy promotion by convenience food marketers is attempting to overcome this. Generally, the convenience food is a 'larder' product; it is a stand-by for 1 or 2 members of the family and is not a group meal. In fact, the increase in use of the convenience meal reflects an increasing breakdown in traditional family meal occasions.

Working mothers, nevertheless, particularly at the younger end of the group, are the prime target. They need convenience and are prepared to pay for the opportunity cost of it. In the larger, older families, the convenience meals cope with the demands of the varied social activities of the family.

Canned vegetables. These are part of the same convenience continuum and the market in 1972 was estimated at £67 million with baked beans and pasta comprising another £44 million. Consumer preferences for canned vegetables in the UK vary by only a few percentage points according to all socio-economic criteria, such as region, age, family size and class. The only exception seems to be in the Scottish and child-orientated families who eat more than their share of baked beans and spaghetti: 12% compared to a national average of 10%. Housewives prepare their baked beans one-third each 'on toast', as a 'side vegetable' and with 'fries and grills'. Heaviest demand for baked beans is in winter[23].

Packaged desserts. In 1969 this was worth £20·8 million and dominated by jelly. Not surprisingly, the presence of children figures in consumption rates so that the two age groups of housewives 25–34 and 35–54 buy the largest amount. Otherwise there are few regional and class differences[24].

Traditional and 'bakery' desserts. This was worth £27·5 million in 1970 and dominated by canned milk puddings. The greatest popularity is in the groups of housewives aged 35–40, in the lowest social groups, in the North West of the country and in households with children. Interestingly, manufacturers say that those 42% of housewives who are current own-label users of milk puddings would be willing to pay an additional 2–3p per can for a rice pudding containing cream. On the other side of the housewife market are those 80% of housewives who use sponge puddings but of whom 40% often make their own and the 85% of housewives who make fruit pies but of whom 80% still make their own fillings.

Convenience foods may be popular but there is still, evidently, a small cell of the more traditional home-makers although this is concentrated into the older age groups [24].

REFERENCES

1. 'Bread', *Retail Business*, 176 (October 1972).
2. 'Potato Crisps', *Retail Business*, 191 (January 1974).
3. 'Natural Cheese', *Retail Business*, 155 (January 1971).
4. 'The UK Market for Biscuits', *Retail Business*, 196 (June 1974).
5. 'Ready to Eat Cereals', *Retail Business*, 152 (October 1972); The Monopolies Commission Report on Kellogs (22 February 1973); *Better Homes and Gardens* Report, Women and Food Survey, Social Research Inc. (1965), The Bureau of Advertising, ANPA (1965).
6. 'The UK Market for Cakes', *Retail Business*, 192 (February 1974).
7. 'Salt', *Retail Business*, 149 (July 1970).
8. 'Fresh Fruit and Vegetables', Part 1, *Retail Business*, 184 (June 1973).
9. 'Meat and Vegetable Extracts', *Retail Business*, 154 (December 1970).
10. 'Fresh Fish', *Retail Business*, 146 (April 1970).
11. 'Jams, Marmalades and Honey', *Retail Business*, 197 (June 1974); 'Jams and Marmalade', *Retail Business*, 153 (November 1970); 'Syrup, Treacle and Honey', *Retail Business*, 137 (July 1969).
12. 'Flour', *Retail Business*, 167 (January 1972).
13. 'Sugar', *Retail Business*, 144 (February 1970).
14. 'Butter and Margarine', *Retail Business*, 161 (July 1971); 'Margarine', *Retail Business*, 144 (February 1970).
15. Vance Packard, *The Hidden Persuaders*, Pelican Penguin Books (1957).
16. 'Beef and Veal in the UK', *Retail Business*, 181 (March 1972); 'Mutton and Lamb in the UK', *Retail Business*, 182 (April 1973); 'Marketing Fatstock in the UK', (2), *Retail Business*, 184 (June 1973); 'Pigmeat in the UK', *Retail Business*, 180 (February 1973).
17. 'Tea', *Retail Business*, 168 (February 1972); 'The UK Coffee Market', *Retail Business*, 169 (March 1972).
18. Frederick E. Webster Jr. and Frederick Von Pechmann, 'A Replication of the Shopping List Study', *Journal of Marketing*, Vol. 34 (April 1970), pp. 61-77.
19. Mason Haire, 'Projective Techniques in Marketing Research', *Journal of Marketing*, Vol. 14 (April 1970), pp. 61–77.
20. 'Retail Outlets for Frozen Foods', *Retail Business*, 198 (August 1974); 'Frozen Foods', *Retail Business*, 198 (October 1973).
21. Noted in the *Grocer* (2 October 1971), pp. 58–86.
22. 'Ready Meals', *Retail Business*, 142 (1969).
23. 'Canned Vegetables', *Retail Business*, 171 May (1972).
24. 'Packaged Instant Desserts', *Retail Business*, 149 (July 1970); 'Traditional and Bakery Desserts', *Retail Business*, 157 (March 1971).

3. Shopping and Shops—the Non-food Market

SHOPPING

The non-food markets which concern the housewife can be roughly divided into:

1. Those small non-food goods such as detergents, soap and toothpaste which can be bought at supermarkets and multiple stores. (Household and hardware sections in supermarkets will be dealt with separately later.)
2. Those larger goods which involve cash and non-cash payments such as durables, mail order goods, items such as clothing and footwear, which usually involve a special shopping trip, and those items which are bought directly from the manufacturer via an agent such as Tupperware and Avon cosmetics.

Shopping for non-food goods can be compared to that for food goods in that there are indications of 'peaking' to the end of the week, particularly Saturday, but this tendency is by no means as marked as it is in the food market. With goods such as tobacco and laundry, for example, expenditure is relatively evenly distributed over the whole week (*see* Table 3:1). As a general rule, we can expect that a product which tends toward the smaller and cheaper end of the non-food scale will be more likely to share shopping patterns with food and grocery goods than bigger and more expensive goods. Soaps and cleaning materials, for example, are bought mainly on Friday and Saturday, but major household durables are frequently bought during other week days. With major household expenditures, such as on housing, travel and communications, there is no major difference between days of expenditure.

In this section, we shall be particularly concerned with those goods which tend not to be 'run-in' with food purchases; that is those in the second group. In this group we find two distinctive features which are not common in the first group:

1. There is a greater propensity for joint purchase, that is, the husband and wife shopping for an item and deciding on its purchase together. Thus, *with certain goods* in this category we may be more concerned

23

with the *influence* of the housewife on the purchase, rather than her purchase *per se*. (Women who buy these goods for themselves and in their own right will be the subject of Part IV.)

2. The simple cash transaction is joined by more credit-orientated forms of purchase, such as direct sales (including mail order), and hire purchase. Women opt for these forms of purchase both for themselves and for their families, and with their husbands. In the latter case it is often the woman who will make the direct weekly or monthly payments where these are not being made by standing order.

The extent to which this second area concerns the female consumer is often ignored and so, within the boundaries of limited data, it will be examined here.

Table 3:1   Main Shopping Day

	Mon	Tue	Wed	Thu	Fri	Sat	Sun
Tobacco	13	13	13	15	18	18	10
Housing	12	13	14	18	20	20	3
Fuel and light	14	13	13	15	21	17	6
Clothing and footwear	10	12	11	14	20	33	1
Major household durables	12	13	15	15	15	28	2
Textiles and furnishing	12	15	14	17	16	25	1
Hardware	13	13	12	14	18	30	1
Soap, cleaning materials etc.	9	11	10	16	29	23	2
Books	15	11	13	11	23	24	3
Newspapers and magazines	9	8	8	11	25	27	11
Miscellaneous goods	11	12	11	14	20	29	4
Petrol and oil	11	12	11	14	18	21	13
Other running costs, motor vehicles	16	16	14	15	17	18	4
All running costs, motor vehicles	13	13	12	14	18	20	10
Travel	15	16	14	14	17	17	7
Communications	18	17	15	17	16	14	3
Entertainment	12	11	11	11	19	28	8
Laundry and dry cleaning	13	12	13	16	22	22	2
Hairdressing	10	11	14	18	26	22	(n)
Hotel and holiday expenses	17	10	6	16	17	27	9
Miscellaneous services	12	11	13	20	25	15	3
Other expenditure	10	6	16	21	17	26	4
Total	10	12	11	14	22	26	5

Source: *Economic Trends*, HMSO (1969), based upon Family Expenditure Surveys (1966 and 1967); *IPC Year Book 1974*.

Direct Selling

This is a method of shopping which relies directly in most cases on the housewife's propensity for communication with any number of other women. Direct selling ranges from the successful and established structure of Avon cosmetics through the gamut of respectability to the traditional door-to-door brush and encyclopaedia salesman. Three of the most common forms of direct selling which are of particular relevance to the female consumer are 'party', 'door-to-door' and 'mail-order' selling. All of these methods rely on an agent who contacts her friends, neighbours and acquaintances.

In the first case, such as with Tupperware containers, and Claire James underwear, the agent arranges parties at which the goods may be examined or tried on in the comfort of a 'home' situation. In the third case, the agent builds up a contact market among her associates; a particularly fertile field for this system is the factory floor where women are confined by space and working hours to a purchase order system. Both shopping methods can offer 'attractive' credit deals which are collected usually in weekly sums by the agents, who in their turn can receive awards for good performance. In the case of door-to-door selling the agent is given a patch, apart from what custom she can dredge up among her friends and family, and in this area she builds up a clientele. It is sometimes possible to take over a patch from a 'retiring' agent. As with other direct sales methods she collects later payments from these customers but it is more often aided than the others by good media campaigns which act as appetite whetters and familiarisers of the company name. Avon is the biggest contender in this field.

Direct selling cuts out the middleman and brings the responsibility for selling, as well as shopping, more firmly than ever into the housewife's lap. She does not just buy for herself; direct selling deals in both personal and household goods to an extent which established retailers have learnt to envy. Retailers have also vigorously opposed the idea of direct selling.

In a report in *Retail Business* (1969)[1] the National Union of Small Shopkeepers was reported as undertaking a campaign against sales parties of all types because these forms of selling were 'contributing to the financial collapse' of other businesses. *Retail Business* wryly notes that this was perhaps an attempt to give respectability to a 'straightforward campaign against competition'. There are, admittedly, some relevant ethical arguments concerned with this selling method. Some observers note that in the Mafia-like atmosphere of a selling party or a mail order group many women buy because of group pressure, an offer they literally dare not refuse, while others note the activities of ingenious, if unscrupulous, groups who were prosecuted recently for holding 'St. Michael' parties with very inferior goods which Marks and Spencers knew nothing about[1]. It has also been noted that the outlawed 'pyramid' selling was only an extension of the direct selling system.

Nevertheless, certain products have always used the direct selling method to women, long before it became as popular as now. Ringtons the tea company, and Spirella 'special corsets' and other corset companies have always sold direct and Avon and Tupperware are only, as we have noted, the smart descendants of the door-to-door encyclopaedia, brush and peg salesman. Companies such as Unigate have just woken up to the possibilities of this sales method and in an astute economic reappraisal of their milkmen's rounds have introduced all manner of commodity groceries into the traditional milk-float ranging from cream, eggs, bread, to potatoes . . . which might make certain bakers wring their hands considering they found the delivery service 'uneconomical' recently and withdrew, to a large extent, the direct sales of bread.

In a recent report on direct selling[2] two groups of factors were isolated as notable to each side of the selling situation.

1. *The manufacturer.* Direct selling means tighter control over pricing and production which are linked more directly to market trends. General demand patterns become 'fluffed' when they are mediated through the high-street middle-men. Also, direct selling capitalises on demand which would otherwise have remained latent. Women who shop through agents are reported to admit they would not have purchased these goods in a normal store situation.

It is these advantages of distribution which are most attractive to manu-facturers because, otherwise, the cost of a direct selling operation is not markedly less than the indirect approach. Sales representatives must still be paid their commission, bad debts are particularly prevalent, and the catalogues which are a basic 'capital' cost are, in this time of increased paper and printing costs, a financial burden. Avon estimate that this 'cost to waste' works out at £500,000 per annum with another £250,000 basic advertising into the bargain. Mail order catalogues which are often given away with no guaranteed follow-up in sales, put the cost even higher.

2. *The consumer.* The main advantage to the consumer is the service aspect. In the days of over-large, impersonal shops and frosty sales-people it is a big perk to some women to find a helpful sales-person who actually wants to sell them something. There is also a wide range of goods which can be seen or handled so that selection is related to choice as opposed to the nearest approximation which might get you from under the sales-person's bored and steely stare. In 1970 Avon had 80–90 items in their catalogue and Claire James offered a range of about 40 items as do similar lingerie companies such as Salamander and Pippa-Dee. Mail order catalogues can offer up to 500 items.

Basically, the main potential in direct selling is that its market is the whole female population while the similar potential for retail shopping is the number of women who regularly go shopping for goods other than necessities. Furthermore, people do not mind being 'disturbed' by a sales representative; a survey by the Direct Sales and Service Association (DSSA) showed that 80% of representative calls were 'friendly'.

Up to this point all the three main types of 'direct selling' have shared the features which have been discussed but beyond this it is easier, for the sake of clarity, to sub-divide the market into two broad sectors—door-to-door and party selling, and mail order—since there are certain features which are common to each but not to each other.

Door-to-door and Party Selling

The housewife is protected from malpractice by operators in this sphere by the DSSA. Formed in May 1965 it claims to represent 70% of the direct sales operators (except mail order) who practice in the UK. Their intention is to squeeze out the disreputable sellers simply by excluding them, and encouraging the reputable ones. Most of the household name sellers are members of this organisation including 'Easifit' covers, Avon, Tupperware, Kleen-e-Zee Brush Company, Pippa-Dee and Ringtons Limited, and each is governed by the rules of the organisation which include prohibition of misleading product descriptions, requirements as to guarantees, and the training of their representatives. The main aims of the association are to protect the consumer and discourage practices that bring the profession into disrepute.

The companies. In mid-1970 the combined sales volume of all the members of the DSSA totalled £310 million with a total market, therefore, (since DSSA represents 70%) of £450 million p.a. Growth in this sector of the industry has been about 15% per annum in the last five years and expansion at this rate is expected to continue, probably in line with the depreciation in the status of the shopping process in the eyes of women and the reduced time available for shopping which coincides with more full- and part-time employment by married women.

Retail Business (1970)[2] has made a brief review of the main companies in the door-to-door and party-selling sector and points out that the growth rate varies by company. Claire James lingerie have maintained sales in the region of £4 million per annum in the four years since the company started operating, whereas Sarah Coventry in the costume jewellery market have claimed an annual growth rate of about 18%.

Avon cosmetics is the biggest UK direct selling company in this sector comparing more than favourably with other big cosmetics companies—holding 15–17% of the £100 million cosmetics market. Their growth rate is estimated at about 16% per annum. The structure of the market is simple, with divisional managers, regional supervisors and a door-to-door force of 60,000 representatives, of whom 80% give up their job every year. A representative can buy an area of 300 houses and a demonstration pack costing £3·10, and buys at a discount of 33% giving her a return of 25% on the retail price. The housewife orders from her and receives, at the same time, the goods she ordered on the last visit. Tupperware are a Division of the Rexall Drug and Chemical Company of Los Angeles and are estimated to be growing at 15% per annum. It is also estimated that Tupperware now have one of its products in four out of every ten British homes. The set-up is similar to that of Avon but the difference lies in the selling method, which is by 'parties'. 10,000 or so Tupperware dealers in the country encourage friends to throw parties at which the dealer demonstrates the products. The party thrower receives a gift and the dealer collects orders. It is estimated by Tupperware that two or three parties a week should produce £9–25 income for the dealer as there is a 33% margin on orders placed.

The saleswomen. The DSSA says that its typical representatives are 'ordinary people, mostly housewives with families, doing a straightforward part-time job'. A survey conducted by DSSA of its 11,149 representatives found that 97·7% of these were women and only 2·3% were male; 94·6% were self-employed and 88·5% were housewives, with 83·5% under 45 years[2]. The survey concluded that the agent is generally an ordinary house-wife with two children who takes an interest in community life. Certainly, they are women with a good standard of living for, as *Retail Business* reports, they are in excess of the national average in terms of their ownership of consumer durables with about 75% owning at least five major items of electrical equipment. They are certainly not working to keep themselves alive. Reasons given for this sort of work all relate to the 'housewife position': it can be fitted into daily routine, to *supplement* income, to get out of the house and meet people, to occupy spare time and as a challenge. The irony must be that women meet women in such numbers and to such important economic effect all for the ultimate purpose of a few clothes, plastic boxes and sticks of make-up. There is in the phenomenon of direct selling a great female energy potential as well as an occupational vacuum which penetrates the lives of women from both sides, the seller and the sold.

Mail Order

This sector had a turnover of £716 million in 1972 which was an increase of £135 million on the previous year—a 24% increase. This was the fastest increase of any retail sector and double the retail trade's average. It is speculated that mail order turnover may soon exceed that of the department store[4].

In 1972 mail order sales as a proportion of the total retail trade reached a new high of 4·2%. Credit accounts for 89·7% of mail order sales and this rose to £642 million in 1972, a 23% increase on the previous year. This amounted to 47·1% of the £1,363 million instalment sales of all retailers[6].

What, however, is of particular interest in mail order selling is the extent to which women contribute to its success. Two different surveys have found that women are agents for and purchasers through mail order to a greater extent than men.

The *IPC /Daily Mirror Survey* of 1973 [3] found that:

1. One per cent of men and 11% of women said they were agents for a mail order firm.
2. Nineteen per cent of men and 36% of women said they had bought through a mail order agent in the last 12 months (excluding agents' own buying).
3. This pattern was further variable by age, class and region in that mail order buying was more common among younger age groups, C2 class and outside London /South East and Scotland.
4. Twelve per cent of men and 16% of women said they had sent for goods by post in the last 12 months (not through agents). One half of each group of purchasers had sent once, one quarter twice, one quarter three or more times. Such purchasing was more common among the AB class and in the South.

A second survey on the mail order market in 1972 [5] found that while the proportion of mail order usage between men and women was slightly closer together, it still tended to favour women (44·3% for men and 55·7% for women). Putting it another way men are more likely *not* to use mail order than women (51·2% compared to 48·8%).

A similar socio-economic distribution of mail order usage was noted in the TGI survey as in the IPC one. The second survey also noted the differing profiles for women in two catalogues. Littlewoods, for example, are biased to a younger and slightly more down-market woman than other mail order houses, while the Janet Frazer user is even younger and further down-market.

Within the range of goods that mail order firms offer, women seem to prefer to concentrate their purchases in the female clothing and footwear area and this, in 1970, accounted for 30·2% of all mail order turnover. The next down on the list, furniture, furnishings and floor coverings, accounted for just over half of the turnover of the women's and children's wear sector, taking 16%.

Women also buy goods for their families through mail order and there is no doubt that a large proportion of boys' and men's wear and hardware are bought by married women in this capacity.

What is it, however, about mail order shopping that women find so attractive? We have already noted that some of its popularity must come from those women who have little time to shop during the week, such as those who work full- or part-time and particularly those in factories where the catalogue can make the rounds in the slipstream of the wage packets.

James Mann (1967)[6] makes some other suggestions. Reasons for its
popularity, he suggests, are the wish to avoid shopping crushes and travelling,
the advantages of low-cost credit in times of inflation and an approval
system so that 'trying on' is in the privacy and mood of home. There
is also a fear and dislike of the rushed and sometimes pressurising sales
assistants and the current trends in shops to one-room changing, for which
privilege one usually has to queue. Shopping for clothes, especially on week-
ends, has become hot and embarrassing and it is probably no coincidence
that the predominance of mail order clothes buying for women has gained
strength at a time when retail shops treat them like cattle at an identity
parade.

In the case of consumer durables, which are often joint purchases, mail
order shopping is an avoidance of the most crowded days at the weekend,
which is when most husbands and wives are free together, and a time
for a relaxed discussion. Dichter (1966)[7] suggested that confirmation of
choice by peers is an important validator of human behaviour and with
mail order there are two opportunities for this process: at the time of
ordering and at the time of receipt, with a lower potential for that most
disturbing of purchase emotions, post-purchase cognitive dissonance[8].

In addition, there is also the pleasing effect that a mail order catalogue
has on women. Mann points out that:

> Mail order catalogues seen for the first time have a remarkable effect, especially
> on women. A catalogue left with a housewife by a representative on a cold call will
> be pored over by the housewife for at least one hour in 85% of instances. If window
> shopping is a pleasurable pastime then the satisfaction that can be derived from this
> may be simulated by examining a large catalogue, with a considerable economy of
> effort and time.

There are problems of delay between the wanting, ordering and delivery of
the goods—usually 2–5 days pass after ordering before delivery—but
this represents an advantage that is not often appreciated. Everyone looks
forward to receiving and opening parcels and when shopping is regarded
as a chore, and some housewives regard it as such, then mail order shopping
can take the form of 'receiving a present' which can be speculated upon
and attacked with relish when received.

'Nice feelings' apart, one of the more tangible reasons for the success
of mail order is that customers usually have a friend or relative who is
an agent. This is offered as the biggest single reason for all mail order
shopping. The catalogue becomes 'my sister's' or 'Joan-Next-Door's' as
opposed to Burlington's or Littlewoods'. The personality of the agent becomes
the personality of the catalogue company. The friend or relative takes the
feared place of the sales assistant and the front living-room replaces the
hostile non-privacy of the sales department. Certainly, as shopping becomes
more self-indulgent and regarded less as duty by women then the operation

of it will cease to hold its glamour of martyrdom and take on the structure of any operation in which the discomfort should be minimised.

Nevertheless, this familiarisation of shopping which characterises mail order holds one disadvantage. Mann says:

> The sales assistant is identified in the eyes of the customer with the selling organisation while the agent, a family friend or neighbour is identified as a peer who, with the customer, faces out from their mutual social group toward the business world. A majority of customers regard agents as being *their* agents in their dealings with the catalogue company rather than the company's agent in its dealings with them.

Mann points out that this duality of roles is often confusing to the agents themselves who have two directions of loyalty; to their companies so that they feel worried about returning goods, and to their customers who obviously trust their judgement and encouragement. This guilt is particularly illustrated by the fact of some agents paying off bad debts themselves rather than letting their companies know about them, as if they were somehow responsible.

There are three types of agents that Mann isolates. There are the 'commission orientated' agents who take orders at any cost and are sometimes poor judges of credit worthiness of customers, the 'socially motivated' ones, whom we have just described who feel a conflict between the personal interest of the company and the individual customer, and a third group who are not motivated at all strongly, who interpret rules on cash and credit very narrowly, use a catalogue for its convenience and so turn in a small and irregular cash turnover from a few friends and family. The more involved the agent with friends and company the better her returns, but also the more anxious and time-consuming her selling activity.

In 1967 there were $2\frac{1}{2}$ million agents whose annual turnover ranged from £30 to four figure sums. Average turnover in 1966 was £150. In 1967 it was Great Universal Stores who held the greatest share of the market by number of agents at 35% with Littlewoods following at 24% and Grattan and Freeman tying in third place at 12% each[6].

Credit Sales

As we have noted in relation to mail order, women do take frequent advantage of credit facilities in their shopping. Nevertheless, mail order is not the only outlet for the female credit contributions. Women also participate in HP and credit sale transactions (48% of women use these methods compared to 65% of men) and check trading (33% compared to 40% of men). It is interesting that it is women almost as much as men who take on the rental for television (33% compared to 40%) although generally women *avoid* credit usage more than men (29% compared to 23%).

One of the reasons for this credit avoidance by women lies, obviously, in the fact that the type of purchases she tends to dominate, such as

food, is not typified by credit sales. The Census of Distribution Report
of 1972 showed that although food sales dominated all expenditure categories,
they represented only £1·5 million of credit sales, although general household
goods, which includes most consumer durables and which came third in
terms of total sales, carried the day at £240 million of credit sales.

Nevertheless, 'women's wear' dominates sales of clothing and footwear
and the total clothing and footwear group came second in terms of credit
sales at £166 million so it is here that the women purchasing alone (as
opposed to purchasing with her husband in the household goods sector)
probably maintains the bulk of her credit purchases[9].

There is no doubt, however, that more women would use credit facilities
if there was not one big social stumbling block in their way. Retailers tend
to refuse credit facilities to women, often because they *are* women but
usually because they are married as well. This has not been noted infrequently, even when women are good salary earners in their own right.

Coote and Gill (1974)[10] recently covered this point in their excellent guide
to women's rights (p. 265).

> When you buy something by HP you have to sign an agreement. Most companies
> that organise HP payments seem to think that women—particularly married
> women—are a bad risk. So if you are married, they will probably ask you to provide
> your husband's signature. If you are single, they may ask you to provide the signature
> of a male guarantor. If you think this is inconvenient, unnecessary or downright
> insulting it is worth making a fuss about it and explaining that you are perfectly
> capable of taking responsibility for the agreement on your own. If you are earning a
> steady wage—tell them so. They may back down—particularly if you tell them
> you have an independent income. If they don't, you can try to find somewhere
> else to buy what you want or you can give up and provide the necessary signature.
> Unfortunately there is nothing in law to prevent companies from discriminating against
> women like this. They are free to refuse credit whenever they like*.

They also quote two women who had replied to a request from the magazine
Which? for details about women who had been refused credit from retail
shops. It is instructive to quote these letters in this context to remind
the reader that although the woman takes considerable economic responsibility in consuming terms there are still many parties who would wish
to see this factor forgotten.

> I have experienced a certain amount of annoyance and frustration when asking for
> 'terms' for some articles, usually in the furniture and electrical shops who will not allow
> me to sign an agreement as I am a woman and therefore not considered to be credit-
> worthy . . . Some shops will allow me to sign such an agreement if I will return to the
> shop with my husband to sign also. I point out that I am a woman earning over
> £1,500 p.a. but most shops are not interested . . . I have asked friends who have
> experienced the same impasse, the separated woman and divorcee has to ask a male
> to back them up too. This backing, although really only a formality, is a bit of an
> imposition and does apparently tie the male to act as guarantor should the lady default.

---

* This will be modified by the Equal Rights Act 1976.

At the beginning of August I saw a coat I liked in a Birmingham store ... As I was not carrying my cheque-book the very helpful assistant suggested I had a credit sale, it wouldn't cost any more during their August-only offer and I had sufficient cash with me for the initial payment. Being the naive type (my husband and I have never previously had any hire-purchase or credit-sale agreement) I expected to sign my name and take the coat home, having duly presented my Barclaycard and Lloyds Bank card as guarantee of credit-worthiness. At the office I was asked to fill in a form which included the name of a friend (for reference only) and given another form to take for my husband to sign. As I was buying the coat by Bankers Order from my own earnings I could see no reason, on thinking it over, why he should have to do this.

NON-FOOD SHOPS

In recent years sales in non-food shops have been increasing rapidly, more so even than in food shops, (*see* Table 3:2). Total non-food sales in 1973 were in excess of £11,900 million, an increase over 1972 of 13·5% by value.

Volume business has also continued to be buoyant as generally higher excess discretionary income has been turned into goods. Within this category of consumer expenditure, Table 3:2 demonstrates furthermore that for 1973:

1. The largest single category of non-food expenditure was on clothing and footwear goods in which we have already noted that the largest sector is women's and children's wear, purchased largely by the housewife. Purchases which are housewife-dominated in this section make up at least 50% of the whole (those italicised). This is, nevertheless, a conservative estimate since it is known that women frequently purchase most of their husband's underclothing and hosiery and they are more likely to frequent haberdashery stores than their husbands.
2. The second category, durable household goods, includes as its joint largest expenditure sub-section, gas and electric appliances. Apart from fires and heating, equipment in this category is dominated by household goods which are predominantly used by the housewife such as cookers, refrigerators and washing machines, let alone the smaller durables such as food-mixers and vacuum cleaners.

Of the other sub-sections, women are also highly likely to have a considerable say in purchase and choice of furniture, floor coverings, soft furnishings and textiles, china, glass, cutlery, hardware, ironmongery and so forth. This would place her influence, if not her direct purchase, into at least 75% of this section.

3. In the third category of goods, 'other household goods', the sectors which are characterised by housewife purchase (those italicised) constitute 3·2% of the 7·2% which this category represents in terms of weekly household expenditure, that is, just over 44% of this section. This, however, assumes that the housewife never buys goods from the other sectors, which is unrealistic. Certainly, it is possible that the contribution of housewife purchases in this sector is between 60% and 70%.

Thus, in terms of the three major non-food categories, we can assume that the housewife plays a significant part in terms of direct purchase of these goods, influence on their choice and the decisions to purchase them at all. This, however, omits the sector of women who buy these goods entirely for themselves i.e. unmarried, widowed or divorced women. Their contribution is noted in more detail in Part IV.

Table 3:2   Household and Housewife Expenditure on Non-food Goods

	All households as percentage of total expenditure	Average weekly expenditure
Clothing and Footwear		
Men's outer clothing	1·5	0·56
Men's underclothing and hosiery	0·6	0·22
Women's outerclothing	2·4	0·90
Women's underclothing and hosiery	0·7	0·28
Boys' clothing	0·4	0·15
Girls' clothing	0·4	0·15
Infants' clothing	0·4	0·13
Hats, gloves, haberdashery	0·5	0·18
Clothing material and making-up charges;	0·2	0·09
other footwear	1·7	0·65
TOTAL	8·8	3·31
Durable Household Goods		
Furniture	1·4	0·54
Floor coverings	1·2	0·44
Soft furnishings and household textiles	0·8	0·31
TV, radio and musical instruments (inc. repairs)	1·6	0·51
Gas and electric appliances inc. repairs	1·6	0·60
Appliances other than gas or electric appliance	0·1	0·04
China, glass, cutlery, hardware, ironmongery	1·0	0·35
TOTAL	7·9	2·84
Other Household Goods		
Leather, travel and sports goods, jewellery fancy goods etc.	0·9	0·35
Books, newspapers, magazines and periodicals	1·6	0·60
Toys, stationery goods etc.	0·9	0·34
Medicines and surgical goods	0·5	0·19
Toilet requisites, cosmetics etc.	1·1	0·42
Optical and photographic goods	0·4	0·16
Matches, soap, cleaning materials etc.	0·7	0·25
Seeds, plants, flowers, horticultural goods	0·4	0·15
Animals and pets	0·7	0·24
TOTAL	7·2	2·69

Source: Family Expenditure Survey, HMSO (1973).

According to data from the Department of Trade and Industry in 1972, most purchases of non-food goods are from: (i) miscellaneous non-food shops; (ii) clothing and footwear shops; (iii) durable goods shops; and (iv) department stores.

Mail order has already been examined; the sales and turnover related to the other outlets are as follows:

Miscellaneous Non-food Shops

These constitute both the biggest sector of shops in turnover terms after food shops and, in value terms, the most important non-food group. Their value in 1972 was £3,700 million and their turnover in 1973 was £4,582 million, a 11·5% increase on 1972.

The shops which fall within this group range from chemists, hardware, paint and wallpaper stores, to hairdressers and laundries. Their biggest sector, however, is the confectioners, tobacconists and newsagents (CTNs) within whose portals consumers spent £2,700 million in 1970, of which £1,720 million went on tobacco, £370 million on newspapers and periodicals and £605 million on sugar preserves and confectionery.

Although weekly family expenditure on all three main commodity items of the CTNs has risen steadily in money terms since 1965, in volume sales they have been dropping since 1967[11].

Clothing and Footwear Shops

Turnover in these shops reached £2,665 million in 1972, almost £275 million more than in the previous year and an increase of 12% for the second year running. Of these outlets, women's wear shops show the most rapid sales increases in the group and account for 64% of the specialist sector's turnover. Footwear and men's wear shops have, on the other hand, shown a consistent below 'all retailer' average over the same period[12].

In 1972 consumers spent £3,279 million on clothing and footwear representing £3 per week for the average household[13]. Expenditure on women's and children's wear lay at £1,813 million in 1972 which then represented 53% of all clothing and footwear expenditure. Women's and girls' wear alone accounted for 41% compared to 16% for men's and boys'[3].

The most popular shops for clothing were Marks and Spencer and C. & A. for women, Marks and Spencer and Burton, for men and Marks and Spencer and Woolworth for women shopping for men. Marks and Spencer were the consistent favourite for men's clothes bought by men, men's clothes bought by women and women's clothes bought by women (*see* Table 3:3).

The most popular shops for women's clothing and footwear also sell other products (Marks and Spencer, British Home Stores, Littlewoods, Woolworth and the Co-op) and in these stores women's clothing was still the most important sector taking 40% of sales (£444 million) in 1970[12].

Table 3:3   Shopping for Clothing

The shops used during the last 3 months   (TG1 1972: 'last 12 months')†

	By men (%)	By women when shopping for men (%)	By women (%)	For men's clothes men (%)	For men's clothes women (%)	For women's clothes (women) (%)
C. & A.	5	2	15	14	11	36
Marks & Spencer	21	17	39	48	39	56
British Home Stores	4	2	8	13	12	21
Littlewoods	2	2	7	10	8	15
Woolworth	2	3	6	1	1	7
Co-op	4	1	7	15	11	12
Hepworth	3	*	–	7	3	–
John Collier	4	*	–	10	5	–
Burton	9	*	–	20	10	–
John Temple	1	*	–	3	1	–
Horne	1	*	–	n.a.	n.a.	–
Jackson	2	*	–	4	2	–
Willerby	1	*	–	n.a.	n.a.	–
Dorothy Perkins	*	–	8	–	–	17
Etam	*	–	4	–	–	7
Richard Shops	*	–	4	–	–	13
Selfridges /Miss Selfridge	*	–	3	–	–	n.a.

* Each group was asked only about the shops for which a response is shown.
† MBRB, *Target Group Index*, 1972.
Source: *IPC Consumer Marketing Manual* (1974).

Durable Shops

Consumers spent over £1,100 million on radio, electrical and other durable goods in 1973, a 14% increase on 1972. Much of this value increase was met by volume sales. Spending on these goods is regionally variable, so that London spent £1·65 per household in 1972 but provincial households spent less at about £1·27. While the traditional distribution outlets for these goods are the consumer durable shops and gas and electricity showrooms, there is now increased competition from the electrical discou nt stores such as Comet, Trident and Argos.

In 1973, refrigerators and vacuum cleaner sales dominated disposals of 'white' goods and, in terms of weekly expenditure, that on gas and electrical appliances was, as we noted earlier, the healthiest of which 'white goods' such as washing machines and refrigerators predominate [14].

Department Stores

In 1972 sales through these shops were valued at £851 million and their share of total retail sales was about 5%. Their biggest competitors are, however, the mail order firms who sell a similar range of goods so that despite recent increases in the value of department store sales they may soon fall into fifth place behind mail order in the non-food sector[15].

WOMEN AND NON-FOOD SHOPS

While we can surmise that women make and influence a healthy proportion of the purchases in the non-food sector, it is not so easy to establish their patronage of the different types of non-food retail stores.

It has already been established that women are important contributors to the sales of mail order companies and in Table 3:3 it was seen that women not only shopped for themselves and their children but for men's clothes almost as often as men themselves. Also, since the range of goods in department stores is similar to that of mail order then we can assume a similar orientation towards a female clientele, but it is with durable goods shops that there is a data gap on women shoppers.

An IPC survey (1970) reports that about 5% of unmarried women, on average, buy such durables for themselves as hair dryers, heated rollers, luggage, record players and tape recorders but these are still a minority market in the consumer durables sector. Thus, we must assume that women *may* make up to 50% of the shoppers in consumer durable outlets for those occasions when they buy smaller durables for themselves, and also when they purchase larger durables for their families both on their own and with their husbands.

Nevertheless, if *awareness* of Gas and Electricity Board showrooms, where durables are often purchased, and other durable stores can be taken as a guide then there is some confirmation of high female patronage in these outlets described by Simmons (1972) who showed that while women knew of the overall availability of Boots stores in 100% of cases, and Marks and Spencer in 96%, they also knew of Currys (electrical goods) stores in 73% of instances and the gas and electricity showrooms in 94% and 97% of cases respectively (*see* Table 3:4).

Before we leave this brief description of non-food categories of shops it is instructive to note one development in non-food retailing which, while it is by no means a significant sector in the non-food market as yet is, nevertheless, of undoubted significance to the housewife purchaser.

This development is the trend towards non-food retailing in the major supermarkets. Women are consistent users of supermarkets for food purchases and it may be that the growth of these non-food goods, which tend to be mainly hardware, household textiles and small durables, will affect the traffic of women to stores which have in the past tended to stock them, such as the larger branches of Woolworth, small electrical wholesalers, drapers, department stores and Co-operatives. The development is still too new to gauge long-term trends from, but some of its current features were noted recently in a report by *Retail Business* (1973)[16].

Table 3:4   Percentage of Women with Retail Chain available for Shopping. January 1971

All women = 1.000	Local* availability (%)	Special† trips (%)	Overall availability (%)
Store			
Boots	70	30	100
British Home Stores	16	62	78
Currys	36	37	73
Electricity Board showroom	66	31	97
Gas Board showroom	66	28	94
Littlewoods	13	56	69
Marks and Spencer	29	67	96
Mothercare	17	50	67
W. H. Smith	32	47	79
Woolworth	70	30	100

* Show card. Which of these stores do you have in your district?
† Are there any others on this card near enough for you to shop at on special shopping trips?
Source: Simmons 1972 (*see* Chapter 1 reference no. 8).

NON-FOOD RETAILING IN SUPERMARKETS

Supermarkets, as we noted earlier, have always offered certain non-food goods which are part of constant household usage and which are linked with food purchases, such as detergents, toothpaste and soap. Now, in many supermarkets, the range has been extended, but is *separated* from the original food section. This new range offers an assortment of products ranging from electric kettles to gardening equipment to table-cloths.

The reasons for the sortie into this sector are various:

1. While turnover per unit space and unit shelving are lower for non-food goods (food to non-food follows about a 2·5:1 ratio and this disparity is even greater for the larger non-food goods) the sales of non-food items are growing faster in the long term than food goods.
2. There is a bigger trading margin for the non-food items: 30% is typical while that for food averages at about 12%.
3. Non-foods are not so susceptible to drastic price cutting as food goods since the brand competition is relatively low.

The size of the supermarket tends to indicate the proportion of space devoted to non-food goods. Those with a floor space of about 10,000 square feet will provide only about 100–1.500 square feet for non-food items while those of 10.000–15,000 square feet will devote up to 20% of the area to non-food goods. Above this, then, non-food usage expands rapidly since there is usually a maximum limit to the size of the food section. The food sector usually provides the nucleus of attraction while the non-food sections are arranged on the perimeter with easy access from the food section. 'Lead' goods such as clothing are placed at the perimeter to attract the housewife into the non-food section.

Tesco pioneered the non-food trend in supermarkets with their 'Home-'n-Wear' sections and they hope that by about 1977, half of the total profits will derive from non-food sales. Fine Fare are the next most important supermarket retailer of non-food goods although in 1973 these items made up less than 5% of turnover. Allied Suppliers have made a first tentative step into this non-food sector, Sainsbury may do so and Safeway are on the verge. Marks and Spencer have already done so with whole ranges of matching rugs, curtains, bed spreads, kitchen containers and cosmetics. On a national basis, over 3,500 supermarket branches in the UK devote 10% of space on average to non-food goods which contribute 4–5% to their turnover.

Also, a recent Institute of Grocery and Distribution survey (on 157 stores operated by 29 organisations) showed that the number of supermarkets devoted to selling non-food goods nearly trebled between 1969 and 1971. In the past few years supermarkets have been reporting that sales of non-food goods have been rising at 12–15% per annum in money terms which is 7–8% above growth recorded for food. Tesco reported that non-food turnover rose by 33% in the financial year 1971–2.

The categories of non-foods which have been particularly significant have been those which the supermarkets rather than the general non-food shops do best in: short-lived and frequently-purchased items bought mainly by housewives. For example, about a third of all health and beauty sales now take place in multiple supermarkets which are also achieving 12% of paint sales and 6% of the tobacco business. They also do well on kitchen hardware for which, in the medium-priced items, the supermarkets have become the major retail outlet, as far as women are concerned; for instance 90% of household glove sales go through supermarkets. Other promising areas are flowers, toys and garden equipment.

Own brands have become as much of a feature in non-food retailing as in food and Tesco sell only its own label in the Home 'n' Wear section where it has extended recently into shoes and electrical appliances. Profit margins are also higher on the own-label goods.

Certainly, the move by supermarkets into this new non-food area is as much a judge of timing as of the potential which still lies in the house-wife's daily shopping routine.

To conclude, non-food consumer response by women is a slower, more discriminate process than can be noted in food purchase. In addition, since it only commences at one end in the 'domestic' area (washing powder, soap, toothpaste) but ends in an interesting and infinite no-man's land of the sparking plug, washing machine, sock and hedge cutter we find that less information exists, relative to the totally domestic food market, on female consumer purchase participation.

Part IV will examine the extent to which the female consumer has developed this sector in her own right but the participation of the housewife passes largely unrecorded. If she buys sparking plugs or dishwashers through her own initiative and effort, financial or otherwise, then she tends to do so anonymously. Where her contribution is recorded, and it would seem on the evidence of published research that the information is practically classified, then it has been built into an examination of a few selected non-food products in the next chapter.

REFERENCES

1. *Retail Business,* 140 (October 1969), Marketing Review, p. 3.
2. 'Direct Selling', *Retail Business,* 154 (December 1970).
3. The IPC /*Daily Mirror* Survey, Food and Household Stores, noted in 'United Kingdom Consumer Shopping Patterns', IPC Publications (1973).
4. 'Mail Order', *Retail Business,* 188 (October 1973).
5. 'The Mail Order Market in 1971', prepared by the Marketing and Research Department of Foote Cone and Belding Limited, London (January 1972), Appendix C, Purchaser Profile Index.
6. James Mann, 'The Pattern of Mail Order', *British Journal of Marketing,* Vol. 1 (1967).
7. Dichter, 'How Word of Mouth Advertising Works', quoted in *Harvard Business Review,* (November—December 1966).
8. For an examination of the research on cognitive dissonance *see* Engel, Kollat and Blackwell, *Consumer Behaviour,* Holt Rinehart Winston (1968) pp. 506—12.
9. 'Credit Trading by Retailers', *Retail Business,* 192 (February 1974).
10. Anna Coote and Tess Gill, *Women's Rights: A practical guide,* Penguin (1974).
11. 'Confectioner, Tobacconist and Newsagent Shops', *Retail Business,* 175 (September 1972).
12. 'Clothing and Footwear Shops', *Retail Business,* 191 (January 1974).
13. Family Expenditure Survey (1970).
14. Family Expenditure Survey (1970): Annual Review of Retailing, *Retail Business.* 193 (March 1974): 'Consumer Durable Shops'. *Retail Business* 196 June (1974).
15. 'Department Stores', *Retail Business,* 187 (September 1973).
16. 'The Growth of Non-Food Retailing in Supermarkets'. *Retail Business,* 180 (February 1973).

4. The Non-food Market—Markets and Sales of Selected Products

As in the section on food products, a random sample of non-food goods can now be examined to illustrate various ways in which the female consumer becomes involved with their purchase, selection, ownership and usage.

The selection will be divided up into smaller non-food goods such as footwear, toothpaste, and detergents, and those consumer durables which are of particular interest to the housewife, which we must assume that she predominantly uses and of which she would have a considerable say in the purchase (details of decision processes in the choice of consumer durables are given in chapter 9). Certain goods such as alcohol, cigarettes, cars, women's clothing, slimming products, cosmetics and sanitary protection are examined as a function of woman purchasing in her own right and for her own satisfaction in chapters 11 and 12.

Here we will be principally concerned with those small goods and consumer durables which involve the woman as a family participant and housewife within the context both of her household work and her outside employment.

SMALL NON-FOOD GOODS

Footwear

In 1969 the footwear market was valued at £387 million of which women's took 50% and children's 25%. Since women are largely responsible for the purchase of both these categories of goods then women purchasers dominated this market.

In 1969 it was found that the peak buying age for women is 16–24 compared to 35–44 for men. The younger women buy about four pairs a year and while there is no connection between high consumption and social class, there is a regional bias in that there is higher consumption by women in the South, South East, and Midlands with low consumption in Scotland, South West and Wales.

In the case of children, there is a close connection between family income, and pairs of shoes bought. In familes with an income of more than £2,000 per annum twice as many mothers bought four pairs of shoes compared to those buying two. This position was reversed in families earning below £1,200 per annum.

Fashion is very volatile in this market with the women's sector particularly so. Very few retailers now commit more than 50% of their women's budget more than 4–6 weeks in advance compared to 80% of men's. (For lovers of useless information, it is a fact of British womanhood that most have feet sizes in the range 4–6, peaking at size 5, while with men, most fall into the 7–9 size range with size 8 carrying the day.)

In 1974 most men's footwear was purchased from Freeman Hardy and Willis (17%) and Clarks (14%) while women's footwear sales were shared by the same two firms (19% respectively) with Dolcis third (14%)[1].

Toothpaste and Toothbrushes

Women buy most of the toothbrushes in this country although in more ways than one it is not a totally healthy market with the average adult using only one a year. Nevertheless, 34 million are sold per annum and these value at around £3·25 million. Its companion toothpaste market, another female stronghold, stood at £20 million in 1974 and represented 2,000 million standard tubes (four tubes per head). Only 20% of men ever buy toothpaste and of the housewife purchasers most of them buy 1–2 tubes per month. Nevertheless, an astonishing 15% of housewives buy between four and six tubes a month although the report, disappointingly, did not speculate why[2].

Household Textiles

Expenditure on soft furnishings and household textiles was £0·29 per family per week in 1974[3] and blankets took £0·8 of this, with some very conservative tastes still operating. Most housewives still prefer, in 40% of cases, to buy white or pale pastel colours but roaring to the fore are a range of newly popular shades including purples, pinks and yellows with cellular types still top of the stakes, especially those with satin-bound hems.

In terms of sheets, women bought 22 million of them in 1972 valued at £40–50 million, about a third of the £140 million household textile market.

It is interesting that slow markets like these rarely catch the marketer's attention yet in 1971 they represented nearly twice the turnover of more public products such as detergents (£82 million: £140 million)[3].

Shaving Products

Women not only buy a considerable proportion of their husbands' and boyfriends' razor blades, about 30 million of the 70 million sold in 1972, but also introduce their menfolk to new shaving methods. This was found particularly with the introduction of the bonded and 'system' razors and blades. In addition, trade sources estimate that women often buy shaving equipment for themselves: 6 million women wet-shaved in 1973 and about 70% of women use their husbands' razors.

In the electric sector of the shaving market, it is estimated that women buy 50% of the electric razors sold each year as gifts and about 50% of these are bought without consulting the receiver. This market was worth £9 million in 1973[4].

Furniture Polishes and Insecticides

The £8½ million household and furniture polish market is again one of those nameless and background markets which women keep quietly ticking over. As a nation, the British do not relish polishing and rubbing compared, for example, to the French and Dutch, and the average housewife buys only 1·28 units of polish a year for her household. AB housewives like aerosols and DE like the traditional solid waxes. Young housewives like the convenience of sprays and a fifth use liquids only; the remaining 40% use combinations of the lot. Convenience and a blind eye seem to be the order of the day[5].

Meanwhile, women still bash away at their household intruders and the £3 million insecticide market in 1970 continues to expand as less messy methods of insect control are tailored to the housewife's needs, such as the new but expensive slow release strips. Generally, aerosols had a 60% penetration of market value in 1970 when strips were worth £1·5 million and aerosols, £1·6 million. Strips are sold mainly to AB housewives and, while there is a similar weighting with sprays, the social distribution is more even. It is mainly, however, younger housewives—some 11 million of them—who buy domestic insecticides[6].

Detergents and Washing Powders

The soap powder market belongs to Lever Brothers, and Proctor and Gamble and their 12 massively promoted brands which take 90% of the British soap powder market[7]. Until 1971 Persil was the market leader but by 1973 Ariel had usurped this position after being on the market for just five years. (This positioning, however, relies on separating Persil and Persil Automatic; if these latter two brands are combined then Persil moves back into first place with a market share of 22%.)

The brands which have most suffered from the introduction of enzyme and 'automatic' (low sud) powders are Omo (which has fallen from a 1968 brand figure of 15% to the present 7%), and Tide (9% in 1968, 5% now). Surf and Fairy Snow are following a slighter but similar trend.

About 17·8 million households in Great Britain now regularly use washing powder, a 98% penetration level. Those 2% non-users are mainly found in the lower socio-economic and older age groups who tend to prefer household soap and a scrubbing board.

Market estimates of value vary; one survey put the market at £82 million in 1971[7] while another more recent one in 1973[8] puts it at nearer £112 million. If these can be compared then the market value increase over the two years must be nearly 36%. Half of the purchases of washing powder are from supermarkets the rest come mainly from self-service stores and grocers. These three outlets together account for about 87% of retail sales.

On a type analysis, of the 17·8 million housewives that one survey found regularly used a washing powder, 5·5 million or 31% claimed that they use mainly a soap powder, 36% or 6·6 million, an enzyme powder and 22%, or 3·9 million, a detergent; 11% did not know[8]. Also, at the time of the interview, 46% of housewives had an enzyme detergent in stock compared to 26% for soap powders, and at least one brand of any type was in stock. Most of the housewives buy one packet of some soap powder every week, notching up a unit total of 7·7 million packets.

According to the Soap Powder Companies, each washing powder has its own type of purchaser so that Persil, according to Lever Brothers, attracts an extremely conscientious woman, dedicated to perfect washing and seeking softness and cleanliness, with time and trouble a secondary consideration. Daz and Omo users are more fickle and need to be kept on the straight and narrow with constant assertions of the whiteness and brightness culture. The enzyme buyer tends to be either a perfectionist seeking complete cleanliness or a woman who simply wishes to complete her clothes washing with a minimum of involvement. Enzyme consumption tends to increase as one moves up the country so that the Scottish housewives are the biggest enzyme users[8].

Own label takes 8–10% of sales, which is surprising considering the media onslaught surrounding the branded products in this market. In 1973 over £7 million was spent by the manufacturers on advertising their products, over 99·5% of which was television advertising. Finally, given this very competitive situation in the market, what makes a housewife choose a particular brand? We have noted usership profiles but, on a more general basis, what do housewives express as the reason for their brand choice?

The overriding factor seems to be the 'quality' of the brand, this despite tests by *Which?* and other organisations which have demonstrated that the differences in performance between brands of washing powder are negligible[9]. Fifty-nine per cent of housewives chose their brand because of its 'quality', 14% of housewives rely on habit in that they use a brand because they have 'always used' it. Economic criteria such as 'special offers' and 'price' were only of marginal importance (mentioned by 7–14% of women respectively)—although the survey which extracted this data from housewives did not look at private label products which might have moved the preferences down the table.

Certainly, it is in the washing powder market that we see brand strategy, and all the imagery and association that that implies, at its best—or worst.

Household Medicines

In the UK in 1966 total expenditure on medicines of all types was £267 million and while £188 million of this was spent in the National Health sector the balance of £79 million was spent by the public on medicines bought without a doctor's prescription. In this huge home market it is mainly women who are the purchasers. It is also a popular market; a recent survey done in Herefordshire and quoted by *Retail Business* (1971)[10] found that individuals using self-medication as opposed to those using prescribed medicines during a given period were in the ratio of 2·6 to 1. Reactions to illness and the onset of it is extremely consistent between males and females and between different adult age groups but it will be the woman who will buy both for herself and for her husband and children. Her purchase will also depend on the perception of the need; for example, a housewife will buy a small pack of analgesic for herself for her handbag, and a large pack for her family.

SOME CONSUMER DURABLES

Electric Food Mixers

The market for electric food mixers has expanded rapidly over the last few years so that it is estimated that housewives in 30% of households are now equipped with one. The basic market of about 700,000 units per annum is made up of roughly 350,000 stand and bowl mixers, 250,000 hand-held appliances and 100,000 large table-top units.

This market was worth £8·2 million in 1973 of which Kenwood held 50% and Moulinex 20%. Ownership tends to be concentrated at the upper end of the social scale with AB and C1 housewives owning the most (59% and 39% of the market respectively). Younger housewives are also a significant sector but this is largely due, no doubt, to the mixer being a perennial wedding present and it is estimated that of the 5·3 million food mixers in the UK, over one-third have been acquired as gifts. The attraction of the mixer to the housewife has also been perceived by the Electricity Boards who give them away as gifts with purchases of larger goods. Future trends favour the liquidiser-mixer and stand-and-bowl varieties but, by definition, since busy housewives cook less, it would be illogical to predict increased mixer usage with less time. It is not so much a labour-saving device if the labour it saves is reduced anyway in times of pressed opportunities.

Nevertheless, increased demand was projected to 750,000 by 1975 and this may come from those housewives for whom cooking has recently been rediscovered in a more creative style. Certainly, sales of recipe books, cards and part-works, have increased tremendously recently so mixers may be part of this trend rather than the labour-saving one. *Retail Business*[11] adds another angle to this when it says that:

The growing acceptance of mixers, particularly the hand-held models with stand and bowl attachments. appear to allow the housewife both labour saving *and a measure of self-participation.*

Mopeds

Women buy 25% of mopeds, a market which in 1973 was worth £11 million. It seems that it is only the demands of child-rearing which makes them leave this market at the age of about 25 years because they return to it when they are about 40. In the scooter market usage by women is at the 30% level and is dominated by nurses[12].

Freezers and Refrigerators

In 1969, 61% of houses had refrigeration and by 1979 this is estimated to be nearer 90%. By 1972, however, the proportion of ownership for the UK was 71% which put her bottom but one to Belgium in terms of comparative household penetration in a twelve-country comparison topped by West Germany at 93% and USA at 90%[13].

Nevertheless, if women have been tardy in their expectations of refrigeration they have been less so in their purchase of freezers. We have already noted the meteoric rise in frozen food sales and the sales of freezers have made similar progress. In 1965 sales of home freezers numbered 29,000 and by 1972 this had been increased 30 times up to 850,000[14]. Thus, by 1972 freezer possession by British housewives put her in tenth place among twelve countries at a 7% household penetration compared to the 60% of the USA and the 27% of West Germany[13].

Estimates for freezer sales suggested that by 1974, 10·6% of households should own a freezer and forecasts for 1980 put the estimate up to 30–35% of homes which represents ownership levels of $6\frac{1}{2}$–7 million freezers. At present, there are signs that it is only particular regions which are interested in freezer ownership since it is mainly the housewives in the South of England and Midlands who tend to own them, while those women in the North of England and Scotland tend not to be so interested.

Home freezers constitute two basic types, chests and uprights, with the latter taking up less space in the generally small British kitchen. The ratio between chests and uprights has changed from 75:25 in 1965 to 60:40 in 1970 with 32:68 predicted for 1974. In the next few years we should also see a rapid increase in the sales of refrigerator /freezers. According to a survey carried out by the magazine *Frozen Foods* in March 1974, 39% of the sample purchased their home freezers from freezer centres, 5% from door-to-door salesmen, 9% from electricity showrooms, 10% from electrical department stores and 17% from electrical appliance shops.

Electric Blankets

Considerable influence is needed from the housewife to purchase this product.

Perceptions of virility are apparently all tied up with male reluctance to admit to being cold in the night. One recent study (1971)[25] noted that there was a 'primitive' pride in men to act as 'cave warmers', so inviting an electric blanket into the bed could be casting a slur on their convector qualities. In spite of this, the market stood at £5 million in 1971 with the underblanket definitely the hot favourite, accounting for 80% of the market. Overblankets, despite a big push by the manufacturers, continue to have less than one-third of the market. It seems that the British like to feel a comfortable mountain of bedclothes above them, which an over-blanket does not require.

An Electricity Council survey in 1961 showed that 19% of UK households owned at least one electric blanket and more recent AGB estimates suggest that the proportion had grown to 51% in 1970. Ownership estimates for 1971 were 53%. Another survey by the Electricity Council notes that there were more than 12 million electric underblankets in use in 1971 and a further 1 million overblankets. Regionally, the spartan Scots lose their image somewhat when one finds that they come highest in consumption rates (70% of Scottish homes in 1970) while lowest ownership is in East Midlands and Manchester/North Wales (45%). Socio-economically, there is a bias towards households in the C2 DE group, and age determines the blanket type with more underblankets used among the older groups and more over-blankets among the younger. Most sales are estimated to be replacements and though the average life of a blanket is supposed to be 6–7 years, most people keep them for 10–12 years[15]. Nonetheless, the instigation for change or initial purchase of the blankets is largely female in origin, the housewife being more practical and less idealistic as regards her husband's heating qualities.

Domestic Washing Machines

The spin-dryer combination and semi-automatic types of machine are the most popular with women for obvious reasons and now that wash-day is no longer the exercise in sweat and martyrdom that it used to be, reduction in inconvenience seems to be a basic goal. The life of the washing machine is estimated at 10–15 years and today 55% of machines are sold to people who have owned them before. It is the need for a change that marketers try to convince the housewives of, and the machine's potential for lasting 10–15 years is a big selling point. The market was estimated by *Retail Business* in 1972[16] to be worth just under £60 million with automatics the largest category at £29 million and twin tubs close behind at £28 million. Hand and power wringers were hardly placed at £3 million. Hoover and BDA (British Domestic Appliances) hold 36% and 25% market shares respectively.

According to a survey by AGB audits throughout the UK in 1972 66% of households owned a washing machine compared to 44% in 1961. Apart from vacuum cleaners this is the highest penetration for any labour-saving device in the UK. There is obviously some connection between the hierarchy of a housewife's work as she perceives it and the extent to which there is household penetration of devices which reduce associated labour. This may account for the low penetration of food mixers and dishwashers but the higher penetration of washing machines and vacuum cleaners. Nevertheless, ownership has not yet reached saturation in the washing machine market. In West Germany the market is 84% penetrated and Holland 80%. Trade sources estimate that growth will continue until 75% of UK households own a washing machine.

Vacuum Cleaners

In 1969 total sales of vacuum cleaners at 1,240,000 units represented an increase of 133,000 units on 1968 and a market value of £13,800,000. Since the average life of a vacuum cleaner is 10–15 years the principal sales, like washing machines, are not made to new users. Most sales are replacements with various new gimmicks such as automatic flex winders, whistles to show the dust bag is full and height regulators for different carpet thicknesses. Estimates, however, put 15% of vacuum cleaners at less than two years old and 24% were purchased between two and five years ago[17].

Unfortunately for the manufacturers the second-hand market for vacuum cleaners is very active and they must be cursing the resilient manufacture of the ancient hoovers which still 'do' for people very efficiently for a few pence from a junk shop. Secondhand vacuum cleaners account for 10–15% of the total number of cleaners sold.

Penetration, as noted earlier, is the highest of all the housewife-dominated durables. The proportion of households owning vacuum cleaners has risen from about 71% in 1961 to 84% in 1969. A household in the UK is more likely to own a vacuum cleaner than an electric blanket, a sewing machine or even a hair dryer. We compare very favourably with other European countries where the Netherlands lie top at 100% penetration and Sweden second at 90%. The UK is third, and West Germany fourth at 80% (the *Financial Times,* 1969). Other relevant points are that:

1. More households own a cylindrical/spherical cleaner than an upright one. The gap between them, however, is narrowing.
2. The 'upright' is more popular with AB households than the cylinder and spherical ones.
3. Household penetration is highest in the North East, in London and the South East.
4. Housewives in the 35–44 age group are more likely to own one than in any other group.
5. Uprights are more popular in the 65-plus age group.
6. Hoover, of course, lead the market, with Electrolux second at 27% compared to Hoover's 56%.

Electric Kettles

A survey in 1973[18] noted that ownership of electric kettles by the British was the highest in Europe related, no doubt, to English tea drinking habits. Only 2% of Dutch households owned one, 6% of Swiss and 11% of French, while the British managed to own electric kettles to the tune of 82%. The survey noted that:

> While the French woman makes her full flavoured aromatic coffee from fresh beans, her average British counterpart is making a pot of tea, or, at best, a cup of instant coffee. Thus, while the electric kettle is more or less essential to the British way of life it is relatively unnecessary elsewhere in Europe.

Over three times as. many households owned an electric kettle in 1973 as did in 1960 with the biggest growth among lower-class households of whom only 54% owned an electric kettle in 1971 but 77% owned one by 1973. Age-wise, ownership and purchase rates are relatively evenly distributed with a slight bias to younger housewives.

This is also a significant gift product; 30% of all electric kettles owned at the time of the survey (March 1973) were acquired as a gift, much like mixers.

A measure of the importance of the kettle to the British housewife was available from answers to the question: 'Assuming that you were setting up home for the first time which five of the listed appliances would you buy?'[18] In reply, 58% mentioned an electric kettle as one of the appliances compared with 79% mentioning irons, 75% vacuum cleaners, 74% refrigerators, and 71% washing machines. By comparison, coffee percolators were rated at 2%, food mixers at 6% and toasters at 5%.

In 1973. Swan (40%), Russell Hobb (20%) and Hotpoint (13%) were the top three brands.

Cookers

The proportion of households owning electric cookers has risen from 30% in 1961 by 1% per annum to 37% in 1968. The ownership of gas cookers has complemented this with a 63% share in 1968; solid fuel cooker sales are negligible at about $\frac{1}{2}$% of the market.

Housewives have long-standingly preferred gas cookers and in the electric market most sales are replacement ones. *Retail Business* (1970)[19] notes that 'For some time the housewife's recognition of the virtues of the electric cookers, in their modern forms has been awaited, but the slow increase in electric cookers' share of the market indicates housewives take a lot of convincing.'

When housewives choose electric cookers they tend to go for the larger ones and sales of those under 5kw have not increased since 1969. The Electricity Board sell 85% of electric cookers and have a strong hold over servicing, promotion and sales policy.

Thus, gas cookers remain the old favourites with housewives and home sales in 1969 were 772,000 units. They were worth nearly £26 million in 1969 compared to the £810,000 of electric cookers in the same year. Similarly, Gas Boards account for 85–90% of sales and oversee the manufacturers; again the market is largely one of replacement.

Domestic Dishwashing Machines

This is an interesting market because no one can quite work out why housewives are not falling over themselves to buy a dishwasher. In the UK over 40 different models are marketed under at least 16 brand names and retail prices range from under £100 to £300 but, although sales of machines have been increasing markedly over recent years, only 51,200 were sold in UK in 1971 and the bulk of these were purchased by consumers in class A. Also, sales in Britain are the lowest compared to five other European countries. Even Italy, which usually consumes lower levels of other consumer durables than Britain, has a 3% household penetration compared to Britain's 2%. So concerned are the manufacturers at British housewife non-response that they have set up an organisation with the unlikely name of 'Dishwasher Development Council' to promote the product.

Retail Business[20] notes that on the surface their task is a simple one: after all, housewives spend 500 hours each year just washing up and they note a contest by Sheila Black of the *Financial Times* in the early 1970s between a dishwasher and a champion woman washer-up which conclusively proved the effectiveness of the machine in terms of time and also spotlessness. Consumer reluctance nevertheless holds on.

Retail Business suggests that there are several reasons why housewives are not helping to expand this £5½ million market[20]:

1. There is a lack of mass market advertising. This is a chicken and egg problem since manufacturers will not use mass market advertising until there is a mass market . . .
2. The product has a luxury image. In 1971 ownership was 16% in the A group, only 1% in the B group and no penetration was recorded in the other classes. In 1971, furthermore, a survey found that only 3% of the population appeared to think that dishwashers were necessities.
3. Product sales of this sort spread most strongly as a result of word-of-mouth communication. With penetration firmly isolated in the AB sector, it is unlikely that those women in the other more mass market groups will get to hear about it.
4. Dishwashing must be part of a fundamental housewife role which the mechanical dishwasher threatens. This is a rather dubious argument. Washing machines have caught on so how is clothes washing less part of the 'housewife role' than dishwashing? Freezer purchases are accelerating and these actually *subvert* the housewife role in terms of regular provision

of food. *Retail Business* goes on to explain that the dishwasher is somehow seen to be lazy and uncreative (dishwashing, creative?).

5. The lack of storage space in the average British kitchen which is notoriously small and already crowded with a washing machine, refrigerator and cooker. The products also, of course, need elaborate plumbing which, since there may already be a washing machine with the same need, is likely to be one demand too many in the limited space available.

Retail Business sums up with a somewhat simplistic analysis of female psychology with the following explanation of why dishwashers are not popular with housewives:

> Despite the popularity of women's liberation, research indicates that the typical housewife still considers the daily household chores her most important tasks. In this task, the typical housewife still considers that quality is of greater importance than efficiency and, furthermore, that this quality is best obtained by the use of the normal traditional methods. The use of mechanical aids therefore develops a feeling of self-indulgence and guilt which is overcome best by the situation where the mechanical aid does the job in a superior manner—as is the case of the washing machine. The dishwasher on the other hand, does not appear to perform better (in terms of quality) than the housewives' own efforts.

Another reason why housewives do not buy dishwashers may also be because they, alone, do not do all the dishwashing.

Surveys by IPC (1970)[21], Joyce (1968)[22] and J. Walter Thompson (1968)[23] have all shown that husbands (let alone other family members) are more likely to help with the washing up than any other domestic activity. Between 70% and 80% of husbands will 'regularly' help with the washing up, a participation which is not seen in any other activity. Help with cooking for example, came to only 25% and help with washing clothes to just 12%. Housewives, therefore, may already have their own dishwashing facilities.

Thus, let us speculate that the unpopularity of dishwashers with the housewife is less to do with simplistic and stereotyped analyses of the 'housewife role' and more to do with perceived necessity, general inconvenience and alien imagery that is associated with the product.

The one statement which indicates that the *Retail Business* report writer was a little more emancipated than he seemed came in the final paragraph. It suggested that of the promotional courses open to the advertiser to promote this product the best one would be to:

> ... tell the housewife that her 500 hours a year can be better occupied than by having her hands in the sink, washing up, and that this liberation from this chore might cause liberation in other wider and perhaps more intellectual fields.

At least to his credit is that the idea is well meant, but it is with cynicism that one realises that this appeal to the housewife's 'more intellectual fields' comes after all appeals to her domestic and menial roles seem to have failed.

The consumer durables which have been examined in the last few pages have been largely housewife-dominated ones, that is, they are likely to be used by, and the influence for the purchase to come predominantly from, the housewife.

As a conclusion to this chapter, it is useful to note the ownership levels of durables of this ilk. A report by European Research Consultants (1972-3)[24] found that ownership of this group of durables is generally lower among younger age groups up to 24 years. Such new households cannot obviously afford these appliances although they have the highest ownership of electric cookers. The 25–34 age group have the highest percentage ownership of small appliances such as kettles and coffee percolators while the 35–44 age group are the greatest owners of many appliances from vacuum cleaners to dishwashers. Deep freezers and fridges are the most popular appliances for the 46–54 age group, the largest family section, while the over 55s show their preference for comfort (with electric blankets) and gas cookers.

These groups reflect the different uses of these appliances, from the advantages of speed and efficiency desired by youth through the economy of middle age to the comfort and simplicity desired by the elderly.

In a hierarchy of general ownership most households will possess an iron, followed by a vacuum cleaner and a kettle. Washing machines, electric blankets and hairdryers follow. Few households, however, own a juice extractor, coffee grinder, dishwasher, or liquidiser (*see* Table 4:1). Ownership,

Table 4:1   Number of Households Owning and Appliances Bought 1972/73

	Number House- holds owning	Number Appli- ances bought 1972/73		Number House- holds owning	Number Appli- ances bought 1972/73
Electric iron	17,017	2,634	Toasters	6,105	641
Vacuum cleaner	16,091	2,136	Food mixer	4,130	712
Kettle	14,276	2,492	and attachments	4,682	694
Washing machine	12,407	2,741	Clothes dryers	3,578	605
Electric blanket	10,039	1,833	Coffee percolator	3,026	267
Hairdryer	10,929	1,638	Deep freezer	2,350	1,244
Cooker (electrical)	8,580	1,513	Dishwasher	819	142
Cooker (gas)	8,491	1,442	Liquidisers	1,745	
Electric shaver	6,924	1,228	Coffee grinder	694	1,139
Battery shaver	1,833	587	Juice extractor	142	
Electric clock	6,533	1,139	Number of H/H in GB = 17,800,000		

Source: Market Research Great Britain (1974)[24].

no doubt, as has been intermittently suggested throughout this section on consumer durables and the housewife, relates to the menial nature of the task and the perceived necessity/luxury of the goods, so that cleaning and washing and ironing are adequately coped with in terms of labour-saving devices, while food mixing, coffee grinding and clothes drying are to a large extent ignored. Nevertheless, the *degree* of tolerance as regards the menial nature of the task and the perceived necessity of the work seem to vary with whichever class the housewife belongs to so that liquidisers and dishwashers, for example, are more 'necessary' in the upper than in the middle and lower classes.

CONCLUSION TO PART I

Female purchase dominates food, particularly, but also non-food consumer sectors. The woman's decision ranges from the total one in cereal, detergent and butter purchase to the predominant one in vacuum cleaners, washing machines and dishwashers. Shops in both sectors rely on attracting her custom for maintenance of steady sales volume and convincing her of value for continuation of money sales and profit levels. She buys using a variety of methods ranging from simple money transactions to extended credit and her shopping trips vary in style, frequency and method depending largely on the nature of the goods to be purchased. What is particularly important is to note that there is no 'average consumer' or 'average housewife' and female consumers make wide-ranging responses to the demands of shopping, and the attributes of products.

REFERENCES

1. 'Footwear', *Retail Business*, 152 (October 1970); 'Clothing and Footwear Shops', *Retail Business*, 191 (January 1974).
2. 'Toothbrushes', *Retail Business*, 138 (August 1969); 'Toothpaste', *Retail Business*, 198 (August 1974).
3. 'Household Textiles', *Retail Business*, 139 (September 1969); 'Blankets', *Retail Business*, 196 (June 1974).
4. 'Electric Shavers', *Retail Business*, 152 (October 1970); 'Razor Blades', *Retail Business*, 196 (June 1974); 'Market for Shaving Creams and After-shave lotions', *Retail Business*, 153 (November 1970); 'Razor Blades', *Retail Business*, 155 (January 1971).
5. 'Floor and Furniture Polish', *Retail Business*, 155 (January 1971).
6. 'Market for Domestic Insecticides', *Retail Business*, 165 (November 1971).
7. 'Detergents and Washing Powders', *Retail Business*, 161 (July 1971).
8. 'Saturated but not static' (an examination of the market for washing powder), Market Research Great Britain (September 1974).
9. 'Washing Powders', a report in *Which?* (June 1968), p. 174.
10. 'Household Medicines', *Retail Business*, 163 (September 1971).
11. 'Electric Food Mixers', *Retail Business*, 181 (March 1973).
12. 'The Market for Mopeds and Scooters', *Retail Business*, 197 (July 1974).
13. 'Frozen Foods', *Retail Business*, 188 (October 1973).
14. The *Grocer* (2 October 1971), pp. 58–86.

15. 'Electric Blankets', *Retail Business,* 163 (September 1971).
16. 'Domestic Washing Machines', *Retail Business,* 177 (November 1972).
17. 'Vacuum Cleaners', *Retail Business,* 157 (March 1971).
18. 'The Electric Kettle: A truly British phenomenon', Market Research Great Britain (March 1974). based on a survey by European Research Consultants (1972).
19. 'Cookers', *Retail Business,* 151 (September 1970).
20. 'Domestic Dishwashing Machines', *Retail Business,* 179 (January 1973).
21. 'Shopping and the Shopper', IPC Publications (1970).
22. T. Joyce, 'The New Housewife', *see* Chapter 8, ref. 26.
23. 'The New Housewife', J. Walter Thompson Survey (1968).
24. 'Electrical Appliances: A summary', Market Research Great Britain. Vol. XIV, Issue 5 (May 1974). p. 6.
25. Noted in Conrad Jameson. 'Theory and Nonsense of Motivation Research', *European Journal of Marketing,* Vol. 5 (4), p. 192.

PART II

Shopping and Consuming Behaviour

'Shopping' and 'consuming' should not be regarded as synonyms for the same process. Shopping is usually considered to be the physical process of purchasing goods which may last minutes or months and often ends long after the purchase of one article, usually by re-appearing as experience in the purchase of another. Consuming subsumes the whole complex of social and psychological factors which surrounds the shopping process, and often the fact of it. The buying or purchase of goods is merely the culmination of the long and intertwined shopping and consuming process and involves a simple financial or credit transaction, the process examined in Part I.

In Part II we shall assume that although we all 'shop', 'buy' and 'consume', these three phenomena have traditionally and economically dominated the role of the housewife in particular. Bearing this in mind, the examination of the behavioural variables behind her shopping and consuming will, where possible, be restricted to those studies and surveys which have taken the trouble to use female samples or observed female behaviour.

5. Attitudes Towards Shopping

Housewives are faced with a real, personal and important problem in relation to their capacity to make use of family resources. They experiment until they establish the mode or organisation which is felt to be reasonable for their personal abilities and suitable for their family. Like commercial firms they do not maximise their situations.

The housewife controls a substantial part of her husband's economic resources and the adequacy with which she manages them, in combination with her own where she works as well, has a significant impact on the mental and physical health of several people. In a way, she is a junior manager whose administrative responsibilities often exceed those of her husband. In addition, her work and the satisfactory completion of it is often as important to her in her perception of role as her husband's success in his work is to him.

A CHORE OR A PLEASURE?

The act of shopping is not the most interesting of the housewife's jobs but neither is it the most boring. Significantly, it is not the act of shopping which is often satisfying so much as the feeling of *stocking* the goods and getting the shopping home. This applies particularly to food shopping since with other goods the act of shopping may be equally as pleasurable as getting the goods home.

This 'stocking' aspect of shopping pleasure was noted by the IPC study 'Shopping and the Shopper' in 1970 and it reflects an about-turn from the source of pleasure in shopping that housewives used to find, that is, the 'social' aspect. The change in the two sources of pleasure has meant a corresponding change in the type and frequency of shopping trips. 'Social' shopping meant more trips for smaller amounts; 'stocking' shopping means fewer trips for larger quantities.

Ann Oakley (1974)[1] in her recent work on the housewife includes data (*see* Table 5:1) which shows that shopping is not the most disliked activity but it still is not as important as cooking.

Table 5:1   Likes and Dislikes of Housewife to some Household Activities

Housework Task	Percentage of 40 women giving answers		
	Dislike	Don't mind	Like
Ironing	75	33	15
Washing up	70	30	8
Cleaning	68	20	38
Washing	65	40	38
Shopping	60	20	55
Cooking	48	18	60

Source: Oakley 1974 [1].

The results of this table are also supported by a similar analysis done on a far larger sample by the IPC study (*see* Table 5:2) which indicates, in addition, that attitudes towards shopping are not homogeneous across all products. Shopping for clothes is more pleasurable than shopping for food.

Table 5:2   Pleasures and Chores—a Comparison

	Most of all	More than Average
Preparing meals	29%	74%
Shopping for cloths	26%	59%
Looking attractive	19%	61%
Washing clothes	11%	52%
Shopping for food	10%	65%
Cleaning and dusting	9%	45%
Making beds	3%	20%
Washing up	2%	20%
Mending clothes	1%	7%

Source: IPC, 'Shopping and the Shopper', 1970.

Also, in the IPC study, of housewives responding to the statement: 'I find that shopping is more of a pleasure than a chore', 35% agreed a lot, 30% agreed a little, 16% disagreed a little and 17% disagreed a lot. Thus, the pleasure of shopping is first, relative to other jobs and second, variable by type. It is also notable that 33% of women find it more of a chore than a pleasure.

IS SHOPPING A SKILL?

Marketers often emphasise the 'skill' of the housewife's job, and politicians and the retail kings alike applaud the ability of the housewife to shop 'skilfully'.

There is, however, some confusion among women on this score. As the following tables show, shopping as an activity is regarded as a skill well below that of preparing meals in relation to 'what is important for a housewife to do well', yet there is considerable agreement with the concept that 'how well you shop makes the difference between a good and bad housewife'. It seems that shopping achieves an average position in the hierarchy of jobs in terms of skill and liking /disliking, but as an activity, as with all of the jobs, it must still be justified as part of the 'good housewife' syndrome (*see* Tables 5:3 and 5:4).

Table 5:3   Is Shopping a Skill?

	There is no real skill involved in shopping for food	*How well you shop makes the difference between a good and bad housewife*
Agree a lot	12%	63%
Agree a little	13%	22%
Disagree a little	26%	8%
Disagree a lot	47%	5%

Source: IPC, 'Shopping and the Shopper' (1970).

Table 5:4   Importance to Housewife of some Household Activities

Activity	*Most important for a housewife to do well*	*More important than average*
Preparing meals	47%	90%
Shopping for food	28%	80%
Looking good	15%	44%
Cleaning and dusting	12%	57%

Source: IPC, 'Shopping and the Shopper' (1970).

There is no doubt that economic conditions also affect the housewife's perception of the skill involved in her shopping so that inflation encourages a more militant and careful attitude. That the housewife is acting like this is supported by a report in the February 1974 issue of *Mintel* which noted, in a rather hurt tone, that the grocery trade should receive 'less blame and more praise' for its efforts to keep prices in check, and that customers are being encouraged by politicians and the media to look upon shopkeepers as people who have to be watched closely and continually suspected of exploiting national economic problems to make unjustified price increases. In the same month the Grocery Trade Index noted in its recent report on the diaries of 12,000 housewives that:

1. The housewife is shopping more efficiently (looking around for price reductions).

2. She has diverted her household spending away from those products which have become very expensive and towards those that have been less affected by inflation.
3. She is spending less in real terms, that is, buying less for her family.

WHY DO WOMEN SHOP?

Women shop because, obviously, they are the chief providers of food and commodities for their household. It is an important economic rhythm in their lives, but to regard shopping as a purely functional activity all the time would be to ignore some of the other important reasons which may intrude on the decision to 'go shopping'.

Tauber (1972)[2] made a useful pot pourri of the various motives and behaviours which surround the shopping routine. He distinguishes between 'shopping', and 'consuming' and suggests that while there are many dimensions of 'consuming' behaviour (which we shall discuss later on) the processes of 'shopping' are neglected. The study which Tauber made was on a relatively small sample (30) and the findings are described as 'hypothesised' motives. They nevertheless give a useful and exhaustive guide to the many reasons for engaging in shopping activity. The 'hypothesised' motives for shopping were:

Personal Motives

1. Role playing. That is, where shopping is part of the traditional housewife role and therefore a woman who takes on the identity of housewife must encounter the sub-roles implied, and 'shopper' is one of them.

2. Diversion. A chance to get away from the circumscribed world of kitchen and kids. Tauber notes: 'The common term "browsing" and the phenomenon of masses strolling through shopping centres reinforces the belief that shopping is a national pastime.'

3. Self-gratification. Boredom and loneliness may propel a person towards a store, or buying may be a form of comfort in times of depression. Several subjects in the study reported that they often spend money on themselves to alleviate depression. This motive for shopping is more widespread than is often realised and is at the bottom of many impulse purchases, certainly with products such as confectionery and cream buns.

4. Learning about new trends. The store is a reflection of wider, social movements. This aspect is of particular importance to those who are innovators. In a study by Rich and Portis (1963)[3] one of the main reasons for enjoying shopping was given as 'seeing new items and getting new ideas'.

5. Physical activity.   Shopping is a simple exercise with an 'implied motive' so that it is not perceived as wasted time.

6. Sensory stimulation.   Handling, seeing and smelling. There is also the stimulation of being part of a crowd in contrast to the controlled silence of the home. This may contribute towards the individual attitude toward the store and be a factor in shop loyalty.

Social Motives

1. Social experiences outside the home.   The market is traditionally a centre of social activity, and women, as Kotler (1972)[4] points out, were the original marketers in historical times peddling the family's wares in the market place. Today, shopping is an opportunity to encounter friends or simply to 'people watch'.

2. Communication with others with similar interests.   Stamps, boats and sports. This is usually a more male approach to shopping.

3. Peer group attraction.   To be with one's own kind and find self-confidence in the process, for example in record shops and boutiques. There may be little intention to buy but where group status is associated with one's holdings or knowledge of a product then shopping may become a form of market research.

4. Status and authority.   The feeling of being waited on and one's every whim catered for by a willing assistant. A mistress/master-servant relationship is created and this sort of motive is characterised by an imbalance between 'shopping' as opposed to 'buying'.

5. Pleasure of bargaining.   This is an extension of the previous principle, but where there is competition between two protagonists who bluff, haggle and insult their way to the act of purchase. This type of shopping is widely regarded as a skill in certain countries. It is notable that where this attitude obtains it is usually regarded as a 'male' activity. Bargaining still operates in some markets in Britain and women are expected to fight the price down in, for instance, second-hand shops and local produce market stalls.

Tauber also suggests that it is possible to have 'impulse shopping' as much as 'impulse buying'. If the shopping motive is only a function of the buying motive then the decision to shop will occur when a person's need for the particular goods becomes sufficiently strong for her to allocate money and effort to visit the store. When there is no economic need then the decision to shop may be on any of the above social and psychological grounds. Thus, the impulse purchase of a packet of chocolate may only be an extension of the same tendency that makes a women suddenly 'pop out' to shop or, when shopping, suddenly dive into a particular shop.

SHOPPING TYPES

A logical extension of the search for reasons as to why women shop has been a search for 'shopper types'. The reasoning is that since shopping is a problem-solving activity capable of variations which are in turn a function of personality then certain personality types should embrace the majority of women shoppers.

The traditional model of 'shopping types' was supplied by Stone (1954)[5] who divided female consumers into four shopping types:

The Economic Shopper (33% of the sample of 150 women)

The behaviour of this shopper is unambiguously directed to the purchase of goods. She is sensitive to the price, quality and assortment of products available and the personnel of the store are completely instrumental to the purchase of these products. Their efficiency is a factor in her decision to purchase goods from a certain store. In Stone's terminology she scores high on 'chain depersonalisation' and low on 'local store personalising'. She is socially mobile and aspiring.

The Personalising Shopper (28% of the sample)

This shopper forms strong relations with the store personnel and these relations are crucial to store patronage. She likes to be treated in a friendly and personal manner by the shop personnel, that is, she scores low on 'chain depersonalisation' and high on 'local store personalising'.

The Ethical Shopper (18% of the sample)

This shopper will sacrifice lower prices to help a small store's turnover rate. She forms strong attachments with stores. She tends to have high social status and long residence in the community and believes the large chains are threats to the local stores. She scores relatively low on 'chain depersonalisation'.

The Apathetic Shopper (17% of the sample)

For this shopper, shopping is an onerous task and experiences in stores are not strong enough to leave any impression on her. Convenience of location is more crucial than price, quality of goods, relations with store personnel or ethics. The cost of shopping is far in excess of value and every attempt is made to minimise her expenditure of effort.

Stone's shopper typologies have formed the basis for other work on female shopper behaviour, such as by Appel (1970)[6] but other attempts to find workable shopper typologies on more precise criteria have met with little success.

Frank, Massey and Lodahl (1969)[7] looked at the potential of psychographics in predicting a household's purchase of beverages (coffee, tea and beer). They suggested that the need for such segmentation was in response to the dissatisfaction that can be expressed at shopping behaviour segmentation by socio-economic characteristics. They were not, however, very successful in their search. They studied 230.000 purchase transactions for the three products from the monthly purchases of 5,000 households from June 1957 to July 1966 on the J. Walter Thompson Consumer Panel. They also took socio-economic and personality data across the sample. They were forced to conclude that:

> The degree of association between socio-economic, demographic and personality variables with household purchasing behaviour is extremely modest. In addition the incremental contribution of personality variables to prediction of knowledge of socio-economic and demographic characteristics is extremely small.

They suggest that a more fruitful area might be to look at the customer characteristics that are idiosyncratic to the customer in relation to a particular product and not to the customer alone. as in the case of general personality variables. They also note the importance of looking at household influences in any female consumer typologies since they had found that the *husband's* personality scores were relevant to his wife's shopping behaviour in certain cases 'although how and at what point his influence is exerted remains a mystery'.

Other studies on personality variables and consumer typologies have not been any more successful when the research was based on general and not product-based personality data. Gottlieb (1959)[8] found only slight differences in personality characteristics of heavy and light users of proprietary medication and Westfall (1962)[9] found only a modest association between personality and customer buying–behaviour in the purchases of cars. The only workable typology of the female consumer seems to be that of Stone's but even this may be usable only because it is very general— then the use may be principally an academic one.

The female consumer is not easily categorised except from the perspective of a particular product which, of course, denotes an infinite typology system, which is, in turn, self-contradictory.

STORE PATRONAGE

Closely linked to the attempts to create shopper typologies have been studies which have investigated the connections between a women's shop loyalty and various psychological and socio-economic variables.

The studies are based on a logic which relates a female's self image to a type of environment where that image is most in equilibrium.

As Stone (*op. cit.*)[5] was able to demonstrate. shopping for purely economic reasons is not all that common while, as the IPC and Oakley studies showed, shopping subsumes pleasure for some women and boredom for others. Thus, it is reasonable to assume that shops may be chosen for reasons which have little to do with simple budgeting factors.

There have been various attempts to relate female self image to shop choice and with varying degrees of success. Dornoff and Tatham (1971)[10] in a recent study on the subject interpret efforts to find a relation between symbolic perceptions of a store and personal image as having met with limited success, mainly because the variables associated with store image have all been measured in such a way as to make comparison with personality variables difficult, if not impossible.

In their study they avoided these variables—friendliness, fashionableness, prestigiousness, reliability, courtesy—and concentrated instead on self perceptions by the female shoppers of 'ideal self', 'perceived self', image of 'best friend' and related these perceptions to the women's choice of favourite shop or group of shops. From this approach they were able to conclude that:

> There was a significantly high congruity in the way that subjects viewed themselves, their friends and [certain] stores ... it appears that the perception of a retail store is merely an extension of an individual's real self, ideal self and best friend.

They found that in the selection of a speciality store, the image of 'best friend' has greater influence than the 'real self'. For the supermarket, the direction of influence is reversed, that is, there is greater 'real self' image than image of 'best friend' in the customers' store-choice decision process. In the case of the department store, the 'ideal self' image has greater influence than the 'best friend' image. While interesting, the results of the Dornoff and Tatham study nevertheless depend on the tenuous and peculiar difficulties of the psychographic study where problems of measurement and the generalisation of results have all been found as stumbling blocks in the practical use of the results.

A wider approach to this phenomenon of store image and patronage was provided by Charlton (1972)[11] who made a useful review of all the factors involved in shop loyalty. He noted that regularities in people's consuming behaviour, for example in the study of brand loyalty, are well documented, but less attention is given to the comparable importance of consumer shop choice. This omission is particularly unsatisfactory, he suggests, now that the importance of the retailer looms up in proportion to the manufacturer in the total marketing process.

First, Charlton makes an enquiry into the definition of shop loyalty: does the consumer who demonstrates shop loyalty favour one shop above all others or is it a question of the frequency with which she changes shops? Can a consumer be loyal while using a stable assortment of shops? Nevertheless, reviewing a selection of approaches he concludes in his review of shop loyalty research that:

1. Shop loyalty is a valid concept, similar in its nature and extent to brand loyalty.
2. As with brand loyalty, no single measure of shop loyalty is adequate, but simple operational measures seem at this stage preferable to the formulation of loyalty indices.
3. Again, as with brand loyalty, shop loyalty does not seem to generalise for the individual across different product fields.
4. No clear-cut relationships seems to exist between psychological traits or socio-economic variables.
5. There is some slight indication of an association between low social class and shop loyalty under the influence of the time available to the housewife to shop. Working women with families are most loyal.
6. There is no relationship between shop loyalty and the level of a customer's expenditure.
7. There is a positive relationship between shop loyalty and brand loyalty in product fields where private label brands are particularly strong.
8. Convenience is a major factor in determining a customer's loyalty.
9. With the move to fewer and larger shops there is no corresponding move towards shop loyalty and, in fact, there may be a decrease.

Nevertheless, despite the potential decrease in shop loyalty among female consumers there have been attempts to relate segmentation strategy to this factor.

Appel (1970)[6], for example, investigated the relationship between those shoppers who preferred the traditional supermarket and those who used the newer one-stop shopping method. He found many similarities but also some important differences. These differences lay predominantly within the two socio-economic categories of age of household head and family life cycle. Shoppers preferring the one-stop shopping tended to be younger (under 40) while only 31% of the conventional shoppers were this young. Also, families with younger children (10 and under) accounted for most of the innovative shoppers and for only 31·3% of the conventional shoppers. Families past this stage of the life-cycle made up 65·5% of conventional shoppers. Other smaller differentiating factors were trading stamp collection: 70% of the conventional group had redeemed them during the last year compared to 48% of the innovative shoppers, and mail order: most of the innovative shoppers had purchased by mail order in the past three months whereas only 41·9% of the conventional ones had. This study by Appel, however, does not distinguish between the individual female consumers, which makes the results of interest but of limited practical use.

A study by Kenny-Levick (1969)[12], nevertheless, did make such a distinction in a study on retail segmentation and his results, based to some extent on the findings by Stone, provide a considerable reinforcement of Stone's findings, while at the same time offering a more detailed and practically useful guide to female consumer market segmentation on the grounds of retail shop loyalty (Stone merely investigated reasons for shopping). Kenny-Levick's study capitalised chiefly on a survey made in 1967, on Liverpool housewives, concerning their shopping motivations and the reasons for frequenting their 'first-choice' store. The reasons given were as follows:

Economic: Lowest prices for the merchandise.

Personalising: Where relationships existed between the consumer and the store, personal contacts were likely to be made and there were ratings of the store in terms of closeness.

Nearness: The 'convenience' factor noted by Charlton (*op. cit.*) in his review of shop loyalty, that is, the nearest shop available because of apathy or lack of time to allocate to grocery shopping.

Quickness in shopping: Where shopping time was at a minimum.

Variety

Ethical: For example, patronising the small man to keep him in business.

Habit: Had used shop for a number of years and saw no reason to change.

Quality

Hygiene: In the way foodstuffs were handled and the general standard of the shop.

Trading stamps

Delivery

Miscellaneous: From joining a savings club to the provision of credit facilities.

Kenny-Levick related these prime motives to 'typical' goals of shop types, so that the shopper typologies were related to retail segments.

Motivation	*Typical goals*
1. Economic consistent with quality	Cut price stores
2. Personalising	Local friendly store
3. Ethical	Co-operative movement
4. Apathetic /concerned only with survival	Handiest store
5. Time saving /given more important motivations to be satisfied	Store where total shopping time is kept to a minimum
6. Enhancement of self image	Prestige store that 'reference' group may be perceived to be patronising
7. Pleasure seeking	Continental delicatessen with wide variety, interesting foods

It is interesting to note that a distinction is made between the 'time-saving' shopper and the 'apathetic' shopper. The former views shopping as a time-calculable activity to be fitted in with a busy routine. Kenny-Levick and Charlton have both noted that this woman is most likely to be busy, usually with a job and also least likely to demonstrate shop loyalty or personalising factors in the shop choice. This type of shopper is likely to become more common with increasing employment of married women. The latter type of shopper, the 'apathetic' one, is merely a housewife who regards shopping as an activity essential for survival and would probably figure in the 33% noted by the IPC and Oakley studies (*op. cit.*) who regard shopping as a chore.

THE RETAILER AND THE FEMALE CONSUMER

Finally, in this overview of retail factors in the behaviour of the female shopper it is instructive to note that, despite the existence of established research on retailer-consumer interaction, the retailer himself does tend to underestimate the potential of researching the female consumer for himself. There are often wide communication gaps between the two parties.

Simmons (1972)[13] in an article on this subject suggests that research by retailers has lagged behind for two main reasons. First, there is the lack of a precedent, so that when a company is successful but has never used marketing research it is dubious about the usefulness of the technique. Second, the retailers, being closer to the consumer, feel that they can spot trends more quickly and accurately than the manufacturers who are often several steps removed.

Nevertheless, a third factor may also be a lack of familiarity with marketing research methods. Simmons suggests, for instance, that while retailers are making more use of their internal statistics, these only show what *was* sold and not *what might have been* sold. They are descriptive and not diagnostic. He says:

> More retailers are realising that their apparent closeness to the consumer can be misleading. Is the decision taken in a large [retail] organisation in fact nearer the consumer than his equivalent in a manufacturing company?

That there is often a gap in perceived views and needs between the retailer and the female consumer can be illustrated by two examples.

First, in a study by McClure and Fryans (1968)[14] it was found in interviews between consumers and appliance retailers that retailers often held considerable misconceptions of consumer beliefs. The strength with which consumers viewed the importance of service and warranty was consistently underestimated, and also the ease of use and style in the appliance purchase decision. Retailers were most accurate in their portrayal of consumers' views on automatic clothes washers and least accurate on kitchen ranges. Retailers also tend to view attributes of competitive brands differently from consumers. These images were either over or under sensitive to specific attributes and seem to reflect historic stereotypes rather than current consumer brand images.

Second, retailers do not often seem to appreciate the difficulties in shopping that women have to face. While it is virtually a truism to note that the typical supermarket shopper is female and frequently a mother, supermarkets and other shops do not provide adequately for women who have to shop with young children. Eirlys Roberts in a report for *Which?* (June 1972) reported on the main complaints which the magazine had received from female shoppers concerning supermarkets. A principle complaint was having to deal with the mechanics of shopping while coping with children at the same time. a problem which is exacerbated anyway by one-man buses, but especially by shops which put children's sections up on the top floor accessible only by a narrow escalator or which do not provide either baby chairs on trolleys, or space inside the supermarket to store the baby while the mother shops. There was particularly no excuse for the lack of chairs in Mothercare whose whole *raison d'être* is supposed to be the mother and mother-to-be.

Perhaps, since shopping is an essential process, retailers have become smug about their provisions for the female consumer and while some stores consider carefully the needs of their women shoppers, it is evident that this is not yet a norm. When decreasing time available coincides with reduced shop loyalty in the future, store facilities and consideration may become important factors in shop choice.

REFERENCES

1. Ann Oakley. *The Sociology of Housework*. Martin Robertson (1974).
2. Edward M. Tauber. 'Why do People Shop?', *Journal of Marketing*. Vol. 36 (October 1972), p. 46–59.
3. Rich and Portis. 'Clues for Action from Shopper Preferences', *Harvard Business Review*, Vol. 41 (March–April 1963), pp. 132–49.
4. Phillip Kotler. *Marketing Management: Analysis, Planning and Control*, 2nd ed, Prentice-Hall (Englewood Cliffs, New Jersey 1972), p. 7.
5. Gregory P. Stone, 'City Shoppers and Urban Identification: Observations on the social psychology of city life, *The American Journal of Sociology* (60) (July 1954), pp. 36–45.
6. Donald L. Appel, 'Market Segmentation: A response to retail innovation'. *Journal of Marketing* (April 1970).
7. Ronald E. Frank Williams, F. Massey and Thomas M. Lodahl. 'Purchasing Behaviour and Personal Attributes', *Journal of Advertising Research*, Vol. 9(4) (1969). pp. 15–24.
8. Maurice J. Gottlieb. 'Segmentation by Personality Types', in Lyn H. Stockman (ed.) *Advancing Marketing Efficiency*, American Marketing Association Chicago (1959).
9. Ralph Westfall, 'Psychological Factors in Predicting Product Choice'. *Journal of Marketing* (April 1962), pp. 34–40.

10. Ronald J. Dornoff and Ronald L. Tatham, 'Congruence between Personal Image and Store Image', *Journal of the Market Research Society*, Vol. 14 (1) (1971), pp. 45–52.

11. P. Charlton, 'A Review of shop Loyalty', *Journal of the Market Research Society*, Vol. 15 (1) (1972), pp. 35–51.

12. C. Kenny-Levick, 'Consumer Motivations: Examples from the grocery trade', *British Journal of Marketing*, Vol. 3 (1969).

13. Martin Simmons, 'Market Research as an Aid to the Corporate Marketing Decisions of Retailers', *Journal of the Market Research Society*, Vol. 14(3) (1972), pp. 152–70.

14. Peter J. McClure and John K. Fryans Jr., 'Differences between Retailers and Consumers Preferences', *Journal of Marketing Research*, Vol. V (February 1968), pp. 35–40.

6. In-store Shopping Behaviour

We move now from the wider field of shop choice to the more heady atmosphere of the in-store interior. Here, female shopping behaviour moves more into the complexities of consumer behaviour, since it is here that she confronts the culmination of efforts from myriad marketers to attract her attention and her loyalty. The packages, the music, the layout, the lighting, the names, the colours, have all been carefully and cunningly designed to lure her one way or the other. For, despite all the massive negotiations, deals. marketing plans and advertising campaigns, the ultimate moment that really matters is when the female consumer actually confronts the product on the shop shelf. If nothing happens in this vital confrontation then all that precedes it, whether with one woman or a million women, has been to no avail.

It would be impossible to cover all the literature on how women and products interact over the supermarket shelf since every brand could tell a different story. What we can look at is how women respond to certain important aspects of in-store shopping.

IMPULSE SHOPPING

A Du Pont series of studies on the supermarket shopper which has been running since 1954 noted that out of 5,500 shoppers in 250 supermarkets, only one in five carried a shopping list. The report in 1954 contended that seven out of ten purchases are decided in the store and that most purchases are guided by the philosophy of 'If somehow your product catches my eye and for some reason it looks especially good—I want it'. This conclusion is perhaps a little journalistic but there is no doubt that other investigators have shown that certain foods. such as cheese, fruit squash and chocolate are particularly prone to housewife impulse purchase. The Du Pont study showed that impulse purchases of products in eye-catching jars. such as pickles, have provoked up to 90% impulse purchase rate.

Christopher, in his book on promotional behaviour (1972)[1], noted from a survey by Gallup in 1968 that the following products attract impulse purchasing at specified rates (in decreasing order of impulse purchase tendency):

Chocolate and confectionery	84%	Meat and vegetable extracts	52%
Cakes and pastries	83%	Paper kitchen towels	52%
Paper handkerchiefs	82%	Breakfast cereals	48%
Soft tissue toilet rolls	67%	Canned soups	45%
Brown bread	62%	Instant coffee	41%
Frozen mousse	61%	Instant milk powder	40%
Frozen fish fillets	57%	Canned cat food	39%
Frozen fish fingers	57%	Butter	35%
Frozen burgers	55%	Teas	30%
Frozen green beans	55%	Margarine	27%
Canned milk puddings	55%		

Nevertheless, despite the prevalence of impulse buying the mechanics behind it are still little understood. To begin with what is an impulse purchase? Is it an impulsive choice by the shopper or is the purchase merely unplanned? Then, what kinds of women are most susceptible to impulse purchase, and does it occur with equal frequency among all customers, or are certain shoppers more likely to make these types of purchases than others? Kollatt and Willett (1967)[2] made a comprehensive analysis of the features of impulse purchase by the female consumer by use of in-store and home interviews. There were 596 store interviews followed up by 197 interviews of the original shopping parties. The results showed that the average customer made eight unplanned purchases while the number of specifically planned purchases was only 2·5. The maximum number of unplanned purchases made by a customer was 40 while the minimum was 0. (Standard deviation was 9·2.)

The incidence of unplanned purchases for women varied greatly between shoppers but in terms of relative frequency the average customer purchased 50·5% of the products on an unplanned basis so that in percentage terms *the incidence of unplanned purchases was greater than the combination of all other intentions—outcomes categories.*

Variables which were found to be associated with unplanned purchasing were few and often achieved significance because they were associated with another master variable, the number of products purchased. For example, the shopper's sex did not predict impulse purchase, men or women were equally likely to indulge in it, but only when the number of purchases were held constant. When this variable was released then women became 'more prone to impulse purchase' but then they also bought more than men. The same effect occurred with days of the week, no day is particularly prone to impulse purchase until the quantity purchased is released then Thursday, Friday and Saturday become good impulse purchase days but also the days when most shopping is done.

What did *not* achieve significance were the wider classes of variables:

economics, demographics, income, number of wage earners, role of housewife in determining budget, occupation and education of household head.

The three major variables to predict impulse purchasing were found to be totally shopping orientated:

1. *Transaction size:* When the number of different products purchased is low then the proportion of unplanned purchases may be high or low, but when the number of purchases is high then the proportion of unplanned purchases is high also. When shopping trips continue to expand and become more infrequent then impulse purchasing will correspondingly rise.
2. *Transaction structure:* Larger and more major shopping trips invoke more unplanned purchases and trips for particular products such as milk and eggs, which have a relatively regular purchase rate, are less characterised by impulse purchase. Drugs, toiletries and desserts, which are more irregular, have a much higher impulse purchase rate.
3. *Characteristics of the shopping party:* These include the presence of a shopping list but in combination with the number of products purchased. If the shopper having a list purchases over 15–20 products then few impulse purchases will be made; with under 15–20 products the list does not affect the percentage of unplanned purchases. Another variable in this factor is the number of years the shopping party has been married: couples married less than ten years have the lowest rate of unplanned purchases and the percentage increases irregularly as the marriage increases.

Kollatt and Willett conclude that much latitude exists in impulse purchase behaviour theory since it is difficult to distinguish between true impulse purchase and mere unplanned purchase. Unaided and spontaneous recall is often used to measure purchase plans in impulse purchasing research and this almost guarantees some items being excluded from normal purchase plans.

RESPONSE TO PROMOTIONS AND DEALS

The in-store atmosphere is riddled with deals, money-off offers, special, bonded or 'flashed' packs, free gifts with special promotions. This 'below-the-line' marketing is designed to promote short-term changes in sales levels of particular products or brands and is a growing sector of marketing expenditure. Christopher (1972)[1] puts estimates of annual promotional expenditure between 1965–9 at between £350 and £450 million compared to the £500 million spent on direct media, for example, press, television and magazine advertising. Below-the-line promotion may even exceed above-the-line in importance within a few years.

Most research on the reactions of housewives only verbalises their *feelings* towards below-the-line activity and Schlackman (1964)[3] noted that there was 'an indication that housewives acted in such a way as to routinise and normalise their shopping behaviour'. That is, the housewife rationalised the price cuts, for example, in such a way that they would fit into her preconceived purchasing framework. The price cuts were not seen as sacrifices in quality where she already had a pre-disposition towards the product or brand, but if the brand was untried and little known, or she had an unfavourable attitude toward it, then she might perceive the price cuts as an indicator of dubious quality. Schlackman also noted that where the housewife was constantly beseiged by such promotional methods as price cutting and offers, then she tended to lose all idea of 'normal' behaviour of the product.

The attitudes of housewives towards marketer promotions in the shopping and door-to-door situation were recorded by the Bradford-Horniblow-Freeman study of 1,000 housewives in the UK. The unprompted evaluations of promotional paraphernalia were recorded in a table by Christopher (1972). (*op. cit.*) (*see* Table 6:1).

Table 6:1　Attitudes of Housewives towards Marketer Promotions

	(%)
Favourable comments	
Think promotions are a good idea /they should have more	10
Like money-off offers, but others just put up prices	8
Like free samples /free samples give you a chance to try new products	6
Think coupons are a good idea /make you buy new products	4
Some are all right but others aren't	4
Promotions are good to introduce new products	3
Lots of goods offered are very good value	1
Other favourable comments	6
Unfavourable comments	
Prefer to have prices reduced instead of promotions	31
Don't like any of these promotions	10
Don't like coupons /coupons are just a nuisance /tend to forget coupons	5
Want more value for money, not free gifts	5
Don't care much for competitions	3
Most of the free gifts are just rubbish	3
Money spent on promotion means an increase in price of product	2
Never know if there is a catch when they say xp off	1
The free samples are good quality, but when you buy the product the quality is not so good	did not reach 0·5
Other unfavourable comments	4

Source: Christopher, (1972)[1].

Response to promotional activity has, as with every other sort of marketing activity, been suggested as a basis for segmenting the female consumer market. Christopher suggests that:

Experience of the promotional process below-the-line quite clearly demonstrates that
segmentation of the market for a product, on a multi-dimensional basis in terms
of differential response to below-the-line, is possible and can be highly profitable.

In order to use response to promotion as a basis for segmentation, however,
knowledge should exist about the nature of the housewife's response to
promotion. Massey and Frank (1965) and the Bradford/HCF Study (1969)
provided two guides to this response.

Massey and Frank[4] examined the purchasing behaviour of one single
food product in one major USA Metropolitan area over a 101-week period
and noted the following characteristics related to housewives and promotions:

1. A significant relationship between the housewife's education and her
   response to such promotions.
2. A small relationship between the working status of the housewife and her
   promotional response, the working housewife being less responsive than
   the housewife at home.
3. Household income made little difference when it came to promotional
   response.
4. Size of household and age of housewife had little effect on their participation in deals.
5. Heavy buyers of a product were somewhat more 'deal prone'.
6. Brand loyalty seems to have no effect on the housewife's response to
   promotions.

The second study ('The Bradford/HCF' Study) conducted among 1,000
housewives in the UK in 1969 by the University of Bradford Management
Centre in association with Horniblow Cox-Freeman Limited found that
'money-off' promotions were by far the most popular with the UK housewife
and those which closely followed in popularity also represented value for
money, that is extra quantity and free samples. These are shown distributed
below:

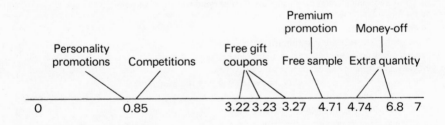

Distance on the continuum may be taken as corresponding to relative
proximity of preference.

The main socio-economic variables associated with response to promotions
were:

1. *Age group differences:* The overall ranking was the same for all age groups.
2. *Regional differences:* Most regions conform to the whole sample. Midland housewives seem to prefer a free sample to extra quantity. South Wales ranked premium promotions higher than free gifts. Scotland produced scores for all promotions which were much closer together and thus suggested indifference between types.
3. *Social Class:* No significant differences concerning promotions were found.
4. *Working status:* No significant differences between full-time, part-time, and non-working women were found.
5. *Family type:* No notable differences for those with and those without children were found.
6. *Attitudes:* No significant differences on attitudes toward shopping and economic attitudes were found.

The American and British studies concur in their estimations of the non-relevance of housewife's age, social class, income, and household size. Disagreement exists on the working status of the housewife, although this may be accounted for by cultural and sample differences.

The only variable of significance seems to be size of transaction, that is, heavy buyers being more promotion-responsive than light buyers, which would tally with the findings of Kollatt and Willett on impulse purchasing. In terms of the British housewife, then, Christopher notes that the group of housewives who are susceptible to promotions, if they were to exist, would be 'under 35 years old, have one child or more at home and live in the North, the North West or the North East of England'.

Finally, there has also been a research area which has looked at the 'deal-prone' consumer. This type of consumer is supposed to be particularly prone to economy offers and price cuts, and has occupied the attention of several large studies. Webster (1965)[5] and Fry and Siller (1970)[6] have both examined features of deal-prone behaviour but add little to the findings already discussed. Webster notes again that deal-proneness increases as the numbers of brands and units purchased increases and suggests, contrary to Massey and Christopher, that brand loyalty tends to increase as deal-proneness decreases. Fry and Siller support the contention of Massey and Christopher that social class is not an important distinguishing variable in itself but notes that deals are more threatening to the working-class woman than to the middle-class one.

Generally, with regards to deal or promotional susceptibility, it would be wise to take note of Kollatt and Willett's guide to impulse buying of any sort, that it happens to almost everyone, at least some of the time, and the distinguishing variables are shopper/purchase related rather than personality or socio-economic related.

STORE ATMOSPHERE

Apart from in-store shopping behaviour, an important facet of the store environment is its mood and atmosphere. Music, colour, warmth and light are features which have been suggested as having an effect on the female shopper, affecting her shopping behaviour and possibly contributing to the high rate of impulse purchase in the shop environment.

Intuitively, one could suggest that the housewife would be under considerable tension in the store situation since she is surrounded by so many purchase choices which must in turn be related to budget and family constraints. Nevertheless, work by James Vicary found instead that the opposite effect is achieved.

He set up a camera to record the blink rate of the supermarket shopper. A normal one is about 32 per minute, that in extreme tension is 50–60 per minute and that for a person who is notably relaxed is around 20 a minute. Vicary found that instead of the blink rate rising, the shoppers' blink rate went down to a rate of 14 a minute which is comparable to the first stage of hypnosis. The women did not recognise their friends or neighbours, walked into boxes, and picked goods off the shelves at random. As they approached the cash-till their blink rate rose to a still subnormal 25 but the sound of the till and the voice of the assistant asking for the money caused the rate to quickly rise to an abnormal 45 a minute. Gerald Stahl of the Package Designers Council carried this finding to the extreme when he suggested that the housewife in a supermarket has so many different choices that she needs a package to 'hynotise' her into picking it up: a good package should transfix a woman like 'waving a torch in front of her eyes'. Reds and yellows, he suggests, are very good colours for doing this.

Another factor which may lull the housewife into a false sense of complancy in the supermarket situation is the presence of music. Nevertheless, there is also evidence which suggests that some women may even be disturbed by this intrusion into their consciousness.

Fisher and Greenberg (1972)[7] have noted that some women find certain music extremely disturbing rather than relaxing and that this is a function of their psychological femininity. Some of the data they review indicates that some women respond to music as if it were an intrusive force which evades their defences and arouses disturbing sensations. Since higher levels of 'femininity' had been shown to correlate with absence of concern at 'intrusion', Fisher and Greenberg hypothesised that the less 'feminine' the woman the more she would be disturbed by outside music while she was occupied by other activities, which is a situation closely parallel to the supermarket situation. The results confirmed that the amount of disturbance produced by music was inverse to the woman's degree of 'femininity'. The results suggest that more 'masculine' women and conversely more averagely masculine men would be disturbed by the presence of in-store music.

Certainly, it is obvious that whatever the cause, music, colour, light or warmth, the female shopper is not in a totally 'normal' state of mind in the shop environment and could well be particularly susceptible to all the marketing cues, more so than in the ordinariness of her own home.

DISPLAYS AND SHOPPER MOVEMENT

Research of every conceivable type, both by the manufacturer and the retailer, has been done on shop displays. Examinations have been made of the varying effectiveness of displays whether end-aisle, end-gondola, eye, knee or waist level, shelf facings or checkout stands. Engel, Kollat and Blackwell (1968)[8] note that much of this research has been accomplished by organisations with vested interests and suggests that much of the 'effectiveness' is overrated in sales value and volume terms. The research also tends to underestimate the tendency of women to 'stock-up' at these displays which will artificially swell their sales effect. Nevertheless, there are certain general 'rules' about displays and their effectiveness in relation to the shopper. For example, it is established that women will be more prone to purchase those products at eye level so that retailers usually put frequently bought, necessity products at knee or waist level where they will be sought and the impulse purchase products at eye level close to related products, such as the evaporated milk near the canned fruits. Small, impulse products will also be placed by the checkout where the woman has a chance to stand and ponder them and certain displays are usually positioned to 'pull' the woman around the shop.

An extension of this principle is the tendency to place necessity food products such as sugar and bread at the back of the supermarket so that the woman must pass many less necessary but more impulse-prone products en route. She may also find her exit blocked at the ends of certain aisles so that she is forced to pass yet another range of goods in order to leave the shop and so be presented with the opportunity to buy yet again. This 'pulling' or traffic of women around the supermarket is the subject of another range of studies on in-store shopping behaviour and these often show that women have distinctive 'pass and buy' rates for certain products. For example, a study in the *Progressive Grocer* (1964)[9] charted up the number of customers in the average supermarket who pass and buy from a major product group:

Out of 100 customers 94 pass and 80 buy fresh meats

93	78	. dairy produce
61	21	. coffee, tea, cocoa
53	20	. fruit, canned
64	19	. meat, canned
66	15	. pickles, olives, relishes
49	12	. snacks
55	22	. soft drinks
55	12	. vegetables, dried
30	6	. housewares

Another aspect to customer traffic is the incidence of occasions when a woman, finding that her favourite brand, or brand colour, or package size is not on the shelf searches for a replacement or refuses to search at all. Reactions to this situation are often dependent on the product involved. Peckham (1963)[10] in an article based on a Nielsen study noted that a quarter of shoppers often left a shop with their wants unsatisified. Fifty-eight per cent on average, over a range of products, would buy substitutes, but 42% did not buy. The reactions to particular products in terms of refusal to buy was:

dentifrice	67%	canned beans	36%
floor wax	57%	tuna fish	36%
instant coffee	57%	vegetable and tomato	
detergents	50%	juices	36%
salts and cooking oils	48%	ready-to eat cereals	34%
margarine	44%	crackers	29%
toilet soaps	41%	toilet tissue	29%
cake mixes	40%		

When the size of brand they wanted was not there, 52% of shoppers would buy another size and 30% would buy another brand, but 18% would not buy at all. When the colour was not available then 69% would buy another colour in the same brand, 20% would buy another brand and 11% would not buy at all.

Finally, in relation to shopper movements and with an eye to the future when more men will be found regularly in the supermarket situation, it is interesting to note that two studies by Henderson and Lyons (1971 and 1972)[11,12] have found distinct sex differences in the ways men and women move in a crowd. The study found that men and women behave as if they belonged to different populations in an otherwise homogeneous group so that male and female curve measurements were displayed from each other by a small but definite amount, the feature being more pronounced for females than for males. In a supermarket of the future we could well find two distinct traffic flow patterns and 'pass and purchase' rates based on the shopper's sex.

Still on this point of sex differences and in conclusion to this section on store behaviour, it is instructive to note that one important trend in shopping behaviour over the next few years will be the involvement of the man, shopping for himself or a family and with or without a woman.

THE MALE SHOPPER

More husbands are helping with every form of family activity. Surveys in 1967 and 1968[13,14] found that husbands helped with shopping in 8% of cases every day or most days and 'helped regularly' with shopping, 35% of the time. This trend to family shopping seems to be part of a general tendency not to delineate roles quite so strictly. After all, according to these surveys, husbands also regularly help with cooking, making beds, and general cleaning and dusting in up to 33% of instances, and 26% wash up particularly frequently, either every day or most days, and 41% some days (*see* Tables 6:2 and 6:3).

Table 6:2 Help Received from Husband with Household Activities

Help received from husband with	Every day /most days	Some days	Hardly ever /Never
	(%)	*(%)*	*(%)*
Shopping	8	39	52
Cooking /preparing meals	9	33	56
Washing clothes	2	12	83
Washing-up	26	41	31
Cleaning /dusting	5	34	58

Source: New Housewife Survey. J. Walter Thompson (1968).

Table 6:3 Husbands and Wives Helping Each Other with Household Duties

	Husbands saying they help regularly with	Wives helping husbands regularly with
Washing-up	69	57
Making fires	51	42
Cleaning shoes	37	26
Shopping	35	25
General cleaning /dusting	33	16
Cooking	25	17
Putting the children to bed	22	21
Making beds	21	9
Washing floors	11	4

Source: NOP Survey (1967)[14].

Nevertheless, this increasing help by the husband has been a long-standing trend. As long ago as 1954 an American survey[15] in Michigan noted that purchases by men alone for the family budget accounted for 13·7% of the total compared to 14·5% for woman and child. It was predicted *then* that:

> With a shorter working week, the men may take over the responsibility of buying the groceries; men are taking an increased interest in the food budget, are becoming more brand conscious and aware of a certain shift in family responsibilities.

Another American survey of the early 1960s noted that the husband not only accompanied the wife in shopping for food 18·7% of the time, but he also prepared food, if only on special occasions 26% of the time, and 'loves to prepare food, and enjoys fixing things himself' in 14·8% of cases[16].

More recently, similar husband involvement has been noted by the NOP survey for the *Daily Mail* which found that he was likely to accompany the wife on shopping expeditions 16% of the time (with greater potential in the ABC1 group) and this represented a regularity greater than the accompaniment of children under four years, who are with the housewife, presumably, all day (*see* Table 6:4).

Table 6:4   Housewife Shopping Alone or with Other People

		Social Class		Age	
	All	*ABC1*	*C2DE*	*Under 35*	*Over 35*
Base	*918*	*280*	*638*	*236*	*682*
	%	%	%	%	%
Alone	51	48	52	28	59
Not alone	49	52	48	72	41
Husband	16	17	15	28	12
Child(ren) under four	12	13	11	39	2
Child(ren) 5–11	7	6	7	16	4
Child(ren) 11–15	3	2	3	0·5	4
Mother	1	1	1	3	0·5
Friend /Neighbour	3	5	3	4	3
Other	6	5	6	1	7
DK /CR	11	11	10	8	11

Source: NOP Survey (1967)[14].

The most recent survey of all in 1974 [17] by IPC, showed that 63% of husbands now do at least some of the major shopping for the household and even larger numbers get involved in food shopping with their wives. This represents a doubling of the 1967 figure by NOP [14]. About 34% of these husbands go food shopping with their wives at least once a week and 17% do the food shopping on their own at least once in that time. The IPC survey notes that there is evidence that this sort of behaviour is a function of a new social movement which is indicated by a variation in age. Husbands with wives over 35 years are less likely to accompany their wives than is the case with the younger couples. As many as 66% of husbands with wives under 35 go shopping with them while above that age the proportion drops to 45%. *Retail Business* comments:

> For some time now a social revolution has been going on in Britain's food shops which seems to have escaped the notice of those manufacturers and advertisers who persist in directing their appeal to the woman of the house, in the belief that she, as purchaser, is the one who must be induced to buy their products.

There are two principal effects on the consuming process for the housewife, of the husband's greater involvement:

1. The limit of purchases by weight alone, is effectively raised. A TGI survey by BMRB in 1970 found that the limit was raised by as much as three-

quarters for those one in four wives they found who took their husbands on the shopping trip with them.

2. The husband can make his product influence directly in the shopping situation rather than vicariously through expressed preferences to the wife. The survey for J. Walter Thompson (1968)[13] found that 8% of husbands have a direct stimulant effect on purchase, that is, encourage their wives to try something new or extra and only 1% act as a brake on purchase. The survey noted that:

> Quite clearly then, the presence of the husband stimulates the housewife to buy more than she would otherwise have done. This may not account for *all* the difference between the spending patterns of the housewives who do and those who do not shop with husbands but it is likely to account for a considerable part of it.

An American survey (1970)[16] found that while the husband 'goes along with' the wife's ideas on food spending for the most part, he acts as damper on spending in 7·8% of the cases but actually is extravagant and spends too much in 14·5%. He is also recorded as expressing preferences for food products in particular (a point which will be examined in greater detail in Part III) in at least 20% of cases and sometimes in 34·9%.

SEX DIFFERENCES IN RESPONSE TO PROMOTION AND SHOPPING

Thus, given that the masculine involvement in the shopping process is not a fad but the start of what looks like being a growing involvement of the husband—not only in shopping but also in other domestic matters—to what extent are we aware of sex differences as a segmentation basis for promotional and shopping response?

Language

Physical sex differences are well documented by, for example, Hutt (1972)[18], King (1974)[19], and Oakley (1972)[20], yet there is no published evidence on investigations of how these differences will relate to promotional response or purchasing behaviour. In addition, as we shall note in more detail in chapter 19, sampling and stratification assumptions of all social scientists tend to militate against the accumulation of data on sex differences. Does the greater verbal ability of women, for example, make them more able to select brand names and take in promotional information compared to men who tend to excel in mathematical ability, and would this greater skill of the man in mathematics make him a more prudent shopper? One area which should be of particular concern to the marketer is that of language, a fundamental of marketing operations both through the sales messages in commercials and the copy lines in advertisements. Men and women have been shown to talk in very different ways both through the structure of their speech and their fluency. Will the male advertiser and copywriter ever communicate effectively to the female consumer? Will the male shopper respond better to a male copywriter than to a female one?

The sex difference in language is one which tends to favour women. Girls learn to talk earlier than boys, articulate better and acquire a more extensive vocabulary. They also write and spell better, their grammar is more competent and they can construct sentences more completely, while boys tend to excel in the grasp of verbal meaning.

Kramer (1974)[21] and Barron (1971)[22] have also made empirical studies on sex differences in language and communication. Barron, for example, suggests that since members of the two sexes experience 'bisocial realities' and language is a system of communication about realities, then language behaviour of men and women would *have* to differ. To support her contention she provided ample evidence of sex differences in language and one finding, for example, was that women produce more 'participative realisations' than men. For example, men will say 'I listen for the bell' women will say 'I hear the bell'; men will say 'father assented to the marriage', women will say 'father approved of the marriage'. Other such words are 'see', 'hear', 'think', 'hate', i.e. the *doer* participates in the verb. Men, furthermore, will use more instances of the objective noun phrase, for example, 'the car looks fine', whereas women produce more instances of the purposive case, for example 'in order to' and 'for'. Generally, the female sample revealed a greater concern with internal psychological states, and the male tendency revealed an involvement with objects and a verbal emphasis on things. She concluded:

> It is now obvious from the results of the study that men and women speak differently— with different emphasis, with different content and in different patterns. Moreover, the sex differences have initally held constant for different socio-economic and racial audiences . . .
> . . . it would seem that the potential of semi-communication between the sexes is grounded in reality: communication differences do exist.

In a recent marketing study by Myers and Warner (1968)[23] it was found that the differences between men and women in the perception of speech also maintained in the perception of certain adjectives. In this study the comparisons were between housewives, business executives, graduate business students and undergraduate business students. The main aim of the study was to present a methodology for determining the psychological meaning to respondents of several commonly-used adjectives for evaluating products and advertisements. The study demonstrated that perception of the quality of the adjectives varied from one group to another—while maintaining a consistent standard within the various groups.

'Delightful' for example, did not vary much between the groups having a range of means across the groups of only 0·32, whereas concepts like 'moderately good', 'nice', 'slightly poor' and 'unacceptable'—in particular did vary between the groups. Among the housewife group the standard deviation was highest in words such as 'terrific', 'very good', 'quite good', 'not very good' while the differences between the executives and housewives were greatest in concepts of 'fantastic', 'exceptionally good', 'all right'. Certain words may also have different connotations for men and women and this is particularly shown in cases of word association tests. It has been suggested, for example, that experiences of males and females in our culture are so different that meanings of different words may be susceptible to much variance. For example, 'mother' and 'marriage' often hold different connotations for men and women.

There are also sex differences in the meanings of fairly simple words, such as the homonym 'bow'. The meaning of the word can be typically sex-interpreted; men see 'bow', for example, as referring to a context of 'bow and arrow', while women conceive its context as decoration (bows and ribbons) or as a sign of deference (bowing to the Queen). [24]

Packaging and Design

Apart from differences in language, sex differences have also been noted in areas associated with packaging and design. Perceptions of shape, for example, can be sex-based. Certain masculinity-femininity tests, such as the 'Franck drawing completion test', base M-F ratings on how men and women complete certain ambiguous line drawings, and in the case of the Terman–Miles test how they interpret certain shapes. This latter factor also lies at the basis of the Rorschach ink-blot test where male and female interpretations of an ambiguous blob indicate 'normal' and 'abnormal' sexuality. It would not therefore be inconceivable that there are sex differences in the perceptions by men and women of certain designs, shapes and packages. This will occur not only in perceptual priorities of the designs, that is, which feature is seen first and retained, but also in the whole area of what the design 'means' and in likes and dislikes.

In the marketing area, there are few published studies on this problem of sex differences, but what studies there are do indicate differential perceptions between men and women. Witkin (1973)[26], for example, found that women are less able than men in picking out a design from a selection, which might indicate that men are better than women in spotting a package design among those of competitors in the supermarket environment. Pilditch (1973)[25], furthermore, found that while children up to seven or eight years react more to colour than to form, adults react in the opposite direction, and men then react more to form than women do. Cheskin (1960)[27] found that certain shapes did appeal more to one sex than to another and found, for example, that men liked triangles but women did not unless the corners were rounded.

Colour

Colour is another problem. One forgets that a high proportion of men are colour blind, one man in fifteen, and even with normal colour interpretation, different colours may mean different things to men than to women.

This was eminently demonstrated in a study on a confectionery product quoted by Turle and Falconer (1972)[28]. The six identical versions of a single product were each covered in wrappers which while identical in design were differentiated by colour. The respondents, all regular purchasers of the product, were tested for their opinions on the products at various stages before and after eating. In every case the wrap colour not only affected the perceptions of taste by each sex but there were strong sex differences in the response. For example, women rated their product wrapped in yellow almost twice as favourably as the men did, while those wrapped in red were perceived twice as well by men as by women (*see* Table 6:5).

Table 6:5   Responses to Different Wrap Colours (post-eating ratings of same product)

Colour	*Total* (%)	*Men* (%)	*Women* (%)	****
Green	54	67	49	*
Yellow	43	25	50	*
Pink	38	33	40	*
Blue	45	50	45	*
Orange	22	58	11	*
Red	35	51	29	*
Base	(101)	(25)	(76)	

Source: Turle and Falconer (1972)[28]
****Significant male/female difference.
Colour labels have been changed.
3000 point scale + 100 − 100.
(The colours are relabelled for security reasons.)

Product Design

In the area of product design, a study by Blum and Appel (1961)[29] showed that male and female perceptions of a product could be variable not only between sex, but also between designer, advertiser and consumer.

This study looked at a gift which was for use by men but to be bought by women. There were eighteen design alternatives and both the female and male consumers, the client's management and the design firm agreed to evaluate the alternatives from what they considered to be the female consumer's purchasing view and the male consumer's ownership view.

The finding, which is of interest to us, was the pronounced negative correlation that emerged between the managers' and designers' perception of a good product design, and that of the women consumers. It seems that not only had the two groups totally misinterpreted the ideal design as far as the female consumer was concerned, but had also perceived an entirely different problem. The designers had originally decided that it was the masculinity of the package which was the most important ingredient but this was irrelevant to the female consumers. They concluded that:

> Had the packaging decision been made on the basis of the recommendation of the design firm and on the pooled judgments of the client's management, the net effect would have been to select the designs which would have had the least appeal so far as the consumers' samples were concerned.

In conclusion, therefore, there is very little evidence available on sex differences in response to promotional and shopping stimuli. What evidence is available and the extent to which it can be academically related to the marketing arena would indicate that men and women might well respond differentially to such stimuli. Certainly, in the whole area of shopping and consuming behaviour, it is a topic which should be resolved since with more male shoppers around in the future what do we know about their behaviour in the originally 'female' environment of the shop?

REFERENCES

1. Martin Christopher, *Marketing Below the Line*, George Allen and Unwin (1972).
2. Donald J. Kollatt and Ronald P. Willett, 'Consumer Impulse Purchasing Behaviour', *Journal of Marketing Research*, Vol. 4 (February 1967), pp. 21–31.
3. W. Schlackman, 'Some Psychological Aspects of Dealing', in *Research in Marketing*, Market Research Society (London 1964).
4. W. F. Massey and R. E. Frank, 'Short Term Price and Dealing Effects in Selected Market Segments', *Journal of Marketing Research*, Vol. II (May 1965), pp. 171–85.
5. Frederick E. Webster Jr., 'The "Deal-Prone" Consumer', *Journal of Marketing Research*, Vol. 2 (May 1965), pp. 186–9.
6. Joseph N. Fry and Frederick H. Siller, 'A Comparison of Housewife Decision Making in Two Social Classes', *Journal of Marketing Research*, Vol. 7 (August 1970), pp. 333–7.
7. Seymour Fisher and Roger P. Greenberg, 'Sensitive Effects Upon Women of Exciting and Calm Music', *Perceptual and Motor Skills* (1972) (34), pp. 987–90.
8. James F. Engel, David T. Kollat and Roger Blackwell, *Consumer Behaviour*, Holt Rinehart and Winston (1968).
9. 'Colonial Study', *Progressive Grocer* (January 1964), p. 91.
10. James O. Pecham, 'The Consumer Speaks', *Journal of Marketing* (October 1963), pp. 21–6.
11. L. F. Henderson, *Nature*, Vol. 229 (1971), p. 381.
12. L. F. Henderson and D. J. Lyons, 'Sexual Differences in Human Crowd Motion', *Nature*, Vol. 240 (8 December 1972).
13. New Housewife Survey, J. Walter Thompson (1968).
14. NOP Survey (1967), *see* chapter 9, ref. 1.
15. Super Valu Stores Study (Minnesota), *see* Hepner (ref. 24) p. 87 and Table 4:1.
16. Social Research Inc. (March 1968), for *Better Homes and Gardens*, noted in, 'The Food Industry', a *Better Homes and Gardens* Report (1970).

17. IPC Surveys Division, 'Husbands and Wives and Food Purchasing' (1974), quoted in *Retail Business*, 193 (March 1974).
18. Corinne Hutt, *Males and Females*, Penguin Books (1972).
19. J. S. King, 'Women and Work: Sex differences and society', Department of Employment Manpower Paper No. 10 (1974).
20. Ann Oakley, *Sex Gender and Society*, Maurice Temple Smith (1972).
21. Chris Kramer, 'Folk Linguistics', *Psychology Today* (June 1974), pp. 82–5.
22. Nancy Barron, 'Sex-Typed Language: The production of grammatical cases', *Acta Sociologica* (July 1971).
23. Myers and Warner, 'Semantic Properties of Selected Evaluation Adjectives', *Journal of Marketing Research*, Vol. 5 (November 1968), pp. 409–12.
24. Noted in Walker Hepner, *Advertising: Creative communication with consumers*, McGraw-Hill (1964), pp. 86–7.
25. James Pilditch, *The Silent Salesman*, Business Books (1973).
26. R. Witkin (Director of State University of New York), noted in Pilditch *op cit*, p. 93.
27. Louis Cheskin, *Why People Buy*, Liverright (1960).
28. J. Turle and R. Falconer, *see* chapter 12, ref. 9.
29. Milton L. Blum and Valentino Appel, 'Consumer versus Management Reaction in New Package Development', *Journal of Applied Psychology*, Vol. 45(4) (1961), pp. 222–4.

7. Prices, Branding, New and Convenience Products

As we noted at the beginning of this chapter, female behaviour in the shopping environment can be approached not only from the more mechanical aspects of simple 'shopping' behaviour, but also from the more diffuse and generalised aspects of 'consumer behaviour' theory. Moving into this territory we encounter more uncertain psychological or 'psychographic' measures of female consumer behaviour and no attempt will be made to note the full range of theory on these subjects. This can be found in any good specialist book on consumer behaviour. What we shall be concerned with is those research findings on aspects of consumer behaviour which can be related to the woman buyer specifically, which have used female samples or which have attempted to relate the research to the female life style.

PRICING

Price Sensitivity and Price Plateaux

Consumers are often more oblivious to the prices of products than the popular press in their lauding of the housewife would care to know. Furthermore, sensitivity to the price of a product seems to depend on the nature of the product itself. In a study by Haines (1966)[1] 25% of shoppers interviewed did not know the relative price of the brand of toothpaste that they purchased while Stone (1954)[2] in a study of surburban Chicago housewives concluded that only 33% of them could be legitimately categorised as economic shoppers primarily interested in price. A study in the *Progressive Grocer*, 'Colonial Study' (1964)[3] found that less than 40% of consumers could estimate within plus or minus 5% the prices of highly advertised food products and Wells and LoScutio (1966)[4] found that price concern varied significantly between products so that it was high for detergents but low for cereals.

Much work on the housewife's perception of prices has been spearheaded by Gabor and Granger of Nottingham University. Since 1961[5] they have made analyses of the price variable in the product mix as perceived by housewives of all denominations. Prices variation, they contend, is only as useful as the sensitivity of the consumer to the standard price of that product. Where price sensitivity is low it would be a waste of effort to aim at high precision pricing.

Two areas they examined were the relative sensitivity of price perception across various products and the use of plateau pricing i.e. using £1·99 instead of £2·00 (1964)[6]. In the former case they say that the price sensitivity of a housewife to a product is, by definition, a function of her awareness and recall of that price. To illustrate this they quote an American study which set up 59 branded articles on tables in stores and customers were asked the price of each item; it was found that the 'correct' price varied with the article from 2% to 86%.

Gabor and Granger set up a similar study and had investigators call on and question 422 British housewives about recent puchases of 15 selected products. Of 15 product groups, 7 could be checked against actual prices and the variation in the percentage correct ranged from 44% to 80% with an average of 59% (*see* Table 7:1).

Table 7:1   Accuracy of Price Recall

	Total	Correct	Wrong	Don't Know	Base: No. of Purchases
	%	%	%	%	
Tea	100	79	16	5	(357)
Coffee	100	68	22	10	(160)
Sugar	100	67	13	20	(397)
Jam and Marmalade	100	60	23	17	(197)
Margarine	100	46	44	10	(252)
Flour	100	36	29	35	(281)
Breakfast cereal	100	35	40	25	(244)

Source: Gabor and Granger (1964)[6].

Comparing tea with breakfast cereal, they found that 95% of the respondents gave a price for tea, with the large majority of the answers correct. For breakfast cereals, more than half of the 75% who ventured to state the price remembered it incorrectly. Gabor and Granger note, however, that variability in price-recall may imply similar variability in sensitivity to price changes and differences, but it does not necessarily follow that the customer who is fully aware of the price will always plump for the cheapest comparable brand or buy it at the lowest-priced retail outlet. Nevertheless, 'the main issue is that the "right" price has wide latitude for some commodities and practically none for others' in the eyes of the housewife.

A second set of studies by Gabor and Granger (1964)[7] echoed these findings. A study in the *Progressive Grocer* showed that 86% of the respondents could get the right price of Coca Cola and 91% were within a 5% error; on the other hand only 2% could recall the exact price of shortening and 34% only were within 5% of the right price.

In another study, Gabor and Granger found that social class of the female consumers affected price sensitivity. They studied 640 housewives over 15 commodities and found that price consciousness was high for some products but there was also a relationship between price consciousness and social class.

Housewives in the highest social class were more willing than housewives in the lower classes to name a price for a commodity, whether correct or not, but the percentage of correct prices recalled was greater for the lower social class groups of the respondents. Thus, in relation to price sensitivity, there is a wide variability in the way a housewife consumer will remember prices and perceive changes in them but the variability is largely product based, although there is some evidence that working-class women may be more price sensitive than their middle-class counterparts.

In the case of the housewife's response to plateau pricing—Gabor and Granger interviewed 3,200 housewives (1964)[6] and concluded that the attitude depends largely on the price structure prevailing in the particular market. It seems that the female consumer comes to regard the prevailing price *method* as the norm for the market, so that if £1·99 is the pricing method particular to a market then £1·83 and £2·00 become 'false' or 'phoney' prices. In markets which do not use this 'penny-below' doctrine then no such idea seems to root in her mind. This is illustrated by two products, one of which uses the 'penny-off' doctrine and the other not. In the first we can see that there is a distinct preference for the prices at the 1p before the plateau; in the second there is no such peaking and the overall range of acceptable prices is smoother (*see* Diagram 7:1).

Diagram 7:1   The Housewife's Response to Plateau Pricing

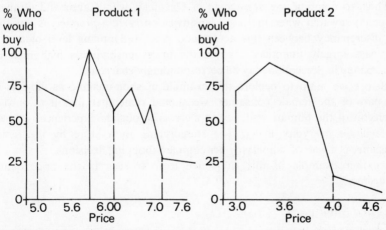

Source: Gabor and Granger (1964)[6].

It is suggested that where marketers create an artificial price standard they are creating a norm for the female consumer and a weighty artifact which could prove lugubrious in later price changes.

Prices and Stores

While Gabor and Granger argue that a female consumer's price sensitivity is a function of the product and the market pricing method, it is also argued that prices perceived as good or bad by the consumer are also a function of the store at which she purchases. It could be said that the store pricing norms become the 'market' norms for the duration of the shopping trip so that the norm is both variable to the commodity, as Granger and Gabor suggested, and variable to the store. Sainsbury and Tesco, for example, may exert norms on the shopper which will alter in relation to shop prices as she transfers her custom from one to the other. This view was propounded by Oxenfeldt (1968)[8]. He suggested that the housewife builds up images of a store by five main channels: words spoken and the tone in which they are expressed about the store by her friends; seeing the store: the quality and content of their promotion; the merchandise displayed in the window, television and magazine advertising; and stimuli from post-purchase contact with the products bought at the store. He suggests that this information is coded over time into an impression of the store, its quality, fairness, cheapness, value, cleanliness and so forth, and this differs with individual women, so that an attitude structure is built up by various individuals who will then differ in their perceptions of the same stimulus. For example, a perception of a store as 'expensive' will colour the perception of a price as 'expensive', although it is no higher or lower than elsewhere. Similarly, a store with a cheap image will be perceived as good value even though the article in question is 5–6p more expensive than down the road at Marks and Spencer.

Thus, to combine the arguments of Oxenfeldt with Gabor and Granger, we could say that when the price sensitivity *on certain products* is low then the discrepancy between this actual and perceived pricing level of a store will pass largely unnoticed. Where the price sensitivity is high then the discrepancy in perception may be correspondingly sharpened.

Before we jump to deplore this example of shop-imaging as illogical on the part of the female consumer, we should remember that it is only an extension of the human tendency to stereotype outside experiences in order to facilitate everyday living. The stereotyping of a store by the female consumer is a way of simplifying her complex shopping decisions.

Another example of this subjective logic is seen in the price/quality syndrome.

Price and Quality

As much as people may take pride in their ability to be 'economic' shoppers there are also shopping situations where the simple economic theory of pricing is turned on its head, where an increase in price may lead to an increase in sales volume. This is a function of the grey area known as 'psychological' pricing, where the price is not merely an indicator of monetary value but of other intangible values, luxury, exclusivity, the good life and, in fact, becomes not so much a monetary appendage as part of the product mix.

This aspect of pricing has not exactly dominated the literature on pricing but work by Fry and Siller (1970)[9] concluded that the tendency of a woman to defer to price as an indicator of quality was primarily a function of her own self-confidence. Those confident of their judgements on quality would be expected to reject the possibility of a price/quality association and purchase a low-priced brand. On the basis of other research findings they had made, Fry and Siller also predicted and found that this observation would favour the middle-class housewife who had been shown to enjoy the challenge of product choice, while the working-class housewife had displayed nervousness and lack of confidence in her ability to discriminate between products on grounds of quality alone. (Such a prediction had also been made by Rainwater, Coleman and Handel (1962)[10].)

This finding, however, should be treated with care since they also found that education level was also related to price/quality consonance. It seems that the better educated housewives in each group had stronger general beliefs that price and quality are related, whether they were working- or middle-class.

While there is no doubt that price in simple monetary terms is often only the most basic guide to the female consumer and that price can be a useful indicator of quality to simplify her decision-making, we should be careful not to over-estimate its importance in the *total* decision. Engel, Kollat and Blackwell in their brief review of price as a 'surrogate indicator' note that price as an evaluative criterion is frequently 'overrated'. In fact, the 'greater the number of alternatives the less important becomes price as an evaluative criterion'.

Prices and Households

The proportion of the household budget that is spent on a particular product or group of products has been well documented. For example, there is the established Engels' Law which postulates that the proportion of a household's expenditure on food will decline as the household income rises. However, what is less known is the extent to which there are household correlates for the purchase price as opposed to the rate of purchase of certain products. Will the housewife's acceptance of a certain pricing norm relate to household characteristics as well as her own shopping behaviour, which is more individually determined?

This is a dubious area in which to work, since general responsiveness to price would logically seem to be a function of the housewife's general shopping behaviour rather than the household socio-economic variables. Frank, Green and Sieber (1967)[11] did, however, attempt an analysis on this subject but with some rather obvious results. They looked at 22 household variables (over a range of grocery products) of which 7 were eliminated because of collinearity with one of the remaining 14.

Those which did correlate were as predicted in the hypothesis:

1. Heavy buyers tend to purchase at lower prices than do light buyers.
2. High income families tend to purchase at higher prices.
3. Large families tend to pay less per unit than smaller families.
4. Car owners tend to pay lower prices than do non-car owners.

Therefore, across 44 grocery products the housewife's reaction to prices was not so much a function of her own status but of the status of the family she represented, with family income and size big predictors of her relative price platform. To say the least, it is a little difficult to see what these results tell us other than it is perhaps better to avoid looking at general household variables in attempting to predict the price responsiveness of female consumers.

Price and Packaging

With some recent controversy over misleading packaging and the relative merits of unit pricing it is interesting to note that in a recent study by Granger and Billson (1972)[12] it was found that women do react to unit pricing by a more economical perception of package size. Granger and Billson asked two main questions:

1. Is price relevant in determining which package size is purchased? If so, can the relationship be quantified?
2. If housewives were provided with value information such as cents per pound, as well as the basic prices, would this affect their purchasing behaviour?

The laboratory experiment used a sample of 200 American housewives and tested their responses to the purchase and perceived value of detergents and popular soft drinks. The conclusions were that prices are of 'clear importance' in determining the selection of package size. Nevertheless, 'many housewives do not have a clear idea of relative value, measured in terms of cents per pound or the like'. When this information was provided a considerable change in choice distribution took place:

> In the aggregate the subjects behaved in the way that economic theory suggests and by applying the theory developed for brand share, a set of specific predictions can be made about the relative share of the market that will be claimed for different sizes at specified relative prices.

OWN BRANDING

A report in *Retail Business* (December 1971)[13] showed that although the growth of own label products was slowing down it still presented a formidable sector in the retail industry. For example, Fine Fare then had 520 own labels accounting for £22 million, about 20% of turnover, while Tesco carried 400 own label brands out of 4,000 which accounted for 20% of turnover. Own label shares also vary widely between different product groups so that private label accounts for 20% of goods in 'women's wear' but only 7% in 'household goods'*.

In some cases, private labels may account for up to 40% of a store's business, for example, Sainsbury, while the Nielsen Researcher (July–August 1969) puts the total annual value of private labels at £300 million. But who among the female consumers are the users of the own brand products? A BMRB report (1970)[14] indicated that, in general, the buyers of own brands were younger (16–34) and more upmarket (ABC1). This was particularly true of Marks and Spencer and Sainsbury. It was suggested that the younger housewife preferred own brands for various reasons varying from cynicism about advertising claims generally, to economy, in that she has the problems of buying for a younger family at a time of relatively low income in the family life cycle. The research also suggested that women often bought own brands as brands in their own right and went specifically to certain shops, such as Sainsbury and Marks and Spencer.

Certainly, there is a fading of the old, poor-quality image of the own brands. In March 1970 an NOP Market Research Omnibus Survey of 1,000 women[15], representative of all housewives in Great Britain, were asked their opinion of the quality of own brand goods. Sixty-two per cent thought own brands were equal in quality to branded goods and only 18% thought they were worse quality: another 18% thought they were better quality. Top of the list of those recognised were Marks and Spencer, and Sainsbury were high in London. Nearly 40% of housewives thought own label products were better value for money than branded items and were generally considered cheaper.

The price factor still remains the important reason for buying own brands and the saving to the consumer varies in estimates from 10–30% (1969 Nielsen Researcher). This gap is now narrowing owing to the big increases in all foodstuffs and particularly in products such as instant mashed potato, fruit squash and plain biscuits (AGB Report, July 1971). Also, as a report in *Retail Business* (December 1971) has pointed out, the onset of decimalisation has made the differences in price seem a little anaemic with three old pence being more attractive than $1\frac{1}{2}$p. This report also notes a survey by TGA in October 1971 which confirmed that over a wide

---

* *See* chap 6, ref. 1.

range of food and household markets, own label price increases were proportionately higher than manufacturers brands in most cases. In 19 major markets own label increases were higher in 10, lower in three, and the same in six.

With the private brand market offering such rich pickings there have been several attempts in recent years to correlate various socio-economic factors with the private brand prone consumers as opposed to those who prefer national brands. The research has had notably little success. Nevertheless, a survey done by Frank (1967)[16] found that the most important variables which indicated whether women would shop for private brands or not were the store purchase variables. Customers who tend to shop in stores with well-developed private brand programmes have a higher propensity to buy private brands than do other consumers. He also found that there were some 'modest associations' between private brand proneness and a household's socio-economic and consumption variables: large families have a higher expected private brand proneness than do smaller ones; the greater a household head's education, the higher is the expected level of the household's private brand proneness: the more cars that are owned the higher the private brand proneness; the higher the household's consumption rate for a product the more likely it is to be private brand prone. Yet the interesting main conclusion that Frank made in this study of forty-four grocery products was that:

> Private and manufacturer's brands meet in head-on competition in the sense that they are consumed by households *with virtually the same socio-economic and total consumption characteristics.*

Weiss (1963)[17] also pointed out that the difference in consumption between manufacturers and retailers brands, in America, was becoming indistinguishable:

> Hiding behind outworn tradition and spurious reasoning is dangerous because the stage has clearly been set for the greatest brand battle of all—the battle between presold labels of all kinds. Who owns the label will be of little moment. What will count will be the skill with which the label is impressed on the shoppers mind.

Frank, Massey and Lodahl (1967)[29] also quote a study by *Good Housekeeping* which revealed brand similarities in facial tissues, canned peas, canned peaches, margarine and salad dressings:

> The overall pattern of results supports the notion that if differences do exist between private- and manufacturer-brand-prone customers, they are relatively slight.

In their own study Frank and Boyd (1965)[18] noted that:

> Our analysis indicated that virtually no segmentation of the consumer market for any of the 44 product categories included in the study has been achieved by means of the development of private branding programmes at retail level.

Generally, therefore, it seems that the usefulness of personal, socio-economic and work variables is slight in the prediction of the private brand prone consumer. There are two main reasons why this seems to be so as noted by Engel, Kollat and Blackwell (1968)[38].

1. A variety of factors may account for private brand proneness but not be strongly associated with other consumer characteristics.
2. Many potential determinants of private brand proneness, such as loyalty to a particular store, price activity, price level, extensiveness of private brand availability and other structural variables have not been analysed. Finally, measures of private brand attitude and proneness may not be valid or reliable.

Brand Image

Branding has frequently been used by consumer behaviourists to explain the orientation of one group of consumers toward a particular product. Self image, they suggest, on all manner of social and psychological variables is the basic link. Britt (1966)[19], for example, says:

> A consumer may buy a product because, among other factors he feels that the product may enhance his own self-image. Similarly a consumer may decide not to buy a product or not to shop at a particular store if he feels that these actions are not consistent with his own perception of himself.

Similarly Grubb and Hupp (1968)[20] note that:

> The empirical data strongly supported the theory that consumers of different brands of a product class would perceive themselves to have significantly different self-concepts. The results also indicated that consumers of specific brands have definite characteristics of others who consume their brand as well as the self-concept characteristic of those who consume competing brands.

The predominant feature in this sort of approach is its mirror-like quality and a dependence on the *status quo*. A brand will only attract the purchase response of the consumer as long as the consumer perceives the image as 'correct'. Where there is a cognitive gap then the brand and the consumer may well go their separate ways. This is an important area to explore in the female consumer market at a time when the self perceptions and 'natural' behaviour of women are now open to so much latitude. Given that branding is importantly linked to the self perceptions of the purchaser, what are the self perceptions of women? Are these self perceptions fairly homogeneous across all products or are they product related? Do they relate to woman as woman, or woman as mother, housewife, wife and worker?

Research by Broverman *et al* (1972)[21] on female stereotypes, self concepts and perceptions of sex roles, and recent reviews of sex role research[22] all stress that while certain extremes of self perception exist in some women which are based on the 'career' woman and the 'mother/wife' there are no easy generalisations for the majority of women who fall between the two poles.

Two studies recently have attempted to link women with products, brands, roles and self perceptions and the results, while by no means providing a total answer to 'what is a woman's brand image?', nevertheless also serve to indicate that no generalisations can be made as to how women see themselves.

The first study by Hamm and Cundiff (1969)[23] on 100 housewives and mothers investigated perceptions of self and ideal images and how certain products fitted in with these images. The sample was divided into low and high 'self-actualisers'. Among the products which came in the top ten of the lists relating to the housewives' 'ideal' and 'self' we find houses, automobiles and dresses, which all the groups share in the ranking positions, but then a deviation. The 'high self actualisers', those women who are concerned with their own development as much if not more than that of their family, rank indulgent, personal products such as perfume, hair shampoo, console hi-fi's, eye shadow, mirror, luggage, nail polish, consistently higher than the 'low self actualisers' who tend to rate household, altruistic and practical products higher in their ideal and self lists. For example, the low actualisers put dishwashers, drapes, canned foods, laundry soap, colour television, bread, consistently higher than the high actualisers.

Where the two groups do agree, it is on those products which are perceived, or so the authors of the study interpret it, as threatening to their roles as wives and mothers and women, such as hormone cream, TV dinners, health foods, or those which 'because of climatic or economic conditions would cause a disequlibrium in equating personal wants with family wants', such as fur coats or necklaces.

Interestingly, the researchers make careful note of the conflicting roles involved in the product associations. They note that there is no one role that all these women respond to, even though the sample was picked for family/household bias. Currénts of personal actualisation, personal perceptions as woman, perceptions of family and mother roles all intermingle in each product perception and by no means could they be said to generalise over all the products. If any of these products, or brands within these products, had to attract a woman's self image, it would have to be researched and examined as an individual item, and could not expect to share other than very general attributes with other products.

This finding by Hamm and Cundiff is ably supported by a more recent study by Wortzel and Frisbie (1974)[24] (discussed in more detail in chapter 17) which allowed women to 'make up' their own advertisements from folio selections of products and advertising images. The women could choose from five roles: 'neutral', 'career', 'family', 'fashion', 'sex object' and 'no preference' and relate them to seven product groups. The study was intended to find to what extent support of the feminist movement indicated which role each woman would relate to which product.

Broadly, the findings indicated that each of the five roles could be assigned in quite clearly differentiated manners to the different product groups. The women saw at least this many dimensions to their roles and self perceptions and by no means demonstrated homogeneity of role across all products. There was also a significant group of women who perceived 'no preference' in terms of the roles offered to them for assignment to individual products, indicating that their role perceptions were wider than the five offered to them. There were also differences noted between women who favoured the feminist cause and those who favoured a more traditional life style. In these cases the evidence also supported the notion that not only did the self perceptions of these groups of women differ, but the differences were further variable over different product groups.

Apart from these studies there is really a dearth of research on women and product /brand /self images. Most studies on brand imagery and branding use male subjects and male-dominated products such as beer (Grubb (1965)[25]) and cars, (Birdwell (1967)[26] and Evans (1959)[27]). One factor, nevertheless, which could also give a guide to which products might lend themselves to branding as far as women are concerned is suggested by Dolich (1969)[28]. He noted that brand image potential is often connected with the public and private consumption of a product. Those products which are consumed publicly and visibly are required to demonstrate more than the more privately consumed ones the ideal self of the consumer, to proclaim to the wider world the potential behind this person. This might, additionally, explain the significance of brand image in cigarettes, cars and beer, which are all publicly consumed.

There are, however, few products which women consume publicly to the same extent as men do, though it should be noted that with increasing consumption by women of 'male' products (*see* Part V on 'Woman Buying for Herself'), marketers would be well advised to look at brand /self perceptions of women in the car, cigarette and drink fields. One would expect that brand /product perceptions are strongest for single women in the same order and type as for men, but for the married woman who owns little in her own right, public consumption may be more prevalent either by proxy—through her children so that their clean clothes and well-kept appearance becomes an extension of her public 'consumption' and her self image—or through those products which she will personally present to the world—such as dresses, coats, cosmetics, perfumes, deodorants and shampoos. Significantly, it is these products which come high on the list of 'self' and 'ideal self' associated products in the table presented by Hamm and Cundiff.

It could well be that the nature of the brand image and its associated role/self image, once individually determined for a product, will be variable in strength by the *extent* to which it is publicly or privately consumed.

Brand Loyalty

A close sister of the concept of brand image is the notion of brand loyalty. Any good book on consumer behaviour will give a good run-down on all the varying definitions that brand loyalty encompasses, but there is very little that can be generalised about the personality correlates associated with it or with the female consumer specifically. There have been attempts to relate brand loyalty to all manner of economic and demographic character-istics but with little conclusive success. If there is any evidence to support this concept then it is usually product based. For example, a study by Frank, Massey and Lodahl (1967)[29] on husbands and wives indicated that for beer, less than 10% of the variation in brand loyalty across customers is accounted for by personality characteristics, for coffee and tea less than 5% of the variation is accounted for and in another part of the same study it was found that there was no link between certain personality variables, brand loyalty and toilet tissue. With regard to economic and demographic variables, the study found that these factors were not related to brand loyalty and Guest (1955)[30] found that there was no connection between marital status, sex, intelligence and brand loyalty although there was a small tendency for respondents in the higher socio-economic strata to have greater preference agreements. Shopping behaviour variables also have produced inconsistent results and no generalisations can be made about the different products. Social class does not predict brand loyalty (Coulson (1966)[31]) and knowledge of brand preferences of other family members does not significantly affect whether respondents have a regular brand that is purchased more than others. Reports on the effects of deals on brand loyalty are also inconclusive; Cunningham (1956)[33] has found that they do, and Frank and Massey (1965)[32] found that they do not affect brand loyalty.

One of the few relevant factors concerning women and brand loyalty seems to be that of shop loyalty, but even then it is variable between products and also between the number of private brands available in that product field. For example, Cunningham found that the only relationship between brand loyalty and shop loyalty lay in the field of instant coffee, where there is a high proportion of private labels. This was supported by Jephcott (1972)[34] who found a clearer relationship between shop and brand loyalty for washing-up liquid than toothpaste, where the former product had far more private label substitutes than the latter. Carman (1970)[35] found shop loyalty to be the single largest factor in the prediction of brand loyalty and in each of the three product fields he looked at, shop loyalty accounted for 60% of the variation in his index of brand loyalty. They were also the fields for which Cunningham found a good relationship, but also high private label activity.

Nevertheless, Rao (1969)[36] excluded private labels from his tests and still found a high relationship between brand and shop loyalty.

It seems, therefore, that to search for a brand loyalty correlate among the female consumers the marketer will have to examine their shopping/shop choice behaviour rather than any murkier, socio-psychological characteristics. Engel, Kollat and Blackwell[38] note:

> At the present time it does not seem feasible to segment markets for grocery products on the basis of attitudes toward, or propensity to purchase, private brands, whether or not purchasers of private brands or other types of products differ from other consumers is, at this point, unknown, and future research in this area would be useful.

INNOVATION

Estimates[37,38] put the failure rate of new products at between 50% and 90%, so it has become particularly important to isolate the special group of women in the female consumer market who tend to be the first to adopt or reject innovation. If these women can be isolated, theorists contend, then by appealing to them directly and specifically the process of diffusion can be stabilised and quickened. These women, by word-of-mouth, example, or by respect of their position as opinion leaders in a community can hasten the acceptance of a product simply because *they* have accepted it.

The work on innovation, opinion leadership and diffusion of innovation is extremely wide-ranging and deals with all manner of products and consumers. There is also a tendency, consistent through many market research reports, to concentrate on male consumers and male products, such as cars[39], owing to the fact that often these are major purchase decisions and lend themselves to easy measurement. With predominantly female products and purchase decisions, the products are often much lower priced and less visible in terms of decision processes, such as food and household goods. For this reason, it is an easy temptation to generalise existing research to the female situation but since the nature of products differs so much this would, for the most part, be unwise. A review which might be helpful, however, is provided by Pizam (1972)[40] who synthesised the results of 37 studies on innovation characteristics (*see* Table 7:2) and was able to conclude that only 16 characteristics were associated with innovation. Certain of these characteristics, however, have also been found in other studies which have made generalisations about women consumers, in particular, those of achievement, motivation and aspiration[41,42] and venturesomeness[43].

Nevertheless, not all the variables which have been associated with innovation tendencies in women have been noted in the Pizam study. Rogers and Stanfield (1968)[41] noted that the woman's education, literacy, income and level of living were also important indicators although these were

Table 7:2   Relationship between Psychological Characteristics and Innovation

Characteristic	Nature of relationship
Achievement conformability	0
Achievement independence	0
Achievement motivation	+
Affective state	+
Affiliation	−
Aggressiveness	+
Ascendancy	+
Aspiration level	+
Cognitive stage	0
Communality	0
Conformity	+
Conative stage	+
Deference	−
Dogmatism	0
Dominance	0
Emotional stability	0
Empathy	0; +
Fatalism	−
Femininity	0
Flexibility	0; +
Impression	0
Intellectual efficiency	+
Interest polymorphism	0
Lability	+
Other directedness	0
Psychological mindedness	0
Responsibility	+ ; 0
Rigidity	−
Self acceptance	+
Self concept (venturesomeness)	+ ; 0
Self control	0
Sociability	+
Socialisation	−
Social presence	0
Succourance	0
Tolerance	0
Well being	0

Source: Pizam (1972)[40].

associated variables rather than causative ones. 'Aspirations for children' was also noted by Rogers and Stanfield which might coincide with the 'aspiration level' of the Pizam study; also, 'knowledge ability' which Rogers and Stanfield defined as 'an awareness of the external world and events in general'. might relate to Pizam's concepts of 'responsibility' or 'empathy'.

Other relevant variables in relation to the innovation tendency of women are:

Communication

Engel, Kollat and Blackwell (1968)[38] in their review on innovation theory noted that there may be a connection between innovativeness and exposure to mass media but it is word-of-mouth communication which offers the richest areas for conclusions. Traditionally and intuitively it has also been accepted that an individual turns more and more to others as she moves through the decision to make an innovative purchase, and this will vary with the perceived risk associated with the product purchase. Risk, in turn, will vary with the perceived newness of the product. That perception of a product as new will vary the risk and increase the tendency for communication, was noted by Frank, Massey and Morrison (1964)[44] and Donnelly (1970)[45], whose research in both cases was on small, frequently purchased food products. Donnelly found that the less new the product, for example freeze-dried coffee compared to powder coffee, the faster it passed through the housewife's diffusion cycle.

It is worth noting, however, that word-of-mouth can work in two directions. Katz and Lazerfeld (1955)[46] found that unfavourable word-of-mouth was more effective in repelling consumers than favourable word-of-mouth was in attracting them. Also, Arndt (1967)[47] found that consumers who received unfavourable communications were 24 percentage points less likely to purchase a new product while those receiving favourable communication were only 12 percentage points *more* likely to buy.

Social Integration

This plays a big part in innovation adoption among women. Arndt found that in the case of a new food product, those housewives who were named most often as a 'relatively good friend' were also among the earliest adopters of the product. Coleman *et al* (1957)[48] found that reliance upon a highly respected member of the group increased with the degree of the risk perceived in the product purchase. This factor of social integration also subsumes gregariousness and this was found to be associated with innovation by Katz and Lazerfeld (1955)[46] and King (1964)[49]. King, in relation to the fashion innovator process, found that the typical innovator had an active life style, visited and entertained friends regularly, attended spectator sports, ate frequently at restaurants and attended many club meetings.

Among other isolated variables which have been found to relate to innovation in women is inner-directedness. Donnelly (1970)[45] found that women who displayed this characteristic were more reliant on their own internal standards and values to guide their behaviour, (related perhaps to Pizam's notion of 'self

acceptance') and they enjoyed risk. Robertson (1967)[43] also found dominance, impulsiveness and activeness were significant variables in innovation
among women.

There is no clear indication that heavy usage indicates a tendency to
innovate and two studies which virtually circumscribe the research in this
area have totally opposed findings. Engel, Kollat and Blackwell (1968)[38]
note that in the case of heavy buyers of millinery they did innovate, but
in instant coffee they did not.

Finally, it is worth noting that the variables that Pizam and others have
remarked as being associated with innovation in women are also those
variables which in masculinity-femininity tests are associated with stereotypical 'masculine' tendencies[50]. Those variables, which we have shown to
be relevant i.e. risk taking, venturesomeness, high education, domination,
aggression, impulsiveness, high aspiration, intellectual efficiency, gregariousness, responsibility and self-acceptance, are not common stereotypical
'female' personality variables and it is interesting to note in the Pizam review
that 'femininity' had no positive relationship with innovation. It is also
notable that women who display these characteristics are also the ones who
receive least representation in contemporary consumer advertising, as we shall
note in more detail in Part VI.

As a footnote to this overview of female innovator types it is useful to
remember that it also may be the housewife who actually thinks up the idea
for the new product in the first place. The *Wall Street Journal* in 1965 ran an
article on consumer innovation ideas and noted that the General Foods
Corporation received 80,000 spontaneous letters annually from housewives.
Could it be that the women who have the 'venturesomeness' and 'aspiration'
to think up these ideas are also the ones who go out and constitute the bulk of
innovators who also buy them?

THE CONVENIENCE-ORIENTATED WOMAN

Convenience foods, as we noted in more detail in chapter 2 are an important
and growing sector in the new food markets. With more married women
working full- or part-time, we can expect more women to indulge in convenience food purchase. Does there exist, however, a woman who has a
particular propensity towards convenience foods? Mauser (1963)[51] noted
that: 'As scarcity of product disappears, the scarcity of time ascends the
value scale.' This theory can be explained as follows:

In an affluent society or group in society, when product availability is
high, time availability tends to be low. This can apply to both men and women
and we would expect that women who hold more than one occupation,
a feature of the more developed societies, would regard their time as more

valuable and thus attempt to reduce their more mundane work. These busy women would, one suspects, be most prone to convenience foods and thus typologies of consumer convenience orientation would then be expected to correlate with features of female affluence and occupation.

This theory does not, however, hold entirely true, according to Anderson (1971)[52]. Anderson found that variety and rate of consumption of convenience foods was largely a *household* characteristic. He found that the degree of convenience food orientation exhibited by the family is significantly related to the presence of and age distribution of children. Stage in the family life cycle was a significantly stronger determinant of convenience food orientation than socio-economic status.

> High convenience food orientation appears typically among 4–5 member surburban families in the early stages of the family life-cycle with the eldest child aged 12 or under. The household head is a well-educated professional between 25 and 40 with annual income significantly above average. Another family type with this orientation is headed by an individual of intermediate occupation and socio-economic status earning average income.

Nevertheless, one should note that the reason why Anderson did not find that any of his results related to the women's occupation, level of affluence and time available, which one might have expected, was largely because *he did not measure these variables.* Admittedly, in this respect he was only being as careless as many of his colleagues right across the social science research spectrum, but in a marketing research study into the use of convenience foods, the omission is particularly frustrating. In fact, to look at convenience food purchase without examining personal variables of the female consumer seems not so much careless as a patriarchial rationalisation of market behaviour gone quite mad. Furthermore, although Anderson's results may describe some features of the convenience-orientated household in 1971 they cannot, since they do not look at the important variables associated with the purchaser, *predict* future patterns of convenience food consumption, a valuable opportunity thoroughly lost.

In the never-ending search for the perfect way in which to categorise the female consumer there have been some fringe and highly specific approaches to pigeon-holing her consuming attributes. It has been worth noting these efforts if only as testimony to the fact that women must be infinitely capable of categorisation, depending only on the ingenuity of the marketer and the research funds and resources available for even more eclectic approaches.

As a conclusion to this chapter, however, we shall note one area of research which will no doubt survive when all other searches for typologies have failed. This area represents the search for the marketers' 'holy grail' and the motive which really underlines all the other approaches, that is, the search for the 'persuasible woman'.

THE PERSUASIBLE WOMAN

The dream of the marketer must surely be that somewhere, somehow, there exists a group of women who are infinitely open to marketing persuasion, who by their very nature are unable to resist the smallest, the most barefaced supplication to her to buy. That the persuasible woman exists is an intuitively 'obvious' fact to most men and to marketers in particular. The research on the subject, nevertheless, does nothing to reassure us of her existence, except in certain highly specific instances. The study by Cox and Bauer (1964)[53] on persuasibility in women is virtually a classic piece in consumer behaviour theory and yet even this is extremely guarded in its conclusions.

The authors noted that while a well-established finding in literature on personality and persuasibility is that males low in self esteem or generalised self-confidence are on the whole more readily persuaded than males high in self-confidence, no similar finding had been held for women. Nevertheless, they noted that people low in *specific* self-confidence with regard to a particular influence situation (a specific task or solving a specific problem) are more readily persuaded in that influence situation than are people high in specific self confidence, and this relationship apparently exists for both men and women. Cox and Bauer wanted to know if women who were high in specific self-confidence but low in general self-confidence would alter a precisely made judgement in a problem-solving situation. They wanted to know whether they would change their judgement in the direction advocated by the communicator (advertiser) in the hope of avoiding social disapproval or whether they would tend to stick to their original judgement because they felt that the judgement was correct.

In the experimental situation subjects were first asked to indicate how good they were generally at judging people, colours, fashions, fabrics and nylon stockings. They were then asked to evaluate two brands of stockings on eighteen attributes. The two brands of stockings were, in fact, identical. Subjects were asked to indicate how confident they were about their evaluation. They then heard a tape-recorded 'sales girls' opinion that one brand was better than the other on six attributes. The subjects then re-evaluated the nylons.

The surprising results were that women who were medium on self-confidence were the most persuasible, not those who scored low. The relevant factor here was thought to be ego defence, that is, if subjects were very confident in their own general abilities then they were not likely to accept the salesgirl's help. If they were really low in self-confidence they were too defensive to accept the help. This left the middle confidence group which could be swayed.

Nevertheless, even with this general guide in mind Cox and Bauer still did not feel that there were yet sufficient grounds to generalise about a 'persuasible woman' and suggested:

For the present time it seems unlikely that subtle personality differences between market target groups for specific products are going to acquire tangible meanings in market research.

CONCLUSION TO PART II

There is little homogeneity about the different components in the house-wife's shopping and consuming behaviour. Many research studies have examined such behaviour from a variety of angles but, in general, one must consider that:

1. Shopping is not a purely economic activity. It is linked with elements of the traditional housewife role but is viewed ambiguously as a skill and a chore, a pleasure and a duty. Shopping is, as an activity, a satisfaction of diverse motives as wide as alleviation of boredom and a reaffirmation of status.

2. Certain shopping areas such as frequency of purchase and certain personality variables such as masculinity-femininity, age, self-confidence and particularly, sex-role perceptions are useful guides to female con-suming and shopping behaviour. These variables, however, have for the most part been shown to be not so much predictive as associative. Of the two variables, the most useful would perhaps be more the mechanical shopping aspect rather than personality.

The most important variable of all, however, will be the product itself and data will not generalise easily, if at all, across all products.

Generally, however, what we need is considerably more imagination in our attitudes to research on the female consumer. Many of the variables which we choose to investigate have been linked uncomfortably to certain cultural stereotypes (the 'apathetic' shopper instead of the 'time-saving' one; the housewifery and child-care variables instead of wider ones such as politics and sexuality). We also omit to investigate as factors in the consumer behaviour of women, those non-obvious personal variables such as psycho-logical masculinity, ambition, aggression, frustration, ambivalence to social role, resentment and generational variables (aspiration and frustrations of the subject's mother). Why these are omitted is open to conjecture but one reason may well be that these variables are widely considered by men to be 'unsuitable' in women, if they are assumed to exist at all. Nevertheless, merely because they are discomforting to conceptualise does not mean that these variables do not exist. In fact, new evidence on sex differences and roles is discovering that they do exist in women both commonly and strongly.

We really must face the fact that existing evidence on female consumer behaviour, for all its effort and elegance, has yielded little that is important or predictive about that behaviour. Much of the research is sterile and unprepossessing. We must look for something new.

Unfortunately, where women are concerned, it seems that the marketer has lost the ability to think either laterally or originally.

REFERENCES

1. George Haines, 'A Study of Why People Purchase New Products', in R. M. Haas (ed.) *Science Technology and Marketing,* American Marketing Association (Chicago 1966), pp. 665–85.
2. Gregory P. A. Stone, 'City Shoppers and Urban Identification: Observations on the social psychology of city life', *The American Journal of Sociology,* Vol. 60 (July 1954), pp. 36–45.
3. 'Colonial Study', *Progressive Grocer* (January 1964), p. 91.
4. W. D. Wells and L. A. LoScutio, 'Direct Observation of Purchasing Behaviour', *Journal of Marketing Research,* Vol. 3 (August 1966), pp. 227–33.
5. André Gabor and C. W. J. Granger, 'On the Price Consciousness of Consumers', *Applied Statistics,* Vol. 10(3) (November 1961), pp. 170–88.
6. André Gabor and C. W. J. Granger, 'Price Sensitivity of the Consumer', *Journal of Advertising Research,* Vol. 4 (1964), pp. 40–44.
7. André Gabor and C. W. J. Granger, 'How Much do Consumers know About Retail Prices?', *Progressive Grocer* (February 1964), pp. 104–6.
8. Alfred R. Oxenfeldt, 'How Housewives Form Price Impressions', *Journal of Advertising Research,* Vol. 8(3) (1968), pp. 9–17.
9. Joseph N. Fry and Frederick H. Siller, 'A Comparison of Housewife Decision Making in Two Social Classes', *Journal of Marketing Research,* Vol. II (August 1970), pp. 333–7.
10. Lee Rainwater, Richard Coleman and Gerald Handel, *Workingman's Wife',* MacFadden-Bartell Corporation (New York 1962).
11. Ronald E. Frank, Paul E. Green, Harry F. Seiber Jr., 'Household Correlates of Purchase Price for Grocery Products', *Journal of Marketing Research,* Vol. 4, (February 1967), pp. 54–8.
12. C. W. J. Granger and A. Billson, 'Consumers Attitudes Toward Package Size and Price', *Journal of Marketing Research,* Vol. 9 (August 1972), pp. 239–48.
13. 'The Development of Own Brands', *Retail Business,* 166 (Dec. 1971).
14. 'Own Brands Seminar', BMRB Report (January 1970), based on Target Group Index information.
15. NOP Market Research Omnibus Survey (March 1970), of 1.000 women representative of all housewives in Britain, quoted in previous reference.
16. R. E. Frank, 'Correlates of Buying Behaviour for Grocery Products', *Journal of Marketing,* Vol. 31 (October 1967), pp. 48–53.
17. E. B. Weiss, 'When is a Label a Private Label?', *Advertising Age* (25 January 1963).
18. Ronald E. Frank and Harper W. Boyd Jr., 'Are Private-Brand-Prone Grocery Customers Really Different?', *Journal of Advertising Research,* Vol. 5 (December 1965), pp. 27–35.
19. S. H. Britt (ed.), *Consumer Behaviour and The Behavioral Sciences: Theories and applications,* John Wiley and Sons (New York 1966).
20. Edward L. Grubb and Greff Hupp, 'Perceptions of Self, Generalised Stereotypes and Brand Selection', *Journal of Marketing Research,* Vol. V (February 1968), pp. 58–63.
21. I. K. Broverman *et al,* 'Sex Role Stereotypes: A current appraisal', *Journal of Social Issues,* Vol. 28(2) (1972), pp. 59–78.
22. *See* chapter 15, refs. 35–43.
23. B. Curtis Hamm and Edward W. Cundiff, 'Self Actualisation and Product Perception', *Journal of Marketing Research* (November 1969), pp. 470–2.
24. Lawrence A. Wortzel and John M. Frisbie, 'Women's Role Portrayal Preferences in Advertisements: An empirical study', *Journal of Marketing,* Vol. 38 (October 1974), pp. 41–6.

25. Edward L. Grubb, 'Consumer Perception of "self concept" and its Relation to Brand Choice of Selected Product Types', in P. D. Bennett (ed.), *Marketing and Economic Development*, American Marketing Association (Chicago 1965), pp. 419–24.
26. A. E. Birdwell, 'A Study on the Difference of Image Congruence on Consumer Choice', *Journal of Business*, Vol. 41 (January 1968), pp. 76–88.
27. F. B. Evans, 'Psychological and Objective Factors in the Prediction of Brand Choice: Ford v Chevrolet', *Journal of Business*, Vol. 32 (1959), pp. 340–69.
28. Ira J. Dolich, 'Congruence Relationships Between Self Images and Product Brands', *Journal of Marketing Research*, Vol. VI (February 1969), pp. 80–4.
29. Frank, Massey and Lodahl in Ronald E. Frank 'Is Brand Loyalty a Useful Basis for Market Segmentation?', *Journal of Advertising Research*, Vol. 7 (June 1967), pp. 30–1.
30. Lester Guest, 'Brand Loyalty—Twelve years later', *Journal of Applied Psychology*, Vol. 39 (1955), pp. 405–8.
31. John S. Coulson, 'Buying Decisions Within the Family', in Joseph Norman (ed.), *On Knowing the Consumer*, John Wiley and Sons (New York 1966).
32. William F. Massey and Ronald Frank, 'Short-Term Price and Dealing Effects in Selected Market Segments', *Journal of Marketing Research*, Vol. 2 (May 1965), pp. 171–85.
33. Ross Cunningham, 'Brand Loyalty: What where and how much?', *Harvard Business Review*, Vol. 34 (January-February 1956), pp. 116–28.
34. J. St. G. Jephcott, 'Consumer Loyalty: A fresh look', a paper read at the Market Research Society Conference, Brighton (1972).
35. J. M. Carman, 'Correlates of Brand Loyalty: Some positive results', *Journal of Marketing Research*, (7) (1970), pp. 67–76.
36. T. R. Rao, 'Consumers Purchase Decision Process: Stochastic models', *Journal of Marketing Research* (6) (1969), pp. 321–9.
'Are some Consumers more Prone to Purchase Private Brands?', *Journal of Marketing Research* (6) (1969), pp. 447–50.
37. *See* Philip Kotler, *Marketing Management: Analysis, planning and control*, Prentice-Hall (1972), p. 466.
38. *See* James F. Engel, David T. Kollat and Roger D. Blackwell, *Consumer Behaviour*, Holt Rinehart and Winston (1968), p. 543.
39. Ralph Westfall, 'Psychological Factors in Predicting Product Choice', *Journal of Marketing* (April 1962), pp. 34–40.
40. Abraham Pizam, 'Psychological Characteristics of Innovators', *European Journal of Marketing*, Vol. 6 (1972), pp. 203–10.
41. Everett M. Rogers and J. David Stanfield, 'Adoption and Diffusion of New Products: Emerging generalisations and hypotheses', in Frank M. Bass, Charles W. King and Edger Pessemier (eds.), *Applications of the Sciences in Marketing Management*, John Wiley and Sons, (New York 1968).
42. Everett Rogers, *Diffusion of Innovations*, The Free Press (New York 1967).
43. Thomas S. Robertson, 'The Process of Innovation and the Diffusion of Innovation', *Journal of Marketing*, Vol. 31 (January 1967), pp. 14–19.
44. Ronald E. Frank, William F. Massey and Donald G. Morrison, 'The Determinants of Innovative Behaviour with Respect to a Branded, Frequently Purchased Food Product', in L. George Smith (ed.) *Reflections on Progress in Marketing*, American Marketing Association (Chicago 1964), pp. 312–23.
45. James H. Donnelly Jr., 'Social Character and Acceptance of New Products', *Journal of Marketing Research*, Vol. VII (February 1970), pp. 111–13.
46. Elihu Katz and Paul F. Lazerfeld, *Personal Influence*, The Free Press of Glencoe (New York 1955).
47. Johann Arndt, 'Role Of Product Related Conversations on the Diffusion of a New Product', *Journal of Marketing Research*, Vol. 4 (August 1967), pp. 291–5.

48. James Coleman, Elihu Katz and Herbert Menzel, 'The Diffusion of an Innovation among Physicians', *Sociometry*, Vol. 20 (December 1957), pp. 253–69.

49. Charles W. King, 'Fashion Adoption: A rebuttal of the trickle down theory', Proceedings of the Summer Conference of the American Marketing Association (June 1964), pp. 108–25.

50. The Minnesota Multiphasic Personality Inventory (MMPI) Masculinity-Femininity Scale; The California Psychological Inventory (Femininity Scale); The Guildford-Martin GAMIN Masculinity Scale; The Terman-Miles Attitude Interest Analysis Test.
    For a factor analysis of the most predictive items in these tests *see* Lunneborg and Lunneborg, 'Factor Analytic Structure of MF Scales and Items', *Journal of Clinical Psychology* Vol. 25 (1970).

51. Ferdinand F. Mauser, 'The Future Challenges Marketing', *Harvard Business Review*, Vol. 41 (November-December 1963), p. 172.

52. W. Thomas Anderson, 'Identifying the Convenience-Orientated Consumer'. *Journal of Marketing Research*. Vol. VIII (May 1971), pp. 179–83.

53. Donald F. Cox and Raymond A. Bauer. 'Self-Confidence and Persuasibility in Women', *Public Opinion Quarterly*, Vol. 28 (1964), pp. 453–66.

PART III

The Housewife and her Family

In food, clothing and footwear products the housewife spends between £6,000 and £8,000 million every year on her family and herself, and these are by no means the only products which she buys in her capacity as household agent. She buys for most of the living and working needs of her family and acts as a kingpin for a system which hinges one way into the vast consumer marketing industry and the other into the household. She is the intermediary channel both for messages from the media and for the more subtle and personalised influences from her husband and children. With the possible exception of certain industrial marketing decisions, there is no other sector in British consumer society where an individual group of purchasers has so much power over spending behaviour.

Yet, although so much importance should be attached to the relationship of the housewife to her family's consuming processes, there has been a tendency to either ignore or oversimplify the subtle web of influences that this involves. Many marketing texts omit this topic altogether and where the subject is discussed at all the findings are often knotted together into some ugly and facile systems which iron out the complexities into 'global' social decision processes.

This section will not attempt to find some generalised model of family decision-making. What it will do is to steer a course through the social and economic pathways which thread through this subject and leave the observer, hopefully, with some clues as to the complex process which binds the woman to her family. There is no easy system which will explain the behaviour of every housewife and every family; there are only tendencies which may characterise some of the families, some of the time. What will emerge, however, is the particular usefulness of product-based systems of family / housewife decision-process and the importance of understanding sex and power role relationships within the family. Above all, the marketer should understand the intricacy behind the elusive simplicity of the final purchase act and remember, as Turle and Falconer* point out, that the household decision-process is a 'masterpiece of complication since the interplay of personalities of husband and wife (not to mention the other family members) necessarily gives rise to an enormous range of interactive positions'.

They note that it is hard to view the family decision-process as a 'practical, predictive instrument' and, taking their suggestion, this is not what will be

---

* *See* Chapter 12, ref. 9.

looked for here—too many disappointed optimists have trodden that particular path.

So where does one begin? As a starter, it is useful to note the succint appraisal of the main physical aspects of housewife purchasing behaviour which were concluded by Lovell, Meadows and Rampley in 1968*. Housewife purchase, they observed, might be made:

1. By herself alone.
2. Accompanied but working from a list.
3. Accompanied but open to impulse.
4. By proxy, that is, giving a list or instructions to a child or the husband.

The items bought may include:

1. Articles for her use alone.
2. Articles that are for family use.
3. Articles that are specifically and only for use by other people.

The purchases and her shopping behaviour will be influenced by:

1. Other members of the household.
2. External influences—advertising and other media; friends and relatives.

The woman buying for herself, and the influence of the media will be dealt with elsewhere. What we shall consider here are the woman's family, friends and relatives in her family purchase-decision, and other relevant factors such as the position of the family in the wider social structure.

---

* *See* Chapter 8. ref. 1.

8. The Family/Household Decision Process

In order to start to understand the complex processes surrounding household decision-making it is important to return to first principles and obtain an objective view of what, for most women, makes up and typifies their household. Upon this basis, the structure of that household, models of its decision flows and social scientific evidence on its operations as a small group act as guides to an understanding of the consumer decisions within.

WHAT IS A HOUSEHOLD?

The structure of 'Household and Family Arrangements' in Great Britain is set out in Table 8:1.

Table 8:1   Household and Family Arrangements (Great Britain)

	Percentage of household/families			Thousands of household/families		
	1961	1966	1971	1961	1966	1971
Households						
No family households	16·8	19·4	22·0	2,724	3,287	3,994
One family households						
Married couple, no children	25·6	25·8	26·5	4,147	4,377	4,821
Married couple, with children	48·1	46·0	43·3	7,790	7,801	7,879
Lone parents, with children	6·7	6·8	6·8	1,089	1,156	1,240
Total	80·5	78·7	76·6	13,026	13,334	13,939
Two or more family households	2·7	1·9	1·4	439	317	254
Total: all households	100·0	100·0	100·0	16,189	16,937	18,187
Families						
Married couple with dependent children	45·7	44·4	44·5	6,362	6,220	6,430
Married couple, without dependent children	45·1	46·1	46·0	6,284	6,444	6,647
Lone parent, with dependent children	3·4	3·6	4·3	474	499	620
Lone parent, without dependent children	5·8	5·8	5·2	805	809	755
Total: all families	100·0	100·0	100·0	13,924	13,972	14,452

Provisional figures based on 1% samples of household Census returns
Source: Family Expenditure Survey, HMSO (1973).

It is important to note the following:

1. A 'household' is not necessarily a family. Most definitions would require some evidence of blood ties before deeming a collection of people a 'family'[2,3]. Those collections of people in dwelling units who are not related, that is, 'no family' households, make up 22% of the total and are often composed of unattached individuals in rented accommodation.
2. 'Family' households make up 14 out of the total of 18 million households. Of these, just over 9 million include children as well as the original one or two members.
3. Out of the total population of 57 million in the United Kingdom, 52 million live in private households. Since just under 80% of private households are family households then we can estimate that about 42 million people in the United Kingdom live in family households of one kind or another.
4. Since there are 14 million households with families, we can estimate that the number of housewives is about the same. There is, however, a problem of definition which Ann Oakley (1974)[4], noted in her recent book. Without going into this too deeply, do we, for example, call a working wife a 'housewife' or are only unemployed wives to be considered as such? Is a women without children and working, as much of a 'housewife' as one with four children who is not? A useful guide may be what women describe themselves as, and Oakley notes that within a random sample of 7,000 women between the ages of 16 and 64, 85% of the women described themselves as 'housewives'.

Generalising this estimate to population figures for Britain in 1973 which showed that there are 20 million women over 15, and adjusting this for the age group 15−16 which is the differential between the two samples, we arrive at a potential housewife population of between 14 and 15 million which tallies with our first estimate based on family households. This gives rise to two observations:

(a) Oakley's estimate of 'housewife' was guided by a perception by the women that they took responsibility for the household in which they lived. Since this tallies with total number of family households, we can conclude that for most mature women in family households, control of those households is perceived by them as their responsibility.
(b) Since we know that 60% of married women also work outside the home in full or part-time employment[5] and since our estimates of 'housewives' so far include most married women, we are forced to conclude that women will describe themselves as 'housewives' even when they are gainfully employed outside the home. Thus our 'image' and definition of the 'average housewife' would be inaccurate if it was circumscribed by a notion of a stay-at-home, domesticated woman. 'True' housewives in the sense of the married woman who does nothing but stay at home

all day with or without children may actually be in the minority. This is one point on which we lack adequate data, probably for reasons associated with the stratification system noted in chapter 19.

Combining point (a) with point (b) we can conclude that women, for the most part, will assume control of household matters *whether they work or not*.

5. Combining point (3) with point (4) we can also conclude that there are about $14\frac{1}{2}$ million women in Britain working both inside and outside the home who define themselves as 'housewives'. These women purchase for the $27\frac{1}{2}$ million people who share the private 'family households' with them.

Thus, we have a ratio of 1:2 for housewives purchasing for other household members and a ratio of 1:3 if we include purchases for herself as additional family member. Putting it another way, in consumer markets every housewife purchase may represent three sets of consumer response.

6. A 'family household' itself may not always cover the immediate nuclear family and in this situation the decision processes become highly complex, mainly because there may be one or two women engaging in buying decisions. These families are in the minority and we cannot be concerned with them here. This situation usually arises where a 'family of marriage' (husband/wife and children) combine with a 'family of origin' (family of husband or wife), and may be further complicated by the inclusion of other relatives—uncles, aunts or cousins. This type of set-up is more common in Europe than Britain and, in terms of buying influences, is under-researched and little understood, if not totally daunting. In Britain, the nearest we approach this situation is in the case of young married couples who live with one set of parents. In a study by Young and Willmott (1962)[6] it was found that a high proportion of young marrieds started life in a parental home, that is, with one family of origin, and with a greater tendency to stay with the wife's parents. There is also a tendency for young married women to set up home near her family of origin rather than the family of her husband. This factor, known as 'matrilocality' may be an important influence on the wife's purchase decisions in early years of the family cycle. A survey by J. Walter Thompson (1968)[7] found that half of all married women under 35 began married life in one of the parental homes, the incidence lower in upper- and middle-class homes, but usually in the wife's mother's home. In this sort of situation, however, we can assume that the original female influence of the wife's mother will be the stronger one and she will perceive the married children as influences on her purchases rather than vice versa.

For the sake of this review on interhousehold influence we will be assuming the most prevalent, and to the marketer the most useful, relationship of a 'family of marriage', where a husband and wife share a household with or without dependent children. We will also assume that the female is the housewife and that she is the main purchaser for the family. Other situations will be dealt with separately.

It is difficult to choose how to approach the family/housewife purchase decision since there are just so many influences operating within it. We will start, however, by looking at three examples of family decision models which have each attempted to illustrate those influences and the patterns they form around the final housewife purchase.

THE FAMILY BUYING DECISION: MODELS AND PATTERNS

In consumer behaviour theory, there has recently been some considerable emphasis placed on the 'flow' or 'process' of buying. Instead of perceiving the act of purchase as an individual act contained within a vacuum of the point-of-purchase, this 'flow' approach takes account of other individual influences which operate before and after the purchase act.

These consumer-purchase models[8] take account one way or the other of the fact that the buying decision is only one act in a larger system that begins before and ends after, often well after, that decision. For example, Kotler (1972)[9] suggests that a subject moves from a recognised relevant need, to information collection and pre-purchase activity, to a purchase decision, then to use behaviour and finally arrives at a post-purchase state with attendant feelings for or against the product. Each stage represents a particular opportunity for marketing communication. These models rely, however, on a generalised or 'global' model of consumer-decision processes, which can be theoretically ubiquitous.

The household buying process could no doubt be readily introduced into these models but certain students of consumer behaviour have also attempted to create models, in varying degrees of complexity, to take account of the vagaries and complexities of the individual household buying process.

Lovell, Meadows and Rampley[1] designed such a model in the paper they submitted for the Thompson Awards for Advertising Research in 1968. Features of this model included a split in the section of 'other members of the household' which demonstrated that there are both *individuals* who are influencing the housewife in their particular ways, and a *collective* influence as a family unit. Similarly, 'purchase' has been split up into components bracketed together; interhousehold influence can affect either the individual elements, for instance where it is bought, what size, what brand, or the fact of the purchase *at all*—or both (*see* Diagram 8:1). The authors point out that the most difficult concept to illustrate diagrammatically is that of time. The box (bottom centre) called 'Comparison of Product over Time' has broken lines to suggest two things:

1. Repeated experience of the product purchases, in relation to alternatives, may effect a different expression of influence on the housewife and her husband from a first-time assessment.

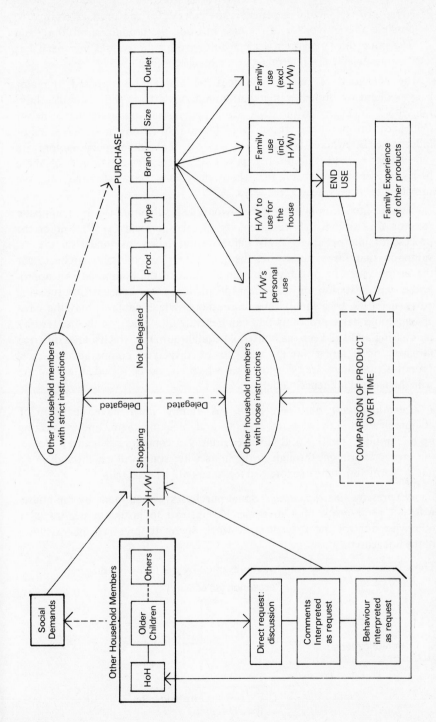

Source: Lovell, Meadows and Rampley (1968)[1].

2. Irrespective of actual experience, the novelty of the product relative to possible alternatives (or of the idea of using the product at all) may help determine the strength of feeling among other household members that is communicated or interpreted as 'influence'.

The likelihood of certain influences being minor as opposed to major is symbolised by broken rather than continuous arrows. For example, those household members with strict shopping instructions will have minor influences on purchase: those with loose instructions may have major influences. Elsewhere, broken lines indicate that some social factors are influencing a housewife in her purchasing decisions by virtue of there being household members, for whom there is a social demand that she provides, in socially acceptable ways.

Another model on household behaviour, also submitted for the Thompson Awards for Advertising Research, by Dr. J. G. Field (1968)[10] notes the process of interpersonal family influence but bases his model on the assumption that for a housewife. the major task is not only purchase, but the maintenance or possibly the manipulation of the household. An appropriate representation of the effect of influence on housewife purchasing may, therefore, be a family interaction model which contains only the most essential and basic processes that can generate and modulate the housewife's purchasing and still keep the household equilibrium, but which allows different families, or different family acts, to be displayed comparatively. Field proposes that there are two processes which should be included in a housewife/household influence model:

1. Communication and perception. A family must have channels of communication with ways of opening and blocking them, and connecting up hierarchies, coalition and alliances (that is, a command structure). Not all the messages will get through to the housewife; some will get through in an altered form and some unexpressed messages will be detected.

2. Expressive–instrumental. Some purchases will be made by the housewife not as a result of a message, but instead to instigate, side-track or otherwise control the influences at work so as to preserve the existence of the household.

These processes may be roughly represented by the following diagram:

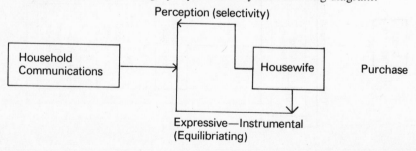

There is a distinction between the source of the 'Expressive-Instrumental' variation on the one hand and 'Communication and Perception' on the other: the former is a more independent source of variation acting on the system than is 'Communication and Perception' which are inter-dependent. This way of looking at the influences on the housewife allowed Field to represent different households or the same household at different stages, in a two-dimensional system.

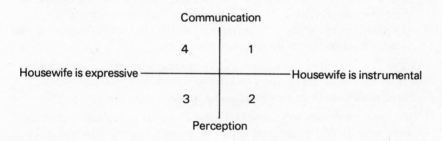

Quadrant (1): Situations in which the housewife is susceptible to every demand of her household (that is not selective in her perceptions), but the household feels constrained not to ask for brands and products that the housewife would find inconvenient to obtain or would dislike herself.

Quadrant (4): The housewife is likewise non-selective and wants to give her family whatever *they* want.

Quadrants (2) and (3): The location for situations where the housewife's interpretation of what was required was relatively high.

In *(2)* the housewife bias in attending to what was required would be self-centred: she would want to manipulate her household (e.g. an encyclopaedia rather than a comic for her child). In *(4)* the housewife would be other-centred, encouraging household members to realise their own aspirations.

A third model, which is worth noting, is by Pollay (1968)[11] who based his design on the distribution of utilities to family participants. He notes that most consumer decision models, for example, those by Nicosia, Howard and Kotler[8,9] concentrated on the individual decision process and related this to other participants only because the individual has goals of 'belongingness and affiliation'. Despite the importance of the family in marketing and particularly to the female consumer, 'little attention has been paid to the process by which family members interact or how the family makes decisions as a unit'.

Pollay's model is extremely complex and cannot be described in detail here but he shares basics with the models noted above by Lovell, Meadows and Rampley, and Field. That is, he emphasises perception of utilities and priorities that the product has for *different* family members. He starts the decision process from the base of an individual product then:

1. Measures the distribution of utilities of that product to various family members.
2. Measures the priorities that the family holds both towards the product and between themselves in decision-making.
3. Matches these two distributions to satisfy the criterion of 'distributive justice', that is, that the players within the decision-making unit should share rewards (receive utility) proportional to the priority structure.
4. Modifies this by 'utility debt formation' that is, the net residual from the family's prior history of decision and behaviour.

From this daunting admixture, Pollay manages to extract patterns and power structures for the decision-making on a particular product.

Features that the three models subsume between them are:

1. Decision processes will vary in terms of power variation, involvement and influence of the different family members *depending on the product being examined.*
2. Influence on the housewife before product purchase may be *overt or non-overt.*
3. The housewife may use purchase decisions to maintain her own balance in family equilibrium and the perceived demands of her family or sex role.
4. The history of decision processes on a product and the relative success of those decisions are taken into account with other products, or in further purchases of the same product.

Sophisticated as these models may be, however, they still do not explain the mechanisms operating behind the physically observable influences within the family. For the subtleties of this behaviour and possible explanation of decision priorities we have to turn to sociological theory and, particularly, that on the flows of communication and influence within the 'small group'.

THE FAMILY AS A 'SMALL GROUP'

The family is the most common occurrence of the small human group and there has been a body of research which has concentrated specifically on behaviour patterns of such groups.

The classic work on this subject is that by Katz and Lazerfeld (1955)[12] who suggested that patterns of communication in the 'small group' tend to be determined by three factors.

1. Group structure.
2. Group cultures or climates.
3. Group situations.

This theory is a useful basis from which to approach the housewife/family consumer decision process.

Group Structure and the Flow of Communication

1. Festinger *et al* (1950)[13] suggested that the more attractive the group was to its members the greater the influence that the group can have on its members. This theory was supported experimentally by Back (1952)[14] who found that when people were more attached to each other, they exerted greater influence over each other's opinions and were also more effective in their influencing. Thus, when the groups were highly cohesive, the number of attempts at changing a partner's opinion were both greater in number and more successful than when the interpersonal relations were less cohesive.

   On this basis we could imply that the more cohesive the family group, then the more interpersonal influence may be exerted and the more this influence may be successful. Extending this concept, we would expect greater interhousehold influence where a family was close together in terms of age, likes and temperament. Conversely, one would expect more autonomy in the housewife decision where the family was less closely structured.

2. Festinger also demonstrated that group cohesiveness was increased by increasing the importance of the goal of the group. This might suggest that there is more tangible and remembered influence on those products which cost or mean more to a particular family. Obviously there is a degree of relativity here. Buying a new hairdryer will mean less to higher-income families than to those on lower incomes and less to a family which owns two than to a first-time purchaser family. It also means that one would expect a more measurable influence on the purchase of consumer durables than on small, frequently purchased food products, a fact which becomes demonstrably clear when we examine the interhousehold influence on different types of products.

Within the scope of this theory which equates to the economic one of diminishing marginal utility, there are myriad semi-important products which are perceived in varying shades of greyness as 'group goals'. Nevertheless, as a general rule, we can assume that the more important the product to the family group, the less important becomes the housewife influence *alone*. Her autonomy will increase in product choice as the group perception of it diminishes, hence the importance of the influence of the housewife in food purchases.

This contention was supported by Sampson (1968)[15] who felt that a hierarchy of products based on price and purchase-frequency would reflect 'low' to 'high' family perception of the product's importance and thereby the extent to which they were 'housewife' as opposed to 'household' purchases. The hierarchy he suggested was as follows:

(a) Low unit price / high purchasing frequency items (such as food products, cleaning products, toiletries).

(b) Low unit price /low purchasing frequency items (such as some proprietary pharmaceuticals, home decorating materials, certain 'specialty' food and drink items, not normally on the weekly shopping list).

(c) High price /low purchasing frequency items (such as consumer durables, furniture, furnishings, floor coverings).

(d) Very expensive items of low purchasing frequency (such as holidays).

(e) Items such as insurance policies, unit trust purchases, involving some measure of investment.

(f) Major items of 'capital expenditure' (such as houses, home extensions, central heating, motor cars).

Sampson explained: 'There would appear to be some sort of hierarchy in this categorisation based upon monetary outlay and therefore, by inference, "importance".'

Categories (a) and (b) clearly would fall within the influence of housewife purchase alone, but moving from (c) to (d) we encounter more and more family influence as well. 'This latter area is likely to be a husband /wife or all family decision with the housewife exerting a "veto" effect.'

Why and when the housewife operates the veto will depend on more general factors of family atmosphere and the degree to which the wife views her role as being tied up with the product involved. Field (1968)[10], as we saw in his family purchase model, believed that this veto is often operated as a means for the housewife to maintain her power equilibrium in role terms within the family. This veto effect was also referred to by Lewin (1951)[16] as the 'gatekeeper' effect in that no matter how much influence circulates within or without the family, including media influence, the final decision to purchase or not will usually rest with the housewife through whom most of these influences are mediated.

3. Other studies have looked at small group information transmission. Back (1952)[14] studied the process of rumour transmission in an industrial situation and found that communication tends to be directed upwards, from lower to higher status members, so that higher ranking members were always targets for communication from those below them in rank. Higher ranking individuals also tend to address themselves to a larger number of group members than do lower ranking members. These studies were corroborated by Bales (1952)[17] who found that person-to-person messages are directed at the most popular members of the group and that these messages move upward in the hierarchy. On the other hand, communication from one person to several others tends to flow downwards. In his analysis of direction of flow Bales adds an analysis of content. This indicates that the high ranking people, that is, those who are the most popular and frequent talkers, are also likely to say different things from the 'low ranking people'. The high rankers tend to proffer information and opinion, and express agreement or disagreement. The infrequent

speakers, in other words, react rather than initiate, while the more frequent speakers seem to make more influence attempts.

Similar findings have been reported by Strodtbeck (1951)[18] in his studies of husband and wife decisions. The implications of these findings is that where husbands and wives or other family members report different degrees of influence in family consumer decisions (this disagreement is discussed in more detail in chapter 18 on research bias), the opinion leaders or the real 'influentials' in the family for a certain product may be determined by observing the pattern of communication flow, while they are discussing the product. It is also interesting to note that Bales found that as the group became larger the opinion leader became more important so that more communication was directed at her/him and less to other group members. Thus, as family size continues to shrink we can expect more democracy in family consumer decisions.

4. Festinger found that the group cohesiveness could increase by increasing the prestige of the group over other groups. This point implies that the greater interhousehold influence might be expected in a household which is conscious of its high status *vis-à-vis* other households. This will again be governed by relativity of ranking both within and between socio-economic groups. Nevertheless, a study by *Printers' Ink* (1958)[19] showed that middle-class families demonstrated the greatest co-operation between spouses in certain buying decisions, while upper- and lower-class families showed the least co-operation.

This was also supported by Converse and Huegy (1946)[20], who found that joint decision-making is more common at the centre of the socio-economic hierarchy, and by Bloode and Wolfe (1960)[27] and Wilkenning (1967)[21] who found a curvilinear relationship between a family's social class and the degree of joint decision-making.

Nevertheless, while elegant, this theory is open to interpretation since it is likely that associated with each social group are cultural sex/power roles between the family members and the husband and wife in particular, which will be stronger and more direct indicators of decision-making patterns than social class alone.

The 'prestigious-social group' theory also does not explain why, although joint decision-making is greater in the middle class, it is reduced in both upper and lower classes[19, 20, 22]. If the social class theory held then we would expect a simple increase in joint decision-making in the family moving from the lower to the upper socio-economic groups. As it happens, this has not been observed; there is, instead, a bunching at the middle sector.

The sex role theory would explain this by postulating that since sex-role delineation is greatest at each end of the socio-economic continuum (Cuber and Kenkel (1954)[23]), so would be sex-role related behaviour. Purchasing behaviour is sex-role related in that a traditional split of sex roles would attribute more involvement for the woman in frequent low-priced shopping decisions and more involvement by the man in high-priced 'important' decisions. Blurring of sex roles would indicate less strict delineation of product involvement on these grounds so that husband and wife would move more into each other's areas: the husband into food shopping, for example, and the woman into consumer durable purchase. There would also be an increase in joint decision-making. Since this blurring of sex roles is more commonly observed in the middle classes than in the upper and lower groups then this might explain the orientation towards joint decision-making in this class as opposed to the others.

The movement of couples into each other's purchasing areas is noted in more detail later while this factor of sex roles will recur throughout this whole discussion on family/housewife influence as an important variable in product purchase decision-processes.

Group Cultures and Climates

We have just argued that social class as a determinant of the climate of the group can be related to sub-variables of sex-role delineation which can dictate the degree to which decision-making may be joint or separate. There are, however, other 'cultural' and 'atmospheric' variables which one can consider. Lippit and White (1952)[24], for example, postulated that whether a group was 'democratic', 'authoritarian' or *laissez-faire* could affect its approach to decision-making. These differences could be a function of a wider national culture, or merely an individual family.

Cooper (1968)[25] used a variation of these distinctions to suggest that types of family and housewife decision-making would depend on budgeting systems that three types of atmospheres would subsume. He called these three types of budgeting 'rigid and controlled', 'loose and controlled' and 'loose and uncontrolled' and related decision patterns to them, as illustrated by Table 8:2.

Table 8:2   Three Types of Budgeting Systems

Variables	Rigid and Controlled	Loose and Uncontrolled	Loose and Controlled
	A	B	C
Decision-maker	Housewife	Family	Family + experts
Sources of Information	Learned skill	Irrelevant cues	Information bought
Quality of decision	Routine	Dramatised	Peripheral or externalised

Source: Cooper (1968)[25].

Strodtbeck in a similar study contended that cultural orientations to patriarchality or matriarchality would dictate generally whether a family decision would be husband- or wife-favoured. He used three cultural types and showed how discussion outcomes were found to favour the dominant partners in 'Navaho' (matriarchial), 'Mormon' (patriarchial) and Presbyterian (more neutral) systems.

Nevertheless, while differences in decision-making noted by Cooper and Strodtbeck have been explained by 'cultural differences' we can note that once more these differences, as with social class, can be related to more personal variables of husband and wife roles.

In Cooper's study the three types of budgeting control could only arise where the housewife was in three states of traditional to non-traditional role ascription. The housewife who keeps rigid control on the family budget, and decides on the basis of learned skill, is obviously demonstrating more rigid, traditional, family-role behaviour than the woman who defers to family and expert, and buys information. The latter is probably characterised by a 'middle class' woman on the lines we have just discussed (most purchasers of *Which?* magazine are middle class) or a busy working mother of any class. In the case of Strodtbeck's analogy, each cultural type again relates to a sex-role delineation in husband and wife partnerships of any culture.

Cultural differences in group behaviour are, it seems, similar to social class differences in that they will tend to subsume sensitive variables on sex/power role relationships between the husband and wife that will generalise to purchase decisions.

Group Situations

Individuals in modern society are usually members of more than one group, and have interpersonal ties in different sorts of situations. Groups of individuals, furthermore, share certain interests on the level of the group as a whole and divide into sub-groups as far as other interests are concerned. Therefore, the same group may engender quite different communications networks to serve different situations.

Katz and Lazerfeld *(op. cit.)* found, for example, that marketing advice and fashion advice flow through different networks and that neither of these channels seems to overlap with the channel for political influencing. While the same people may or may not be involved in these different spheres of influence the patterns of communication-flow in each case take different shapes.

Within a family, the husband and wife may form a sub-group whose common interests are the purchasing of the larger, more expensive types of household appliances where the husband or wife may take the role of the 'influential'. Another sub-group within the family may be the mother and children whose common interest may be the buying of children's clothing, certain foods and children's durables. Joyce's research on the housewife

(1967)[26] found that even the young housewife's mother may be a formidable influence on the planning or preparation of certain activities, such as parties, recipes, meals, and in the purchasing of certain groceries.

Thus, to summarise:

1. The autonomy of the housewife decision is greater in larger, loosely-knit, less democratic families where she operates within a more traditional and rigid female family role. There are indications that this will occur most frequently in lower and, to some extent, higher socio-economic groups.
2. The family will take more part in consumer decision processes in smaller, more cohesive, more democratic families where the housewife has to a varying extent moved away from her traditional female family role. This is most often found among working women who combine two roles and, particularly, in the middle socio-economic groups.
3. In terms of products, there will be more family involvement, particularly by the husband, in those purchase decisions where the product is perceived of as important to the family as a whole, or is more expensive and less frequently purchased. There will be more housewife influence operating on those products which are small, inexpensive and more frequently purchased which the family tends to take for granted, for example, food and household goods.
4. The family may attempt to exert influence on the housewife both individually, in that the purchase will perhaps have particular significance for one family member more than another, and collectively, where several members will see a joint benefit. This influence will vary with the different products or brands and will be overt or non-overt.
5. The housewife may use her power of veto in the family purchase decision for reasons which relate to the maintenance of her equilibrium in the family power structure or to her perception of her role.
6. Different product decisions may involve different sub-groups in the family where influence differentials will vary by family member. In these cases, the main influencers and high and low status group members can be observed by patterns of communication flow during discussion.
7. Past experience in decisions on products and the outcome of those decisions will play a part in other purchase decisions for other products or repeat purchases of the original product.

Overall, two factors are particularly notable:

1. The importance of viewing a purchase decision from the perspective of the individual product and not attempting to generalise family decisions to all purchases.
2. The importance of the housewife's perception of her role in the family, and the balance of sex-role behaviour (and the power patterns that this generates) between her and her husband.

Moving now to the specific study of the husband and wife purchase-decision we shall find this final point on sex and power roles particularly relevant.

REFERENCES

1. M. R. C. Lovell, R. Meadows and B. Rampley 'Inter-Household Influence on Housewife Purchases', Gold Medal Paper, The Thompson Medals and Awards for Advertising Research (1968).
2. Family Expenditure Survey, Department of Employment. HMSO (1974).
3. *Social Trends,* Central Statistical Office, HMSO (1974).
4. Ann Oakley, *Housewife,* Allen Lane: Penguin Books (1974).
5. *See* footnote on page 247.
6. M. Young and P. Willmott, *Family and Kinship in East London,* Pelican Books (1962).
7. 'The New Housewife', Survey by J. Walter Thompson Company (1968).
8. Arnold E. Amstutz, *Computer Simulations of Competitive Market Response,* MIT Press (Cambridge, Mass. 1967). John A. Howard and Jagdish Seth, *The Theory of Buyer Behavior,* John Wiley & Sons (New York 1969). John Howard, *Marketing Analysis and Planning,* Richard D. Irwin (Homewood, Ill. 1963).
   M. Francesco Nicosia, *Consumer Decision Processes: Marketing and advertising implications,* Prentice-Hall (Englewood Cliffs, N. J. 1966), p. 156.
9. Philip Kotler, *Marketing Management: Analysis, planning and control,* Prentice-Hall (Englewood Cliffs, N.J. 1972).
10. Dr. J. G. Field, 'The Influence of Household Members on Housewife Purchases', Gold Medal Paper, The Thompson Medals and Awards for Advertising Research (1968).
11. Richard W. Pollay, 'A Model of Family Decision Making', *British Journal of Marketing* Vol. 2 (1968), pp. 206–29.
12. Elihu Katz and Paul F. Lazerfeld, *Personal Influence,* The Free Press of Glencoe (New York 1955).
13. Festinger *et al* 'Theory and Experiment in Social Communication', collected papers, Ann Arbor Institute for Social Research (1950).
14. Kurt Back, 'Influence Through Social Communications' in Swanson, Newcomb and Hartley (eds.) *Readings in Social Psychology,* Henry Holt (New York 1952).
15. P. Sampson, 'An Examination of the Concepts Evoked by the Suggestion of "Other Members of Household" Influence over Housewife Purchases', Gold Medal Paper, The Thompson Medals and Awards for Advertising Research (1968).
16. K. Lewin in D. Cartwright (ed.), *Field Theory in Social Science,* Harper Row (New York 1951).
17. Bales R. F., 'Some Uniformities of Behavior in Small Social Systems' in Swanson, Newcomb and Hartley, (eds.), *Readings in Social Psychology,* Henry Holt (New York 1952).
18. F. L. Strodtbeck, 'Husband and Wife Interactions over Revealed Differences', *American Sociological Review* (16) (1951).
19. Anon, 'Family Buying Decisions: Who makes them, who influences them?', *Printers' Ink* (1958) pp. 21–9, Report of the Conference at the University of Michigan.
20. P. D. Converse and Huegy, *The Elements of Marketing,* Prentice-Hall (New York 1946).
    Mirra Komarovsky, 'Class Differences in Family Decision Making on Expenditures', in N. N. Foote (ed.), *Household Decision Making,* New York University Press (New York 1961) pp. 255–65.

21. E. A. Wilkenning *et al* 'Dimensions of Aspirations, Work Roles and Decision Making of Farm Husbands and Wives in Wisconsin', *Journal of Marriage and the Family*, Vol. 29 (4) (1967), pp. 703–11.

22. Elizabeth H. Wolgast, 'Do Husbands or Wives Make the Purchasing Decision?', *The Journal of Marketing*, (October 1958), pp. 151–8.

23. J. F. Cuber and W. F. Kenkel, *Social Stratification in the United States*, Appleton Century Crofts (New York 1954), p. 249.

24. R. Lippitt and R. K. White, 'An Experimental Study of Leadership and Group Life', in Swanson, Newcomb and Hartley (eds.) *Readings in Social Psychology*, Henry Holt (New York 1952).

25. Peter Cooper, 'The Decline in the Status of Household Decision Making', *British Journal of Marketing* Vol 2, (1968), pp. 179–84.

26. T. Joyce, 'The New Housewife', A Comprehensive Social Survey, ESOMAR and NOP Market Research Ltd., Random Omnibus Survey Amongst Housewives (July 1968).

27. Robert O. Bloode & Donald M. Wolfe, *Husbands and Wives: The dynamics of married living*, The Free Press (Glencoe, Ill. 1960).

9. The Husband/Wife Decision Process

While the investigation of marital decision-making has provided a fruitful area of research for social scientists and marketers alike, there has been missing from marketing, in particular, a classification system to organise the research in this area. On the basis of the research available, however, one such system could be assumed to congregate around two broad research approaches which attack the marital decision from two levels. These two broad approaches could be noted as the 'product' approach and the 'sex-power role' approach.

THE 'PRODUCT' APPROACH

This approach is mainly a descriptive one. It takes a product or brand and investigates the husband/wife influence on purchase either in 'gross' terms, that is, notes the extent to which the housewife is aware of her husband's influence on the product, or in 'net' terms, that is, how each partner affects the product decision in various stages up to the time of purchase. The main use of this method is that it provides a quick and accurate idea of whom to aim media strategy at and whom to attract in pack, brand and name design. Its main weakness, which is also the main strength of the 'sex-power role approach' is that it cannot explain why differential influences in the husband/wife decision on the product, come about.

Nevertheless, as we shall see from examples of this approach, one evident advantage of this method is its clarity in mechanical influence measurement, particularly in grocery products where it would be virtually impossible because of the diffuse nature of the decision processes surrounding these products, to measure reasons why a husband (or other family members) is important in purchase influence. Examples of the 'gross' approach to product based observations of husband/wife influence are provided by a NOP shopping survey on groceries[1] and two studies by Nowland and Company for *Life Magazine*[2].

NOP Shopping Survey (1967)[1]

This survey on a nationally representative sample of 1.000 housewives showed, for various classes of groceries, for whom the housewife shops and the incidence of influence from the husband and other family members, (*see* Diagrams 9:1 and 9:2).

Diagram 9:1

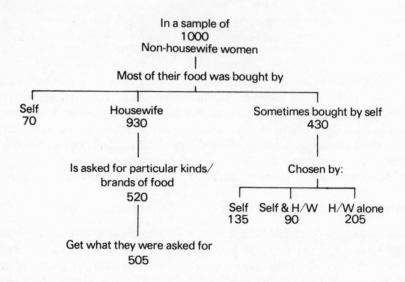

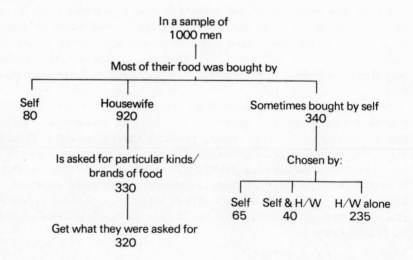

Source: NOP (1967)[1]

Diagram 9:2

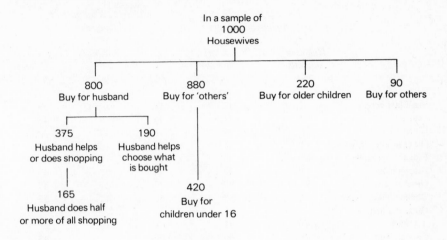

In a sample of
1000
Housewives

| 800 | 880 | 220 | 90 |
| Buy for husband | Buy for 'others' | Buy for older children | Buy for others |

375
Husband helps
or does shopping

190
Husband helps
choose what
is bought

165
Husband does half
or more of all shopping

420
Buy for
children under 16

A second part of the NOP study took a slightly different but still somewhat 'gross' angle to husband influence when they asked housewives how often their husbands suggested the purchase of different products, and how often they went on to buy what he suggested. The results are given in Table 9:1.

Using results from this survey we can see that to the extent that the husband is the initiator in suggesting the purchase of certain products this appears to be relatively greater in the cases of cheese, pickles and sauces, breakfast cereals, meat pies and sausages, toothpaste and biscuits. It is low in tea, coffee, canned fruits and desserts.

Perhaps results from just one survey should be treated carefully, but the fact that this study has managed to depict fairly accurate patterns of husband influence is indicated by the extent to which the results are supported by other surveys. In the case of toothpaste, for instance, Jaffe and Senft (1968)[3] found that the husband was of particular importance in choice of the brand while they and the NOP survey also find his influence relatively low in the case of coffee.

Furthermore, in a more recent study by IPC (1974)[4] it was noted, as it was in the NOP survey, that husbands were particularly important in the influencing of purchases of pickles and sauces and toothpaste. In the case of bottled sauces, 62% of the housewives claimed to know their husbands' preferences and were convinced that any change from this would be unfavourably received. In the toothpaste sector, 72% of the housewives knew their husbands' brand preferences and 37% felt they would object if a different brand were purchased.

Table 9:1   Influence of Husband in certain Purchase Decisions

| | All buying for husbands and buying the product | | All buying what husbands suggest | | |
	Husband suggests (%)	Husband doesn't suggest (%)	Usually (%)	Sometimes (%)	Hardly ever (%)
Breakfast cereals	18	82	59	17	24
Tea	9	91	45	6	48
Coffee	11	89	46	14	40
Other hot beverages	14	86	42	18	40
Frozen vegetables	12	88	29	19	52
Frozen fish	13	87	31	27	42
Other frozen food	13	87	32	21	47
Canned baked beans	12	88	52	12	35
Other canned vege-tables	9	91	20	14	66
Canned fruit	11	89	38	20	43
Other canned food	13	87	44	17	38
Meat pies, sausage etc.	18	82	57	23	20
Pickles and sauces	19	81	56	22	22
Cheeses	20	80	59	23	18
Soup	13	87	47	17	35
Fresh and dried fruit	12	88	54	15	32
Biscuits	17	83	51	24	25
Slimming products	11	89	27	–	73
Cakes	14	86	40	27	33
Desserts	8	92	38	10	53
Jam and marmalade	14	86	53	5	43
Ice cream	10	90	46	18	35
Toothpaste	18	82	55	10	35
Soap	10	90	40	6	53

Source: NOP (1967)[1].

The Nowland Studies[2]

These studies illustrated husband/wife influence from a mechanical angle similar to the NOP study, but expressed the numerical findings, which the NOP study provided as raw data, as descriptive statements on husband/wife product and brand influence. For example, selected findings from the two studies note that:

1. There is an advantage of pre-selling both to the husband and the wife of about 8:5 of selling to the wife alone.
2. When brand consensus within the household is not achieved, the husband has about one-third of the purchasing value of the wife.

3. Heaviest purchasing takes place when both husband and wife shop together.
4. When they shop alone, husbands have a great deal of latitude as to the specific brands they may purchase.
5. Consensus is usually lacking in a majority of homes.
6. In these homes the brand on hand is the husband's brand almost one-third as often as it is the wife's.
7. In these homes where consensus is lacking the brand on hand is much more likely to be the husband's brand if he shops for it alone.
8. If he shops with his wife, his preference prevails one-fifth of the time; if she shops alone, she follows his preference about one-tenth of the time.

Nevertheless, interesting as these findings from NOP and Nowland & Company are, they only, as we have noted, measure 'gross' influence of the husband on the wife. They do not illustrate, for example, when and how this influence took place during the total decision. When the housewife reports that her husband suggested that she buy a particular breakfast cereal or soup, and husbands according to the NOP survey 'suggest' these 18% and 13% of the time respectively, one could ask, 'when does he "suggest" them?'

To answer this sort of question we have to turn to the more subtle 'net' approach of investigating husband influence on the housewife and an excellent example of this is provided by a model by Jaffe and Senft (1966)[3]. These researchers based their work on the assumption that different influences are brought to bear on the housewife by her husband at the different stages which lead to a product decision. Using this approach, they were able to predict the degree to which the husband or the wife was the major influence in products as wide ranging as coffee and paint.

The original model, on which the study was based, had set out first, to measure the extent to which various roles are performed in households in the consumption management of certain product categories, and second, to determine how husbands and wives compare in the performance of these roles, paying particular attention to any overlap in role playing between them. Focusing on the household as a consumption unit, husbands and wives were assumed to perform various consumption management (that is, purchasing decision) roles at different points in time. The specified role hypotheses were:

1. Information Seeking Roles

    (a) Information gatherer via people, i.e. the one who finds out from people about the product.

    (b) Information gatherer via the media, i.e. the one who uses various media as sources of information about the product.

2. *At the Latent Phase*

   (a) The initiator, i.e. the one who originally gets the idea to look around, to change past behaviour, who starts the process going.

3. *At the Purchase (Adaptive Phase)*

   (a) Suggestor of type or style, i.e. the one who sets broad requirements within a product class, who specifies the product.

   (b) Suggestor of brand, i.e. the one who has a very specific requirement with a product class, who specifies the brand.

   (c) The budgetor, i.e. the one most concerned about the cost of the item, the budget etc., who specifies the general price level for the expenditure.

   (d) The shopper, i.e. the one who goes to the market place, either alone or with a spouse, to check what is available and to satisfy the consumption needs of the household.

   (e) The purchaser i.e. the one who makes the actual purchase.

4. *At the Use (Goal Seeking) Phase*

   (a) The processor, i.e. the one who converts the product to usable form.

   (b) The consumer (satisfied), i.e. the one whose needs for the product have been satisfied.

   (c) The consumer (dissatisfied), i.e. the one whose needs for the product are not fully satisfied.

5. *At the Consolidating (Integrative) Phase*

   (a) The process validator (satisfied) i.e. the one who thinks the entire process was right and would repeat it the same way next time.

   (b) The process validator (dissatisfied), i.e. the one who thinks something in the process was wrong and would change the process the next time.

Jaffe and Senft said of their model:

Because a system of consumption has developed for each product or type, each spouse has learnt to play specific roles with respect to each system or product. A different psychological climate exists in each phase. These set up certain constraints which enable us to set up probabilities for certain actions (marketing).

A form of Markov chain analysis can emerge throughout various stages of the product's decision process. Jaffe and Senft in a later work combined a social action theory with this model and gave their *broad* results which are set out in Table 9:2.

Also, using a projective technique (the Thompkin-Horn Test) they were able to elaborate on these results and found that, for example, in the case of coffee, husbands and wives appeared equally important in the role of 'initiators', but with toothpaste, the husband was found to be less important.

Table 9:2 Convenience Foods and Toiletries

Coffee	Housewife purchases in
Frozen orange juice	the true sense
Toothpaste	
Pet food	
Household Items	
Rugs & carpets	Household purchase rather
Paint	than housewife
Sterling Silver & tableware	
Motor Cars & Appliances	
Motors Cars	Housewife and family
Refrigerators	purchases
Vacuum Cleaners	

Source: Jaffe and Senft (1966)[3].

However, when it came to actually suggesting the brand the reverse was true, in that the husband was found to be relatively more important in the case of toothpaste and less important in the case of coffee (which supports our earlier observations). With paint and floor coverings it was found that the husband is relatively more important in the case of all purchasing phases for paint, although the housewife retains an important role in 'planning'.

Thus, to summarise, the 'product' approach to husband influence on wife purchase describes, in the case of the 'gross' approach, the *incidence* of influence in a mechanical way, whereas the 'net' angle can suggest where this influence takes place at various stages along the decision route. What, however, this 'product' approach does not do is explain *why* influences form, and clues to this may be found in the next section on 'sex/power' roles.

Before we move to this section, however, it is important to note that the reason why this 'product' approach does not tend to explain influence is because it is often used in investigations of grocery products which are characterised by the most daunting family influences of all. Coulson (1966)[5] attempted to explain the variability of influence on different grocery products by a 'visibility' factor in that those products such as beer, deodorants and cold cereals which were visible in their unaltered form during consumption by the family would be a source of greater family influence than, say, cake mix, which is considerably altered from its original form by the time the family consumes it. This is an interesting and valid theory and could be developed further but other explanations of husband–family influence on grocery products are, to say the least, thin on the ground. The main reason for this is that generally, grocery product purchase-decisions are not at all notable or measurable compared to, say, consumer durables. There are three main reasons for this:

1. For the most part, several people may be involved in the influencing of a single grocery product or brand while in the consumer durable purchase it is usually only the husband and wife who are involved. The involvement of so many influences in the grocery decision process renders it hopelessly complex for research purposes where multi-stage, multi-variate models would have to be used.
2. While durable goods are relatively expensive and infrequently purchased, with much easily measured and recalled deliberation and consultation, the grocery product is often cheap and frequently purchased so that decision influences are transient and easily forgotten.
3. The decision influence in groceries differs not only by product but also by brand which makes for a virtually infinite scale of family influence within one shopping basket of goods. Every marketer, for every brand has, no doubt, his own little cache of data on family influence but to collate all this information into an influence typology would be a gargantuan task. With consumer durables, on the other hand, there are fewer products and even fewer brands within each product group than we tend to find in groceries, and experience has also shown that it is possible with consumer durables to generalise influence patterns over whole groups of products, such as Joyce's (1967)[6] and Gisler's (1948)[7] finding that the wife's influence is relatively more important than the husband's in vacuum cleaner purchase because this product is more clearly linked to her sex-role than his. We could not safely make a generalisation like this on reasons for the influence of a family member on, say, the whole market for chocolate.

THE 'SEX/POWER' ROLE APPROACH

While the strength of the 'product approach' to husband/wife influence lies in its simple, mechanical description of influences which, we specially noted, was the most viable approach in the complex influences of the grocery market, so the strength of the sex/power role approach lies in its ability to describe why a balance of influence between a husband and wife comes about, particularly in the more visible decision surrounding consumer durable purchase. The basis of this theory is a recognition that husbands and wives will differ in the deference that each gives the other's influence in a product choice on grounds of how they relate to each other in role terms, which may be simple 'dominant-submissive' or based on more complex variations of the cultural sex role.

We have already shown in the discussion of social class and family decision-making that sub-variables associated with sex roles provide better indicators of joint as opposed to single sex decision-making, than social class alone. The sex/power role theory of husband/wife decision-making is really a re-affirmation and elaboration of this.

The sex/power role factor in marital decision-making is really a sociological concept of longstanding, and sociologists already have a considerable body of research on the subject. They have tended to approach marital decision-making from two extremes. At one extreme is the contention that the sex/power role factor in a marriage influences decisions in a continuum from 'matriarchality' to 'patriarchality' so that decisions more to the matriarchial end, for example, will tend to be dominated by the wife rather than the husband. The rigidity of this differentiation depends, of course, on the degree to which the sex roles are traditional (rigid) or contemporary (flexible)[8]. At the other extreme is the belief that within the marriage, there is not unidimensionality, but several sub-roles each of which contain a 'male-female' continuum. Farber (1949)[9] for example, saw two sub-roles of policy and household decisions, while Herbst (1952)[10], on the other hand, saw four sub-roles: household duties, child care and control, social activities and economic activities. Each sub-role is assumed to have one dominant partner who might or might not allow encroachment into the decision by the other.

A third approach, by some researchers, is to go the whole hog and produce academically interesting, if theoretically useless, 'power typologies'. Winch (1958)[11], for example, divided families into four random groupings varying from the wife-dominated 'Thurberesque' marital relationship to the husband-dominated 'Ibsenian'.

Description	Winch's Typology Husband	Wife
Thurberesque	inhibited	uninhibited
Mother–Son	dependent	dominant
Master–Servant	ostensibly dominant really dependent	subservient but strong
Ibsenian	dominant	dependent

This sociological 'sex/power' role theory can be generalised to husband/wife consumer decisions by suggesting that:
1. Some products are seen as wife or husband dominated in the sense that they are 'masculine' or 'feminine' e.g. power drills and sheets. The degree of perception of 'maleness' and 'femaleness' will dictate the degree to which either partner takes the dominant role in the purchase decision.
2. Some products are seen as related to specific family activities as per Farber and Herbst's sub-role theory. Where the particular partner takes responsibility for those activities then the product decision will be dominated by her/him.

Of course, a theory such as this one depends on two big factors:
1. An accurate representation of the 'sex' of the product (*see* Stutteville on the sexuality of products in chapter 11).

2. An empathetic understanding of sex-role delineation within any social group and, most important. a good idea of where and when sex-role descriptions are changing. Old concepts of 'domestic' woman and 'working' man went out of the window some time ago and what we have left in contemporary western culture is something far more complex and sophisticated in its variability. Sex-role behaviour is no easy thing to categorise any more.

Nevertheless, validation of the sex/power role theory in explanations of husband/wife consumer decisions can be found in two contexts:

1. In examination of the delineation of husband and wife decisions over certain products as illustrated by a synthesised table by Field (1968) (*see* chapter 8 [10]).
2. Examination of the changed 'sex' of cars over time and the corresponding change in car purchase influence balance between husbands and wives.

Field's Table of Decisions

In his study of household behaviour for the Thompson Gold Medal Awards, Field illustrated the influence of sex-roles in certain product purchases with a table he synthesised from three research studies by Gisler (1948)[7] Nye and Hoffman (1963)[12] and Foote (1961)[13]. This is set out in Table 9:3.

A sex/power role approach to the husband and wife decision would interpret the results as follows:

Part A

1. Those products which are bought by a husband-dominated decision are clearly masculine in nature i.e. plugs, tyres and oil (mechanics); drink (masculine sociability) and shaving goods. Those bought specifically by wife-dominated decisions represent female activity in the household i.e. aspirin (household medicine); soft drinks (food provision) and shampoo (cosmetics).
2. Those products which fall in the joint areas alone are those which tend to be 'consumed' by both parties and which do not have a strong 'sex-image' (vacations).
3. Those products which are joint purchases but with a balance to wife or husband indicate those situations where use, or results of use, are joint but where a 'sexual' image balance still exists in favour of one spouse or the other i.e. insurance and cars benefit both parties but finance and driving are more 'male' activities. Similarly, while the benefits of vacuum cleaners and toasters are felt by both spouses they are still wife-dominated (cleaning and cooking).

Nevertheless, this theory, while seductive, does not explain everything.

Table 9:3   Influence of Sex Roles in certain Product Purchases

PART A	Population Sample US, Gisler (1948)[7]	Husband	Mainly Joint	Wife
	Plugs, tyres and oil	+	0	0
	Alcoholic drinks	+	0	0
	Shaving goods	+	0	0
	Insurance	+	+	0
	Heating	+	+	0
	Cars	+	+	0
	Vacation	0	+	0
	Washing machine	0	+	0
	Refrigerator	0	+	0
	Vacuum cleaner	0	+	+
	Toaster	0	+	+
	Aspirin	0	0	+
	Soft drinks	0	0	+
	Shampoo	0	0	+
PART B	Difference between matched Working— non-Working Wives	*Husbands of Working Wives		Husbands of non-Working Wives
	Nye and Hoffman (1963)[12]			
	Food shopping	+		0
	Medical care	+		0
	Furniture	0		+
	Cars	0		+
	House purchases	0		+
	Vacation	0		+
	Insurance	0		+
	Financial matters	0		+
	Really important decisions	0		+
PART C	Purchase decisions in general Foote (1961)[13]			
	Families with pre-school children	+	+	0
	Younger couples	0	+	0
	Lower social grade	0	0	+
	Middle social grade	0	+	0
	Upper social grade	+	0	0

*This section of the table shows the direction of the differences.
Source: Field (1968) *see* Chapter 8, reference 10.

For example, why do refrigerators and washing machines which are, intuitively, 'feminine' not appear in the 'joint-wife' decision area? It seems that this theory must be modified by one other variable, and this could be finance. Adding this to the sex-power role theory then we could postulate:

1. Where the products are not expensive, then sex-role differences are clearly present. e.g. plugs, tyres and oil, and shampoo.
2. Where the product is more expensive then the decision becomes more joint but still retains a sexual bias, e.g. in insurance and vacuum cleaners.
3. Where the product is particularly expensive or totally sexually neutral (vacations) then sex biases are abandoned and the product becomes a joint decision.

The theory is still based on sex/power roles but becomes a little 'tighter'. Certainly, financial factors alone could not explain the division of decisions. (This still does not explain why cars do not fall into the totally joint decision but this is explained later.)

Part B

This part of Field's table supports the sex/power role theory from another angle. Here we have decision outcomes from the perspective of husbands of working wives and non-working wives. If perception of sex roles leads to a 'division of labour' in the husband/wife decisions, we would expect that where the balance of sex-role changes, whether in the marital relationship or in the 'sex' of the product, the balance of the husband/wife decision would also change.

In Field's table, when women in the sample are noted as working, that is, moving out of their traditional 'domestic' role, then their husbands correspondingly move into the former 'female' purchasing areas. As can be seen in the descriptive results of Nye and Hoffman's study, the husbands of working wives both move into the 'female' shopping areas of food and medical care *and* out of specific male-purchase areas of, for example, house purchase, insurance and financial matters. The husbands of non-working or 'traditional' wives stay firmly put in product decisions which circumscribe a traditional 'masculine role' and leave food and medical care to their wives.

This supposition can also be supported by Kenkel (1961)[14] who hypothesised that the extent to which the husband is perceived to perform the role of family provider will also be a determinant in the role he plays in the family decision-making. Where income contribution is shared then there will be a relative decline in the traditional husband and wife roles. This is also noted by Wolfe (1963)[15] who found that the employment status of the wife affects her role in the decision-making. Generally, the influence of the wife is greatest if she works outside the home.

Part C

Here we find more evidence to support the theories of sex role and social class that we noted earlier in the chapter. Middle-class and younger couples, those which one would expect, both intuitively and from evidence already noted, to be most flexible in their sex role behaviour, demonstrate the most joint decision-making compared to, for example, lower and upper social class groups.

All in all, Field's table tends to give support to sex/power roles as a valid indicator of patterns in certain husband/wife product decisions.

The Changing Sex of the Car and the Marital Purchase Decision

As further validation of the sex/power factor in marital consumer decisions, we can now turn to purchase patterns of the car.

We have shown that where sex-role perceptions change, so may the corresponding patterns in product purchase. Can this phenomenon be related to a product? If the sex-role image of a product was known to be moving from one sex-role area to the other then would we not expect, under the sex/power role theory, that the purchase emphasis would move correspondingly from one partner to the other?

Taking the car as an example, we can see that this is, in fact, exactly what can happen. Tracing research on the car, the earliest known study on it as a durable in husband/wife decisions was over twenty years ago in work by Wolgast (1953)[16]. She found that while decisions over household appliances were housewife-dominated, those for the car were husband-dominated. In addition, in patterns of 'decisions to buy' while the intention to buy durable goods was usually mentioned as the 'wife's' plan it was usually the 'husband's' in relation to cars.

During the 1950s and 1960s more and more women took full-time employment and more bought their own cars or learned to drive and used their husbands'. By 1959 Martineau[21] was noting that at least 1 man in 5 took his wife along when buying the car and 3 in 5 looked for her approval before the purchase decision. By 1972 Newman and Staelin[17] and Doyle and Hutchinson[18] were noting that women had started to take a considerable interest in the car purchase so that differential perceptions of one model and differing attitudes towards brands by husband and wife had intruded extensively into the car purchase decision.

By 1974, in the most recent study, Cunningham and Green[19] in a direct comparison with earlier results on car purchase decisions by Sharp and Mott (1955)[20] found that the influence of the wife in the family car purchase was not only considerable but had reduced the incidence of husband domination in car purchase by 18 percentage points over the 20-year period. It seems that in 1955 Sharp and Mott had found that the automobile decision was husband-dominated in 70% of the cases and joint in 35%, while in the 1973 study this balance had changed to 52% and 45% respectively. Cunningham and Green[19] conclude that:

> The most dramatic change in decision roles found in the study occured with respect to automobiles. Here the data indicate that a basic change in market composition has occurred. Formerly a male bastion, the automobile purchase appears to be increasingly becoming a joint decision in the family ... Both husband and wife have vested

interests in the selection of an automobile since both use the car in the performance of their roles. An alternative explanation of the shifts in automobile decision-making might refer to *increasing egalitarianism in the husband-wife relationship. Major economic decisions, such as those relating to automobiles are becoming more shared and less controlled by one family member.*

To conclude, then, on the husband/wife decision process:

1. Influence on the housewife's decision by the husband can be measured by the more mechanical method of 'product-based' research. This involves a 'gross' measure which merely notes the incidence of influence by the husband on a particular product decision and the 'net' measure which breaks this influence down into significant stages of the decision. It is usually used in investigating grocery products where the influence is difficult to explain and evaluate. The product-based method can be used on family, as well as husband, influence measurement.

2. Joint husband and wife decisions çan be evaluated, particularly in the larger consumer durable purchase, by recourse to sex/power role measures. These attribute relative influence of the husband and wife on the product decision to factors associated with balance of the sex roles and the power relationships that this subsumes within the partnership. This approach can be generalised to other family members only in the sense that family sex roles may generate sub-roles which move a decision from the husband and wife to, for example, mother and daughter.

In short, product and marital factors should always be at least considered in investigating the husband-wife decision process in a purchase, and the potential influence of the wife in the husband's decision and the husband's in the wife's decision *should never be ignored.*

REFERENCES

1. NOP Grocery Shopping Survey (1967).
2. 'Family Participation and Influence in Shopping and Brand Selection', Phases I and II, conducted for *Life Magazine* by Nowland and Company Inc., Greenwich, Connecticut (June 1964 and May 1965).
3. L. J. Jaffe and H. Senft, 'The Roles of Husbands and Wives in Purchasing Decisions', in Adler and Crespi (eds.), *Attitude Research at Sea,* American Marketing Association (1966).
4. 'Husbands and Wives in Food Purchasing', IPC Publications (1974), noted in *Retail Business,* 193 (March 1974).
5. J. S. Coulson, 'Buying Decisions Within the Family and The Consumer-Brand Relationship', in Joseph W. Newman (ed.), *On Knowing the Consumer*, John Wiley and Sons (1966).
6. *See* chapter 8, ref. 26.
7. C. R. Gisler, 'Is the Buying Influence of Men Underestimated?', *Printers' Ink* (24 September 1948), p. 39.
8. *See* Ernest W. Burgess and Harvey J. Locke, *The Family,* New York American Book Company (1960).

David M. Heer, 'Husband and Wife Perceptions of Family Power Structure', *Marriage and Family Living* (36) (February 1962), pp. 65–7.

David M. Heer, 'Dominance and the Working Wife', *Social Forces* (36) (May 1958), p. 341.

Bloode and Wolfe, *Dynamics of Married Living*, The Free Press, (Glencoe 1960).

9. Bernard Farber, 'A Study of Dependence and Decision Making in Marriage', unpublished doctoral dissertation. University of Chicago (September 1949).

10. P. G. Herbst, 'The Measurement of Family Relationships', *Human Relations* (5) (February 1952), pp. 3–35.

11. R. F. Winch, *Mate Selection: A Study of complementary needs,* Harper and Row (1958).

12. F. I. Nye and L. W. Hoffman, *The Employed Mother in America*, Rand McNally (1963).

13. N. N. Foote (ed.), *Household Decision Making,* New York University Press (1961).

14. W. F. Kenkel, 'Husband-Wife Interaction in Decision Making, *Journal of Social Psychology* (54) (1961); pp. 255–62.

15. D. M. Wolfe. 'Power and Authority in the Family', in R. F. Winch. R. McGinnis and H. R. Barringer (eds.), *Selected Studies in Marriage and the Family*. Holt Rinehart and Winston (London 1963).

16. Elizabeth Wolgast (1958), *see* chapter 8, ref. 22.

17. Joseph W. Newman and Richard Staelin, 'Pre-Purchase Information Seeking for New Cars and Major Household Appliances', *Journal of Marketing Research* Vol. IX (August 1972), pp. 249–57.

18. Peter Doyle and Peter Hutchinson, 'Individual Differences in Family Decision Making', *Journal of the Market Research Society*, Vol. 15 (4) (1972), pp. 193–206.

19. Isabella C. M. Cunningham and Robert T. Green, 'Purchasing Roles in the U.S. Family 1955 and 1973', *Journal of Marketing*, Vol. 38 (October 1974), pp. 61–8.

20. Harry Sharp and Paul Mott. 'Consumer Decisions in the Metropolitan Family', *Journal of Marketing*, Vol. 22 (October 1956). pp. 149–56.

21. Pierre Martineau, *Business Week* (December 1959), p. 79.

10. The Influence of Children and certain Significant Others

THE INFLUENCE OF CHILDREN

Over the last couple of decades children have become an important marketing segment. Goulart (1970)[1] notes that in 1939 only 300,000 dollars was spent in America on advertising to young people on network radio. In less than 20 years the budget for youth advertising, on television, rose to over 100 million dollars. In 1970 children in America represented yearly gross sales that have been estimated as high as 50 billion dollars. Several billion more were to be had from adult sales *influenced by child pressure*. The biggest markets of all were those for toys which took $2\frac{1}{2}$ billion dollars, soft drinks at $3\frac{1}{2}$ billion, sweets at $1\frac{1}{2}$ billion and bubble gum at 25 million dollars.

Meanwhile, the breakfast food industry persuades children to consume 650 million dollars of dry cereal annually while the 35 million comic books that children read every month represent an annual income of 48 million dollars. Wells (1969)[10] assures us that American children consume, every year, enough peanut butter to coat the Empire State Building three feet thick, enough soft drinks to fill the Queen Mary ten and a half times and enough bubble gum to blow a bubble the size of the Rock of Gibraltar!

Children are big business and, it seems, mainly because there are just so many children and young people in America.

An article in *Business Week*[2] notes that over half the American population is now under the age of 27. Removing the young adults and young marrieds, over 70 million Americans are, thus, in the under-18 group. The older child market, that is, the 'college' market (records, books, clothing, sporting goods, travel) now consists of over 7 million persons who account for direct spending of over 45 billion dollars annually and who *influence the purchase* of another 145 billion dollars worth of goods.

As befits their status as consumers, children in America are assaulted by the media and consumption industry from their earliest babyhood and Riesman (1950)[3] observed that the long-range object of mass media assault on children was to build up in the child 'habits of consumption he will employ as an adult'. In the 1960s, social anthropologist Henry[4] pointed out that all

142

cultures train children 'for the roles they will fill as adults'. In western society 'the central aims of our culture . . . are to sell goods . . . create consumers . . . educate children to buy.' As it is with America so it is in the United Kingdom.

Retail Business reports[5] on the new pre-teen market, 'the previously unrecognised awkward gap between being a genuine child and a genuine teenager', that there was now £126 million to be shared out among the manufacturers 'who can latch onto the pocket money market'.

Children between the ages of 5 and 15, it seems, are reckoned to receive this amount of pocket money annually and something like £24 million of this goes on ice-cream and confectionery and £9·25 million to the publishing trade for magazines and comics. Morley (1968)[6] gives a breakdown of the source of children's pocket money and it is evident that the bulk of it, £92 million, is contributed by parents and other relatives. It is the smallest proportion (£33 million) which is earned.

At the older end of the child age range, the *Retail Business* report notes that there is also considerable expenditure on clothes so that for every £1 of their own money that these children spend, they help in varying degrees in choosing for themselves several more pounds of clothing paid for by parents and themselves. At the other end, there is the baby and toddler sector, where women spend £10—12 million p.a. on baby toiletries and £15 million on pram and nursery equipment. Baby hygiene is a growing sector and in this women spend about £4 million per annum on baby pants and disposable nappies, while the huge baby food sector notches up nearly £48 million a year[7].

The British birth rate is, however, falling[7], and baby food manufacturers are thus trying to move their goods into the later baby years to retain their market value, although the general market for baby goods should not suffer too much since these products are bought anyway for the first child and are used by successive children. Other observers suggest that the whole children's market may even benefit by the falling birth rate both because most children's goods will be bought at a time of greater family prosperity, and because this new trend is also coinciding with a greater gap between marriage and the first child and first child and successive children.

Those markets which are particularly important in terms of child influence (0—15 years) are illustrated in a table drawn up by Morley (1968)[6] (*see* Table 10:1) and the results of a survey by NOP on housewife-child influence*. It seems that children dominate the consumption and frequently suggest the purchase of breakfast cereals, clothing, bread, biscuits and cakes, ice cream and confectionery in particular.

Certainly, the main importance of children lies in the food sector and a marketing man of a large frozen food company, quoted by Goulart

---

* NOP Survey on Shopping (1967) (*see* chapter 9 ref. 1).

(1970)[1] notes that: 'Few people are aware of the depth of children's influence on food buying.'

He estimated that school-age children influence 15% of all family food purchases.

Table 10:1   Estimates of Expenditure for Child Consumption (these generally cover all 13·5 million children aged 0–15 inclusive, in the United Kingdom)

Product Groups	Annual Expenditure (£ million at market prices)	Source
Boys' clothes	69·9	(a)
Girls' clothes	69·5	(a)
Children's footwear	63·6	(b)
Bread	43·0	(b)
Breakfast and other cereals	35·0	(b)
Biscuits, cakes etc.	54·0	(b)
Confectionery	105·0	(c)
Ice cream and lollies	32·5	(d)
Toys and games	61·0	(e)
Soft drinks	22·0	(b)
Books and magazines	21·0	(b)
Poultry, sausages, canned meat etc.	65·5	(b)

(a) Family Expenditure Survey (1966) average annual household expenditure grossed up by 17,577 million (Registrar General's mid–1966 estimate of UK households).
(b) Extracted, by comparison of difference in family unit consumption, from Family Expenditure Survey (1966).
(c) The Confectionery Market: surveys by Social Surveys (Gallup Poll) Limited. Source (b) not used since basic data acknowledged as unreliable by compilers.
(d) Trade estimates of 50% child consumption of £65 million market. Source (b) not used as basic data acknowledged as unreliable by compilers.
(e) Toy Manufacturers Association Limited estimate of £66 million home production, less £15 million exports, plus £11 million imports. Source (b) for toys, games plus paper and stationery goods gives expenditure of £72 million.

To say the least, the children's market has encouraged a great deal of marketing interest in the last few years and testament to this can be found in the plethora of research articles on how to interview children for marketing research studies [8,9,10,11]. There has also been a proliferation of children's research agencies and new codes on how not to advertise to children, while the responsiveness, interest and cynicism of children towards commercials have been frequently measured along with their particular likes and dislikes. Feldman and Wolf (1974)[9], for example, found that while food commercials were both the most liked and disliked by children, the extent of like/dislike varied according to the age of the child; 5–7-year-old children were more likely than any other age group to pan food commercials while those in the 8–10-year-old group were most likely to classify them as 'favourites'.

The child, however, unless she/he is spending money earned by herself/ himself is obviously still going to need to make some reference to the mother, in particular, and the family, in general. Even pocket money for the child's own consumption is still going to be donated and to some extent influenced by at least one parent and, in the case of other markets such as food, cereals and confectionery, it is obvious that the mother is going to be a strong brake on the child, by choosing to buy or not buy what the child likes or by vetoing a purchase that the child wants to make. Yet, on balance, the influence of the child should not be underestimated. Rippel notes in his study of the influence of the child on the housewife's decisions: 'The child has ceased to be simply the recipient of the educational efforts by its parents and has become a member of the family and is not infrequently asked for its opinions.'

How, therefore, do we balance out influence by the child on the family purchases and the 'gatekeeper' effect by the mother on the child's behaviour? For this we have to turn to the, admittedly few, studies on the child and mother in the purchasing situation.

STUDIES ON THE CHILD AND THE MOTHER

Berey and Pollay's study (1968)[12] on the relative influence of children in the purchase of breakfast cereals is the one most quoted in relation to this subject. Previous studies by Wells and LoScutio (1966)[13] and Garnatz (1954)[14], had looked at the interaction of mother and child at the point-of-sale but did not describe the *reasons* behind the observed mother-child behaviour. Berey and Pollay investigated why a child should influence its mother's product choice and examined this from the angle of child-orientation of the mother. They made two hypotheses:

1. The more assertive the child, the more likely the mother will purchase the child's favourite brands of breakfast cereal.
2. The more child-centred the mother, the more likely she will purchase the child's favourite cereal.

They also tested the dependence/independence of other related variables. Their results were interesting. First, none of the control variables was dependent on the child-mother interaction, that is, the mother's purchase behaviour was independent of the child's age, the number of other children in the home, the mother's outside employment, the number of trips to the store the child made alone, and the number of trips to the store made by the child accompanied by her/his mother.

Second, although the association between the child-centredness and purchase was significant at the ·05 level, the direction was *opposite* to that previously hypothesised. Instead of child-centred mothers showing a greater tendency to purchase their children's favourite cereals, they had a tendency to purchase these cereals *less* frequently. (In the case of the other hypothesis, the child's assertiveness compared with the mother's purchase behaviour did not yield a correlation that was significant.)

The conclusions that the researchers drew from these contradictory findings were that the mother who is more child-centred has a greater tendency to purchase cereals following her view of what is 'right and health-ful', while the low child-centred mother may be more likely to purchase the brands the child prefers to placate the child. The researchers comment:

> Though child-centredness of the mother may increase her receptivity to influence by the child, for cereals there is apparently the stronger effect of the mother being in strong disagreement with the child over what brands to purchase. Awareness of the strength of this 'gatekeeper' effect has some strong implications for firms marketing any product with which the child is eventually involved. Given that the mother is not only a purchasing agent for the child but also an agent who super-imposes her preferences over those of the child, it is clear that a lot of advertising would be well directed at the mother, even if the mother is not a 'consumer' of the product. Without such advertising, the child's influence attempts may be largely ignored if the mother thinks the brand desired is an inferior good.

As a rider, the study postulates that a rejection of the child's influence may also stem from the mother's perceptions of the quality of the information the child possesses, that is, she may see the advertisements aimed at the child through her own adult eyes and not like what she sees. The child's attempts to influence the mother would then be a function of the mother's opinion of the promotional stimulus that initiated the child's interest. 'A commercial the mother perceives as silly and unconvincing may cause her to discredit the product.'

Ward and Wackman (1972)[15] attempted to take up where Berey and Pollay left off and while supporting some of their findings also added some new ones related particularly to conflict and media exposure. The study on twenty-two heavily advertised products indicated the following broad features on child/mother purchase influence:

Child Influence Attempts

Children most frequently attempted to influence purchases for food products, but these attempts decreased with age. Durables which the child used directly were the second most requested category. Younger children made frequent influence attempts for game and toy purchases while older children con-centrated on clothing and record albums (11–12 year olds). Across all product categories, purchase influence attempts by the children decreased with age.

Parental Yielding

The older the child, the more likely the mothers were to yield to influence attempts 'perhaps because the older children generally asked for less'. Ward and Wackman, in line with the Berey and Pollay findings noted that the greater influence of the older child could be attributed to the mother ascribing greater competence in making judgements to older children. Food also figured highly in levels of parental yielding. Mothers were most likely to yield to influence from the child on food purchases, the same products that the child most often asked for. This is related to a slight correlation between a tendency for those children who asked for most to be yielded to most.

Conflict

There was an indication from the data that a significant positive relationship existed between conflict and influence attempts, suggesting that purchase influence attempts might be related to a general pattern of disagreement and conflict between parents and children. Few parents, however, were found to actually punish their children by consciously refusing to yield to purchase influence attempts.

Media Use

There seems to be a general 'strict' and 'loose' continuum operating in this connection. The more restrictions that the parents place on a child's televiewing the less they also yield to its purchase influence attempts. Nevertheless, this form of control does not restrict the number of attempts at purchase influence that the child will, optimistically, make. Related to this is a finding that mothers with more positive attitudes towards advertising were more likely to yield to purchase attempts than mothers with less favourable attitudes.

A third study by Rippel (1968)[11] investigated how children judged products as a basis for assessing differences in product perception between parents and children. One of his findings, which relates to both the Berey and Pollay study and the one by Ward and Wackman was that children tended to judge products on more emotional grounds than their parents who used criteria such as price and usefulness. This would support the parental belief that children are usually not fit judges of product desirability and the contention by the child-directed mothers of both studies that children's product decisions are motivated by irrationality.

One particularly interesting finding of the Rippel study was that children, for all their influence attempts, are very often totally unsure about the possible outcome of their pleadings. Twenty-two out of fifty-four children were unable to picture the future conduct of their parents, that is, whether or not they would be prepared to buy the product under consideration. Of those children who did picture the outcome, they were often much more pessimistic than their parents. The parents were more often in favour of the product than the children had forecast, in fact twice as often.

Wells, (1966)[16] finally, in his study of the purchase influences of children divided their purchase attempts into four main types.

1. *Personal purchases.* Here they relate to their parents in a contrary fashion by buying what is considered unnecessary or evil (sweets, gum, soft drinks, comic books and inexpensive toys). This is from the age of about six.

2. *Direct requests at home.* These, as Ward and Wackman noted, were mainly requests for food and toys, but also dog food, shoes, bread and other isolated products which fell generally into the main 'child' categories noted by the NOP survey and the results of PAS, Morley (1968)[6] (Table 10:1 indicates these categories).

Wells, in line with Ward and Wackman, found that direct requests tended to diminish with age. He notes that the simple 'mummy buy me . . . ' request reaches a peak in elementary school and after this changes to the third form of influence.

3. *Passive dictation.* This is a form of non-verbal communication and depends on the mother observing what the child consumes willingly and what they resist. 'At times this passive dictation governs product choice and brand choice for the whole family. If the other family members, including the mother, have no objections the child is likely to carry the day.'

4. *In-store influence.* This is found to follow a similar pattern to that which Wells observed in the home and which Berey and Pollay, and Ward and Wackman also observed in their studies, that is, younger children ask for many things but they do not get everything they ask for. The parents act as dampening intermediaries. Older children are more selective and more circumspect but still effective especially if they are going to consume the product themselves.

Thus, to summarise the main results of the studies by Berey and Pollay[12], Ward and Wackman[5], Rippel[11] and Wells[16] on child/mother influence in purchase decisions:

1. The *age* of the child is a most important variable in purchase influence in that the older child is more likely to be successful in his influence attempts. This age factor is related to the fact that:
2. Mothers, especially those who are particularly child-orientated, tend to perceive a younger child's perception of products as irrational and influences working on her/him to buy, as irresponsible. The older child is perceived by such mothers as being more capable of decision and less open to irrational influences and this will allow her/his opinions to figure in her purchase decisions.
3. Children watch most advertisements, and make most influence attempts, for food products. Mothers are also likely to yield to more influence

attempts in food products, possibly as a function of the greater number of influence attempts.

4. Conflict between the mother and child may stimulate her operation of the purchase 'veto' (*see* Field *op. cit.*, chapter 8 [10]).

5. Mothers who are exposed to less media and who have a less favourable attitude toward advertisements are less likely to yield to purchase influence by their children than those who are exposed to more and have a favourable attitude.

6. Children may make frequent attempts at influence but this is part of an optimistic bombardment policy since they have been shown to considerably doubt the effectiveness of their influence attempts.

7. Child influence on the mother can be overt and non-overt.

In conclusion, children are a constant and valid influence on housewife purchase, quite apart from purchases in their own right, and this influence takes place both in the shop and in the home. Mothers, however, as they have since time immemorial, generally have the final and important say.

TWO FINAL VARIABLES

The family has now been examined from a variety of approaches for angles on how it influences the female consumer. Two other influences should be noted, however, before we conclude this section and these are related first, to extra-family influences, and second, to an important family variable, that of time.

Extra-family Influence—Mothers and Friends

It would be unwise to omit the housewife's mother and mother-in-law from this study of household-housewife purchase influence for, especially in the early years of the marriage, both are of considerable importance to the wife in certain domestic decisions. For example, Joyce (1968)[19] noted that young housewives turned to their mother for advice on buying groceries 29% of the time compared to 21% to their friends and 18% to their husbands. A study by J. W. Thompson (1968)[17] also noted that a third of married women under 35 live within walking distance of their parents and over half of these see their mothers at least once a week.

The influence of the mother-in-law is also important to the young housewife but is not as important as that of the mother to whom the housewife tends to turn in situations such as looking after the baby, buying groceries and arranging a party. The influence of mother and mother-in-law diminishes, however, with the length of the marriage. Sampson (1968)[18] comments:

> In early married life the influence of the mother is quite substantial, whether the mother lives in the household or not, and the question of the children hardly ever arises. At later stages of the life cycle, the housewife is likely to become 'more experienced' in executing her role as housewife and mother, and rely upon her mother less.

With the reduced importance of the mother as the marriage progresses, another party tends to creep in to maintain balance and this is the housewife's friend. Her influence tends to increase steadily with the number of years the housewife is married. Joyce noted that both the mother as an advice source and the 'novelty' of the husband diminish with time, and then friends play an increasing role in purchase influence. In fact, in the later marriage years friends influence things such as shop choice 8 percentage points more than the mother.

Nevertheless, generalisations should be avoided in relation to extra-family influence since Joyce[19], IPC (1970)[20] and Katz and Lazerfeld (1955)[21] all find that this influence is highly variable not only by length of marriage but also by product. Ideally, in fact, extra-family influence should be measured primarily from a product perspective.

Life Cycle

Life-cycle theory in relation to family purchasing behaviour is a tacit acceptance of the fact that dynamics of influence and power in the family will change over time. As people change over a period of years so then will their personal relationships and priorities. New power and influence equilibria are formed.

Wells and Gubar (1966)[22] point out that although the concept of life-cycle as an independent variable is a relatively new idea in marketing research, it is not new in sociology. They cite evidence from research that the life cycle ought to be a more sensitive indicator than chronological age, and suggest that it would be profitable to use 'life cycle' instead of age in marketing research studies involving family consumer behaviour where inter-active positions of family members do change over time. For example, children become a more important influence on purchase as they get older. There are, however, important problems of definition. There is no standard form of 'life cycle' and while the different definitions tally, each nevertheless puts different emphasis on slightly different variables e.g. age and number of children, occupation, year of marriage etc. Wells and Gubar (1966)[22] and Joyce (1968)[19], to compare but two, use similar but differing structures. The 'life-cycle' definitions of each research study are set out below:

Wells and Gubar[22]

Stage 1   The bachelor stage: young single people
Stage 2   Newly married couples: young, no children
Stage 3   The 'full nest' I: young married couples with dependent children
          —the youngest child under six
          —the youngest child six or over
Stage 4   The 'full nest' II: older married couples with dependent children
Stage 5   The 'empty nest': older married couples with no children living with them

        Head of household still working
        Head of household retired

Stage 6   The solitary survivors
        —still working
        —retired

Joyce[19]

1. Single/unattached
2. Single/planning marriage
3. Married/no children
4. Married/eldest child under one year
5. Married/eldest child 1–5 years
6. Married/eldest child over six years

Nevertheless, despite the problems of definition, there are still indications that life-cycle theory is a valuable way to approach family decision-making since it charts the different roles and skills of husband and wife over time and we have already seen that role-playing is an important variable in such decision-making.

Kenkel (1961)[23] and Wolgast (1958)[24] have both, for example, used life-cycle theory linked with data on 'expressive-instrumental' behaviour and ages of children, to explain why and how wives take more part in family consumer decision-making as they progress through the marriage. Its main use to the marketer is that it presents a dynamic image of the housewife and mother and helps to see factors such as employment as recurring rather than absolute factors in her marriage cycle.

CONCLUSION TO PART III

The degree to which a woman makes her own purchasing decision or is influenced by her family or husband is a complex area and Part III should serve to end all sweeping criteria based on 'a housewife buys what her husband wants', or 'women control the housekeeping purchase'. It is also impossible and Utopian to conceive of an 'average' housewife influenced in some general and predictable manner, by an 'average' family. Family influence on the housewife is highly variable. If there are any important factors to note then they must be ones which we have noted already in other contexts in previous chapters. These are that:

1. Different products/product groups encourage different housewife/family influences. In fact, how the woman is influenced in her purchase should be a product-by-product study followed by a within-product decision analysis. Supporting this, Engel, Kollatt and Blackwell (1968)* say: 'Marketing

---

* Chapter 7[37].

executives should base strategy decisions on product or brand role structures describing overall decision-making in the family,' while in a very recent study, Cunningham and Green 1974* concluded that:

> ... it is difficult to generalise the impact that changes in the environment will have on family purchasing patterns. While family decision-making roles have been changing in response to environmental change, all products apparently have not been affected in the same way.

> Thus, it would be a mistake to base any marketing decisions that are affected by family decision-making patterns on information concerning general role shifts within the family; product-specific information should be required.

2. The perceptions by the housewife of her role as woman, worker, sexual partner, mother and wife will:

(a) Combine to form a powerful mediating variable in the family purchasing decision that can as easily takè the form of veto as of approval.

(b) Synthesise into a perception of power balance in product decisions, particularly in those which involve the husband.

The important factor in this perception of role is that of change. As family structure dissolves and female role perceptions modify, so will the family / housewife decision and sex /power roles in product decisions gradually restructure in an attempt to regain equilibrium.

Overall, however, there are probably few other areas in marketing where purchase decisions and influence processes are quite as complex as in the relationship between the housewife and her family. In fact, it is perhaps in recognition of this complexity that one can find the key to understanding it. Controlling or predicting it is another thing altogether.

REFERENCES

1. Ron Goulart, *The Assault on Childhood*, Victor Gollancz (London 1970).
2. 'Getting Across to the Young', *Business Week* (18 October 1969), pp. 88–90.
3. Noted in Goulart *op. cit.*, p. 15.
4. Noted in Goulart *op. cit.*, p. 15.
5. 'The Nursery Market', *Retail Business* Report, 176 (October 1972).
6. John Morley, 'Marketing to Children', *British Journal of Marketing*, Vol. 2 (1968), pp. 139–46.
7. *Retail Business* 176, *op. cit.*
8. Scott Ward, 'Children's Reactions to Commercials', *Journal of Advertising Research*, Vol. 12, No. 2, (April 1972). pp. 37–45.
9. Shel Feldman and Abraham Wolf, 'What's Wrong with Children's Commercials?', *Journal of Advertising Research*, Vol. 14 (1) (February 1974), pp. 39–43.
10. William D. Wells, 'Communicating with Children', *Journal of Advertising Research* (1965). Vol. 5(2), pp. 2–14.

---

*Chapter 9 [19].

11. Kurt Rippel, 'The Child as Test Person'. *European Market Research Review*, Vol. 4(2) (1969). pp. 37–46.

12. Lewis A. Berey and Richard W. Pollay. 'The Influencing Role of the Child in Family Decision Making', *Journal of Marketing Research*, Vol. V (February 1968), pp. 70–2.

13. William D. Wells and Leonard A. LoScutio, 'Direct Observation of Purchasing Behaviour', *Journal of Marketing Research* (3 August 1966), pp. 227–33.

14. George Garnatz, 'Children Have Market Influence', quoted in unpublished paper, Kroger Food Foundation (Cincinatti 1954).

15. Scott Ward and Daniel B. Wackman, 'Children's Purchase Influence Attempts and Parental Yielding', *Journal of Marketing Research*, Vol. IX (August 1972), pp. 316–19.

16. William D. Wells, 'Children as Consumers', in Joseph D. Newman (ed.), *On Knowing the Consumer*. John Wiley and Sons (New York 1966), pp. 138–45.

17. J. Walter Thompson (1968). *see* chapter 8, ref. 7.

18. Sampson, *see* chapter 8, ref. 15.

19. T. Joyce (1968), *see* chapter 8, ref. 26.

20. 'Shopping and the Shopper'. IPC Publications Ltd., (1970).

21. Katz and Lazerfeld, *see* chapter 8, ref. 12.

22. William D. Wells and George Gubar, 'Life Cycle Concept in Marketing'. *Journal of Marketing Research*. Vol. III (November 1966). pp. 355–63.

23. Kenkel. *see* chapter 9, ref. 14.

24. Wolgast, *see* chapter 9, ref. 16.

PART IV

Woman Buying for Herself

Woman dominates the huge household and food markets and in this capacity she buys both for herself and for her family. There is, however, a whole sector of markets wherein she purchases chiefly for her own satisfaction and subsistence. These markets may vary from the traditionally feminine, such as those for cosmetics and sanitary protection, to areas where she has virtually crossed the sexual frontiers to make a formerly neutral or masculine market, her own.

Housewives and unmarried women both figure in these areas, and the spending power of the single girl in particular, is a growing force to be reckoned with. For example, an IPC Survey in 1973, 'Teenagers and Young Housewives' noted that women between 15 and 29 spend £460 million a year on clothes, £42 million on confectionery, £141 million on cigarettes and £90 million on toiletries and cosmetics, not to mention their expenditure on consumer durables and appliances, drinks, holidays, sport and entertainment activities. The women buying for herself constitutes an economic sector which the man buying for himself cannot compare with, for even in the male product area the main purchasers are often women buying *for* the men in their lives, for example, after-shave lotion and underwear.

To be sure, there are 'men's' markets and there are 'women's' markets, but these bastions of sexual rigidity are fast eroding with the onset of more indistinct sex-role behaviour, so that the time is coming when it will be increasingly difficult to assign strict sexual characters to behaviour, preferences or buying patterns.

The signs of unisexuality are noted in widely differing contexts. Dr. Brown of Mount Sinai Hospital* suggests that interpretations of the Rorschach Inkblot test show that sex differences are blurring, so that both males and females are giving the female or 'abnormal' interpretation, a finding which indicates a narrowing of the stereotypical sex-role differences. In a marriage contract noted in *Nova* in 1973† a clause covered the *equal* responsibility of husband and wife for the financial and social upbringing of the children and maintenance of household and marital dues. In the *Guardian*†† a report on the preferability of *male* au-pairs noted that they were more hardworking and better at some household

---

* Carol Ashkinaze, the *Guardian*, 23 November 1971.
† *Nova* Marriage Contracts between David Marsden and Alison Ryder of Birmingham in *Nova*, 14 March 1973.
†† The *Guardian*, 8 August 1973.

jobs than their female equivalents. Rosemary Piper in an article in the *Guardian** notes that there is an upsurge in domestic science courses in schools for boys and girls, with an 'A' level in parenthood proposed for both sexes. Finally, a study by Wilmott and Young† showed that only one in seven professional men now get by without doing anything in the home (compared with one in four of the unskilled and semi-skilled) while in the chapters on 'Shopping' we observed that men now participate frequently in the shopping activity, as a matter of right.

Strict delineation of markets on sexual grounds is a tradition which may be next to crumble and in certain product groups, it already has.

---

* Rosemary Piper in an article by P. Pigache 'Since Lads Will be Dads', the *Guardian*. 30 January 1973.
† *See* chapter 8, reference 6.

11.   The Female Erosion of Traditionally Male Markets

Some markets are traditionally 'female' and others traditionally 'male' but increasingly these days no one can be quite sure about which these markets are and how long they will stay so carefully divided.

'Masculinity' and 'femininity' are socially flexible concepts. Ultimately, true outward 'maleness' and 'femaleness' rests entirely on hormone balances and since both males and females contain each others' hormones and each others' physical potential—men even have a vestigial womb—differences are never entirely clear. We create sex differences for a variety of socially convenient and prejudicial reasons, and those which lie in the products we buy are only as strong as the social acceptance that these differences should be maintained.

Stutteville (1971)[1] showed how certain products can even be sex-typed within their appropriate categories, cars being a classic example. He shows, on the diagram below, how sexuality in the image of a car can cause it to fall into specific market segments (*see* Diagram 11:1).

Diagram 11:1

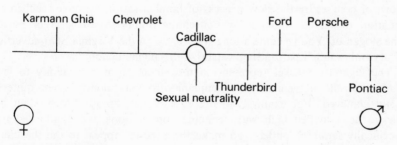

Source: Stutteville (1971)[1].

157

The use of a 'feminine' car will not, however, seriously damage a male sex-role image, although the car may be recognised as having a female image, possibly because this is a product which has become 'neutralised' with time, a mechanised eunuch whose sexual notation is merely illusory so that it is not emotionally unacceptable for one sex to drive the car with the opposite-sexed image.

> Although the Pontiac is perhaps one of the most masculinely identified production cars, a woman can be seen driving it without any risk of seeming to be Lesbianishly hard. Volkswagen's Karmann Ghia is so strongly feminine that its ads even call it 'the Pussycat', yet many 'He-man' types drive the Karmann Ghias but perhaps with more image danger than the female who drives the Pontiac GTO. The other cars cluster around neutrality.

He suggests that neutrality is reduced to some extent by factors such as colour; light pastels 'shove' a car to femininity, and strong, bold and dark colours 'nudge' a car to masculinity. ·

Stutteville noted other products can, however, be too strong in their taboos to allow a comfortable use of them by the 'wrong' sex. An example he gives is attaché cases. Women, even in business and educational establishments, still prefer the more feminine image of a smart bag to the 'over-masculinised' image of a brief-case.

Nevertheless, there are also the products which had this strict sexually-divided image once but which by time and familiarity crossed into the ownership of the 'other side'. A good example of this is the cigarette. Stutteville notes that in 1905 a woman was arrested on New York's Fifth Avenue for smoking in a car and when a Madame Schuman-Heink was used by George Washington Mill to plug Lucky Strikes in an advertisement she had many of her USA engagements cancelled, and was viciously attacked by the outraged Methodist Board of Morals for undermining the health and morality of American women and girls. Stutteville comments:

> Apparently smoking by women was seen as masculinising in a rather narrow but highly dangerous vector; namely it was a scarlet badge brandished by brazen women who were thereby announcing that the sexual freedom of masculinity was now theirs.

Now, of course, by the slow process of familiarisation we have reached the situation of mixed smoking by consenting adults in all sorts of places. The slogan of 'You've come a long way, baby' in the Virginia Slim advertisements makes full, if patronising, capital of this phenomenon.

The cigarette market represents a movement from masculinity to femininity but the movement from femininity to masculinity is not quite so easily achieved. For example, in the case of hair sprays the product has always been loaded high with feminine connotations and channelled into specifically feminine outlets. To make the product appeal to the masculine market it had to be completely recharged with masculine symbolism, packs were changed from pinks and white to reds and blacks and the odours to 'male' smells of pine, spice and leather. The promotion appealed shamelessly to aggression, defiance and over-stated masculinity. Yet, rarely is this extreme change in promotional style needed in the progression of 'masculine' products to the feminine arena. Remarking upon this contradiction, Stutteville drew up an interesting diagrammatic representation of the flows from masculinity to femininity and vice versa, in the consumer marketing field (*see* Diagram 11:2).

Diagram 11:2

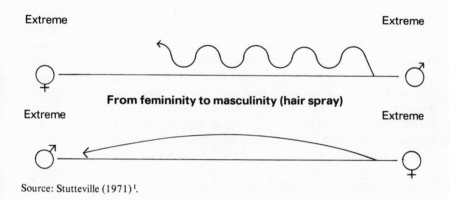

From masculinity to femininity (cigarettes)

Extreme   Extreme

From femininity to masculinity (hair spray)

Extreme   Extreme

Source: Stutteville (1971)[1].

The flow from masculine polarity to femininity is *not* comparable to the reverse flow. The flow from masculinity to femininity proceeds at a slow, gradual pace. 'The impression of such communication is provocative and suggestive, not of present reality but of what might be.' The reverse flow is notable for lack of gradualism and subtle exaggeration of what might be: 'The flow is dramatic, exaggerated and total.'

Stutteville also notes that:

> The status differential between the male and female role in American society suggests that the flow from masculinity to femininity is easier to accomplish. The reverse flow requires heroic efforts to assure males that the previously feminine symbol is really, after all, intensely masculine — hence that chest pounding.

The different emphasis on sex roles means that, given a set budget, it is more reliable to extend a campaign over a longer period to get women to buy a man's product than to risk everything in the one do-or-die campaign to get men to buy a woman's product. In the latter case, it is a clear success/failure story quickly; in the former it is a slow but more certain success story.

The reason for the change in the metre of flow may be found in the different conceptions of masculinity and femininity. Roger Brown[2] explains it thus:

> In spite of American distaste for ascribing status there remains a difference in rank between male and female. Women have not always had the vote and have not yet produced a President. It's a little better to be male than female. A girl who acts like a boy is, therefore, doing something we find more understandable than is the boy who acts like a girl. We can think of the girl's behaviour motivated by a wish to improve her status rather than by compulsion to act like a male. The sissy, on the other hand, is mimicking a group that ranks below himself. There is nothing in our values that will make his behaviour acceptable or even comprehensible.

The emphasis on 'our values' is perhaps the significant point and, perhaps, is a question of 'traditional' values. It tends to be the traditional *status quo* which places women in their passive situation and which tends to distrust the female-mimicking man. In the more 'alternative' line of thinking where women are regarded in much more equal terms, more because it would be illogical to do otherwise, we find a corresponding uncaring attitude towards 'correct' sex-role behaviour. Men and women wear perfumes, bracelets, kaftans, make up, earrings, embroidered shirts, longer hair—all features of 'femininity' in establishment culture. As sex-role standards slip closer together we may well find a similar androgyny in product markets.

Stutteville explores this at length and contends that the status differentials between sexes are collapsing along with many other social differences. It is not a question of undifferentiated roles but of reduction in status of one role *relative to another,* that is, masculinity in relation to femininity. This will not only make it easier to transfer one market to the other but will mean that there will be less chest-beating to put an idea over to men and fewer of the romantic/sexual fantasies for women.

Returning to hair spray again, Morris and Cundiff (1971)[3] in a study on the sexuality of products, used this product as the basis of a theory that a male's sex-role identification and anxiety levels are significant variables in his consumer behaviour. They analysed the relationship between two variables: psychological femininity and manifest anxiety in relation to the hair spray as a product with a defined feminine appeal. Their results showed that the inter-action of the two characteristics of femininity and anxiety was significant at the $\cdot 0427$ level. A high feminine identification by a male interacted with level of anxiety about the products so that the higher the anxiety level of the high feminine male the more unfavourable his attitudes to the product. The significance of these tests is that the more one is secure in one's sex role the less one is anxious and, by deduction, threatened by products with a marked cross-sexed image. Morris and Cundiff conclude: 'The introduction of a new male product with a feminine image might be best directed toward more "masculine" or less anxiety prone groups to gain initial acceptance.'

Applying this logic to the female market, it follows that those women who are most stable in their basic femaleness are those who will feel least anxious and most willing to try masculine products, and those who feel less secure will keep to classically feminine products. It is paradoxically possible, that those women who smoke pipes, who were the first to try cigarettes, drive cars and consume alcohol were not 'masculine' as was supposed but so concretely and basically female, with minimal role conflict, that trying these products was merely a neutral experience just like any other. The first woman to carry an attaché case on campus—using Stutteville's analogy—could be the one who is the most stable in her femaleness and the most 'feminine' one there.

Conversely—those women who persist in purchase of myriad feminine products, who use hair spray and cosmetics and certain frilly items most of the time, or at least very regularly, are those women who might be most anxious and insecure in their own femaleness. The outer layer of femininity becomes a surrogate for an unfelt psychic femininity. Certainly, women who use a great deal of make-up are often those who feel most insecure in their own sexuality and even in their own sex. This is a contradiction that is not widely appreciated and there is a tendency among marketers, men and women alike, to think of the woman who does not display feminine behaviour according to the social norm as 'unfeminine', and the man who rejects social norms of masculinity to be 'homosexual'. This is not only illogical, it is inaccurate, and it is used as a basis for all manner of social, psychiatric and employment bias.

It is an interesting thought that the intelligent marketer should consider, and consider the implications of, that the man who supports the liberation of women from their traditionally feminine role may be demonstrating a strong and secure masculine sex role; he is not threatened by 'masculinised' women. Those marketers and advertisers who resist the emancipation of women or who persist in portraying women in stereotyped or inferior roles may well be expressing an anxiety about their own masculinity.

This topic will be considered in greater length in a later chapter, but in the light of the theory, findings and suppositions examined above it is now instructive to look at those markets where the women have, as female consumers purchasing in their own right, moved into some of the traditionally masculine areas.

THE MAJOR AREAS OF EROSION

Cigarettes and Smoking

By 1971 the British population was spending just under £1,500 million a year on cigarettes which accounted for 85% of tobacco sold (by weight). Within this market women have been making a growing contribution; in 1960 they consumed 1,620 cigarettes per head which, by 1970, had risen to 2,230. In the comparable period the consumption per head for men has correspondingly shrunk from 4,030 cigarettes per head to 3,890 in 1970 [4].

In terms of brands, a recent survey (1974) [5] has found that among the female smokers Embassy is the favourite with Players No. 6, runner-up.

In other sectors of the tobacco market, however, the female emphasis is insignificant. In the hand-rolled cigarette market, for example, while the Tobacco Research Council estimates that 1% used this smoking method, *Retail Business* [4] points out that this is 'an extremely working class, male habit'.

In the area of pipe-smoking, which has been declining as a market over the years, women do not figure at all and another report by *Retail Business* [8] notes stiffly that 'pipe smoking is a male prerogative and the incidence of female smoking is too small to be statistically significant' [6]. Nevertheless, marketers could have a look at the female influence in this market, since in earlier ages and in certain cultures now, women have smoked pipes and enjoyed them. In the case of cigars, which have made considerable progress in volume and value terms recently, it is difficult to estimate the participation by women. Nevertheless, industrial sources estimate that 250,000 women smokers have now changed to smoking cheroots in America and in Sweden the proportion is even higher.

In recent years, the tobacco manufacturers have recognised the importance of the woman as a smoker and in his justification for emphasis on the supermarkets as future outlets for cigarettes, P. Middleton of W. D. and H. O. Wills (1970) [7] cited the following facts: (i) 43% of all women over 16 smoke; (ii) 87% of women smokers are housewives, and (iii) 35% of the total cigarette and tobacco market is accounted for by women.

Alcohol

Women have always drunk some alcohol but never to the extent to which they now consume it. Reasons for alcoholism or extreme consumption of alcohol often relate, in women, to sex-role conflict and comprise a complex area of study [8]. Thus, what we will specifically consider here are the more everyday and moderate excursions into the formerly male bastion of drink.

A report in *Retail Business* (April 1971) noted that women are influencing the buying, dispensing and consumption of drinks more than ever before. They have more importance in the selection and use of drink and are also more inclined *to talk about it* than men.

> This factor seems now to be of sufficient importance to cause the major companies to bear in mind the feminine buyer when designing their packs and planning their promotion. With Women's Liberation on the march, it will be a delicate task for the ad-men to evolve a promotion for the women's drink.

A survey carried out for IPC Magazines in 1970 showed that 43% of individual drink purchases for the home are made by housewives who make a third of them through grocery or supermarket outlets and who in three-quarters of the purchases decide themselves which brand they buy. In 38% of the purchases the money for drink comes out of the housekeeping [10]. Drink, it seems, is becoming a feminine responsibility, coinciding with the increased weekly expenditure on alcohol from 4·1% of average weekly expenditure (£0·86) in 1964 to 4·6% (£1·47) in 1972 [9].

In the case of beer, for example, *Retail Business* (1972) notes that among significant trends in its growing popularity is the number of women drinkers which has increased from 25% to 33% of the total adult female population during the last 10 years. In the related lager market, 20–25% of female beer drinkers also drink this product. In addition, most sweet-stout is drunk by women [11].

In the market for cider, the single woman devotes 2% of her expenditure to this drink compared to the 18% of the single man and the 5% of husbands and wives. In the table-wine market, women are more and more responsible for choosing some of the 450 million bottles sold every year. *Retail Business* [14] notes that:

> Since it is usually women who shop in supermarkets and since women do not drink as much beer as men, the wine trade is increasingly slanting its promotion towards encouraging women to buy and drink wine.

A report in *Self-Service and Supermarket* in August 1971 on the wine market [12] also noted that part of the 350% increase in wine consumption in the UK over the last 20 years can be attributed to the interest of the housewife and her housekeeping money. There are those women who buy only for a special occasion and those at the other extreme who buy top name sherry and chateau wines for investment: but in between is the army of housewives who dominate the bulk purchases of wine by regularly spending between 50–100p a week on it. The *Grocer* (25 September 1971) also noted that the female supermarket purchases are taking business from the traditional outlets: supermarkets take 21% as opposed to the 26% from pubs and 29% from off-licences [13].

Also, men and women may shop together for alcohol but it is notable that even when men make the choice of drink, their wives pay in 20% of cases. On 60% of occasions it is the wife rather than the husband who makes the decision to buy [13].

The situation with spirits is slightly different but the trend is still notably female-orientated. Consumption of spirits is low, about 3·4 proof-pints per head of population in 1972, and in 1974 it was noted [9] that less than half the population ever drink any individual type of spirits. For women, it tends to be a special-occasion activity only. Nevertheless, in 1971, 32% of women made the decision to buy gin: 24% whisky and 35%, liqueurs.

Cars and Petrol

More and more women are using cars—and buying them. This tendency, as with other consumer durables, is likely to continue with the increased employment, lower childbirth rate and higher salaries for women. In a study by BP in *Retail Business* (June 1971)[16] it was noted that there are 4·5 million women motorists on the road consisting of:

1. Married women using their husbands' cars for shopping or taking their children home from school.
2. An increasingly important group of women who buy their own cars and own petrol. This group are in high socio-economic groups and half are under 35.

These two groups of women take no less than 12·5% of all petrol purchases, that is, £160 million per annum. Interestingly, their attitudes to promotional offers influence them less, it seems, than the willingness of the attendants to check tyres. They mostly buy 3-star petrol and pay cash.

BP has set up a panel of six women motorists to advise it on policy and there is a possibility of greater emphasis on tights, cosmetics and other 'female' products. 'With toward half a million potential customers gazing into space while the attendants deal with their cars some advertising opportunities could also be seen to be around for the taking.'

A more recent report on women drivers in *Marketing* (March 1973) suggests that the number of women motorists is higher, at around 6 million, and notes that half of the people taking driving tests today are women. In addition, 30% of oil purchases (a £60 million market) and 25% of batteries are bought from supermarkets by women who also account for £80 million in petrol sales each year in their capacity as owner-drivers. Female owner-drivers drive less than the national average but represent half of the drivers in the low mileage section, that is, those who own small cars in the 1,000 cc section. The report in *Marketing* notes that 'Despite representing a significant market in this sector women are completely ignored as far as the advertising and promotion are concerned.'[15] This is illustrated by car advertising, which is notably male-orientated; the driver is usually a man with a woman typically in the passenger seat. Yet, the Target Group Index noted, in response to the question of who makes the decision to buy a car, that the decision was contributed to by 40% of women.

In a survey of the women's market by IPC recently, owner-drivers were estimated at around one million and 40% of women between the ages of 17 and 34 are now drivers. There is also a close association between the growth in the number of cars and the trends in shopping, and eleven of the fourteen major grocery outlets (accounting for 80% of retail turnover) are developing extensive car parking facilities. The survey suggested that women will buy a significant proportion of the 5·9 million extra cars on the road by 1976[15].

In a recent survey of petrol retailing, however, women were excluded from the major part of the sample although they were acknowledged [17]. The survey estimated that 27% of women lay in the 0–4,999 miles per annum category and that 16% of purchases were made by them. In a survey by JICTARS, which it quotes, there was an indication that of all those who buy *most* of the petrol for at least one car, 18% are women.

'Do-it-yourself'

The DIY phenomenon, once a fertile source for the cartoonist, has now become established and respectable. Today it has a culture all of its own, with magazines, clubs, tool trade names and workshops and, to the observing public, a specifically 'male' image. In a recent report [18], however, reference was made to the 'DIY *household*'. The report says:

> In the previous report |three years before| the market was seen in terms of the amateur handy man who undertook all the work and purchasing involved even though he was probably spurred on by his wife. However, with the *increased participation of women, it is now more realistic to look at the market in terms of households where both husband and wife work jointly.*

Most DIY takes place in the early stages of home ownership, the 25–34 age group, and where the house is under mortgage (Family Expenditure Survey 1972). Readership of DIY magazines is often about 40% duplicated and only about half of the serious handy men and women read DIY seriously and regularly. There are $7\frac{1}{2}$ million people and 6 million households who are interested but what of the women among them?

It is noted that women have always been important in encouraging their husbands to get on with decorating and repair work and they have also played the more important role in changing the decorative materials. Evidence now indicates that a large number participate with their husbands in doing the work. One DIY magazine claims that over half of its circulation goes to women and one TV programme is aimed directly at women. 'They therefore have much greater influence on the handtool and the non-decorative market than is often supposed.'

The *Retail Business* report showed that paint brushes and hand tools are now designed with women in mind.

> Manufacturers of such mundane articles as screws, fillers and grout now realise that women are almost as likely to apply and are more likely to buy their products than men and are altering their instructions and packaging accordingly.

Interestingly, *Retail Business* are careful to note that DIY knowledge is passed down—not from father to son, but from 'father and mother to son and daughter'.

A lot of the recent emphasis by women upon DIY has been a function of leisure patterns. A survey issued by the DES ('Planning for Leisure') in 1969 showed that the DIY urge for women is only a continuation of trends in their leisure time to 'crafts and hobbies' which now take second place to television in women's leisure priorities. In addition, 'decorating and house maintenance' take as much average percentage of their leisure time as 'drinking' and 'cinema and theatre' combined.

So what jobs do these handy women participate in with their husbands? A survey at the DIY Exhibition in 1972 [18] found that the tasks are much more complex than before. Women instal central heating, loft and roof insulation and place ceramic tiles all over their kitchens and bathrooms. Many (about a quarter) still like the traditional painting and papering, while 32% of the women made kitchen, bedroom and bathroom furniture, fittings and shelves, 4% installed double glazing and 2% were able to tackle floorings and electrical work. *Retail Business* comments:

> Many of those connected with the DIY market tell amazing stories of people with no experience, *including many women,* successfully tackling the installation of, for example, a complete hot water and central heating system.

How come we get the impression that this side of the woman as housewife is not exactly represented in the advertising we see directed at the female consumer?

What we have examined in this chapter is only a small sector of those markets into which women, spending by and for themselves, are venturing. No doubt, in the coming years similar analyses will be made for other areas which to us now seem unutterably masculine. Is it inconceivable, after all, given the rapidity with which sex roles are modifying, that we should soon find sizeable female markets for such products as football, cricket and tobogganing equipment; cigars and pipes; stereo and fine engineering machinery and the faster, more powerful cars?

Women have only reflected the social expectations of their behaviour. With the expectations becoming more and more pragmatic, the marketing delineation of products into those which are and are not sex-appropriate may soon be blown wide open.

REFERENCES

1. John R. Stutteville, 'Sexually Polarised Products and Advertising Strategy', *Journal of Retailing,* Vol. 47(2) (Summer 1971), pp. 3–13.
2. Roger Brown, *Social Psychology,* Macmillan (1965).
3. George P. Morris and Edward W. Cundiff, 'Acceptance by Males of Feminine Products', *Journal of Marketing Research,* Vol. VIII (August 1971), pp. 372–4.
4. 'Changing Patterns of Smoking', *Retail Business,* 172 (June 1972).
5. Market Research Great Britain, Vol. 14 (March 1974), pp. 18–22.
6. 'The UK Pipe Tobacco Market', *Retail Business,* 173 (July 1972), and ref. 4.
7. *See* 'Marketing Review', *Retail Business,* 147 (May 1970), p. 3.

8. *See* chapter 15, refs. 52—4.
9. 'Changing Patterns of British Drinking Habits', *Retail Business*, 192 (February 1974); 'Trends in Spirit Consumption', *Retail Business*, 193 (March 1974).
10. IPC Report 1970, quoted in 'Marketing Review', *Retail Business*, 153 (November 1970).
11. 'Brewing and the Beer Market', Part 1, *Retail Business*, 174 (August 1972); 'The Beer Market in the UK', Part 2, *Retail Business*, 175 (September 1972).
12. 'Women Leading the Wine-Buying Boom', *Self Service and Supermarket* (5 August 1971).
13. 'Drinks—the Housewife's Choice Grows Stronger in Buying Decisions', the *Grocer* (25 September 1971).
14. 'Table Wines', *Retail Business*, 191 (January 1974).
15. 'Women's Market Survey', IPC Publications Ltd. (1973).
16. *Retail Business*, 160 (June 1971), Marketing Review, 'BP Cherche La Femme', p. 2.
17. P. L. Atkinson and A. J. Ogden, 'Sample Surveys of the Point of Sale: A case history from the petrol market', *Journal of the Market Research Society*, Vol. 16(2) (1974).
18. 'Do-it-Yourself', Part 1, *Retail Business*, 182 (April 1973).

12. The Psychological Markets

It is often overlooked that women buy in their own right and for themselves as female human beings certain products in which men do not figure at all. It is also notable that it is in this market that we find the greatest potential for the exploitation of woman in terms of her self-confidence and her femaleness, ranging from the devious and sneaky strategy of the vaginal deodorant manufacturers to the open and self-delusive strategies that men employ in the marketing of cosmetics and slimming products. There are other markets, too, and they will be examined in chapter 13, but these three, in particular, deserve careful and critical attention.

THE SANITARY PROTECTION MARKET

Menstrual Protection

Women between the ages of 12 and around 45—50 will, with few exceptions and allowing for individual differences in starting and completing the cycle, (puberty to menopause) menstruate once every month for a period of 3—7 days. This is a messy, important, ego- and sex-role connected, private and profitable phenomenon. It is profitable particularly to those manufacturers who market and manufacture products which women use to cope with and control the menstrual flow. By definition, the market is limitless and a function of the total female population. It can also produce some secondary off-shoots such as discharge deodorisers, special 'panties', perfumes and talcum powders which can be variously used to 'cope with' the vagaries of the female sex organs. (It is strange how men 'have' sex organs but women must 'cope' with theirs.) It is, furthermore, a market which will be constant over a number of years for every woman so the brand loyalty potential for each woman is enormous. Every woman who menstruates 12 times a year for at least 25 years (15-40 years to be on the conservative side) and allowing for pauses for childbirth, will experience menstruation at least 300 times. There are 10·7 million women between the ages of 15 and 44 in this country at present. Thus, among women alive at the moment there are $300 \times 10 \cdot 7$ million opportunities for menstruation. These would average at around 3,200 million allowing for pregnancy and individual variation. And even allowing for the latitude of these estimates they still represent a huge and captive market for the marketer of sanitary protection.

It was comparatively recently that menstruation was not only a taboo topic but women who were in this state had to retire from public view, although *Retail Business* assures us that the earliest recorded sanitary towel, as such, was Smith and Nephew's Southall brands which can be traced back to 1880. They became the first sanitary towels to be advertised in 1897. Kimberley-Clark marketed the first disposable towel in 1920 closely followed by Southalls in 1927. The towels constructed since then have been in the same basic form with recent variations on the theme in the form of plastic backing (Kotex) and the introduction of panties to hold the towels thus eliminating the 'torture of belts and pins'. Sanitary towel manufacturers even have their own association, the Association of Sanitary Towel Manufacturers, who co-ordinate sizes and details of solubility[1].

The most recent and dramatic change in the market has been the advent of the tampon. These were developed by a doctor just over 30 years ago and marketed by the American Tampax Company, who now market this product worldwide. One of the most recent competitors in this section is Lilia-White (Sales) Limited who market the Lillets non-applicator tampon and it is no secret to marketers that Tampax and Lillets have been engaging in some pretty virulent competition in the last couple of years, with one advertisement, in particular, being injunctioned recently for various legal reasons. It seems that the battle for the brand loyalty of women in this market is not as ladylike as the company images would suggest. It is all made worse by the fact that Lillets, after a mere 10 years in the market compared with Tampax's 30, have been rocking the brand-share boat.

Estimates put the 1973 sanitary towel market at £25 million and since towel users dominated the markets in 1969 at 60/40 split with the tampon users, the total market must be worth about £40 million. During each menstrual period, women use, on average, 12 towels or 11 tampons. However, consumer usage of towels was declining at approximately 1% per annum in 1969 and has probably speeded up since then with the huge increase in promotional expenditure by the tampon manufacturers in the last few years. The change to tampons was accelerating in the 16-24 category in 1969 and was also stronger among the ABCs. In both of these categories, according to ETU, there are fewer inhibitions about trying new ideas. Generally, there are fewer phobias, too, about tampons; for example, that a young girl will lose her virginity if she uses them. Still, in an estimate by Smith and Nephew, the split in favour of towels is strong even in the more advanced and socially 'permissive' societies such as Sweden and the USA where 3 in 5 women still use them.

In terms of the emergency market, Southalls (Birmingham) seem to have this cornered with a 95% share in 1969 and the private labels are coming into their own with Boots and NPU accounting for 6% (1969).

Most of the products are sold through retail chemists which take 53% of purchases (all grocers take 23% and all other, 24%). There is also a growing emphasis on self service, although many customers, understandably, still feel reticent about standing at a checkout flourishing their packet of Dr. Whites at the rest of the queue.

Sanitary protection purchases for young girls between 12 and 16 are usually made by the mother, who protects her daughter from embarrassment and holds the purse strings. Young women buy for themselves when they have a certain amount of financial and personal freedom. This is the group that the marketers are waiting for and they are approached mainly through the young female weekly and monthly magazines.

A recent report in *Campaign* notes that Lilia White are now aiming £250,000 specifically at young girls. Advertising expenditure is high and growing every year at about 10–13% representing £400–£500,000 at 1969 prices. The style of promotion recently has become more open. 'let's all be honest about it', with graphic illustrations of tampons in test tubes with roses sticking out of the top—which can pass as symbolic if not exactly aesthetic. Lillets are pushing their width-ways expansion as opposed to the length-ways expansion of Tampax, a contrast which brought the companies to commercial blows in early 1974 when both started sneering at each others claims and putting out knocking copy to prove it. Media strategy is difficult to spot but there is obviously much effort expended in 'getting them while they're young' and trying to grab the brand-disloyals on the other side—the floating voter of the consumer market. Much effort has gone recently into free samples, talks to schools and explanatory leaflets. It is also the only promotional style of advertising to women which shows them in athletic, active, and energetic roles instead of indulging the typical media woman's bovine leer. One feminist remarked recently that in advertisements for Tampax, you get the only example of women functioning as normal, active people at the time, the only time, in the month where they feel least like it. However you look at it, it is strange that the only time of the month when women have the ultimate reinforcement of their femininity, the marketers are falling over themselves to show women how to indulge freely and fearlessly in the most 'masculine' of pursuits.

Vaginal Deodorants and other 'Sanitary Protection'

A very profitable market has sprung up in recent years in the wake of the tampon and menstruation market. that of the vaginal deodorants. This is an emotional area for those who see marketers as basically exploitive of women and, to be fair, the marketers have nothing to be proud of in this connection. We have here an example of blatant appeal to insecurity and anxiety in women, an appeal which is infinitely self-reinforcing.

As a product, vaginal deodorants have been around since about 1968 and a report in the *Grocer* (6 February 1971) reported that in that year they were used by about 3% of women, and by 1970 15% of women were using them. They were particularly popular among 16–18 year olds, with 40% usage. Horrifyingly, 11% of the 13–15 year olds were using them too, compared with 30% of the 19–24 year old group and 17% of the 25–34 year olds. At least in the latter two groups one could see some possibility of why these women should need them—but 13–15 year olds? These products have also had a big following in the AB social groups, closely followed by the Cs (20% AB, 17% C1, 16% C2, 10% DE).

What is so amazing is that this product was viewed as potentially harmful even in the days before consumer opinion turned against the product. The American journal *Science* reported in 1972[2]:

> The market for vaginal deodorants, most of which contain hexochlorophine as a principle active ingredient, has grown from nothing five years ago to a business worth $53 million p.a. and involving 24 million women. Probably more than half of this growth occurred since mid-May 1969 by which date the Food and Drug Administration knew both that hexochlorophine was ineffective as a vaginal deodorant and that it was potentially damaging to mammalian brains.

The American Magazine. *Ms*, came out strongly against the vaginal deodorants on the grounds that they were 'psychological' products. It seems that in America in 1970 some 24 million women spent $50 million on these products. At the same time, sales of flavoured and scented (raspberry, champagne, jasmine, orange blossom) liquid douches flourished. Also, related products such as deodorant tampons, douching appliances and vaginal wipes climbed on the bad-smell bandwagon. The problem, as author Judith Ramsey pointed out, was the centuries-old, male-chauvinist prejudice that identifies the vagina with impurity (menstruation, child-bearing, sexual intercourse and urination) and the tendency of modern women to be neurotic about cleanliness so that they worry about a real or imagined smell. The irony is, it seems, that these products are completely unnecessary. The article quotes *the Medical Letter,* an authoritative publication that evaluates drugs and other therapies for physicians, as saying:

> It is unlikely that commercial deodorant feminine hygiene sprays are as effective as soap and water in promoting a hygienic and odour-free external genital surface.

Why these products are so popular with some women is suggested by psychiatrist Sara Sheiner:

> A woman wants to conform to her own self-image of what is beautiful, and she associates vaginal odours with something undesirable. She's afraid she won't receive love and approval if she smells the way she actually does.

One is forced to wonder if women worried or wondered like this *before* the onset of the vaginal deodorant?

Natalie Shainess, a psychologist in the area of sex differences and female psychology, testified before the Senate sub-committee on the promotion and advertising of over-the-counter drugs and said of the implication behind these products:

> While fostering an overt image of a feminine 'sexy' woman, the implication of need for such a spray conveys a message of woman as being dirty and smelly. This is extremely damaging to a woman's sense of self-esteem and self-worth as well as to a man's view of her.

Despite this, however, there are still the admen who remain convinced of the product as a feminine necessity, though necessary to whom, is not clear. There is Jerry Della Femina of Femininique who says 'the sprays are a psychological product. They fill a need — real or otherwise — that certain women feel.' Asked if he felt the product was performing a useful service he said:

> Think of the women who are now going at sex with gusto and confidence. If there were a Nobel Prize for Peace for more and better orgasms, I think I would qualify.

Nevertheless, Judith Ramsey catalogues some of the more harmful side-effects that have been associated with vaginal deodorants. For example, there is vulvitis, which is known to start in many women when they use vaginal deodorants. The unpleasant symptoms (itching, redness, blisters) nearly always disappear once the product is discontinued. In a letter to *Obstetrics and Gynaecology*, Dr. Bernard Davis of Montreal reported that he had treated 20–25 cases of vulvitis associated with the sprays; another doctor reporting in *Medical World News*, a weekly magazine for doctors, puts the casualties at about 10% of usage.

Manufacturers and marketers persistently deny that there is anything really wrong about the product or its physical or psychological side effects and Judith Ramsey quotes a spokesman for Alberto-Culver who says that 'Consumer complaints fall within the accepted range for a cosmetic, about six per million sales.' But even at that date, apparently, Alberto-Culver had already received reports of 107 women who complained of irritation, allergic reactions, burns, infection, dermatitis of the thighs, stinging, swelling, itching, inflammation, a lump and a burned hand associated with use of FDS deodorant spray, according to consumer reports.

Robert Schaffer, (a top Food and Drug Administration administrator) was concerned about the fact 'that the rate of reported consumer injuries for feminine hygiene sprays is the second highest among cosmetics in terms of sales volume.' This is 48 per 100 million units per deodorant sales, which seems low until you remember that not every woman who has had a complaint bothers to write in; and how many are sufficiently aware to write of the psychological damage and insecurity that the product brought to their lives?

Nevertheless, the signs are, in Britain anyway, that sales of this product are declining. According to the IPC Cosmetics and Toiletries Survey of 1974, use of vaginal deodorants has fallen from 17% in 1973 to 10% in 1974. Furthermore, only about 12% of women used vaginal sprays in August and September of 1973 and this usage rate was down to 9% by May of 1974. In this reduced market, Femfresh is still the brand leader with a 44% share, followed by Bidex with 14%, Avon with 8%, Elle with 6% and Boots and Cosmea with 4% each.

Yet, although vaginal deodorant sales are plunging, it seems that some manufacturers are still trying to jump onto the same bandwagon. In the *Guardian* (20 April 1972) Jane Alexander reported the latest in the long line of female exploitive products with the introduction of Fastidia mini-pads. These are made by Smith and Nephew, who pioneered the sanitary towel, and are disposable pads to absorb 'day in and day out vaginal discharges'. Barry Tarry says of the research that it was 'positive and enthusiastic': 30% of women questioned admitted to having problems of vaginal discharge outside their periods, including females of 9 and 72. The advertisements were going to read: 'Sprays and talcs, tissues and lotions are half the answer. You need something absorbent to complete your every-day protection.'

Jane Alexander comments:

> It seems to be piling another damaging con onto the vaginal deodorant: the implication is clearly that even the notorious deodorants are not control enough for female genitals — you've got to wrap them up in a pad every day as well . . .

It was only after the conference with the journalists, some of whom were somewhat scathing, that the manufacturers conceded that it might be somewhat dangerous to suggest to women that vaginal discharge was somehow normal and just to be 'wrapped up'. They finally promised to print a warning on the back of the pack — next time round. Jane Alexander concludes:

> . . . the promotion is going to make a sizeable contribution to the commercial exploitation of women's hang-ups about their sexual organs, especially with that poor little nine year old |on the pack| with 60 years ahead of her of wrapping up her sex.

COSMETICS

In 1972 the cosmetics market in the UK was worth just over £65 million. The biggest sector by value at retail prices was perfume and cologne at £15 million, closely followed by face creams at £11 million; face powder and eye make-up took £10·6 million each. The total market was still growing and had added nearly £10 million to its retail sales value since 1966, a growth rate per annum of 4–5%[5].

Net profit in the industry overall worked out at around 14·8% according to a NBPI Survey in 1968, with raw materials and packaging taking an enormous 28·2% of total cost (selling and distribution took 18·6%, advertising and promotion 14·2%). Even this profit figure represented a *drop* in net profit in the period from 1965–8. In 1970 Max Factor was sharing the market lead with Avon at 17% each and the others varied from the 3% for Coty and Rimmel to the 8% of Yardley, but each company holds different places in each market sector. The premium-priced sector includes Helena Rubenstein, Revlon and Charles of the Ritz, the middle sector holds the larger companies such as Max Factor and Avon, while the cheaper market holds Rimmel, Outdoor Girl and Miners.

There are at least 17–20 big household cosmetic brands in Britain—many of them American-based or, like Max Factor, distributed by direct accounts from a parent American company. Distribution is mainly through the multiple and private chemists (24% and 28% respectively), while direct selling, the most important recent development, accounts for 23%. Advertising and promotional policies are mainly aimed at maintaining or extending market shares—not by price competition since the three tiers of the market preclude this—but by establishing brand or house identities. As much is spent below-the-line by cosmetics companies as above, and in the latter category the women's press is of particular importance; the weeklies take about 50% of the appropriations and the monthlies 25% with the teenage magazines left with 15–20%. Newspapers take up some of the small amount of slack. Television advertising is little used except by Avon who use it in a 'missionary salesman' capacity, since the selling methods are rather like those of the industrial market. In 1973 expenditure on all advertising by cosmetics advertisers was £32,628,000 (MEAL).

And what of the future? A report in *Campaign* on a market forecast by James Morell and Associates on 1 June 1973 noted: 'As incomes rise the proportion of people's disposable volume income that is spent on toiletries and cosmetics tends to rise faster.'

The forecast suggested an expenditure of £515 million on this market by 1977. In one of the recent surveys by IPC on cosmetics, the stranglehold of the market on women was illustrated by the fact that 50% of women between 13 and 64 wear some make-up even when they are alone and nearly two-thirds use it every day, with some regional variation. While 70% of women in London and the South East use it everyday, in the North West the figure is only 58%. Another survey published by IPC in 1972, the Cosmetic and Toiletries Survey (1971), revealed that 11% of women have six or more different types of eye shadow. Two-thirds using lipstick or nail varnish have more than one type in their handbag or on their dressing table and 70% of those using eye shadow are not content with just one; 14% use six or more different types of eye shadow.

Meanwhile, women are buying more and more for their menfolk in the cosmetics industry, according to the IPC 1972 survey, particularly after-shave for which the number of women buying for their men is rising. Nine out of 10 women under 65 made such a purchase within the 12-month period under question. Women in Wales, the South West and the Midlands are more likely to buy these products as gifts than women in other parts of the country. Old Spice was the brand leader in after-shave and shared the leading position with Avon in the deodorant market. (According to the *Retail Business* report on toiletries, the after-shave market is worth £5·7 million.)

Cosmetics do not always, however, have their own way. The French Government was recently urged by scientists to introduce laws making it compulsory for cosmetics manufacturers to list ingredients on their products. The 150,000 tons of chemicals per annum used by French cosmetics manufacturers are causing skin diseases in women and, furthermore, the Co-operative Analysis Laboratory is demanding that labels on cosmetics be reworded so as not to encourage sales. Manufacturers are resisting the move to list ingredients because they say neither the public nor the doctors would be able to understand them but the matter's seriousness is illustrated by the fact that France is likely to bring the matter to the attention of the Council of Europe in Brussels. In our own Houses of Parliament the cosmetics industry was hounded during the reading of the Fair Trading Bill in May 1973 for the deception in the packaging of their goods. Matters brought to the attention of the House were the prevalence of fake or false bottoms, and giant boxes containing minute tubes of toothpaste. Abuses were particularly rife in cosmetics where there were jars within jars and the inner jars contained only a tiny proportion of the total volume.

What, however, do cosmetics do to, or for, women? Are they used for superficial glamour or for deeper reasons associated with personality and self-image? *Campaign* (1971)[3], in a recent report, suggests that the balance is towards superficiality combined with masculine manipulation:

> The irrelevant fantasy perpetuated in so many cosmetic advertisements comes directly from men. The marketing men in the beauty companies and often the creative men in agencies have become convinced they are selling glamour and promise. This may have been true in an earlier era, it may have been shown in research once, but it is handed down with that authenticity that unproven facts have and it is still the philosophy that most beauty products are sold by.

Barbara Attenborough of Boots No. 7, the new intruder on the cosmetics market, suggests that the realistic woman of today does not buy a product thinking she is going to look like the woman in the advertisement, but Elliot of Dorothy Gray probably represents the bulk of male opinion in the business when he says with touching certainty: 'she is buying the package, the pretty-pot, the aura: she doesn't want to know what it is or how it works.'

Nevertheless, a study by Wax (1957)[4] suggests that make-up is, as a conscious process, employed not only in relation to sexuality, but also to denote status or role in relation to observers or prospective observers. A study by Gloye (1965)[6] supported Wax's observation and also suggested that make-up may operate on an unconscious or semi-unconscious level as a means of experiencing a certain status or role *when these are not fully established.* So, cosmetics become a means of preparing a self for the consumption of others, in interpersonal relationships. He suggests that make-up is a function of and functionally independent of social roles. It is a vehicle for expression encouraged by (i) 'prescriptive statements presented through mass media under the auspices of the cosmetics industry', and (ii) widespread tendencies toward making casual personal assessments on the basis of observable features.

The study by Gloye aimed to develop descriptions of various types of college women in terms of their use of cosmetics and then test these descriptions by asking subjects to assign personality traits. It was found that lack of make-up is accepted as a sign for lack of social responsiveness. Heavy make-up is associated with great socialbility. There was also an age difference in the factor associated with make-up; younger women (as supported by Wax) tend towards casualness in their make-up while older women seek 'control'. Non-college students more quickly adopt the make-up habits of older women. Stereotypes of various make-up styles were built up from the results. For example:

> This girl wears an average amount of make-up but it is not applied with skill or taste so it leaves a poor impression. She changes her make-up and hair style often. Her hair is artificially styled and coloured and usually poorly groomed.

This stereotype was described as 'disordered, self-centred and indecisive'.
In another profile:

> This girl wears little or no make-up. She has dark hair worn in a natural casual way with a tendency toward poor grooming.

She was described as 'emotional, quiet and disorderly'.
These stereotypes persisted through personality types. Gloye concludes:

> Overall implication of the results supported the interpretation that make-up signals operate with consensus and uniformity. These signals have established associations with personality traits and discrimination among them on the part of college students takes in a complex of variables associated with cosmetics.

Thus, each product in the cosmetics market may be assumed to have some particular significance to the female consumer so, using the *Retail Business* reports as a guide, it is interesting to examine the consumer in the light of her purchases, using examples of the main products[5].

Lipstick

This has achieved the highest rate of acceptance among consumers with over 85% of UK female cosmetics users regularly wearing it; 70% wear it every day. Annual consumption of lipsticks, if that term can apply, is now around 30 million units per annum at about £8 million. Average purchases per head have been about two a year but, despite this, women tend to possess 3–4 at any one time and younger women buy 4–6 units per year. Promotional methods, therefore, revolve around fashion and the younger woman. In terms of consumer profile, there are some distinct class and age differences and EIU estimate that everyday users are strongest in the 25–54 years category, while the AB dominates 'everyday' and 'regular' users of lipstick.

Nail Polish

Nail care is the smallest of the individual markets, worth only £3·6 million in 1970 with nail polish and remover taking most of the honours. About 12 million units of polish were sold in 1970 and 5 million of remover; in real terms, growth has been 8% p.a. over the last few years, which seems surprising. The market is dominated by younger consumers; women under the age of 34 (about 25% of all adult women) account for 50% of sales. Usage is concentrated into AB and C1 both for weekly and total use and, with the exception of Scotland which uses very little, there is not much regional bias.

Eye Make-up

This is the fastest growing sector of the cosmetics market and over the last five years, the overall average annual growth rate in sales has exceeded 15% per annum. It includes different products which have different growth rates, with eye-liner and eyelashes growing at about 20% per annum but mascara and eye-shadow growing at 10% (3·2 and 2·5 million units respectively). Eyebrow pencils, until very recently, noted a negative growth rate and were the smallest sector at 0·8%.

Eye-shadow sales are strong in the ABC1 group, and are the most important market in terms of absolute sales. They are used by 25% of women in the country. Different makes have different profiles. Max Factor appeal to older women, and Avon make most of their sales to women over 25. Outdoor Girl and Miners are very popular in the C2 and DE social groups. Mascara is relatively unused by those in DE social class; usage is highest in London and South East but very low in Scotland. Eye-liner has a similar profile, only this time Max Factor sell well to the 19–25 age groups and ABC2 while Avon do an about-turn and sell mostly to the C2 and DE women. Eyebrow make-up varies directly with social class, with Max Factor and Miners also achieving their normal old-young pattern. Boots is the newcomer and is doing well among the AB social groups. False eyelash wearers predominate in the ABC1 categories and are most common in London and the North West, and least common in Scotland.

Perfumes and Toilet Waters

Estimates from *Retail Business* are that 75% of all perfume sold in the UK is also produced in this country, the remainder being imported from France and the USA. In 1971 the value of perfumes and toilet waters to manufacturers in the UK at MSP was £9·8 million and the total market retail selling value in 1971 was £16 million. Real growth in this market over the years has been negligible or nil, with most value increases taken up by higher prices unmatched by volume.

Which women use perfumes and toilet water? It seems that nearly all of them use fragrances of some description regularly; about 70% at least once a week and 80% at least once a month. Women between the ages of 16–25 are the heaviest users, and then usage declines with age so that women over 55 are the least important users. Similarly, usage varies directly with socio-economic grouping. Over 90% of AB women use fragrances regularly whilst this is reduced to 70% for DE groupings. Regionally, consumption is uniform with the exception of the South West, Wales and Scotland where figures are much lower: in other areas about 84% of women use fragrances regularly.

Make-up and Complexion Treatments

This sector is also growing and is attributable to the growth of all-in-one make-up which has compensated for the decline of the fluid make-up market. In 1971 sales of make-up in the UK came to £7·8 million and of this, liquids accounted for £2·2 million, all-in-one for £4·5 million and highlighters and blushers for about £1·1 million. Total unit sales are over 20·5 million packs per annum.

About a fifth of women use liquid make-up and a further third use all-in-one; about 40% of all women use it regularly. There is little duplication between consumers for the two types. Age bias is slight up to 55 although usage is marginally higher in the age range 18–24. Large differences occur by social grouping; women in the AB group consume about twice as much as those at the other end of the socio-economic scale.

Face Creams and Skin Care Products

The current retail value of this highly segmented market is £11·9 million including under its umbrella, cleansing creams, foundations, beauty creams and astringents, along with all manner of wrinkle, hormone and all-purpose creams. Ponds, in the face of high competition, maintain a lead with Boots, Max Factor and Avon, in that order, battling for its 26% share by value.

Over a quarter of all women use cleansing creams daily and half of all women use them regularly, but usage decreases with age and falling income. About 2 women in 5 use foundation cream. Usage, as in all the stable and declining markets, is by older and higher socio-economic groups of women. Beauty creams are expensive, so usage tends to be weighted up-market. Women in the 25–40 age group are the most frequent users. Only 17% of all women are regular users of beauty creams. Over half of all women regularly use all-purpose creams and usage is uniform across all groups but the 25–44 age group less than the others; they use the more specialised 'beauty' creams, being more beauty conscious and more age-conscious. All-purpose creams are used by low rather than high income groups; C2 and DE women account for 80% of sales.

Tissues

The domestic disposable paper product market is currently estimated to be worth about £40 million per year at retail prices. This includes facial tissues, toilet tissues and kitchen rolls. The facial tissue market, worth £11 million in 1968, has been growing at 17–20% per annum since 1965 and now takes about 30%. It used to be a product for colds and showed a marked seasonal development until the potential for its use as a make-up remover was realised. Now the major use for facial tissues is make-up removal for women, for family use in cars, and as a general piece of kitchen equipment. All manner of promotional ideas have been aimed at women, including the recent development by Kimberley-Clark of 'boutique' tissues, boxed in cuboids. In fact, boxed tissues account for 90% of the market and can be bought in all colours and in patterned varieties. Man-sized tissues, which, incidentally, are used by many women too, accounted in 1968 for 40% of the market.[5]

Toilet Preparations

Toilet preparations are one of the smallest sectors of the chemical industry but in terms of the retail market are a fairly large sector with sales of over £130 million per annum. Toilet preparations in the UK account for £122 million, including hair preparations, and sales of toiletries to the female population account for the dominant sector amounting to around £110 million. In addition, wives also purchase a large proportion for their husbands' use and this amounts to a further £10 million.

Toiletries for Women

Three main toiletry markets remain almost exclusively feminine: hair sprays and lacquers; conditioners and hair dressings; perfumes and toilet waters. The hairdressings and conditioners are worth £1–1·5 million and are dominated by Estolan and Vitapointe, while hair sprays and lacquers, with sprays the dominant product, have no particular brand leader. Perfumes and toilet waters have been noted in detail already. In the more general toiletries market, dominated again by women, the largest of the combined markets is the one for shampoo, worth £15 million. The growth is slow in volume terms but 60% of sales are through the supermarkets. Talcum powder also falls into this market with a value of £7 million but has made no great changes or progress over the years with Avon sitting triumphant with the largest share of £1–1·5 million. The market is slightly larger in the third sector, deodorants, at £6–7 million. Sales of male deodorants account for some £2–2·5 million although usage by men is somewhat higher possibly because some men use their wives' products, such as 'Mum' and 'Body Mist', the latter holding the largest share of both the women's and the combined market for deodorants. According to the recent IPC study on cosmetics (1973) the deodorants market has risen from £3·5 million five years ago to £14 million today, with 76% of women using them compared to 69% in 1966.

FOOD AND CONFECTIONERY

Eating and the purchase of food are areas fraught with psychological significance for women. Food is not merely an instrument of life sustenance; it has all manner of symbolic loadings which woman cannot and will not ignore. Problems associated with food: anorexia nervosa, worrying about weight, compulsive eating in times of stress, food preparation for the family and food purchase are predominantly female events and the food factor is a significant part of the female consumer's life-style.

In 1950, writing on the 'Role of Science in the British Economy', R. L. Meir suggested that new developments in food technology will require the building up of a group of specialists who can undertake studies of the psychology of food prejudice and allied activities. E. M. Forster observes in *Aspects of the Novel* that eating is grossly neglected in favour of love as a form of human activity to write about.

Roland Harper in an article on the sensory bases of foods[7] comments that:

> Systematically recorded information about the sensory qualities of foods and their function in determining whether or not particular foods will appeal to us is only just beginning to reach appreciable proportions, and much data of interest probably remains on the confidential files of food manufacturers and marketing organisations.

Harper also notes a contention by a Professor E. H. Gombrich in the context of a discussion on the role of texture in art that there is a psycho-analytically-orientated response to foods; 'biters' and 'suckers' are distinctive personality types.

One good example of food psychology can be found in the confectionery industry where it is established that certain products have high psychological loadings, particularly those which are known as 'count lines'—single chocolate bars wrapped individually. The eater is prevented by social ostracism from offering it to her/his companions for the obvious reason that while one can offer a sweet from a pack one cannot offer a friend a 'bite' from a bar. This makes the eating of the bar a strictly personal sensation. These types of confectionery are particularly popular with women who eat them with a variety of states of mind. In the case of one well known 'count line' with a hard centre it was found to be consumed when the eater experienced problems and tended to externalise her worry. A softer, squelchier version was also eaten at times of stress but by those people who internalised their worry. Certainly, Gombrich's 'biters' and 'suckers' do exist among women in the confectionery market.

There is also a fair quantity of guilty reaction among women in the confectionery area; sweets are children's things, they make you fat, they spoil your complexion and your teeth, yet they make life easier and comfort in times of stress. They comprise a means of lavishing attention on oneself when no one else does. Often, there are considerable differences between the groups of women in a certain confectionery product market and they fall into certain well-delineated and established personality groups. Males tend to have a less emotive and more taciturn response to chocolate and react similarly to girls rather than to women. Girls, in their turn, respond more 'normally' to these products. One researcher noted that (in the case of women eaters):

> Greed for food can be unconsciously close to overexcited sexuality . . . fatness and spots to pregnancy, satiation to the loss of capacity for sexual satisfaction.

Confectionery eating is a dominant housewife trait; estimates put the largest single consumer group of count lines and chocolate bars in 1970 as housewives over 35 (35%). Males of the same age take $22\frac{1}{2}$%, females under 16 only take 5% and males of 16–34, 10%.

An article by Turle and Falconer (1972)[8] noted that there were marked differences in taste and colour preferences by sex when the wrapper colour of a well-known chocolate bar was changed and both men and women saw different colours as being positive for them. There are also quite different psychological correlates for the consumption of other chocolate products between men and women, with women tending generally to the extreme on such measures as 'neuroticism', 'obsession' and 'romanticism'.

If we note the catalogue of reasons why these confectionery products are eaten by women, and similar effects have been noted for the consumption of peanuts and crisps, we can see that food for women is not simply a nutritive component. Research by the Tavistock Institute in 1958 and 1964 noted that such sweets carry 'ancillary psychological and social reasons'. They are eaten for:

1. Alleviation of distress, whether from specific events or less obvious causes within the housewife herself. Also, disappointment and boredom play a part.
2. Ease of unfamiliarity and transition periods. They are eaten when people are temporarily separated from their usual food supplies, such as home or mother. They can be substitutes for love and can counteract feelings of loneliness, deprivation and boredom.
3. Harm avoidance-attraction. There are fears for the harmful effects of the sweets but this makes the self-indulgence all the sweeter. There is thus a need for justification so these sweets may be described by the eaters as 'meal substitutes' and the 'need for quick energy'.

It is interesting that the market for certain chocolate products and the market for cigarettes for women show some marked similarities. Both products are highly emotive and both involve some high oral satisfaction and, for women, the two markets both peak in the 35–55 year category. That cigarette ex-smokers tend to put on weight is often more due to food providing a substitute than to other mysterious factors, as they often claim. The pipe smoker, the cigarette smoker, and the compulsive chocolate eater are all nearer their mother's breasts than they would care to imagine.

It is significant that the housewife is the main victim of these compulsions and it is notable that for cigarettes and count lines the single woman and the career woman both have a lower rate of compulsion and consumption.

We have looked at the individual significance of food for the woman but obviously this extends to the more family-orientated food purchases. The significance of food purchase for women in the family context was noted by Dr. Cyril Sofer (1965)[9] of the Tavistock Institute. His study showed that food served functions other than the physiological—there were psychological and sociological intrusions in the motivations for purchases. He asserted that there were so many values, ideologies and social relationships involved that it was probably impossible to understand food consumption without understanding the social structure which accompanies it. Furthermore, this helps to explain why nobody eats the food which is nutritively the best available and why we eat much we know to be harmful. He suggests that food is used, for example, to express love in the household, provide treats, parties, entertainment, recreation and negotiation. Different foods are prescribed for men, women and children both on cultural and family levels. We use food to mark off changes in status and segregate special and everyday foods.

Central to all this is the housewife to whom the symbolic importance of satisfactory food provision in her traditional role is difficult to over-estimate. Its importance can only reduce as her traditional role becomes less circumscribed, as it is showing signs of doing. The more that food shopping becomes perceived as a chore, the more we will know that the traditional role structure of women is narrowing and weakening.

SLIMMING FOODS

As a corollary to the food market, there is the equally female-dominated slimming market. It is almost an extension of the cosmetics market and can trade on the same principles as the vaginal deodorants.

There are two categories of slimmer; the long-term weight watcher who is continually weight conscious and the serious 'one-off' slimmer who is trying to lose a lot of weight in one go. The total market was worth £34 million in 1970[10] with slimming breads accounting for almost 65% of it. It seems that consumers of slimming bread are predominantly over 35 and often over 45. Married couples with younger children are under-represented and the bulk of sales go to the AB and C1 groups with the C2 and DE taking most of the ordinary bread, so the markets tend to complement each other. In terms of individual parts of the slimmers bread market, the important other sector is crispbreads which were worth almost £7 million in 1969, about 27% more than in 1965. Slimming rolls are a small market worth about £1·1 million in 1969 and are of minority interest, but crispbreads are steady and popular sellers all the year round. The leading brand is Ryvita, at 44% of crispbread sales by value, with Energen second at 30%. There is a seasonal peak in crispbread with late spring the best period and it is directly competitive with bread.

The consumer profile covers the main army of female weight watchers, mostly in the 25–45 age-group, and the range ABC1 is fairly evenly represented with no regional bias. Most of the sales of Ryvita, 88%, go through grocers and only 2–3% through chemists but, with Energen, 10–15% goes through chemists with 70% through grocers. Marketing of all crisp-breads, and bread and roll substitutes, is aimed at women through television and the women's press.

But bread is not the only slimming aid. There are also a whole range of foods, such as biscuits, drinks and sweeteners, which have a cumulative importance of their own taking £13 million a year between them.

Slimming aids or foods can take two forms: food substitutes or food supplements. There is also a category called 'dietary preparations' which were worth only £750,000 in 1970. The biggest entrant in this sector is Complan, marketed as a food substitute by Glaxo. Another product in the dieting market is the slimming biscuit and this market was worth £5·3 million in 1971. The Bisk range is a supplement for the nibblers and is regarded as an appetite depressant although most biscuits, such as Limmits, now attempt to provide the slimmer with a complete meal. The biscuit market is domi-nated by Pfizer and Fisons who account for 80% of the market for slimmers biscuits between them, with Pfizers Limmits the brand leader with 40% of the market. Fisons make Bisks which take 30%.

Artificial sweeteners are also big business and a stable market. In 1970 this was worth about £2·8 million with Sweetex, the brand leader, at about

55% share. Saxin is second and Hermesetas, a Swiss product marketed by Anestan, is so close as to be identical in share.

Slimming drinks are typified by PLJ of Beecham which probably accounts for £2·6 million of this £4 million segment of the market. The typical consumer of PLJ, according to *Retail Business,* is in the 35–44 age group and in the social groups AB and C1 although DE account for 33% compared to the 48% of the AB.

Slimming tablets are the last main category and the principal ones are Slim Disks and Intrim from Tentham Laboratories and Ayds from Cuticura. They mainly work to depress the appetite. Ayds are the most active sector with a spectacular rise since 1968 and now claim 10–15% of the total slimming aids market. Sales from 1969–70 show an 138% increase[11].

Consumption Patterns

Patterns of consumption of slimming products vary considerably from one slimming product to another but since half of the population of the UK is said to be over their ideal weight, there are some 29 million or so potential slimmers in the country. This figure is split equally between men and women, yet it is significant that the slimming market is predominantly female. There is also a marked correlation between overweight and age: 65% of men and women in the 50–59 age group are overweight although they do not form the important part of the slimming market. There is also a marked seasonality about the market with late spring being a time for acute self-consciousness about winter weight gain in the light of summer nakedness. Women, of course, worry far more than men do, and at all other times. *Retail Business* estimates that over 80% of slimming food sales are made to women and among them, the largest single group are women in the 25–45 age bracket. Only one section stands out as male dominated: the artificial sweeteners section of which 40% of sales are estimated to be made to male consumers.

Slimming and Women: a Special Relationship

The appeal to slimming in women may be as much of a psychological appeal as that which goes through the marketing of vaginal deodorants. Dieting and slimming and being slim are a particularly female phenomenon and have been exploited mostly unconcernedly by manufacturers for some time.

A study by Dwyer, Feldman and Mayer notes the special significance of dieting for women. They suggest that the greater concern for women is motivated by several reasons[11].

1. Weight deviations are more of a social liability for women than men. A successful career man may be obese and even have star quality but the wives of successful men and successful businessmen can rarely take the same freedom.

2. Aspects of appearance are more intertwined with the self-concept in females than in males. Their looks are their whole personal value to many women who have never been taught or encouraged to value themselves in any other way, so the smallest gain in weight is a reduction in their social exterior and a reduction, therefore, in their worth. Seeing the weight accumulate is to see their personality and self identity disappear proportionately inside it. Studies by Huenemann *et al* (1966)[12] indicate that women weigh themselves more than men and know their weight more constantly and consistently than men do. Fatter girls showed a tendency to report weights on questionnaires that were markedly less than their actual weights, while boys, who obviously had less to lose, in one sense anyway, reported theirs accurately.

3. Obesity is more visible in females than males. *Normal,* young, mature females have twice as much fat on their bodies as men do and it is distributed more conspicuously on the hips and chest while men tend to put it on their torsos. Women's fat is a source of embarrassment but by its distribution is more visible, thus creating a merry-go-round of self-consciousness.

4. Women tend to underestimate the contribution of build rather than fat and may spend many unhappy weeks trying to get rid of what is really healthy body structure. Since all women should be small-boned and slight, the big woman, in order to move towards a more 'feminine' standpoint, attempts to diet to what is basically an unhealthy weight. The cultural stereotype has more to be blamed for than most people realise.

5. If the fashionable stereotype of women was fat and broad, as it is in Turkey and has been over the history of Europe, then women would not worry so about their weight and manufacturers of dieting foods would be without a market. Nevertheless, the modern woman is trapped by a stereotype of femininity, which emphasises a woman's worth by her closeness to the stereotype and not for any more tangible or personal qualities such as intelligence or ability. Thus, she can lose on both sides, both in psychological terms when she feels her image is unsuitable, and by the fact that this is, nevertheless, the only way to be socially accepted. Even if she should forget her predicament, advertising is always there to remind her. That women worry about this 'Catch 22' is documented by many surveys. Dwyer and Mayer (1970)[14] in an analysis of several public opinion polls, revealed that concern about weight and dieting behaviour was much more common among adult women than among men. Weight is also perceived as much more of a problem by teenage girls than boys. Huenemann *et al* (1966)[13] classified 25% of a sample of both boys and girls as being overweight, yet he still found that 50% of the girls classified themselves as obese compared to less than 25% of the boys. In a similar study [16], 16% of girls and 19% of the boys (high school seniors) were overweight but over 80% of the girls and 20% of the boys wanted to weigh less than they did.

If this phenomenon exists on a national scale then we have an epidemic in psychological weight terms that can only be equalled, as far as the woman and the female consumer are concerned, by the use of the vaginal deodorant.

Other studies noted in the review by Dwyer, Feldman and Mayer indicate that there are distinct sex differences between men and women in their hang-ups about weight, but both sexes have clear ideas about the stereotype of slim women. Dwyer *et al* (1969)[13] in a famous study on college students asked them to rate six female silhouettes for their 'ideal' and as the most 'feminine'. A majority picked the slim, slender, female mesomorphic-ectomorph as their ideal and as the most feminine. Thus, social and sexual problems are certain to arise for the obese woman in fitting into our present rigid, cultural standards, and these women can have pathetically negative, self-images. Monello and Mayer (1963)[15] found that the obese girls showed personality characteristics such as passivity, obsessive concern with self-image, expectation of rejection and progressive withdrawal, all strikingly similar to the traits of ethnic and racial minority groups, due to their status as victims of prejudice. They also accepted the common, negative attitude towards obesity in our society, so that they also gave compulsive responses concerning weight in such things as sentence completion tests even when there was no connection in the task.

It is within *this* context that we should view the concern with slimming, slimming products and the high incidence of anorexia nervosa which several spokesmen recently have been likening to a growing epidemic. For women the causes of weight obsession are complex but are usually tied up along the way with estimations of femininity, denial of womanhood and extreme anxiety at the social image of women and how they fit into it. Obesity, as Dwyer, Feldman and Mayer note, is often in the eyes both of the beholder and the beheld, and the eyes are glancing constantly at the ever-present media images.

Anyway, if the vaginal deodorant enigma is anything to go by, the manufacturers will justify their role in the slimming problem until such time as the slimming environment becomes unprofitable. Their contribution to the problem is difficult to estimate, but the direct promotion of slimming products must also be coupled with the more indirect promotion of a stereotype of 'media woman' which is out of line with 'real' woman.

That manufacturers have tended, in the past, to overstep the ethical mark in the slimming product market is testified to by the fact that the CAP committee had to bring out a special bulletin to control the advertising of slimming products (August 1972). It seems that advertisers had been pulling little fast ones, like using temporary expulsion of water from the body as 'slimming' and touching up 'before' and 'after' advertising pictures. Still, incitement to slim by threats to an individual's self-worth, and exploitation of cultural prejudices do not yet make up sufficient grounds for unsuitable advertising according to the CAP standards. When they do, the slimming food marketers may lose some customers, but at least only the really obese women will be their target instead of those many non-obese, healthy women who diet merely because they cannot accept themselves as they naturally are.

The sanitary, cosmetics and slimming markets are strange phenomena. Together they probably typify everything bad, yet something prevalent, about female consumption: compulsion, guilt and obligation. Yet, the strange thing is, these are the very markets where one consistently finds the marketers falling over themselves to note that it is they who are doing the women a favour, rather than vice versa. It is as if they, in some way, need to feel responsible for, and in control of, the two essentially female processes which objectively they have no right to: the mystery of female beauty and attraction and the spectacular phenomenon of female menstruation and procreation as centralised in the vagina.

This proprietorial leeching onto two of the basic re-affirmations of femaleness is typified by a remark made by a marketer, quoted by Friedan[20]:

> Properly manipulated—if you are not afraid of that word—housewives can be given the sense of identity, creativity, the self-realisation, even the sexual joy they lack—by buying things.

In other words, is the implication, women should be grateful. They should rejoice in their identity by courtesy of the marketer, their femininity by the goodness of the manufacturer.

Yet, to what extent are we viewing here, in the marketing industry, the mass projection of a phenomenon which is gaining more and more theoretical acceptance, that is, the principle of womb envy? Gregory Zilboorg[17] writes that womb envy on the part of man is far older and far more fundamental than penis envy on the part of women, while the psychiatrist Horney notes that[18]:

> When one begins to analyse men only after a long experience of analysing women, as I did, one is surprised by the insensitivity of their envy of women. Is it really remarkable that so little recognition and attention are paid to the fact of man's secret dread and envy of women? It is even more remarkable that women themselves have so long overlooked it.

Gould-Davis further notes that:

> In civilised societies today this clitoris envy, or womb envy takes subtle forms. Man's constant need to disparage woman, to humble her, to deny her equal rights and to belittle her achievements—all are expressions of his innate envy and fear. In earlier times, and still in primitive societies where the instinctive dread and awe of women has not yet turned to fear-plus-hate men have sought to imitate the dreaded object.

She concludes that, on the basis of anthropological, cultural and psychological evidence[19]: 'Sexual envy is exclusively a masculine phenomenon.'

Is it therefore so unlikely that marketers and advertisers, in their unique position of male-female control, their peculiar power to note and manipulate the vulnerabilities of women, are demonstrating some symptoms of this sexual envy, this womb envy principle? Can we conjecture that through their coveting of the female principle, their femaleness by proxy, their control of women by control of the essences of femininity, they are, in effect, only acting out a more primeval fear?

REFERENCES

1. 'Sanitary Protection', *Retail Business*, 142 (December 1969).
2. Also, *see* 'Give us this day our daily dose of hexachlorophene', *Nova* (July 1974), p. 33 and 'Deodorants: The hidden dangers', *Sunday Times* (12 November 1972).
3. *Campaign* (5 November 1971), p. 36.
4. M. Wax, 'Themes in Cosmetics and Grooming', *American Journal of Sociology*, Vol. 62 (1957), pp. 588–93.
5. 'Facial Tissues', *Retail Business*, 137 (July 1969); 'Toilet Soaps', *Retail Business*, 138 (August 1969); 'Cosmetics. Part 1, *Retail Business*, 167 (January 1972); 'Cosmetics', Part 2. *Retail Business*, 169 (March 1972); 'Cosmetics', Part 3, *Retail Business*, 170 (April 1972); 'Toilet Preparations'. *Retail Business*, 156 (February 1971); IPC Cosmetic and Toileteries Survey (1970-3); *Retail Business*, 182 (April 1973), Marketing Review, p. 3.
6. Eugene E. Gloye, 'Make Up as a Signal System for Personality Traits', *Psychology*, Vol. 2(2) (1965), pp. 7–14.
7. Roland Harper, 'The Appeal of Food and its Sensory Bases', *Advertising Quarterly* (Spring 1967), p. 17.
8. J. E. Turle and R. Falconer, Communications Research Ltd., 'Men and Women are Different', *Journal of the Market Research Society*, Vol. 14(2) (1972).
9. Dr. Cyril Sofer, *The Sociology of Distribution*, Tavistock Institute Publications (1965).
10. 'Slimming Foods', Part 1, *Retail Business*, 151 (September 1970); 'Slimming Foods', Part 2. *Retail Business*, 157 (March 1971).
11. Dwyer. Feldman and Mayer, 'The Social Psychology of Dieting', *Journal of Health and Social Behaviour* (1970), pp. 269–87.
12. R. L. Huenemann, R. L. Shapiro. M. C. Hampton, B. W. Mitchell and A. R. Behnke 'A longitudinal study of gross body composition and body conformation and their association with food and activity in a teenage population: views on teenage subjects on body conformation, food and activity', *American Journal of Clinical Nutrition* (18 May 1966), pp. 325–38.
13. J. T. Dwyer, J. J. Feldman, C. C. Seltzer and J. Mayer 'Body Image in Adolescents: Attitudes toward weight and perception of appearance', *Journal of Nutrition Education* (2) (Fall 1969), pp. 14–19.
14. J. T. Dwyer and J. Mayer, 'Potential Dieters: Who are they?'. *Journal of the American Dietetic Association*, 56 (June 1970), pp. 510–14.
15. L. F. Monello and J. Mayer, 'Obese adolescent girls: An unrecognised minority group', *American Journal of Clinical Nutrition* (13) (1963), pp. 35–9.
16. H. Canning and J. Mayer. 'Obesity: An analysis of attitudes, knowledge and weight control in girls', *Research Quarterly* (December 1968), pp. 894–9.
17. Gregory Zilboorg, 'Male and Female', in Harold Kelman's 'Introduction' to Karen Horney, *Feminine Psychology*, Norton (New York 1967), pp. 8–9.
18. Karen Horney, *Feminine Psychology*, Norton (New York 1967). p. 62.
19. Elizabeth Gould Davis, *The First Sex*, Dent (1973).
20. Betty Friedan. *see* chapter 15, ref. 14.

13. *Woman Buying as Woman—Clothing and Hair*

In the previous chapter we examined three markets where, to all intents and purposes, the marketers controlled and framed the female consumer response. In this chapter, we shall look at two other markets which are remarkable both for size and consistency. Both these markets, for clothing and for hairdressing, concern the female appearance yet, while there is evidence of compulsion, this element is to a greater extent controlled by the women themselves.

WOMEN'S CLOTHING AND FASHION

Women's clothing has been, to the casual observer, a consistent source of historical fascination and this is an emphasis that women have been no less enthusiastic in ascribing to themselves. Yet, at no time in history has this fascination translated itself into such regular and extensive expenditure. This is particularly illustrated by an IPC survey in 1973 which noted that young women in Britain spent well over half of their money on clothes. In fact, the 5·4 million women in the 15–24 age-group spent £462 million on clothing, more than 60% of the £750 million they spent on themselves.

Single women spent more than married women although there were large variations in different categories. Single girls at school, for instance, spent an average of £57·3 a year while single working girls, between 19 and 29 years spent £114·4 during the same period. Generally, it was women in the lower socio-economic groups who bought clothes most frequently. Only 11% of the women in the AB groups had bought 6 or more dresses in the last 12 months, while 20% of those in the C1 and DE groups had bought more than 6 [1].

The clothes market in the women's personal purchase sector is evidently of enormous importance and since there are still only 13% of women who regularly make their own clothes and 42% of whom 'never do', it is reasonable to conclude that the purchased clothing item must still be almost totally unsubstitutable [4].

189

In financial terms, women's skirts and dresses were, in 1971, the most profitable sector in the British clothing industry, registering profitability of 13·3% (compared to 10·9% for children's wear and 10·2% for shirts and nightwear). In 1972 one estimate suggested that this market was worth £1,812 million representing an increase in expenditure of more than 20% on 1966, while IPC puts the retail sales value for 1974 at £1,150 million. (Within this total value, knitted outerwear and dresses / skirts /suits took £270 million respectively; coats and rainwear, £220 million: underwear /nightwear, £150 million; stockings, £140 million and foundation garments, £100 million.) By way of comparison, the estimated expenditure on the men's clothing market in 1973 was about half the value of estimates for the women's market, £680 million[2*].

In terms of retail outlets for women's clothing, there is no doubt that Marks and Spencer leads the field and their £395 million turnover in clothing and other non-foods in 1972—3 represents a significant proportion of the sales which go through multiple chain stores (53% in 1975).

Women's Outerwear

The TGI of 1972 /3 found that women who had bought items of outerwear did so in the following proportions:

Raincoats	38%	(8% bought more than one)
Cardigans, jumpers	68%	(24% bought four or more)
Dresses	72%	(40% bought three or more)
Overcoats	33%	(10% bought more than one)
Trousers and jeans	53%	
Suits	32%	

Items of underwear and lingerie had, by contrast, been bought in 60% of cases and 24% of women had bought four or more items which, within the total women's clothing market, puts these garments in third place in terms of purchase frequency.

Simply in reference to the outerwear market, however, it is evidently dresses, trousers /jeans and jumpers /cardigans which are the principal sectors in a market which represented some 175 million garments in 1972[4].

Dresses. Within the total women's clothing market women's dresses account for the largest share of sales, 40% in 1972, according to DTI figures. There are about 5,000 manufacturers of women's clothing in the UK and it is difficult to quantify those who are in the clothing market specifically for dresses. Estimates put the market at about £20 million representing between 30—60 million dresses per annum[3]. The younger women,

---

* *IPC Consumer Marketing Manual* (1974) (compounded from several sources).

according to *Retail Business*, account for the highest purchase rate which also declines with age. The single largest age group with the highest *per capita* rate of acquisition is that composed of the under 20s (15–20) while women between the ages of 20–29 tend to purchase at a marginally lower rate. The two groups together, that is, all women under 30, purchased approximately five dresses *per capita* in 1972, while women over 30 and under 50 bought three. In 1970 and 1969 the 15–20s *per capita* consumption was around $3\frac{1}{2}$ per head with a consumption of $2\frac{1}{2}$ for the 50–59 group and one for the 60 + group. Collectively, women under 30 who make up only a quarter of the female population, purchased the largest proportion of dresses, 40%, although buying frequency is also an important factor in the under 20s group. Advertising for women's dresses tends to fall into four types covering: (i) the garment maker alone; (ii) the fibre company in conjunction with the manufacturer; (iii) the fibre company in conjunction with the manufacturer and retailer; and (iv) the manufacturer and retailer.

Distribution is almost equally divided between the independent retailer and chains (35% and 33% respectively). Departmental stores and mail order take 10% and 12% respectively[4].

Trousers. Estimates are that 15–20 million trousers were purchased by women in 1971 and the average *per capita* consumption doubled between 1969 and 1971 from half a pair per year |*sic*| to a whole one between 1969 and 1971. An indication of the penetration of trousers into the feminine culture is that purchasers are getting older. While 15–20 year olds still retain a quarter of the trouser market and half of the jeans market (equivalent to an eighth of the total trouser market), the most noticeable shift has been from the late-teen to the middle-aged woman as an increasingly important consumer. From 1969-70 *per capita* consumption was nearly doubled by the 20–30 age group. On average, however, 14% of women acquired jeans in 1974, 8% stretch slacks and 33% ordinary slacks with an average price paid of £3·12, giving an estimated total expenditure of £53,300,000, £11 million of which were on the 'ordinary slack' category[4].

Brand-wise, Marks and Spencer took 22·9% of branded sales, principally through the 'ordinary slack' category, with Slimma taking 5·4%, Levi 8·0% and C&A, the only other chain store apart from Marks and Spencer which took any noticeable share, taking 3·6%.

Knitwear. Of the knitwear market, the most popular item is the sweater which 53% of women acquired in 1974 compared to the second popular garment, the cardigan, which 35% of women purchased. Unhappily for the spectre of English-womanhood-past only 3% of women bought a twinset, the same proportion which bought a knitted trouser suit, a fact which is perhaps a sign of the times.

The spending on the two principal items, the sweater and the cardigan, notched up nearly £80 million in 1974 representing some 45 million garments. Nevertheless, even Britain cannot beat the consumption rate of knitwear of the German women who purchased 418 items of knitwear per 100 women in 1974 closely followed by the 374 of French women. Britain came third with 352 per 100 women[4].

Girls Outerwear

Little girls, it seems, still wear a lot of dresses and, as *Retail Business*[3] says defensively:

> Dresses are very much the largest selling item of clothing, let there be no mistake about it. and a large number of manufacturers of girls clothing still produce large ranges of dresses.

Nevertheless, many manufacturers, it seems, have also diversified into trousers, trouser suits, tops and skirts in response to the demand for more casual wear. Fashion is important too, and this is reflected in the upgraded standard of display in children's departments and shops, aimed at attracting the child's attention as well as the mother's. The total market size in girls wear (14 and under) is £5$\frac{1}{2}$ million for tailored outerwear (including slacks and overcoats) and just over £7 million in light outerwear in terms of value of production (not r.s.p.) making £13 million worth of what little girls are made of. In 1971 about 20 million girl's dresses were purchased and about six million trousers (trade and EIU estimates), representing about three and one garments per head respectively.

Most garments are distributed via the independent retailer—especially dresses, skirts and coats. Chains such as Marks and Spencer, British Home Stores and Littlewood account for a growing share along with Mothercare. Dresses accounted for just over £3$\frac{1}{4}$ million in 1971, skirts £540,000, blouses £360,000, slacks £1,270,000, overcoats £2,804,000 and suits including trouser suits, £600,000.

Women's Underwear

The women's underwear market has a curiously sensible–sordid image which is circumscribed by the Marks and Spencer ethos of clean, bright 'undies' and the *Tit-Bits* world of crutchless, nippleless creations which owe less to function than to titillation. Nevertheless, respectability in an understated way seems to be the general key-note of this £100 million market which finds its biggest sectors in the brassiere and corset purchase and its smallest sectors in the region of the swimming costume and the panty*.

---

* In 1972, vests, slips, petticoats etc. took £14$\frac{1}{4}$ million; knickers, panties and briefs, £6 million; corsets, £23 million; brassieres, £26 million; nightwear, £26 million; housecoats, £11 million; swimwear, £4 million.

Undoubtedly, it is also a market which is held firmly by the spotless reins of St. Michael and underwear provided the largest source of revenue for Marks and Spencer in 1973 with 42% of sales of foundation garments and 19% of stockings and tights going through that shop[4].

If the women's movement has promoted any major changes in the underwear front then it is certainly not over-visible as yet, although there are some indications that sales of brassieres have diminished slightly per 100 women and it is now accepted by some sources that there is some unisex going on in the panties/underpants sector, while the use of tights as bone-warmers by male football observers is now, apparently, rife. *Retail Business* further assumes some effect of the sex revolution when it notes as a main reason for the embryo movement to the use of the cod-piece ('Makes the well-armed tidy and the not-so-well-off unashamed of his small stature'): 'one menswear speciality that is safe from mass female adoption'.

Nevertheless, women's underwear seems relatively untouched by the ravages of unisexuality and still tends to see itself principally as conservative. In fact, apart from some original ideas in packaging, there have been no really revolutionary changes in the market since the garments were devised, except, perhaps, the sector of disposable panties which has been little heard of since a glowing *Retail Business* report on its growth rate in 1969[6]. Body stockings died a death somewhere round about the model girl era of the nineteen-sixties while formless bras were merely a logical repurcussion against the boned and pointed discomfort of contouring in the nineteen-fifties. Women's underwear is, it seems, contented and changeless and sees itself, if market research reports are anything to go by, as divided into its two principal sectors; foundation garments, and stockings and tights.

Foundation garments. There have been difficulties in estimating the size of this market but IPC, in a recent report using the 1965 retail value of £65 million, suggest that the current value of the women's foundation market is around £100 million[7]. According to European Research Consultants (1972), slightly more than half of this expenditure, 54%, is on brassieres, while the remainder is on corselettes, high-waisted girdles and pantie-girdles, the last taking over 25% of sales[5].

The distribution channels of these garments have remained relatively fixed over the years with drapers and smaller clothing shops still finding a market of sorts, but the doyenne of female underwear sales, Marks and Spencer, is still going from strength to strength with a stranglehold on the market of 42% of all sales. department stores taking 20% and mail order 13%[5]. Obviously, therefore, an analysis of brand shares finds St. Michael reigning supreme with 39%, closely followed by Playtex at 14% and Berlei at 8%, and just to demonstrate how seriously the branded goods take the St. Michael threat, Berlei, Playtex and Silhouette are shown to have spent just under £2 million on press and television advertising in 1972, only £216,000 of which was spent in the press.

In terms of underwear usage, the British woman follows a trend noted generally throughout Europe of buying at least 2–3 foundation garments a year; only in Spain do women attain an average purchase rate of four. Prices are relatively low in Britain and the highest prices paid for foundation garments are in France and Germany, where the two markets between them were worth an estimated £627 million in 1973 or 53% of total European retail sales value. In fact, in Europe as a whole, 350 million foundation garments are bought every year, 211 million of which are brassieres (60% of sales), 77 million are pantie girdles and 62 million are of some other type.

Several reports have recently examined the underwear market in Europe[5,4] and details about usage and purchase rates tend to be variable. Purchaser rates per annum for brassieres, for example, vary between the 75% of the TGI sample in 1973 to the 60% of the Euro-Monitor Survey in 1975 and it is difficult to tell whether this represents sample differences or actual reduction in brassiere usage. Nevertheless, between the surveys various interesting facts can be gleaned:

1. Engaged women are heavy purchasers of all sorts of underwear. They were particularly well represented among the 34% of women who bought three or more brassieres in 1973.
2. One per cent of French women regularly purchase rubber underwear although the favourite material among 70% of French women is lycra.
3. Seventy-two per cent of French women prefer full-cupped brassieres. Only 28% like the half-cupped variety and 8% prefer them strapless.
4. The most important feature in the choice of a foundation garment for British women is 'comfort' (30% of women noted this), followed by 'figure control' (28%), 'good-wearing properties' (17%), 'attractive appearance' (15%). Price only figures in 11% of cases which suggests that foundation garments are far from luxury products.
5. Forty per cent of women prefer their foundation garments to be lightweight and IPC notes that the heavier 'controlling' garments are rapidly losing popularity, even among older women.
6. White is still the most important colour in underwear, noted by 56% of women in one survey to be their favourite. flesh colour followed at 22%, pastel at 10%, black at 8% and multi-coloured at 4%.

In fact, to conclude, few surprises can be found within the foundation garment market and inertia seems to be the operative and metaphoric key-note, a fact which may be modifying in the light of female, social emancipation but which trends have yet to pick up.

Stockings and tights.   Estimates put the size of this market at around £140 million in 1972 of which the biggest sector by sales was women's tights and panty-hose, put at 542 million units in the same year. The *Grocer*[7] which made this estimate also puts sales of women's stockings at 74 million pairs of which the seamless ones made up 66 million and the seamed, 8 million. According to the TGI in 1972, the St. Michael brand leads in both stockings and tights (with 22% of sales for both) with Pretty Polly and Aristoc notable among the stockings shares at 15·6% of sales and Woolworths, in the tights market, coming second to St. Michael at 11% of sales. Channels of distribution are, for the most part, drapers, multiples and department stores, including Marks and Spencer, which takes 19% of trade. Interestingly, bazaars and markets take 8% of sales in this market and supermarkets are steadily increasing their 10% share.

Usage of tights and stockings is again a fairly consistent European phenomenon with tights in the ascendant: 2,343 million pairs are bought every year in Europe as against 553 million pairs of stockings. Demand per 100 women for tights is highest in Germany and the Benelux countries and lowest in Italy. Conversely, Spain, in line with other market observations that this country tends to contradict European trends in women's clothing, represents the biggest market for stockings.

In Britain, specifically, the TGI for 1973 tells us that 13% of women are heavy users of tights and these tend to be in the 15–24 age group and biased toward the C2 class.

Again, engaged women seem to be heavy users of this garment; they made up 35% of the 'heavy' group in 1972. Stockings, however, have been registering a steady decline since the 1960s and an increase in tights purchase has been parelleling this. While 17% of women bought five or more pairs of tights in 1972 this had risen to 30 by 1974. In 1969 the average woman bought 16·8 pairs of stockings; by 1970 this had dropped to 3·0. The current market for stockings is less than one-third of that for tights; $5\frac{1}{2}$ million women wear stockings and buy them an average of 12 times a year compared to the $17\frac{1}{2}$ million women who wear tights and buy them 30 times a year.

WOMEN'S FASHION

'Fashion' is one of those hard to define, amorphous characteristics of the female clothing market that seems to be dying the death with a tendency for women to choose their ways of spending by more random and autonomous means. It still exists as an important and necessary indicator for many women, particularly in the very young and very upper-class strata, but the death of fashion as dictator has been traced back by several observers to the birth of the midi. This was particularly noted by Reynolds and Darden (1972)[8]:

> ... the midi failure points out that no amount of promotion will ensure the success of a new style whose design is incongruent with the characteristics desired by the markets.

(They then go and spoil everything after this militant little conclusion by commenting in relation to the women's fashion market, 'The consumer is still *king*.')

Another article in *Marketing* (December 1972) was more forthright in its comments. It said:

> The coming of the midi marks the end of an era. The days when haughty fashion designers could tell a woman what to wear are over.

The article tells the story of how American manufacturers of dresses and textiles became disenchanted with the very popular 'mini' skirt, 'the favourite fashion of a century', because it offered little opportunity for variation and, anyway, hardly used any material. Less and less business appeared available for the established firms. So they decided to sponsor the midi to create an entirely artificial style but using a concept and a force which, unknown to them, had lost its potency—fashion.

In the spring of 1969 the rag trade took the plunge but by the autumn it was evident that all was not well. Women not only did not buy, they protested at this manipulation in the first display by women of its kind. There was FADD (Fight against Dictating Designers), GAMS (Girls against More Skirts) and POFF (Preservation of our Femininity and Finances). *Rags Magazine*, an avant-garde fashion publication, published an attack on the midi entitled 'Fashion Fascism'. The industry was in a state of complete disaster with the $8,000 million investment of the American rag trade wasted. Price was not the only factor; it was the idea of being manipulated that got to the female consumer for the first time and in a way that has still not really been duplicated. Things were never quite the same again, and now fashion is not so much a dictate as something one appraises, and takes snippets from here and there, a taste of this and a fillip of that, but in tune with its relevance to one's own gestalt. *Marketing* noted:

> Today's style-conscious woman wants a fashion which will be an expression of her own personality, the life she leads and the things in society which amuse and delight her ... The midi mess is proof enough she doesn't want to be told what to wear by anybody.

Nevertheless, apart from the observation of the midi debâcle and the subjective comments of fashion correspondents there have been few surveys which have attempted some quantification of 'fashionability' and placed some value upon the movement away from fashion-as-dictator. What surveys there are, however, do tend to support the contentions of the observers. One survey noted, for instance, that: 'To most women it [fashion] forms a guiding influence rather than a dogma', while another concluded:

On the whole the survey results have shown that the British woman does not blindly follow fashion but she tends to try to adapt the fashions in a way that is suitable to her individually.

A third survey found that in 1973 64% of women agreed with the statement that they 'try to be fashionable but it has to suit me' compared to 4% who 'always follow the fashion' and the 32% who disregarded fashion completely [4, 5, 9].

The bones of fashionability, a subject which for all its popularity has really been under-researched, were investigated recently in the context of the European market, and the interesting findings underlined the fact that fashion could change its nature and degree by nationality and by class/age criteria giving wide variations in emphasis. For instance, on investigating the proportion of women following fashion, the survey found that Netherlands and Spain led the field while Britain came last. Of those disregarding fashion completely, the proportions were, however, one in four in Germany, one in three in Great Britain and two in five in Belgium, Netherlands and Spain. The first two countries mentioned, in the main, that they 'try to be fashionable but it has to suit me'.

In all the countries except for Spain, the upper-class women tended to have the biggest proportions of the fashion-conscious. Spain had the reverse distribution with the upper-class women showing the least interest in fashion and the lower-class the most. Without exception, however, the younger groups were the most fashion conscious. In Great Britain, only 6% of the 14–18 year olds disregard fashion compared to a national average of 25%. This fact has also been supported by a recent profile of the women's clothing market in Great Britain [9] which found that over half of all women over the age of 50 years claim to disregard fashion and dress in what suits them best, whereas 90% of 14–18 year-olds try to be fashionable provided it suits them, with 5% following fashion regardless. In investigation of the 'fashion leaders' in the European bloc it was found that four out of five countries gave the leadership to France while the fifth country, Britain, chauvinistically nominated itself. In the other four countries, Great Britain came second but way behind France, if far ahead of other rivals.

Time of purchase was also investigated by the survey and, predictably, it was found that the upper-classes purchased more often at the beginning of the season. Generally, however, this was a minority in every country, and most women purchased clothes when they needed them, particularly in Great Britain but less so in Belgium. Colour-wise, there was great consistency in favourites between all the countries. Blue is still the most popular colour right across the board, followed by brown in the Benelux countries, red in Germany, green in Great Britain and black in Spain. The choice of blue as favourite is also borne out by other surveys on women's clothing, one of which noted colour favourites for slacks, rainwear and knitwear to be blue in every case [9].

WOMEN'S HAIR

Havelock Ellis notes that hair is the most generally noted part of the
female body after the eyes, while Millum in his critique of the image of
woman ascribes to hair, in particular, a strong symbol of libido and quotes
Berg, a psychiatrist, who went so far as to note that, in Freudian terms,
'short hair is in the nature of castration'. Millum [10] goes on to note:

> Hair is not merely an accessory to the face but a most important and integral part
> of the facial image. Hair is a very potent symbol, and as such is more amenable to
> alteration and adaptation than is the face; for it can be dyed different colours. made to
> stand on end or hang down. cut into shapes or removed altogether . . . Apart from its
> symbolic qualities it is both aesthetically satisfying to look at and a pleasure to touch.

It is small wonder, then, that hair interest and care should, as with clothing,
have developed from a widespread personal obsession to the subject of
extensive marketing.

This sector will examine the two sides to this marketing: the hair salon
sector which, while financially the greater, is of less interest to the marketer
since it does not utilise many consumer retail products, and the home hair-
care market, the more private and profitable world of woman and her hair
which spawns an ingenious range of 'individualised' products and a seemingly
infinite potential for permutation and change.

Professional Hairdressing

According to the National Income and Expenditure Report in 1972, about
£230 million was spent by consumers in hairdressers' shops. As a product
it varies with income: households with an income above the national average
spend less than the national average on hairdressing and, with the exception
of the more affluent South East, women and men both use hairdressers
but women dominate the spending pattern. In 1966 (nearest Retail Census
of Distribution figures) women spent nearly $4\frac{1}{2}$ times as much on their
hair as men. *Retail Business* did some calculations for 1972 and estimated
that expenditure might well be of the order of £230 million in total. of which
women take £188 million and men £42 million [11]. What, however, goes on in
hairdressers to warrant this expenditure?

In the women's market in 1973, shampoo and set accounted for 55%
of customers and 45% of turnover; shampoo and blow dry took 14% and
11% respectively, and colouring and bleaching were high in the turnover
figures at 19% although this attracted only 10% of customers. A feature
of the hairdressing market is that the number of operations does not need
to tally with the turnover since prices vary widely with each operation [11].

A survey by IPC on women and their 'shampoos and set' (Cosmetics
Survey 1973) showed that 66% of women visited a hairdressing salon for
a shampoo and set in 1972 while the rest did their own at home. Most

of this 66% were either very regular visitors (weekly or fortnightly) or very irregular. Young women, in particular, showed very little demand for the regular shampoo and set and over half of them paid no visits at all in the year. This trend is further borne out by the IPC study on spending habits of young women in the 15–29 age bracket for 1972, where we find that three-quarters of British teenagers and young wives have an electric hair dryer at home, and hair dryers and heated rollers are popular gifts for young women[15] (a factor examined in more detail later in this chapter).

In 1972 40% of women demanded a perm and they were marginally concentrated in the upper-age brackets, low-income brackets and industrial North and Midlands. Fashion waving recently may have increased the demand among young women for these type of perms. Women requiring no perm at all in the course of a year have moved up steadily from only 7% in 1966 to 60% in 1972.

Interestingly and obviously, hairdressing, like direct selling, is one of those trades where women do unto women to an unprecedented degree. They also receive very low wages, according to the *Retail Business* survey, and are still un-unionised. Their median weekly wage in April 1974 was £12·40 or 32p an hour compared to the median weekly wage of £18·69 paid to *all* women in full-time employment. Most of the women, 827,000, are in women's hairdressing, though in the census of distribution in 1966 there were 86,000 women in mixed hairdressing and 23,000 in men's hairdressing of all types.

Home Hair Care

Presently, the home hair-care market is reckoned by *Retail Business*[12] to be worth in the region of £80 million—still a fragment of what is spent in the salon market but very much a product-intensive, expanding market—especially with the trend towards more 'anti-salon', natural hair fashions. Obviously, this trend has been greatly helped by improvements in the quality of home products so that disasters such as the common 'orange hair' and 'candy floss' effects, so well known and well hated just before and after the war, are generally avoided these days. In addition, more women enjoy the time-saving aspects of their own hair care particularly in this time of the working housewife and the career girl who cannot just skip off to the hairdresser for a weekly set—a much more common occurrence in the 1950s and 1960s.

Overall, the chemists catch the brunt of this market, taking a 30% share in which Boots only narrowly leads the 'others'. The grocery retail sector has increased its share but wholesaling is declining slightly, although it is still significant since independent chemists and grocers still take a considerable proportion of the total sales. The amount sold through hairdressers is still very small.

The key to this market, however, is very much one of fashion. This generates changes in emphasis on the different products within the market with interesting irregularity. If 'control' is 'in', then perms and sprays leap to the fore; if we are all 'back to nature' then these are out and conditioners and blow-wave setters are in.

In this market examination we shall look at two main sectors: the associated products (dryers, heated rollers, ornaments) and the direct products (shampoos, colourants, conditioners). It will be seen that, as with clothes, the historical interest in hair has really changed little. What *is* different is the mobilisation of forces by the marketers to take advantage of this phenomenon.

WOMEN'S HAIR MARKET: THE DIRECT PRODUCTS

Hair Sprays

The hair spray is a product very much prey to hair fashion, more so than many other goods in this field; the 'beehive' and the 'natural look' are virtually on different planets, one requiring all and the other nothing of the hair spray. Sixty per cent of women use this product, representing expenditure of £27·5 million and usage is highest in the 25—44 age group. Nevertheless, over a quarter of women have never used a hair spray. In terms of brands, Sunsilk holds the field at a 20% market share with Silvikrin creeping up behind at 15%. Advertising expenditure on hairsprays reached £1·8 million in 1974 of which £1·7 million went on television promotion. Only Wella concentrates on the press to any great extent.

Setting Agents

This market is valued at £5 million and is currently expanding at about 20% per annum. The usage is encouraged by the blow-drying phenomenon and some setting lotions are marketed specifically for this. The brand leader is Beecham's Amami with a 20% market share followed by Polyset and Twice as Lasting at 10% each. These firms lead the advertising expenditure stakes which in the total market reached £1·4 million in 1974, of which £0·8 million went to television and £0·6 million to the press. About 20% of women use a setting lotion, although this number tends to be substitutable with the usage of home or salon perms. Nationally, 29% of women have salon perms regularly while 10% use the home variety.

Colourants

Despite recent publicity that hair colourants may be carcinogenic and there are moves in America, in particular, to curtail their use (the vaginal deodorant syndrome re-visited?), they are a consistently popular product taking an estimated £14 million a year in retail sales, particularly from women under 25 years of age. Semi-permanents account for 40% of the market, permanent colourants taking about a third. Lighteners and bleaches together take another 15% of the market while temporary colourants, the smallest sector at present, account for between 12 and 13%.

The recent *Retail Business* report on hair care notes that while demand for colourants as a whole rose very rapidly in the 1960s, the rate of growth seems to have slowed down since then, a fact supported by an IPC survey which notes that while 25% of women used colourants in 1965, only 18% did so in 1972–3[13]. Perhaps hair colour, as with style, is following a 'natural' philosophy. Nevertheless, the market remains buoyant enough to take a considerable portion of trade from the salon. Only 14% of women visited a salon for colouring in 1972 and only about 1% of women wanted the service as frequently as once a month.

Conditioners

Conditioners have been a recent addition to the home hair-care market and a relatively dynamic one. *Retail Business*, nevertheless, now notes that the market is levelling out. There are two main sorts of conditioners. There is the creme rinse which is mainly a short-term, comb-in repair job which takes over 70% of conditioner sales, and the cream conditioners which aim to do more basic preventative and repair work to the hair structure. The market is currently estimated to be worth about £5 million.

Shampoos

While this product probably typifies home hair-care more than any other, there is little volume growth in this market now. Saturation has brought value growth through inflationary factors rather than anything to do with sales levels. It is a heavily segmented market, with an astonishing capacity for permutation. At the moment, the medicated shampoo type accounts for about a third of sales with the more 'cosmetic' varieties (such as lemon, herbal, protein), catering for an infinite variety of hair types and colours, taking the rest. There is a very high level of penetration in the shampoo market. Only about 3–4% of the population have never used a shampoo, but this is higher in the older age groups.

The main manufacturers are Beecham and Elida Gibb, whose brands of Silvikrin and Sunsilk respectively take 9% of the market. Otherwise, there is really very little to choose between the shares of the different brands. In terms of advertising, media expenditure on shampoos reached a massive £25 million in 1974 of which £2·1 million went through television. As with the detergent market, advertising level is the key to maintaining market share for, like the detergents, the shampoo is basically almost totally substitutable between brands, a fact that women buyers, it seems, must not latch on to.

WOMEN'S HAIR MARKET: THE ASSOCIATED PRODUCTS

Hair Dryers and Heated Rollers

Market Research Great Britain notes that in 1972 1,171,000 hair dryers were put on the market in Great Britain, at a value of £4,001,000. Of the total, 696,000 were manufactured in this country, 496,700 were imported models of which Moulinex took 40% share[14]. The main outlets are through direct sales but mail order or stamp catalogues take a third of all deliveries. Only 215,000 out of 860,000 went through the independent retail trade in 1971. Chemists and chains take 10% respectively and are increasing their share, but independent outlets are fast losing their hold on their 25% share.

Since 1968, ownership of hairdryers has increased from 50% to 54% in 1970, to the 1973 figure of 61%, but what has altered more dramatically has been the distribution of different ownerships by brands. While Morphy Richards remains the clear leader slicing over one-third of the market, the nearest competitor being Pifco, both these brands have suffered over the years in the face of competition from Ronson, Philips, Moulinex, Hoover and Boots.

Breakdown by class and age shows that there are differences in preferences among women for the different hair dryer types. The table model is popular among the upper-class and middle-aged women and the hood model among the under-24 age group. The general trend to the simpler, cheaper models is most noted among the lower socio-economic and older age groups. In general, the hand model has declined somewhat in importance, despite the fact that many new designs have been introduced. The table model, conversely, has increased from holding a 2% share of the market in 1966 to a 7% share on all appliances owned in 1973. With increasing affluence, the hood variety has increased in popularity from 8% in 1966 to the 1973 figure of 17%.

With heated hair rollers, demand may well be set less fair than with hair dryers. Indications are that the boom period has eased off and demand correspondingly suffered. Nevertheless, the original manufacturers— Carmen Curlers—have maintained a clear lead in the market and account for 62% of ownership while Boots, the most successful competitor, has about 10%[16]. Women acquired most of their heated hair rollers during the middle 1960s compared to hair dryers, of which nearly one-fifth of those in use today were acquired before 1960. Only 15% of hair dryers and 16% of hair rollers were bought in 1972 and 1973.

Overall, 18% of households own a set of heated rollers although, as with hair dryers, the ownership levels are higher in the upper socio-economic groups. While one in three upper-class households own them, less than one in seven of lower-class households do.

Age comparison can also be made between the two products. The peak in ownership for hairdryers among the age groups is in the 35–44 age group, the group with the lowest ownership of heated hair rollers. Generally, however, hair rollers are much favoured by young people with a secondary, surprising peak in ownership among the 55–64 group who may find a fond resemblance in them to the old heating and crimping irons. Finally, it should be noted that with both rollers and dryers, an important aspect to this market is that of gifts. One survey in 1973 found that of all hairdryers owned, 38% were acquired as a gift while the corresponding figure for heated rollers was 34% [14].

Hair Ornaments and Attachments

According to a trade paper [13], the hair ornamentation market (excluding wigs) has been described as the 'fastest growing sector of the total hair-care field' and by another as 'a high profit line with a very fast turnover'. The market, which covers hair bands, slides, rollers, grips, combs and ponytail holders for women and girls, is now worth about £3 million, about 25% of the total hair-care market. Of this, about 40% is taken up by private brands, Boots and Woolworth in particular, while the remaining 60% is controlled by six main branded ranges.

A product manager in the market notes that in the late 1960s hair ornamentation represented 12% of the total hair-care market. Over five years it has increased by £2·15 million (360%) which is, on average, a growth rate of 72% per annum. Over this period it is the chemist in particular who has benefited. In the late 1960s the chemists (excluding Boots) took 30% of the market (£0·2 million) which by 1973 had risen to 63% (£1·7 million). Interest in this market has been attributed to an upsurge in hair fashion generally, but the more important factor is probably the use of attractive floor stands in self-help displays. Newey Goodman who hold the largest share of this field, 41% compared to the 25% of Lady Jane, say that the 'look of the article is important to them' and as a matter of policy they use a white gloss card with gold and black design for some of their ornaments 'so as not to clash with the bright colour of the product'.

The other side to the hair ornament market is that of the wig and the hair-piece. Usership of these products is much higher than is popularly supposed and is regionally variable. For instance, nationally, one woman in 20 owns more than three wigs whereas in the Midlands only one in 100 owns this many. Women in Wales and the South West are the greatest purchasers of wigs. Nevertheless, ownership of wigs does not always tally with usage. Whereas Midlands wig owners are less prolific purchasers, only one Midlands woman in five owns a full wig, they are more likely to wear them once purchased. Nationally, 12% of women wear their wig once a month but in the Midlands 4% of women wear them every day. It is the woman in the South East who seems to like her purchase the least; the purchaser in this area is more likely than average to throw it in a drawer and forget it. In retail terms, only 25% of wigs are now bought in salons and 7% in 'wig' boutiques; it is the large chain stores with large displays and trying-on areas which are expanding their sales.

CONCLUSION TO PART IV

The woman who buys for herself is a creature visibly swelling in strength and financial integrity, and represents for marketing one of those very few areas which can only grow more viable with the coming years. With increased social and political emancipation, better contraception and child-care facilities, more women will work, and work longer, expect to be paid more and tend to resist roles which curtail financial freedom. In evolutionary terms, this can bring enormous benefits to women. In financial terms, the marketer, cheerfully stoking the markets she patronises, can hardly complain.

Yet, within this situation we find the seeds of an interesting irony. On the one hand, the markets for women's personal expenditure, that is, those which appeal to the woman as woman, can only grow stronger with economic liberation and the curtailment of traditional roles. On the other hand, marketers for decades have adopted as their *raison d'être* the depiction and maintenance of women in economically powerless and fully traditional roles, that is woman as dependent, as housewife, mother, wife and domestic.

In the past, marketers could neatly sidestep this contradiction in policy, to appeal to woman as woman, or woman as altruist, by claiming that the two markets were mutually exclusive. Woman bought as woman until she married and 'settled down' when she sublimated the personalised aspect in favour of buying for the family, hearth and home. There were really two main markets, two types of women, no problem. But all this has changed. Woman can now buy as woman and as any other role *at the same time*. The separateness is blurring, the markets crossing, the female consumer no longer obligingly classifies herself into two identifiable segments. The housewife will be a car buyer and cigar smoker, the career woman will be a detergent and nappy purchaser, the mother will want to buy investment, sparking plugs and cosmetics.

The question is, can the marketer cope with this new creation, this paragon which breaks market barriers and denies categorisation? Or is he so stuck with his old, stereotypical markets that only a major re-formulation of his attitude to women will help? Either way, the woman buying for herself will be something the marketer should watch carefully. On all the evidence she is working by fewer sex stereotypical rules than he is and, it seems, is leaving him behind.

REFERENCES

1. 'The Clothing Market', IPC Publications Ltd (1973). quoted in the *Financial Times* (13 July 1973).

2. Target Group Index. BMRB (1973); National Income and Expenditure HMSO (1973); 'Men's Outerwear', *Retail Business*. 150 (August 1970).
3. 'The Market for Women's Dresses in the UK', *Retail Business*, 186 (August 1973), 'Children's Clothing—Outerwear', *Retail Business*, 180 (February 1973).
4. 'A Profile of the Women's Clothing Market in Britain'. Market Research Great Britain, Vol. 8(7) (1973).
   '. . . and Clothing', Market Research Great Britain (January 1975), p. 22.
   National Income and Expenditure. HMSO.
   Retail Business Nos. 112, 121 and 177.
   Target Group Index (1972, 1973), BMRB.
   The *Financial Times* (29 November 1972), reporting on the Report of the Economic Development Committee for the Clothing Industry (1971).
   Eurometer estimates of the value and volume of the clothing market in Great Britain (2) (11 April 1975).
   'The Women's Trouser Market', *Retail Business*, 177 (November 1972).
5. 'The UK Market for Socks and Stockings', *Retail Business*, 147 (May 1970). *Retail Business*, 112.
6. Marketing Review in *Retail Business* (July-December 1969–70).
7. The *Grocer* (12 August 1972).
8. Fred Reynolds and William R. Darden, 'Why the Midi Failed', *Journal of Advertising Research*, Vol. 12(4) (August 1972), pp. 39–44.
9. 'A Fashionable Consideration', *Euro-Monitor* (October 1973), pp. 11–20. and *Euro-Monitor Review* VII (2) (April 1975).
10. Trevor Millum, *Images of Women: Advertising in Women's Magazines*, Chatto and Windus (1974).
11. 'Hairdressers'. *Retail Business*, 195 (May 1974).
12. 'The Home Hair Care Market', *Retail Business* 207 (May 1975).
13. 'Hair Ornaments—Fast Selling, Fast Growing'. Supplement to *Chemist and Druggist* (May 1973).
14. 'Home Hair Care Appliances', Market Research Great Britain (1973).
15. *Retail Business*, 154 (December 1970), Marketing Review, p. 4.
16. 'Mrs Britain and her Hair', *Hairdressers Journal* (22 September 1972).
   The Cosmetics and Toiletries Survey, IPC Publications Ltd (1971–2).
   'Home Hairdressing—A source of profit', Supplement to the *Chemist and Druggist* (28 June 1969).
   'Salon Goldfield', *Hairdressers Journal* (13 October 1972).
   'Home Hair-Care Appliances', Market Research Great Britain (1973).
   Radio and Electrical Retailing (October 1972).
   Electrical and Electronic Trader (21 April 1972).
   'Hair Ornaments: Fast Selling, Fast Growing'. Supplement to the *Chemist and Druggist* (May 1973).

PART V

Women, Media and Media-woman

Communicating to the female consumer is a business in its own right. The professional communicators, the agencies with their design and copy teams, account directors and managers, creative heads, media buyers and planners are all working to make sure that the buying message goes faithfully not only to the female consumer but the right female consumer, at the right time and in the right place.

Women and media are strange bedfellows. The relationship is both ascetic and professional with its JICTAR ratings, its weighted, exposure levels, its costs per thousand, its frequency/expenditure patterns while at the same time it is emotive, manipulative, coercive and ingratiating. The communication is at two levels, mechanical and personal.

Noting the mechanical part is one of observation. Which women are exposed to which medium in what proportion and in what particular patterns? The first part of the section will do this.

The personal part of the communication is not so simple. We are living in a time of dynamic sex-role perceptions and social change. We cannot simply observe the messages and images that the advertiser is sending to the female consumer and make some functional analysis of their nature; re-define and politely re-state the *status quo*. Along with the simple 'when?' 'where?' and 'how much?' of women's exposure to media we must also look carefully at the 'what?' and the 'how?' of the interaction. What, for example, is the advertiser saying to the woman along with his suggestion about the product? What is he telling her about herself, about the place of women, about her life-style, her potential, her norms? How, for example, is he saying this: by example or by prescription? How are the images and messages he creates a function simply of the selling message, the products' attributes, and how much his interpretation of a wider, more amorphous set of cultural assumptions?

Guides to the marketing content of the advertisements have been covered in the previous four sections. This, if you like, has been the statement of the ground-rules, the raw materials. Here we shall start to take a more critical look at the communicative side to the female consumer and marketer/advertiser interaction, and note to what extent the interaction veers from business policy into the more treacherous and controversial areas of socio-cultural and psychological influence. In other words, we see woman, not only as consumer, housewife, mother, careerist and purchaser but also simply in the context of woman as woman. First, however, we shall make note of the extent to which women are exposed to media and the commercials and advertisements thereby subsumed. The structure of these advertisements will come later.

14.   Women and Media

Women are exposed to virtually every medium that men are—sometimes a lot less, as in the case of certain newspapers: sometimes much the same as with television and sometimes considerably more, as with women's magazines. As Table 14:1 illustrates, exposure to media categories has been found to be inclusive of 70% of women in the case of a national daily paper, and 27% in listening to Radio Luxembourg. This table also shows, for example, that 12% more men than women read a national daily paper, both watch television to a similar degree (94% of men and 93% of women although this balance fluctuates), while between 25 and 40% more women than men read women's magazines.

Table 14:1   Media Categories as a Vehicle for Advertising to Women

Percentage of men and women who read any	Men	Women
National daily paper	82	70
National Sunday paper	89	84
Evening newspaper	51	46
Newspaper colour supplement	23	18
General weekly magazine	59	55
General monthly magazine	54	36
Women's weekly magazine	20	61
Women's monthly magazine	27	54
% of men and women who ever view TV	94	93
Ever go to the cinema	55	50
Ever listen to Radio Luxembourg	34	27

Source: National Readership Survey (January-December 1973).

ADVERTISING BY PRODUCT CATEGORIES (FEMALE-DOMINATED PURCHASES)

Advertising expenditure is particularly impressive on those products which are bought principally by women, that is (using product groupings from MEAL), food, toiletries, clothing and household goods (*see* Tables 14:2 and 14:3). Food, which is the most frequently purchased product by women, is also the largest category of advertising expenditure, equalling that of financial, motor, tobacco, and publishing advertising combined.

Table 14:2   Advertising Expenditure of certain Product Groups

Product group	Percentage of all advertising expenditure	Placing in list of 23 product categories
Food	19·1	1
Retail and mail order	10·9	2
Household stores	7·0	3
Toiletries and cosmetics	7·0	3
Household appliances	3·1	12
Household equipment	3·7	10
Pharmaceutical	3·1	12
Wearing apparel	2·2	15
TOTAL	56·1	

Source: MEAL Statistics (1973).

Each of these product categories will have a different balance of expenditure through television and press (*see* Table 14:3). Food and household stores are, for example, principally advertised through the television while household appliances and equipment, and retail and mail order use the press, for preference.

Table 14:3   Advertising Expenditure through Press and Television

Product group	Total (Press and TV) (£)	(%)	Television (£)	(%)	Press (£)	(%)
Food	89.159,000	100	78,605.000	88	10.554,000	12
Retail and mail order	50.672,000	100	7,545.000	15	43.127,000	85
Household stores	32.655,000	100	28.078	86	4.578,000	14
Toiletries and cosmetics	32.628,000	100	21,990.000	67	10.638,000	33
Household appliances	14.460,000	100	6,188.000	43	8.272,000	57
Household equipment	17.230,000	100	5,537.000	32	11.693,000	68
Pharmaceutical	14.729,000	100	7,469.000	52	6.810,000	48
Wearing apparel	10.049,000	100	3,592.000	36	6.457,000	64
TOTAL	261.582,000		159,004.000		153.992,000	

Source: MEAL Statistics (1973).

WOMEN AS MEDIA AUDIENCES

Television

The chief leisure activity for both men and women is watching television[1]:

23% of both sexes claim it is their most important leisure category. Nevertheless, given this homogeneity, there are considerable differences in interest and exposure within different age and socio-economic groups, particularly for women.

Women aged 19–22, for example, prefer to put television in fourth place after participative sports, crafts and hobbies, excursions and walks; single women of 23–30 put it in a similar order of priorities but married women of 23–30 years put it into second place after crafts and hobbies. As more and more children arrive then television becomes more important so that, as a general rule, the television as diversion does not achieve any significance in a woman's life until she reaches about 23–30 years, is married and starting to have children, that is, enters strongly into the 'housewife' category. Housewives, in fact, are among some of the heaviest television viewers. Of all housewives, 26% have claimed to be heavy television watchers compared to 23% medium-heavy and 9% light. In comparison 22% of men watch heavily, 22% medium-heavy and 15% claim to be light viewers (Table 14:4).

Table 14:4   Intensity of Viewing ITV

	Adults (41·2m) (%)	Men (19·7m) (%)	Women (21·5m) (%)	Women 15–24 (3·8m) (%)	Housewives (18·4m) (%)
Heavy	22	18	25	25	26
Medium-heavy	22	22	22	20	23
Medium	22	22	21	21	21
Light-medium	16	18	15	16	14
Light	12	15	10	12	9
Never	6	5	7	5	7
Total	100	100	100	100	100

* For greater detail see NRS, JICTAR Reports, BBTA Bulletins etc.
Source: National Readership Survey (January–December 1973).

Seasonally, women (over 15 years) watch less in August (14·7 hours on average) than in February (16·7 hours) with men of a similar age watching less but with more differentiation between the two seasons (10·0 hours compared to 14·7). This data, however, while interesting, should be treated with care since this type of broad grouping does not refer only to adult men and housewives but also to the teenage group who do not watch as much television as adults.

Regionally, (using standard ITV regions), London has 7,390,000 women viewers and the Midlands 4,739,000 compared to the 295,000 in the Border region and 839,000 in the North East. The North East includes most women in the 0–15 age groups, while London has most of those in the 25–44 age group (by a very marginal difference) while the greatest proportion of housewives with children are found in the Ulster, North East. Border, and Central Scotland areas.

In terms of coverage, the National Readership Survey estimates television will cover 93% of all women: the remaining 7% includes those who have no television set for ITV, those who say they never watch television and those who never watch ITV. JICTAR estimates[2] that the archetypal television viewer is a 40-year-old housewife whose husband is a skilled, manual worker.

Nevertheless, this coverage figure will not measure attention factors and although women are frequently exposed to television this will not guarantee careful concentration on commercials. According to IPC, 31% of women viewers are doing, or looking at other things while the commercials are on which, as the report notes, makes these commercials 'an expensive sound track'. In contrast, 80% of these women will give all their attention to women's magazines with average page traffic scores of 90%.

How much influence does the mother have in choice of television programme or channel? Wand (1969)[3] has noted that the success of the individual in viewing his/her choice was related to his/her role in the family. Where the mother had a subordinate role then her viewing preferences tended to come relatively further down the list compared to other family members. On average, however, in a situation of choice conflict between parents, this will be resolved by the dominant choice of the mother. In conflicts between the children, however, the parents will have roughly equal say in the outcome except in families with older children where the mother seems to withdraw from the conflict and leaves the resolution of programme and channel choice to the rest of the family.

Cinema

The frequency of cinema visiting is fairly similar between samples of men and women for the obvious reason that most frequenters of cinemas go in couples. If anything, men are slightly more likely to go to the cinema alone and so this lifts the male proportion of all cinema going (regular, occasional, infrequent, never) to slightly above that of women.

This is not a very popular medium; 48% of all adults say that they 'never' go to the cinema and 40% say they go 'infrequently'. Women are more likely to go 'never' or 'infrequently' than men and this is particularly so in the case of housewives, 56% of whom 'never' go and only 1% go 'frequently'. Of the women's sample, the most regular cinema frequenters are those in the 15–24 age group who go 'occasionally' and 'regularly' in 38% of cases, the highest proportion of all groups, male and female.

In numerical terms, the National Readership Survey estimates that of the 11 million women over 15 recorded as cinema-goers by the survey in 1972–3. about one-third were aged 15–24. Only 2¼ million women go to the cinema at least once a month. In terms of class. women in the C1 category are most likely of all the classes to go 'once a month', those in the AB category most often in the 'once a year' category. Those in the ABC1 category go most often 'once a quarter' and those in the DE category are the most likely 'never to go at all' (1972)[4].

Commercial Radio (Radio Luxembourg)

There is little data on this medium which is broken down into sex differences. Nevertheless, the National Readership survey in 1973, estimated that women were more likely 'never' to listen to Radio Luxembourg than men (73% compared to 66%) and housewives, in particular, do not seem to favour this medium (79% never listen to it at all). On the other hand, it is women in the 15−24 age group who are the most 'regular' listeners, with 35% of them listening 'occasionally' and only 38% 'never'. As yet, the effects of local and commercial radio on the housewife listener are relatively unknown quantities.

Giveaway Magazines and Free Sheets

The 'giveaway' magazine is a peculiar medium, neither below-the-line nor in the full category of direct media, such as press. Yet its audience is principally the young employed woman in the larger conurbations, and its function primarily one of advertising. These publications are financed largely by advertisers and are handed to women in the street or through the subway systems. They are usually in the magazine format with some editorial matter, some 'advice' and lots of advertisements.

In 1973 there were three principals among these magazines which appealed to the under-35 working girls. In London, the biggest (in 1973) was *Miss London Weekly* (the first of them and now nearly six years old). Then there was *Girl About Town* and *Sophisticat,* the latter launched in April 1973 as a partner for *Memo,* a magazine for typists and secretaries. *Miss London* and *Girl About Town* claim circulations of 100,000 each, and *Sophisticat* 80,000. They all have basically the same image, with *Girl About Town* the most trendy. The advertisements range from those for products, holidays and special offers to those for jobs. The other side of this market is that for free sheets. These are single pages or small papers which contain nothing but advertisements, are paid for by the advertisers and distributed free to households. Housewives, rather than the young employed woman, are the principal market for these. The usefulness of these sheets is dubious and there is little research evidence on their sales effectiveness. Nevertheless, research in the Tyneside area among housewives in 1971−2 showed that the average noting score for advertisements in the *Tyneside Champion,* a free sheet, was 56·7% against 49·6% in the *Newcastle Evening Chronicle,* a paid-for evening newspaper[5].

Housewife or career girl, the markets for these free sheets and giveaway magazines are a good source of advertising revenue. The Advertising Association estimated that the revenue from these free sheets in 1972 was £3 million.

By 1973, estimates were that this would have risen to at least £4·5 million
with a total circulation of about five million (1973)[5].

Press

1. Newspapers.   Contrary to popular belief, women do not read newspapers
all that less frequently than men. In 1972, the National Readership Survey
noted that 70% of women read a national daily paper compared to 82%
of men, 84% read a national Sunday paper compared to 89% of men,

Table 14:5   National Press: newspapers and colour supplements

Group and Publication	Circulation ('000) July-December 1973	Adults	Men	Women	Housewives
'Average issue' readership (%)					
NATIONAL DAILIES					
Daily Express	3,290·1	23	26	19	19
Daily Mail*	1,729·7	13	14	11	11
Daily Mirror	4,291·3	33	38	29	27
Daily Telegraph	1,419·5	9	10	7	7
Financial Times	194·3	2	3	1	1
Guardian	345·8	3	3	2	2
Daily Record	578·8	4	5	4	4
Sun	2,966·3	26	33	20	19
The Times	344·8	3	3	2	2
LONDON EVENINGS					
Evening News	818·8	6	7	5	5
Evening Standard	492·1	4	4	3	3
NATIONAL SUNDAYS					
News of the World	5,943·9	39	42	35	35
Observer	795·0	7	7	6	6
Sunday People	4,423·5	32	34	30	29
Sunday Express	4,096·1	26	28	25	25
Sunday Mirror	4,543·2	33	36	30	29
Sunday Telegraph	774·8	5	6	5	5
Sunday Times	1,516·3	10	11	9	9
Sunday Mail	757·0	6	6	6	5
Sunday Post	Over 1,000·0	11	11	12	12
NEWSPAPER SUPPLEMENTS					
Observer	795·0	8	9	7	6
Sunday Times	1,516·3	11	13	10	9
Telegraph+	1,497·6	10	12	8	8

*Average issue circulation (January–June 1973).
Sources: Rates: *British Rate and Data* (March 1974) and other announcements of changes.
Readership figures: National Readership Survey, (January-December 1973).
All circulations based on ABC figures, except those marked+ (audited net sales).
For greater detail on audience data, see NRS and publishers' surveys.

46% an evening newspaper compared to 51% of men and 18% a colour supplement compared to 23% of men. Furthermore, in the 24-million total circulation sales of Sunday newspapers, there were 18 million women readers and their average consumption was 1·3 copies each compared with 1·0 copies each of the national daily morning newspapers which had a total of 15 million women readers. In the case of evening newspapers, the average readership by women is about 46% but there is considerable fluctuation by area, from 37% in London and the South East, to 69% in the Midlands and 57% in the North.

Taking each category individually, women read four daily papers in particular. The order and penetration is similar for both 'all women' and 'housewives' (*see* Table 14:5). The favourite is the *Daily Mirror* followed, in order, by the *Sun,* the *Daily Express* and the *Daily Mail.* Of the Sunday papers, women prefer the *News of the World* (which attracts more women readers than *Woman* magazine), followed by the *Sunday People* and the *Sunday Mirror* equally, then the *Sunday Express* and the *Sunday Post.* According to a recent survey by the *Sunday People,* they reckon to attract one million mothers every week. If there are any preferences for the Sunday supplements, the *Sunday Times* is marginally the favourite with women.

General magazines.   The most important sector of the general magazine market is that which encompasses the two programme magazines, the *Radio Times* and *TV Times.* In December 1973 the circulation of the *Radio Times* was 4,046.000 and this was divided equally between men (27%), women (28%) and housewives (27%). A similar pattern occurs with the *TV Times* although 'all women' have a marginal preference for it (30%) compared to men (28%) and housewives (29%). (These are 'average issue' readership figures.) Of the other general interest magazines—women prefer the *Weekly News* and *Weekend* in that order, followed by *New Reveille* and *Tit-Bits* (*see* Table 14:6).

Of the general monthly magazines (those above were 'weekly' issues), women and housewives prefer only the *Do-it-Yourself* magazine and the *Practical Householder* to any great extent, although 23% of 'women' and 'housewives', compared to 28%, of men like to read the *Reader's Digest.* Of the more female-orientated magazines in this sector, which are not specifically women's magazines, the most significant one is probably *Slimming* on which readers spent £249.000 in 1972.

Women's magazines.   The women's magazine market is probably the single most important sector of advertising media for women. While women may report reading other printed media and are exposed to television and cinema, it is with women's magazines that we find the highest attention factor. The page traffic, as we have already noted, is particularly high at around 90% with women giving their full attention to the magazine in at least

Table 14:6 Most Popular General Magazines

Group and Publication	Circulation ('000) July-Dec. 1973	'Average issue' readership (%) (selected magazines)			
		Adults	Men	Women	Housewives
GENERAL WEEKLIES					
Radio Times	4,046·1	28	27	28	27
New Reveille	717·5	9	10	8	8
Tit-Bits	548·0	7	8	6	6
TV Times	3,915·0	29	28	30	29
Weekend	1,034·9	12	13	12	11
Weekly News	1,300·1	12	11	12	12
GENERAL MONTHLIES					
Film Review	112·4	4	4	3	2
Car Mechanics	187·9	6	11	2	2
Do-it-Yourself	146·0	8	11	6	6
Practical Householder	157·8	6	8	4	4
Practical Motorist	165·4	7	12	2	2
Reader's Digest	1,605·7	25	28	23	23

Source: *IPC Consumer Marketing Manual* (1974).

80% of instances. It is a market which seems infinitely capable of fragmentation and new entrants on the market sink or swim in a seemingly random manner.

The basic formats of these magazines have not changed much since the last century and White (1970)[6] and Frankl (1974)[7] have described in considerable and painstaking detail both the evolution of these magazines and the extent to which they tend to reflect the changing social perceptions of women. Both works note that there are stirrings in the air of these journals and the purely domestic image has both given way to a more wordly approach in existing magazines and spawned a host of new ones which reflect the tastes of the 'new woman', intellectually, as used to be with *Nova*, sexually with *Cosmopolitan,* and in terms of total feminism with *Spare Rib.* Side by side. we find variety and homogeneity. Each magazine is that much different. has that much varied a market and is that slightly different in approach, yet they are all moving away from stereotypes and more into a vast. middle area wherein abortion mixes uneasily with recipes; tips for working women with babies' illnesses; and problems of the educational and political system with fashion. Only magazines such as *Woman's Realm* and *Spare Rib* hold faithfully onto a fairly undiluted version of the female potential. domestic and emancipated. Certainly, advertisers should keep a careful watch on the content of the magazines because times. in editorial terms, are changing, and there is special irony in the fact that we often find in magazine advertisements a more stereotypical and reactionary attitude towards women than the text of the magazine would reflect. In *Nova*, for example, there were occasions when the coy and frilly tone of the advertisements leapt into farcical relief against an acerbic article on some aspect of the Women's Movement.

Nevertheless, the publishers need the advertisers as much as vice versa and in 1973 it was estimated that women's magazine publishers rely on advertising for about 55% of their revenue and for most of their profits. Advertisers' expenditure on women's magazines is currently about £30 million per annum (1973). Of this, 15% is paid to advertising agencies as commission and the balance of £25·5 million is the revenue that publishers receive[9]. A recent report on women's magazines in *Retail Business* (1973) noted that this revenue for women's magazines is currently under extra pressure from television from two fronts. Colour television is now in 2% of households and growing fast (colour was something that magazines always used as an edge over television), and the extra broadcasting hours for television and /or local radio have an almost exclusively female audience[8].

The products which benefit most from the women's magazines market are those in the food, toiletries and cosmetics, clothes and household equipment markets, although with the weekly magazines it is the first two product categories which are most important (*see* Table 14:7) since the long lead-time of the monthlies makes it difficult to plan for promotion of product changes or innovations. Conversely, the monthlies are more important for the equipment sector where market changes are slower. Of the other products, retail and mail order firms reach most of their important female customers through the weeklies, while monthlies are preferred for drink products.

Table 14:7   Percentage of Revenue Derived from Different Categories of Consumer Products

	Weekly Magazines	Monthly Magazines	All Women's Magazines
Food	27	16	23
Toiletries and cosmetics	26	18	19
Clothes	9	13	10
Household equipment	5	15	9
Retail and mail order	9	5	7
Pharmaceutical	7	5	6
Household stores	6	4	5
Tobacco	7	2	5
Household appliances	3	5	4
Drink	2	4	3
Other	2	4	3
ALL PRODUCTS	100	100	100

Source: Trade Estimates quoted in *Retail Business* (January 1973)[9].

Taking the magazines in more detail, there are about 30 regularly published and nationally distributed women's magazines in this country, including the 'story romance' section which is one of the fastest growing areas and now accounts for 8% of all women's magazine consumer expenditure. IPC dominates the publishing of these magazines with 68% of the consumer expenditure. with D. C. Thompson at 17%. None of the others accounts for much above 5% of the copies sold.

In terms of expenditure per consumer, women spent £34·5 on magazines in 1971, a sum which has been growing steadily since 1966 at 6% per annum. The number of copies sold, however, has fallen by an average of 2% per annum. The women's weeklies still claim the largest single part of expenditure on women's titles (68%) but have suffered a loss in circulation of 11% in five years.

Although, in absolute terms. the main part of the market growth in the last five years has come from the magazines for the adult woman (£5·7 million in five years) the largest percentage growth has been shown by young women's titles (68% in five years), and reflects the trend we have already noted to catch the prosperous and unattached female market. In 1971, this latter group took 20% of all money spent on magazines by adult and young women compared with 14% six years before. Between 1966 and 1971. £2·5 million extra consumer expenditure was attracted by new young women's titles compared with £1·2 million from new adult women's titles. The largest sector growth of all, however, has been that in the romance and 'real life' stories which have made a 128% increase between 1966 and 1971[8].

Women's weekly magazines.   This is the most important group accounting for 68% of all expenditure on women's titles. The top circulating paper in this category is *Woman* followed by *Woman's Weekly* and *Woman's Own (see* Table 14:8). Nevertheless, these circulation figures do not tell the whole story since readership figures may be much higher. Estimates from a *Retail Business* report in 1973 put the readership of *Woman* at 6,282,000 (compared to the circulation of 1,875,700), *Woman's Own* at 5,690,000 (1,691,400), *Woman's Weekly* at 4,092,000 (1,784,600), *Woman's Realm* at 5,852,000 (962,100). *My Weekly* at 4,092,000 (885,900) and *People's Friend* at 1,542,000 (705,700). The ratio of readership to circulation varies between 3:1 and 2:1[8].

Table 14:8   Most Popular Women's Magazines

WOMEN'S WEEKLIES	*Circulation*	*Women*	*W15–24*	*W25–34*	*Housewives*
My Weekly	885·9	13	12	11	14
People's Friend	705·6	9	5	6	9
Woman	1,875·7	30	38	33	29
Woman's Own	1,691·4	30	37	31	29
Woman's Realm	962·1	19	19	19	19
Woman's Weekly	1,784·6	22	18	18	22

Source: *IPC Consumer Marketing Manual* (1974).

The weekly sector of the market contains the magazines which have traditionally tended to fall more into the 'domestic' category, the prime example being *Woman's Weekly*. In November 1971 [9] it was celebrating 60 years in publishing and over a five-year period it had been the only magazine to put on substantial growth, gaining a 317.000 circulation between 1966 and 1969. The editor likens the readership to a club and notes that the basic ingredients are still two serials, a story, several knitting patterns, recipes, a little beauty and fashion and two advice columns. 'The models are pretty and comfortable and the food is basic rather than exotic.' Advertisers, however, have to watch their step, 'because of the trust our readers have in us'.

Nevertheless, despite a certain homogeneity, these domestic magazines, as with all women's magazines, have slightly different tones and readerships. *Woman* and *Woman's Own* cater more for the woman as woman and gives a great deal of information, disturbing true-life stories and special features; they have a worldly air which is strengthening every year. *Woman's Weekly* and *Woman's Realm* are both more directed at the woman as housewife, with the former, as we have noted, more extreme in its homeliness. *My Weekly* and *People's Friend* are strongly biased toward Scotland and the North, and appeal particularly to older women and the lower socio-economic groups.

Women's monthly magazines.   This market tends to be more inhomogeneous than the weekly one, further up-market, and orientated towards work rather than the home (*see* Table 14:9).

Table 14:9   Selected Women's Monthly Magazines 1973

SELECTED WOMEN'S MONTHLIES

	Circulation '000s	Women	Women 15–24	Women 25–34	Housewives
Argus Women's Group	484·6	14	28	18	13
Family Circle	1,050·2	18	23	28	18
Good Housekeeping	284·2	12	11	12	12
Homes and Gardens	193·5	7	6	8	8
Honey	210·6	5	16	5	4
Ideal Home	185·5	10	10	12	10
She	326·6	8	11	13	8
True Magazine	223·9	7	15	9	6
True Romances	179·7	10	20	13	9
True Story	207·7	10	18	12	9
Woman and Home	740·6	16	12	15	17
Woman's Journal	180·2	5	4	4	5

Source: *IPC Consumer Marketing Manual* (1974).

Sixteen per cent of female magazine expenditure goes on titles in this group and it contains the important new development of the supermarket magazines. *Family Circle* and *Living*. These two papers have been notable publishing successes and over eight years have been distributed entirely through supermarkets and grocery shops. *Family Circle,* for example, takes a circulation of 1.050,200 which puts it well into the lead in the women's monthlies. Two-thirds of the readers of these supermarket magazines are under the age of 44.

The other women's monthly magazines can be sub-divided as follows:

Fashion magazines ('Vogue', 'Harpers/Queen').   This is exemplified by *Vogue* and is altogether a luxury, up-market part of the magazine market for women. Most women's monthly magazines have duplicated readership. This can range from 4 to 12 readers per copy. but *Vogue* romps home at 21, the highest of the lot. It is more of a luxury purchase than a magazine and is usually kept and passed on, rarely just thrown away. Nevertheless, despite its prestige, this group carries only 3% of spending on women's titles.

Home/interior design ('Ideal Home and Gardening', 'Homes & Gardens'). These are up-market too. They account for 4% of consumer expenditure on women's magazines, and *Homes & Gardens* is the highest to circulate in this group at 187,000 copies per issue. Readership per copy again averages out high at about 10 per copy. *Retail Business* notes that this is the segment most likely to be affected by economic conditions.

Craft magazines ('Pins and Needles', 'Stitchcraft', 'Golden Hands').   These account for 3% of consumer expenditure in women's titles and represent an expanding area. They have an older profile (most of their readers are over 45) and a large proportion of readers from the C2DE classes.

General interest magazines for young women ('Honey', 'Mirabelle').   These have a high fashion and beauty content and reflect the prosperous younger market with a somewhat South-East tone. *Honey* age profile is slightly higher than *19* and also has a high male readership. Women over 34 make up half the readers of *Honey*. The cheaper, young, 'pop' market is catered for by magazines such as *Mirabelle*, which has changed its emphasis on cartoon love stories to features on pop stars and fashion. It is significant that those women who read *Girl's Crystal* and *School Friend* just 7–10 years ago are paralled by readers of *Mirabelle* today, while the old *Mirabelle* readers would now read *19* and *Honey*. Official readership figures today do not include those under 15 but there is no doubt that readership penetration for this age group is significant. As a group, this young women's sector carries 12% of expenditure on women's titles. (Fairly detailed analyses of the readership of these magazines can be obtained from Adams (1971)[11]; White (1970)[6]; and from IPC.)

As a conclusion, it is interesting to note that the popularity of the woman's magazine for the female consumer market is a fairly consistent international phenomenon. In Germany, for instance, the female and parental interest magazines such as *Brigitte* and *Ettern* cover 12% and 10% of the population respectively, figures which are only exceeded by the television and radio magazines, *Horzu* and *TV Horen und Sehen* (30% and 12% respectively). These women's magazines also take the bulk of food, toiletry and household advertising.

In a special report on women's magazines in Germany (1974)[10] it was noted that the marketing prospects for women's magazines, and the editorial and advertisement style were changing away from the traditional housewife image:

> Increasingly, young German women receive a better education and are offered more chances for professional and other activities than previous generations. More young married women continue to pursue their career instead of becoming full-time housewives.

Brigitte, the top women's magazine in Germany in 1973 published a 'Frauentyplogie' based on 4,000 interviews. This gave a breakdown of Germany's 14·87 million female magazine readers (14–49 years). These were categorised into:

Traditional housewife	19%
Intelligent, active woman	14%
Old-fashioned modest woman	12%
Aspiring but not accomplished lady	12%
Well-groomed but frustrated woman (!) |sic|	12%
Smart career girl	10%
Fashionable woman, who loves to improvise	10%

The report notes that 'in the future, existing women's magazines would be well advised not to miss emancipatory trends. The classical women's magazines have started to extend their contents to brief news on economics, legal, social and education issues. This type of information is still given in small doses but will certainly become more prominent in the next few years.'

It would be wise for the marketer to keep a good eye on what is happening in the German women's market because it is here that many of the stronger trends in behaviour of the modern female consumer are well highlighted, including employment, attitudes to equal pay and rights, possession of household consumer durables and shifts in the editorial and advertisement content of the women's media. Nevertheless, shifting our attention back to Britain and given the set of observations on women's exposure to all media types, of which television and women's magazines emerge as the most important in reaching the female consumer, we can now concentrate specifically and critically on the advertisement itself.

REFERENCES

1. *See* DES Survey 'Planning For Leisure' (1969).
2. Frank Jefkins. *Advertising Today,* International Text Book Company (1972).
3. Barbara Wand 1969. 'Television Viewing and Family Choice Differences', *Public Opinion Quarterly* 32 (1968–9), pp. 84–94.
4. 'The Cinema Industry', *Retail Business,* 177 (November 1972) and the *IPC Consumer Marketing Manual* (1974).
5. Michael Goldman, 'The Market for Free Sheets and Giveaway Magazines'. *Advertising Quarterly* (Autumn 1973), p. 23.
6. Cynthia L. White, *Women's Magazines: 1693–1968,* Michael Joseph (1970).
7. George Frankl, *The Failure of the Sexual Revolution,* Stanmore Press Ltd., Kahn and Averill (1974).
8. 'The Market for Women's Magazines', *Retail Business,* 179 (January 1973): 'Consumer Magazines', *Retail Business,* 187 (September 1973).
9. 'Sixty Years of Happy Endings', *Campaign* (5 November 1971). p. 55.
10. 'Women's Magazines in Germany', *Marketing in Europe,* 135 (February 1974).
11. Adams, *see* chapter 16, ref. 38.

15. Media Woman—the Stereotype

Whom does the female consumer confront in advertising media? Is the woman she sees a relatively truthful replica of herself or some idealised, prescriptive 'media woman' who is the perfect consumer, but an imperfect woman? To what extent does the female consumer see in advertisements, as she does in more general media, an image that bears less resemblance to herself than to the archetypal, masculine, mother/lover fantasy?

The advertiser and marketer cannot be unaware of recent criticism by feminists and civil liberty groups that the female media stereotype is insulting, and that it promotes negative and wasteful social perceptions of 51% of the population. Yet do they know how much empirical and observational data support these contentions? And given these contentions, the extent to which the images are accurate, inaccurate or simply guilty of deception by omission?

There are three good reasons why the advertiser and the marketer should take a closer look at this problem:

1. Similar criticisms preceded major changes which advertisers in America were forced to make in their images of cultural minorities, such as that of the black (which will be discussed in more detail in the next section).

2. As long as media images are inaccurate in their reflections of the woman as person this, by definition, must indicate both inadequate knowledge of the female potential and life style and point to a break in communications between the industry and woman as consumer.

3. The advertiser has some responsibility for such imagery and cannot pretend that a perpetually distorted image will have no effect on those who receive it. Concentrating imagery into one particular group over an extended time-period must have some effect on self-perceptions and self-value.

Knowles (1971)[1], for example, has already documented the acquisiton of 'residual' imagery from media which adults carry from their earlier to their later life, while Hovland, Lumsdaine and Sheffield (1949)[2] and others[3] have all made testimony to the 'sleeper' effect which describes how a single image or idea may have little immediate effect but has a cumulative 'latent' effect on total perceptions. 'Passive learning' from media has also been noted by Krugman and Hartley (1971)[4] to occur best in conditions which compare uncomfortably well to those in which advertisements are viewed; that is, an effortless, calm, non-resistant atmosphere, while Cadet (1967)[5] and Henry (1959)[6] have made eloquent observations on the ability of advertising to create and reinforce self-images, and its inevitable tendency to utilise the stereotype.

Content analyses of advertising media by Millum (1974)[7], Courtney and Lockeretz (1971)[8], Wortzel and Frisbie (1974)[9], and Wagner and Banos (1973)[10] have matched polemical and descriptive work by Bardwick and Schumann (1967)[11], Embree (1970)[12], Florika (1970)[13], Friedan (1963)[14], Grant (1970)[15] and others in their isolation of factors which typify the advertising media stereotype of women. These works have been paralleled by examinations of the image of women in more general media by, for example, Katzman (1972)[16], Kinzer (1973)[17], Long and Simon (1974)[18], and Sternglanz and Serbin (1974)[19].

Whether in general media or in advertising media specifically (and it is useful to compare data from both), the images of woman have been noted to fall into two broad, almost totally contradictory areas, in each of which several associated contentions are subsumed. These could be expressed as follows:

1. A woman's goal in life is to attract and attain a man which subsumes:

(a) Women are always attractive; they are sexual objects.
(b) Women operate alone; they do not relate with other women, only to men.
(c) Men are intelligent; women are not. Men do not like intelligent women (who are 'unfeminine'). Women have inferior ability.

2. Women are ultimately and naturally housewives/wives and mothers which subsumes:

(a) Women do not work outside the home.
(b) When women work outside the home, they are not successful; they do not do 'male' jobs.
(c) Women are happy doing housework; it is satisfying.
(d) Men and women have strictly delineated sex roles and household duties.
(e) Little girls grow up to be housewives, wives and mothers.

To what extent, and how have these contentions been observed in both general and advertising media and, ultimately, how true are they?

A WOMAN'S GOAL IN LIFE IS TO ATTRACT AND ATTAIN A MAN

Women are always attractive; they are sexual objects

Long and Simon (1974)[18] in their review of American television programmes found that women, more so than men, were extremely similar, mainly fortyish or younger and well-groomed. Thirty of the 34 women they noted were thin, tall, attractive and nicely dressed. Men could be fat, short, unattractive and bald. Women were consistently concerned with appearance; they exercised and tried beauty routines. In interaction with men they were seen as sex objects whose bodies and appearance would be judged, commented on and rewarded.

Courtney and Lockeretz (1971)[8] and Wagner and Banos (1973)[10] in their studies of magazine advertisements made a similar finding in that the women in their samples were primarily pictured in a non-working role and when in this state, their function was likely to be 'decorative' and 'recreational', more even than 'family', (*see* Table 15:1). In addition, the incidence of the decorative role had increased between 1970 and 1972 by 25 percentage points.

Table 15:1 Comparison of Non-working Activities of Women shown in General Magazine Advertisements

	1970* per cent of females			1972† per cent of females		
	Alone or with females	With males	Total	Alone or with females	With males	Total
Proportion portrayed* as non-workers	90	92	91	66	90	79
Roles of non-workers						
Family	21	25	23	0	13	8
Recreational	9	64	46	5	55	36
Decorative	70	11	31	95	32	56
TOTAL	100	100	100	100	100	100

* Courtney and Lockeretz[8].
† Follow-up study, January 1972[10].
Source: Wagner and Banos (1973)[10].

Courtney and Lockeretz concluded that 'men regard women primarily as sex objects. [This is indicated] by the plethora of decorative roles assigned to women more than men. The effect is also heightened by showing men and women sharing recreational activities but not work and by showing women in relatively few working roles'.

Kinzer (1973)[17] in her study associated with 'soap operas' found that of the occasions when women were found in the home, which was nearly all the time, 38% of this time they were adjuncts to men and 17% as pure sex objects. Similar conclusions were recorded by Millum in his study of advertisements in women's magazines when he noted that most women were captured in pictures which tended to emphasise 'mannequin' and 'dummy' expressions with the appearance 'sophisticated' rather than 'plain' or 'involved'. He also found that in terms of appearance, women were more likely to be 'sophisticated' and 'naïve' than men who were more often 'plain'. In terms of expression, women most often demonstrated a 'catalogue', that is, 'dummy-like', expression, devoid of personality, while men most often demonstrated a 'thoughtful expression' implying some intellectual processes.

Millum also emphasised this reification of women by a ranking of the roles which he found women to assume in advertisements (*see* Table 15:2). Women were in an object, decorative and service role three times in the first four placings while the males only fulfilled this sense once, that is as a mannequin. The last two roles were insignificant roles for both men and women. Millum also noted the two opposed sets of characteristics most frequently noted for the female actors in these advertisements (*see* Table 15:3).

The 'outward/concrete' role most typified the maternal/practical/house-wife role: the other extreme, 'inward and self-involved' and, to some extent, the neutral position were both highly emphatic of appearance, narcissism, self-involvement, and inactivity, that is, the sex object role.

Table 15:2   Portrayal of Roles of Men and Women in Advertisements

Female	*Male*
1. mannequin	1. husband and father
2. self-involved woman	2. friend/boyfriend
3. wife and mother	3. mannequin
4. hostess	4. specific work roles
5. friendly, carefree girl	5. buffoon
6. career/independent woman	6. he-man hero

Source: Millum (1974)[7].

In all, Millum noted seven *major* roles in which women in British magazines could be conceptualised (*see* Diagram 15:1). Of these seven, the hostess, and mother and wife will be noted later; of the remaining five, four (society hostess, narcissistic woman (1), narcissistic woman (2), mannequin) emphasised a woman's servant and sex object characteristics. Only in the remaining role, the minor one of 'carefree girl', did the woman achieve any activity, freedom of movement and life style and this, Millum notes, is circumscribed by the qualifying feeling that this is a transient period before she 'settles down' into her domestic and sexual capacities. The diagram Millum uses is a

Table 15:3   Typical Portrayal of Women in Advertisements

Inward/self involved	*Outward/Concrete*
attention to self, middle distance	attention to objects, people
tactility to self	tactility
narcissistic, soft expressions	practical maternal expression
domestic/relaxed	functional poses
narcissistic poses	moulded, non-blonde hair
freeflowing blonde hair	informal or office wear
exotic clothes and lack of clothes	uniform
younger	older
sophisticated	plainer

Neutral
attention to reader
no tactility
catalogue, carefree, cool expressions
dummy, carefree, composed poses
shaped hair
exotic informal office wear

Source: Millum (1974)[7].

combination of the 'inward' and 'outward' characteristics already mentioned, and the two sides to the basic roles of women: the social side (the operation of her sexual and domestic role in the world outside the home) and the personal side (the operation of these roles inside the home).

Diagram 15:1

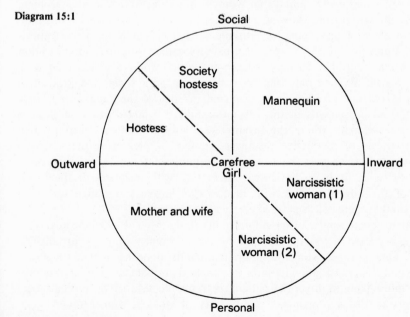

Source: Millum (1974)[7].

Each role implies the following qualities:

Society hostess	Hostess	Mannequin	Mother and wife
lady of leisure aware of fashion and good taste, cool composed, clothes, exotic children, rare surroundings, wishful	surroundings familiar and practical, more carefree; the little homemaker wanting to be modern, hardworking, with kids. clothes, informal office wear	sophisticated, competitive beauty on display, cool, composed, dramatic, exotic, wishful /fantasy	housebound and practical, dutiful, plain, older, in conventional interiors, everyday, familiar, unsophisticated

Narcissistic woman (1)	Narcissistic woman (2)	Carefree girl
completely self-involved, sensual, soft expression, narcissistic poses, lack of clothes, free blonde hair; in exotic sometimes fantasy surroundings	romantic and idyllic, sometimes with men, self involved; less sensual, more youthful and naïve, soft /kittenlike free blonde hair, surroundings romantic	not a woman; a girl in the last transient period before she settles down, energetic and youthful, energy rarely seen again

Women operate alone; they do not relate well to other women, only to men

The goal of women to attract a man is paralleled by an assumption that women should also compete with, dislike and ignore other women. They can relate to men or be alone.

Courtney and Lockeretz in their earlier study that was later replicated by Wagner and Banos found that women rarely interact with other women. Of the advertisements showing only women, only 11% showed more than one. In eight of these nine advertisements the women were in illustrations for clothing firms and so were in proximity rather than in communication with each other. No women were shown as co-workers unless men were also present. Women only interacted with men on a social and productive level. Mixed-sex advertisements occurred in 34% of the sample and while only 30 advertisements of the 729 used showed a mixed group with more than one woman, where the groups were mixed, women talked to men in two-thirds of interactive instances. In fact, if men were the sex who got on with their own kind, women certainly did not. Men were more than twice as likely to be shown interacting with members of their own sex; of the advertisements with men, 19% showed more than one man wherein they were consistently likely to be co-workers.

Millum made similar observations in his study. Men alone in the advertisements occurred 5·5% of the time whereas 'women only' occurred 70% of the time: in these, women were predominantly alone. Men, in all situations, were more likely to give attention to people than women were, and women were more likely to direct their attention to middle-distance or to themselves. There was also a pronounced self-tactility of women; women touch themselves in 32·3% of cases, objects 29% of the time, but other people only

7·9%. Male actors, in comparison, touch themselves only 12% of the time and objects and other people for 27·2%. Putting it another way, Millum found that in analyses of attention direction, women were more likely to be 'inner-directed' than men (65% of the time compared to 35%).

Courtney and Lockeretz also noted that women rarely ventured far from home by themselves or with other women. They did not smoke, drink, travel, drive cars and use banks, but on those occasions when they did it was in the company of men. This seemed to take the independence from the action. In fact, in those exceptional cases when women were shown in a male world without a man then they were in a decorative or 'sex object' role, such as displaying an automobile. That is, their independence was reduced to something which was for the benefit and titillation of men and therefore not dangerous.

Another side to this isolated, self-involved factor in media woman's behaviour has also been observed by Oakley (1974)[20] who noted the 'private, self-defined' outline of the housewife world:

> Housework is an activity performed by housewives within their own homes, the home is the workplace and its boundaries are also the boundaries of family life.

She noted that the housewife is typically isolated from other women, and this is why there are no rules or frames of reference to housewifery. Housewives could not 'unionise' because they have no fusion or co-ordination. In fact, she suggests, the media image may be the only definition of mass housewifery at all. 'Housewives' would not exist as such, without the media to give them an identity. The media create an homogeneity and a composite whole where none exists, and then monopolise all its rules and regulations. To side-track a little, it is interesting to note here a suggestion by Embree (1970)[12] that an extension of the persistent image of woman alone in her home is the need for her to defend it against the outside world. This place is her castle and she is the sole guardian. Embree says that the theme of 'containment and control' runs consistently through the advertising imagery sometimes in relation to the woman's body (hair and figure) but especially through products for home use. The aerosol was the best example of this defence mechanism. This theme has also been taken and developed by Florika (1970)[13] who equates the aerosol in the home with the forces of social control outside:

> The aerosol spray, both as a weapon and as a product, has created a new distinction in social behaviour between the rioters and the consumers. Between those who have to be controlled and those who've learned to control themselves.

Men are intelligent; women are not. Men do not like intelligent women (who are 'unfeminine'). Women have inferior ability

In her article on advertising to women, Ferguson (1973)[21] quotes Anne

Burdus, head of research at McCann-Erikson who has philosophically noted the tendency of executives to denigrate the consumer: 'in their eyes the consumer is often little short of a cretin.' Ferguson comments:

> Think about a few of those ads showing eager mums going into ecstasies about detergents, or grovelling around on shining floors or floating about the kitchen like Mary Poppins and you'll see what Anne Burdus means.

The stereotypical, female, intellectual vacuum, is approached by the mass media through three main channels but each of them arrives at some point near where Anne Burdus took off. These three channels are:

1. An indication that women cannot do difficult things on their own; they need male help and male money.

Courtney and Lockeretz, and Wagner and Banos noted this particularly and, in fact, one of their three main conclusions was that 'women do not make important decisions or do important things'. This was illustrated by the way that women in advertisements were rarely shown in activities outside the home and were limited in household decision-making. They operated independently in small purchases but the more expensive these became, the more likely the male was to become involved. This was demonstrated by their isolation of a hierarchy of products (Table 15:5) which were 'male' or 'female'.

In their work on imagery in general media Sternglanz and Serbin found that women were usually portrayed as 'silly, over-emotional and dependent on their husbands or boyfriends'. The women always made deference to male authority and 12 out of the 14 women were shown consistently in obeisance to their husbands. In only two cases were husband and wife shown as sharing authority and responsibility, that is, where both parents were shown confronting situations of stress and counselling their children, but in these situations both women did all the housework. In 12 plot situations, four showed women asking, begging or trying to trick their husbands into giving them money. When they had it they had to account for it.

2. The consistent use of males in various professional or service capacities to show women how to work appliances, use powders and liquids and to explain how these products work. Kinzer, in her study on stereotypes in soap operas, reiterated a finding by Hennessee and Nicholson[22], that woman in advertisements was a more extreme version of woman in general drama, that she was 'stupid and incapable'. When she had problems:

> such as cleaning the toilet bowl, keeping left-over food palatable or making dishes shiny [then these were] solved by an off-camera male voice or a man who flies through the window, with a booming voice like Zeus atop Mount Olympus or Wagner's Siegfried passing through the Ring of Fire, and the omnipotent male rescues a befuddled female from her dilemma.

The irony of the expert housewife in her *pièce de resistance,* housework, which males never normally stray into, being instructed by those males has been noted by Komisar[23] who says:

> There is a special irony in the fact that women, who presumably spend most of their waking hours in the kitchen or laundry room, received instructions about how to do their housework from men: Arthur Godfrey |American actor| who probably never put his hands into soapsuds, tells women across the country, why they ought to add still another step to their washing routine with Axion Pre-soak. Joseph Daley, president of Grey advertising says that men are used because the male voice is the voice of authority. Others add that while the execution of housework is only menial, thus female, the development of detergents and polishes is scientific and therefore male.

Cadwell of Cadwell-Davis, puts another angle to this male-female interaction. She thinks that Greek gods, white knights and other human versions of the white tornado themes are sex symbols that housewives use to assuage their own guilts and neuroses. The connection of sexual fantasies with soap and cleaning reached brave new heights with the Lever Brothers' commercial in America which tried to project a virtual love‚affair between housewife and soapsuds. The product was called 'Hero' and the housewives had a liaison with him while their husbands were at the office. The commercial even had hordes of women bearing baskets of washing and worshipping at his feet. Cadwell notes that the commercial was withdrawn because people found it religiously disturbing but not because it was such a blatant humiliation of women[24].

Komisar (1971)[23] also raises the interesting point that men and women are only shown in the interaction of instruction where the work is deemed to be of a sufficiently menial nature. Where the work involved is of any status or advanced social use, women are excluded from the interaction.

> The image of women in advertising is as much defined by the ads that omit her as those that exploit her. Business executives and doctors, for example, are always men. Even the language is male-orientated like the General Electric 'Man Helping Man' on an ad that discussed the development of nuclear plants.

A good example of this is also seen in the advertisement series for Bayer Chemicals in which one of the ads shows a father and son walking together down a country lane, with the son on the father's shoulders. Entitled 'The World's Most Powerful Man?' it reads:

> By tradition the father's role is to provide for his family. Another provider is the farmer. He has to provide for the family of Man. *Their combined efforts will decide the future of Mankind:* the father by feeding the minds of his children. the farmer by nourishing their bodies.

So what happened to mother?

3. The use of the sexual joke. Media woman is often caricatured into the time-old dumb blonde. She is beautiful and brainless and is both the archetypal mindless woman and the original sex object, sexually useful but intellectually and practically useless. In fact, we could conceptualise the dumb blonde stereotype at one end of the media woman's intellectual continuum, at the other end of which lies the housewife and mother, who is full of Common Sense. Originality, creativity and intelligence do not figure on the continuum; these are 'male' concepts and a woman who demonstrates these qualities becomes by implication 'non-feminine'.

Komisar records an advertisement published by the Dictaphone Corporation of America which pictures a pretty blonde woman who, wearing a micro-mini-skirt, is sitting at her desk polishing her nails as four worried men try to arouse her interest in some calculator. Says the copy: 'Our new line in calculators goes through its final ordeal. The dumb blonde test.' She also notes the advertisement by IBM which talks about a businessman and his secretary: 'If she makes a mistake, she types right over it. If her Boss makes a revision she just types the revision.' 'Somehow', says Komisar, 'secretaries, who are always women, make mistakes; bosses, who are always men, make revisions.'

Recent advertisements on British television have shown a vacuous lady who knows that the juice she is drinking is not real 'because it does not contain any pips': one mentally defective blonde who cannot get her lines right for a deodorant commercial and another blonde woman who dances prettily in a sequinned dress to advertise her investment in a building society, thereby, one assumes, neutralising the masculine, and thereby threatening, aspects of such canny, financial behaviour. Justification for this form of stereotyping is that it is 'all a joke'.

WOMEN ARE ULTIMATELY AND NATURALLY HOUSEWIVES, WIVES AND MOTHERS

Oakley encapsulates this contention, which was noted in every content analysis and set of observations on women in advertising. She says:

> In the social image of a woman, the roles of wife and mother are not distinct from the role of housewife. Reflections of this image in advertising and in the media generally portray women as some kind of statistical mean of the three roles combined ... Housewife can be an umbrella term for 'wife' and 'mother'. Women's expected role in society is to strive after perfection in all three roles.

The 'natural' role of housewife and mother is implied by the following assumptions in advertisements.

Women do not work outside the home

Courtney and Lockeretz found in an examination of advertisements in seven general-interest American magazines that only 12% of the workers shown in these advertisements were females: if entertainers were excluded, this proportion dropped to 7%. Approaching this from a breakdown according to sex, 45% of men were shown in working roles, compared to 9% of women. When women were shown alone or with other women, 90% were in non-working roles. Wagner and Banos in their follow-up study of the Courtney and Lockeretz analysis found that while there had been a slight improvement in this omission of working women, it was still not representative of the actual number of working women in the USA, which is nearly 40%. In 1972, they found that 21% of the women shown in general magazine advertisements were in working roles compared with only 9% in April 1970. Millum, in his study of British women's magazines in 1968, made similar observations. Advertisements which showed the career woman were usually for nursing or the armed services and in these instances the world presented to women was: 'complete and self-validating in the way that the world of the wife and the mother is'. These roles were grudgingly offered in the light of implication that they excluded any alternative:

> They can be the complete opportunity for opting out for anyone who cannot meet the demands of the other roles because they offer a total identity, a world which is completely self-validating. It is significant that in this way, the career becomes irreconcilable with other roles, with being married, with having a good time, good taste etc.

He concluded [7]:

> From the picture presented by these illustrations one could not begin to grasp the fact that one-third of the total labour force is comprised of women. The working woman is simply omitted from the world of meaning of the illustrations.

Wight (1972) [25] made an almost identical observation in his recent book on advertising and consumerism. He said:

> The advertising industry tends to present the housewife as though carrying out the traditional role was still the norm. Who would ever guess by looking at the television commercials that one in three women worked?

The omission of working women has also been noted by Bardwick and Schumann (1967) [11] who refer to it as a 'denial', an interesting angle which presumes that the media promoters have made a psychological involvement in omitting the working woman:

> One of the most striking examples is the curious TV denial of the fact that 25 million women work outside the home. Even the occasional woman in a lab coat is shown reheating coffee—which she could do just as well wearing an apron. Otherwise women on TV are comedy sterotype figures . . . the TV woman is housebound. While

the time-saving products that are extolled as reducing labour are probably desired most by working women who are time-harried, the purchasers in these ads are not working.

Embree (1970)[12] quotes an advertisement by IBM which declares that: 'Your wife's office is probably better equipped than yours' and pictures a youthful housewife surrounded by wall ovens, electric stove with greasehood, blender, rotisserie, four-slice toaster and electric coffee pot. She comments:

> Nearly half of the women in this country work, but you wouldn't think so to look at American advertising. A woman's place is not only in the home, according to most copywriters and art-directors, it is in the kitchen or laundry room.

So media woman does not work other than in the confines of cultured domesticity. Yet, is this consistent throughout all media? Outside of the advertisement breaks, are women in the working environment then? Long and Simon, and Sternglanz and Serbin conclude that they are generally not. Nevertheless, the former study found that the proportion of married women with jobs was better than in advertising media: 14 of the 24 married women with or without children did not have jobs which puts the proportion of working women portrayed at 45% which, although gleaned from a very small sample compared to those which formed the basis of the advertising media content analyses, is still a considerable improvement on the 21% that Wagner and Banos noted for advertisements. In spite of this, however, Long and Simon note that, although these women had jobs, they were implied rather than demonstrated. Except for two women (a writer and a news editor), all the women, married, widowed or single were actually seen almost exclusively in the roles of homemakers and/or parents.

It is interesting to note that a further implication of the non-applicability of women to the great outside can be taken from the actual numerical incidence of her appearance in various media types. In more general media, that is, most television programmes, mass circulation non-female magazines and newspapers, women occur consistently less frequently than in real life. As the nature of the media moves towards the 'domestic', such as with television commercials, 'family' comedies, women's magazines, more women appear and men, correspondingly, start to vanish.

For instance, in Millum's study of advertisements in women's magazines, he showed that there was a predominance of female actors, and women without male companionship occurred in 70·3% of the advertisements, compared to 5·5% of men alone and 24·2% of men and women together. When, however, as in the studies by Courtney and Lockeretz, and Wagner and Banos more general magazines are analysed, men are found to predominate, so that in the former study, for example, men alone are present in 40% of the advertisements, women alone in 26% and both sexes together in 34%.

In general television programmes, Long and Simon, and Sternglanz and

Serbin also find that women are not adequately represented. Long and Simon, for example, in their initial sample of 50 television programmes had to abandon 8 because they did not have any regular female character, if they had one at all. Of the 15 women in non-leading roles, seven were seen for only a third or a quarter of the time available; and the others for less than a quarter of the time.

In the study by Sternglanz and Serbin, four out of the original sample of 10 programmes had to be excluded because they did not regularly contain at least one female figure. They also made two major hypotheses on programme content, one of which was that the sample of programmes would reflect the American population at large; that is, depict 51% female incidence and 49% male. This hypothesis was rejected: the sample was broken 33% female and 67% male which was significantly different from the population at ·001 level.

Women are not successful in work outside the home. They do not do 'male' jobs.

To underline that women *should* be housewives, when they are shown to work outside the home, they do not achieve positions of authority. In the case of general media, Long and Simon noted specifically that where women worked outside the home they played their roles in 'subservient, dependent and less rational ways than their male counterparts'. Women did not occupy positions of authority in or out of the home. In fact, taking participation in television programmes themselves. only 8 of the 34 female characters were in leading roles. Men were more positive and successful.

Sternglanz and Serbin found that while males were significantly more likely to be aggressive, constructive, succorant. emitting more total behaviour and to be rewarded for their actions in whatever occupation they filled, women were significantly more likely to be shown as deferent and they were often punished for showing a high or successful level of activity. Also, the outcome of female behaviour was invariably scored as neutral, that is, the behaviour of women had no environmental consequences. (This, anyway, has some base in reality since O'Leary, Kent and Tonik (1973)[26] have already found that this happens frequently in the school situation, that is, teachers are more likely to respond to the behaviour of boys than the same behaviour performed by girls.)

The sister studies of Courtney and Lockeretz, and Wagner and Banos made particular note of the lack of success of women in working roles in advertising media. Both studies found that no women were ever shown in high-level business executive positions and only 4% were shown in a professional position in 1972 compared to none in 1970. The number shown as entertainers and professional sportswomen had dropped by nearly a half

over the two sets of data and there was a slight improvement in the representation of women in the sales, middle-level business and semi-professional
levels. Nevertheless, the non-professional, white-collar role of the working
woman: clerk, typist, secretary, nurse, airline hostess etc., had actually
increased (*see* Table 15:4).

Table 15:4 Comparison of Occupations of Working Women shown in General Magazine
Advertisements

	Per cent of females	
	*1970**	*1972+*
Proportion shown as workers	9	21
Occupational categories		
High-level business executive	0	0
Professional	0	4
Entertainers, professional sports	58	23
Sales, middle-level business, semi-professional	8	15
Non-professional, white collar	17	46
Blue collar	17	12
TOTAL	100	100

*Source: Courtney and Lockeretz[8].
+Follow-up study, January 1972[10].
Source Wagner and Banos[10].

Similar findings have been made by Katzman (1972)[16] and Kinzer (1973)[17]
in their content analyses of American 'soap operas'. Women were housewives,
mothers and wives, and men were professional workers. Where women
strayed into male areas then they made a 'womanly' mess of it. If they
worked competently it was in a female profession. Katzman, for example,
found that in 14 'soap opera' episodes during the week of 13 April 1970,
60% of men were doctors, lawyers or businessmen. Less than 5% of the
women were in these categories. Of the women, 62% were nurses, secretaries or housewives. She concluded:

The afternoon soaps foster an ideology based on female passivity, ineptness and
subservience. Even independent women of the highest professional stature manage to get
themselves in the damnedest messes, from which only strong, brave, intelligent males
can extricate them.

Women are happy doing housework: it is satisfying

The advertisers cannot consistently suggest to a woman that she is naturally
and infinitely a housewife, wife and mother and also demonstrate that this
work is dirty, humiliating, menial and boring. To overcome this contradiction
they must deny something, so they make a continual assertion that housework
is fun, satisfying and pleasant. All women always enjoy it. Of the American
version of this piece of fast footwork, Embree[12] says:

In a country where the low status of maids cannot be matched, where the more than one and a half million household workers (98% female; nearly two-thirds black) have a median. year-round, full-time wage of $ 1,523—they are excluded from the federal wage laws—it is an amazing feat of hocus-pocus worthy of Tom Sawyer and Phineas T. Barnum to lovingly declare that domestic labour is the true vocation of women wearing wedding bands.

Bardwick and Schumann refer to this glorification of domestic labour as one other 'denial' in the work of media woman.

Even the reality of her labour is denied in TV wonderland. Although she is surrounded by mountains of laundry, TV ads show her how she can dance through washday with good cheer.

Friedan (1963)[14] devoted almost all her book on the 'feminine mystique' to an attack on the lie behind this spurious pleasure in domestic labour and accused advertisers of propogating a huge Parkinson's law syndrome, whereby housework expands to fill the time available in order to create its own markets. The work, under the glamourised exterior, has no importance at all:

The glorification of 'woman's role', then, seems to be in proportion to society's reluctance to treat women as complete human beings; for the less real function that role has, the more it is decorated with meaningless details to conceal its emptiness.

These 'meaningless details' are viewed by Embree as synonyms for labour-saving devices. She also believes that the 'housework is fun' contention is faced by the contradiction inherent in labour-saving devices that domestic labour should be reduced if possible. She compares the use of these devices to the use of cosmetics: to keep up with cosmetic fashion and to keep up with domestic labour demands. more and more products are needed with increasingly elaborate means of application/use. Both products, she suggests, are subtle means of keeping the housewife involved and preventing further occupation which would. in turn, reduce time in the house and the markets for other domestic products.

Another prevailing myth of the consumer economy is that the new innovations create leisure time for the consumer. This is especially true of the housewife consumer. The special cleaners for windows. floors. carpets, sinks. toilets. furniture etc. are supposed to release women from household drudgery. Cleaning the house becomes more and more a highly specialised routine linked to the consumption of highly specialised cleaning products.

One maniac feature of the 'housework is fun' contention, noted by Embree[12] and Trahey[27], is the exaggerated delight that women display when confronted by inanimate domestic objects. Embree notes dryly:

If television commercials are to be believed, most American women go into uncontrollable ecstacies at the sight and smell of tables and cabinets that have been lovingly caressed with long-lasting, satin-finish, lemon-scented spray-on furniture polish. Or they glow with rapture at the blinding whiteness of their wash and the green-eyed envy of their neighbours. The housewife in the Johnson's wax commercial hugs the dining room table because the shine is so wonderful . . . Bold detergent shows one woman in deep depression because her wash is not as bright as her neighbours.

Trahey puts this ideology into the realms of farce. She again notes the compulsive table-caressing and refers to an advertisement for Mr. Clean which [27]

shows a woman who has gone quite bonkers over her dining room table waxing job. She sits at one end of the table and rubs it lovingly. If her husband found her this way, he most certainly would either return her to her mother or, if he were kind, suggest a shrink.

Men and women have strictly delineated sex roles and household duties

The marriage of media woman is one which operates on strictly traditional lines. Parallel to the contention that she does not work outside the home, is the one that the husband does not work *in* the home. She is infinitely domestic, he never is. This strict delineation of marital roles into domestic (female) and professional (male) is compounded by the continuous association of domestic products with female usage and larger more important products with male usage. Millum made observation of this factor by a classification of all the products found in women's magazines. Those products which had a family and domestic air were related to female acts and female usage. Men were not involved. Men were only related consistently with those products which had an external air to them.

Courtney and Lockeretz classified products into 'male' or 'female' in terms of the sex portrayed most often in association with them. Evidently, larger or non-domestic products such as alcoholic beverages, cars and banks were male: cleaning products, food and beauty products were female. By this sort of sex-typing, they note, women are inescapably associated with the interior activities and men the exterior ones. Cross pollination does not exist (*see* Table 15:5).

This ideal is found in both general and advertising media. Sternglanz and Serbin, Long and Simon, and Kinzer all note that men do not participate in or help their wives with domestic work. Children are theirs by implication only, for they show only minimal affection and little or no nurturant care. Millum suggests that, in its way, this denial of the involvement of a man in his children and family's welfare is as much a source of pathos as the denial of intellect and ability in women.

As husband, he is seized, waited on and ministered to, the guest in the wife's house . . .
He is the man whose main business and concern is elsewhere: his work is somewhere

'out there'. . . . To the father who cannot cope by himself, the father who is really just a kid himself, the buffoon who spills things and acts the fool, the boyfriend who is a slave and suitor, to these, woman is superior, she is in control of the situation.

Table 15:5   Product Categories and Sex Roles

Product Category	Sex portrayed most often	Ratio of ads showing males /ads showing females
Cleaning products	Female	·00
Food products	Female	·45
Beauty products	Female	·60
Drugs	Female	·66
Furniture	Male	·71
Clothing	Female	·76
Home appliances	Female	·86
Charity	–	1·00
Travel	Male	1·30
Cars	Male	1·37
Alcoholic beverages	Male	1·63
Cigarettes	Male	1·90
Banks	Male	2·11
Industrial products	Male	2·17
Entertainment /media	Male	2·33
Institutional advertisements	Male	2·50

Source: Courtney & Lockeretz (1971)[8].

The embarrassment of the non-involved father and husband, his stupidity and assigned clumsiness are seen by Bardwick and Schumann as ways of opting out of the domestic confrontation by a rationale of elimination by incompetence. Nevertheless, when this image is no longer useful, that is, when he is outside the house and the domesticity is behind him, then he assumes strength, confidence and ability:

The . . . father and husband is portrayed as passive, stupid, infantile and emasculated . . . the TV mother protects, provides and pampers. Only in the purchase of expensive items like a car or a colour TV set is the housebound American male pictured as the rational and competent decision-maker. In the house his wife caters to him, even his razor blades spoil him, so that he doesn't seem to resent his apparent loss of authority. The theme song of Mr. Average seems to be a meek 'Why did you have to go and make trouble?'. . . But outside of the house, trouble is what he is looking for. Swift as a panther. free as a mustang. stealthy as a cougar, he speeds to his rendezvous with independence and violence. While TV commercials portray women in a confused and predictable way, the double life of men seems consistent.

In Britain we have our version of the American husband in the Philip and Katie advertisements for Oxo in which we see the strict delineation of roles operating through Katie the cook and Philip the worker, the handyman,

the source of meal appreciation if not preparation. Purser (1965)[28] compares
the Philip and Katie couple with other media marriages, such as the George
and Kate of 'Marriage Lines'. Purser asks:

> |Isn't| the favourite posture a rueful one with hubby caught out by wifey and having
> to hang his head boyishly and a bit mischievously, so that she—and with her, every
> soft-hearted female in the audience—could only pretend to be cross. Wasn't the appeal
> to the maternal instinct, and isn't it about time we had a more assertive, grown up
> image for the national husband?

Nevertheless, along with the denial of male involvement in domestic activities,
and the recourse to childish caricatures to avoid this involvement, there
are occasions where the role delineation in the media marriage becomes
sadly clear and much less coy. This is reflected in those occasions when,
for example, the man dogmatically refuses to eat, or sample, food of which
he disapproves, or fails to turn up at the church because his fiancee cannot
make a good cup of coffee on which her use and value as a person obviously
depends.

The stereotype is of a man squatting in his armchair while an obviously
neurotic and deeply anxious woman begs him to notice her or, if not
her, then at least the pie that she is holding. It is the tactless husband who
takes one mouthful of some lovingly prepared food and throws it down
in disgust and stamps off in the rain while the tearful wife stands alone
in the porch.

Luce (1967)[29] in his review of masculinity in America contends that
such denial of caring and domesticity in men is as notable as the denial
of professional competence in women. In his study of masculinity and
media he further notes that:

> . . . it is true that the advertising industry has tremendous influence in creating values and
> public stereotypes which in turn are used by those individuals whose value systems are
> weak and whose identities are diffuse. Better to identify with a stereotype than to
> experience the anxiety of no identity.

What, he argues, is so disturbing about these media images, is the trivialisation
of non-stereotypical aspects to masculine behaviour; the caressing of the
child, the delight in helping a loved woman, whether it is in washing up
or mending a car together, the expression of the gentler emotions. The
caring father, the mature, nurturant and participating male are abandoned
in favour of an easier and cheaper 'masculine' image which is harmful
because it denies one more time the 'rightness' of caring interaction for
those men who need the reassurance of a stereotype. Every 'easy' stereotype
in media, advertising or general, compounds a retrogressive image of
masculinity, as it does with femininity.

... an additional part of our thesis is that fantasies of masculinity reinforced by our cultural stereotypes are also changing the masculinity concept from a personal to an impersonal one—the latter being more difficult to recognise for what it is i.e. regressive or a compensatory device for ego-inadequacy ... stereotypes often represent isolated, uncommitted males, incapable of tender love for the opposite sex. Their masculine capability is usually typified by the unfeeling brutality of casual violence. The superficial, almost photographic, appearance of masculinity replaces competent, mature responsibility. The stereotype acts like someone else but does not feel like himself. In this sense, he is as much a robot as the deified computer—robots being defined as people who function effectively in limited situations totally without feeling.

Little girls grow up to be housewives, wives and mothers

If sex-role stereotyping occurs in advertising and general media for adults, then it also does so to an even more blatent extent in media directed at children. To be fair, however, the advertiser is only being as careless in this respect as his colleagues in other sectors of the information industry. Collier and Gaier (1958 and 1959)[30] found, for example, that children's heroes and heroines in their favourite story books frequently reflected strictly masculine and feminine occupations, behaviours and interests, while Chiu (1973)[31] found that male and female children were persistently encouraged to read stories which were 'appropriate' to their sex rather than to their interest. Oakley notes a set of American books which put the goal of the little boy as 'President of the United States' and that of the little girl as 'mother of children'. There is also that astonishing list of statements found in an American children's book called, *I'm Glad I'm a Boy: I'm Glad I'm a Girl* (1970)[32] which says:

> Boys are stronger: girls are graceful
>
> Boys are doctors: girls are nurses
>
> Boys are football players: girls are cheer-leaders
>
> Boys are pilots: girls are stewardesses
>
> Boys fix things: girls need things fixed
>
> Boys build houses: girls keep houses
>
> I'm glad you're a boy: I'm glad you're a girl!
>
> We need each other!

Advertising media manages to convey similar role models to the growing child but usually by depicting interactions of the children with toys and with each other. Boys, for example, tend to demonstrate to girls who are usually the passive parties, the recipients of knowlege, the lookers-on. Little boys are the doers, the creators, the curious ones. Furthermore, toys have strictly delineated masculinity–femininity images which relate to outside, active, mechanical things (masculine) or nurturant, child-caring, domestic and passive activities (female). Oakley notes a list of toys which were rated by 20-year-old psychology students for masculinity (low scores approaching one), neutrality (scoring under five) and femininity (high scores approaching nine) (*see* Table 15:6). The assessments by the students were a good indicator of which toys boys and girls felt were 'appropriate' for their use.

Table 15:6   List of Toys Rated for their Masculinity-femininity

Toy	Rating
wheel barrow	3·2
cleaning set	8·4
plane	1·7
sports car	3·6
teddy bear	5·8
rocking horse	4·6
skipping rope	7·0
blackboard	5·3
dish cabinet	8·3
football	1·5
construction set	2·7
tool set	2·0
sewing machine	8·2
dumper truck	2·5
banjo	4·5
cosmetics	8·8
dolls pram	8·5
telephone	5·6
racing car	2·2
alphabet ball	4·9
roller skates	5·3
paddling pool	5·0
tractor	3·0
doll wardrobe	8·7

Source: Oakley (1972)[33].

Sex-typing in children's advertisements has a more organised and vocal opposition in America than in Britain. Whether this is because such sex-typing is more extreme, or because parents are more aware of the potency of such modelling, is open to debate. Komisar, for example, draws attention to a protest demonstration by a group of women in 1969 against Mattel toys who had run an advertisement in *Life Magazine* to promote its lines in the children's Christmas trade. The advertisements are worth quoting as archetypes of the sex-role stereotype in children's advertising:

> Because girls dream about being a ballerina, Mattel makes Dancerina ... a pink confection in a silken blouse and ruffled tutu ... Wishing you were older is part of growing up ... Barbie a young fashion model, and her friends do the 'in' things girls should (*sic*) do—talk about new places to visit, new clothes to wear and new friends to meet.

Later in the advertisement it said: 'Because boys were born to build and learn, Mattel makes Tog'l' (a set of building blocks for creative play). Another illustration showed a boy playing with a telescope:

> Because boys are curious about things big and small, Mattel makes Super Eyes, a telescope that boys can have in one ingenious set of optically engineered lenses and scopes ... that ... create dozens of viewing devices—all for science or all for fun.

Komisar notes that advertising imagery of this type

> ... begins stereotyping males and females very early in life: the little girl who was taught to want to be a model or a ballerina and imbued with the importance of how she looks and what she wears, grows up to be a 30-year-old Barbie doll with advertising still providing the cues.

Goulart (1968)[34] in his detailed and intensive study of the children's toy and marketing industry reaches similar conclusions. He explores the wider morality of advertising contentions as well as imagery and its effect on children. Of the effect of domestic imagery directed at little girls, the Barbie doll, the little cooker, the vacuums and sweepers just like Mummy's, the doll's house, the little knitting and sewing sets, he questions the right of advertisers and marketers 'to allow children to be constantly enticed to abandon their search for themselves, to allow them to accept a pre-packaged ready-to-live life ... The arbitrary domestication of all young girls is wrong.'

THE FEMALE CONSUMER: THE REALITY

So how do these images compare with the reality of life for the female consumer? Obviously, there is some grain of truth in all of them; even caricatures, to be effective, must bear some resemblance to the figure from which they derive.

Many women, it is true, are housewives; the proportion may be as high as 70% of all women (*see* chapter 8). Women often are narcissistic, isolated and do find it difficult to relate to other women. Men often receive a better education than women or are trained to higher levels and attain more posts of authority. Some women have been known to spend their entire lives in domestic work, principally inside the marital home and it is true that where women are skilled, these skills tend to concentrate into semi-professional posts such as secretarial and clerical work. Some women on some occasions have enjoyed certain types of housework and historically, men, in some cultures, have avoided contact with their children and domestic work.

Yet, is this the whole story? All these facts depend on the maintenance of the historic sex role and the definition of a sex role has always been a dynamic one. Can we any longer be sure that what held true for women once, any more than for men, is going to remain stable and unchanging for much longer?

The advertiser spends a great deal of time and money in investigating the family and consumer behaviour of the woman as buyer. How much time has he spent looking at woman as woman? To what extent are his perceptions of the female consumer built on a shaky base of rusty cultural expectations, personal prejudice, and to what extent on empirical evidence?

Over the last five years a considerable body of literature has been developing round the sex-role concept and the female-role concept in particular. A lot of it is new; some of it is a reformulation of data which has been around for some time. The data on women have looked at her history[35], physiology[36], mental health[37], abilities[38], dual roles[39], anthropology[40], social contribution, politics, economics[41] and sex-roles[42]. Importantly, many of the findings and reformulations within this data have made complete contradiction of existing expectations about women[43].

How much of this does the advertiser know about? How far has he ever delved into this body of research which is as important in understanding the truth and potential of the female consumer's life-style as his engineer's handbook to the working of his factory machinery? Would he attempt to utilise his plant with a screen drawn over the heart of the engine in the same way as he will perceive the female consumer's buying behaviour without ever looking at the mechanics of her psychology, physiology, abilities and expectations?

Thus, given the fact that many of the images that we have shown to characterise female media stereotypes contain grains of truth, what else might we add to make us question the right of these images to represent a total picture? The advertiser should be aware of the following realities, for example.

Appearance and Beauty

Not all women, obviously, are attractive; in fact very few are. Women can be ugly, haggard, wrinkled, worried, untidy and maintain other undesireable, unwanted, hated and utterly human characteristics. Yet women, after centuries of emphasis on their visible worth, have forgotten to recognise that they can value themselves, as men do, by other criteria. Thus, the gulf between attractiveness and the often plain reality holds an enormous potential for simple human unhappiness. This has been particularly notable among older women[44] but many researchers[45] have made particular note of the mental tragedies associated with the woman who is simply ordinary. Seidenberg[45] suggests, for example, that because of the cultural stereotype, the plain woman is often discriminated against in job opportunities and notes some case studies where the women's unconscious feelings of failure were associated with their looks, which led them into a whole gamut of marital difficulties and psycho-somatic illnesses. In chapter 12 we made reference to the numerous studies which catalogue the negative self-images and personality problems faced by the healthy but plump woman who continually tries, but can never succeed, in attaining the slim ideal. and studies have made close associations between the attractive female stereotype and the incidence of, and deaths associated with, anorexia nervosa among young girls[46].

Ability and Intelligence

Female abilities have been demonstrated in as many areas and strengths as the culture will allow her to. In ancient civilisations she could be a great poet. mariner, painter, writer, architect; in the mediaeval years she would run farms, cottage industries, be merchant, guild craftwoman. business woman, executor in her own right[35, 40]. In Russia today she will make up the bulk of doctors, dig roads and design bridges, while in China she will lead party programmes, local militia and, as in many other countries, fight. Fundamentally, her abilities can be as capable. developed and diverse as those of men.

Oakley (1974). Hutt (1972) and King (1974)[38] in their reviews of sex differences in ability and intelligence conclude that, for the vast majority of men and women, there is no difference in levels of intelligence. Such findings are recorded by standard intelligence tests such as the Stanford-Binet, but other researchers have found that approaching the concept of intelligence from the level of individual ability shows that male and female strengths can be differentiated and will dovetail into each other to form this homogeneity. The findings are multi-faceted, but it is generally agreed that females perform better than males on verbal tasks, arithmetical tasks, clerical skills, some types of verbal reasoning. rote memory and fine manual dexterity. Males perform better than females on spatial tasks, on mathematical problem-solving, on mechanical tasks and practical abilities. Nevertheless, all these results are gleaned from directions of averages in very large samples. For the average man and the average woman, such differences are less evident than educational differences, and it is this factor of education rather than that of intelligence which is the important one. Women still receive consistently less education, and to lower levels than do men. They are still encouraged away from skills such as architecture, mathematics and engineering because these are 'masculine' areas and, once qualified, still find difficulty in attracting employment equal to their ability*.

And what of the sexual joke about the thick woman, the dumb blonde, the empty-headed dollie? The advertiser should remember that this reveals more than a stereotyped sense of humour; it is also a recognised outlet for hostility and fear about women.

See Tables 80. 83 and 88 in *Facts in Focus*, HMSO (1974) and Table 120 in *Social Trends*, HMSO (1974).

Freud[47] suggested that while dreams symbolically fulfill a wish, wit expresses an aggressive trend in disguise. Similarly, the sexual joke is a special form of sexual aggression which is released by ridicule and laughter. Fry (1972) and Grotjahn (1972)[48] suggest that men's sexual jokes reveal their anatagonistic attitude toward women and isolate three such attitudes that appear in jokes concerning them. These are the hard, practical woman, even when in the throes of passion, the sensuous woman whose appetite is insatiable and finally the 'dumb blonde'. All these images figure in men's 'jokes' about women in attempts, they reason, to defuse the female image and to reassure men regarding their own masculinity. It is also true that this sort of humour as an expression of social fears and prejudice has been studied in the context of the negro in the white culture, where jokes about the low mentality, fear of the supernatural and the exaggerated sexual proportions and ability of blacks have been interpreted for some time as outlets for fear and envy of the negro[49].

Changes in Family Role Behaviour

There is no inarguable reason why women alone as opposed to men, or both men and women together, should occupy the role of 'mother'. Historical and anthropological evidence[35,40,42] indicates that men can be just as good in the job, and, in fact, in certain cultures it would be as unlikely for women to take this role as it is for men to do so in our culture. There are many caring, affectionate, gentle, 'maternal' men in our society who are being wasted as there are competent, aggressive, intelligent women. Given this cross-cultural rider, nevertheless, we can note the following of our society of the mid-1970s.

The woman at work.   Women do work outside the home. Women make up over a third of the working population in Great Britain and two-thirds of these women are married, that is, the archetypal housewives. Thirty-one per cent of these women are members of trade unions, and most work part-time, combining worker and housewife roles. It is not uncommon for some of these women to work up to 12 and 15 hours a day[50].

Many of these women are skilled workers and in 1971 1·5 million of them were self-employed, managers, forewomen and supervisors. They work in all industries and not just the 'female' ones. They work in service industries, mining and quarrying, clothing and footwear, electrical engineering, the distributive trades, in catering and in medical and dental services. They are reliable workers and their job mobility is only slightly higher than that of men over a 10-year period; in addition, 60·7% of women have been recorded as being 'very satisfied' with their work, compared to 47·2% of men. Most women who have worked once will work again, and while they will pursue paid employment up to the birth of their first child, they will also work a second period from the school age of their last child until their retirement. The Department of Employment considers the increase in the number of married women workers to be the most significant factor in employment trends in the next decade[51]*.

Furthermore, it is not 'unnatural' for women to pursue two roles in this way. In fact, the 'unnaturalness', on historical and cross-cultural evidence, lies in the designation of housework as women's sole activity. Several studies[35,40] have shown that in twentieth-century western culture we have for the first time in any known society, women who have occupied themselves solely with housework and motherhood and nothing else. This work, as a separate activity, just has not existed in this way before; women have always had several roles.

The woman at home. As an obvious corollary of the previous point, housework and child-care alone do not make all women happy all the time. Oakley[39] and Friedan[14] have made careful and disturbing analyses of the trauma and boredom that women have found in this work. Crawford and Hooper (1973)[52], Curlee (1969)[53] and Wilsnack[54] have also noted the growing level of female alcoholism and have been able to relate it to role-crises, inactivity and loss of identity associated with children leaving home and the sudden absence of domestic usefulness. A whole new set of research[55] is now studying the psychological traumas among women who, when attempting to strive, succeed and develop, cannot cope with the effort in a stable manner because such activity contradicts cultural norms which equate female success and achievement outside the home with 'non-femininity'.

Men and women will only have strictly delineated marital and social, domestic and non-domestic roles, if a culture insists on such delineation. We should note, however, that in our present culture Harrell-Bond (1969) and Rapoport and Rapoport (1969)[56] have noted the trend to, and the role-blurring of, the new dual career family, while Biller (1971) and Hetherington (1973)[57] have recently underlined the importance of recognising the essential contribution of the more involved father in the upbringing of his children, in particular for the social and sexual stability of daughters.

Anyway, there is no rule which limits women to work within the home and men without. In fact, as long as married women continue to work, then the evidence is that domestic rules will have to change.

Maternal employment, as concluded in reviews of the extensive literature by Wallston (1973) and Siegal and Haas (1963)[58], is a big arbiter of change.

These reviews show that there is no positive evidence to indicate that

---

*See the editorial 'Social Commentary: Men and women', in *Social Trends*, HMSO (1974); *Annual Abstract of Statistics 1971;* Economic Progress Report (November 1974); Audrey Hunt, Survey of Women's Employment, HMSO (1968); General Household Survey 1974; Amelia Harris, 'Labour Mobility in Great Britain 1953-1963': ref. (51).

the working mother, *per se*, is harmful to her family and, in fact. through greater satisfaction of the mother and more self-reliance among the children might be, in many cases, beneficial.

The most interesting effects, however, to come from such employment are a definite shift in family-role behaviour, more shared domestic responsibility, and more help from the children with domestic work. Furthermore, the family tends to get smaller and, most interestingly, the children tend to grow up with highly flexible notions of sex roles, usually anti-traditional, and the daughters, in particular, follow less domestic-orientated occupations, demonstrate more non-feminine ambitions and aspirations and often follow their mother in combining two roles[58].

The influence of the media on children.   Mass media do not merely glance off the life-style of children in some neutral, benign manner. They have become a force comparable to that of teacher and parents in acting as a modelling stimulus in the child's life and, by implication, learning of sex roles. More children are now watching more television and reading more magazines than ever before. Estimates[59] are that the American child spends 64% of his waking hours watching television and by the time the child leaves school at 16 has probably spent 2,000 more hours in front of the television than in front of his teacher. The European child has also seen 2,000 hours of television *before* he goes to school and, when he gets there, will pay as much attention to the television set as to the teacher.

The tendency of children to pick up incidental learning from mass media has been well documented[60] along with the importance of modelling learned from play situations[61]. The socialisation of children through mass media has been conceded and investigated by Maccoby and Wilson (1957) and the Defleur studies[62] among many. We cannot assume that the presentation of sex-role stereotypes will have no effect on the self-images of the growing girl and boy. As it is, Defleur and Defleur[62] have already noted about children's acquisition of stereotyped occupational data, that television is a:

> ... more potent source of occupational status knowledge than either contact or the general community culture ... Any learning source which distorts reality concerning this aspect of the social structure and the child's generalised other may be laying the foundations for difficult personal and social problems.

Female Psychology

As a postscript to this brief resume of data on female sex roles, we should note one fact which will run as an undercurrent through all the points we have just noted. If sex roles are dynamic with social values then so is female psychology.

Women have never had a psychology which is immutable and absolute. Psychiatric contentions about female behaviour have reflected social prejudice about women as much as Szasz (1972)[63] finds that they once did with blacks. Consequently, female mental ill-health is often found, on historical analysis, to be a euphemism for non-'feminine' activity and Weisstein (1970), Sherfey (1970), Shainess (1970), Friedan (1963) and Chesler (1974)[64] have all documented frightening examples of bias, deliberate misinterpretations of female psychiatric data and twisted logic in the treatment of female mental problems. In line with this, one should note that, while Freudian psychology is still indispensable for its interpretations of the subconscious and childhood experience, many of Freud's findings about women should be treated with extreme care. All the psychologists mentioned above and also Suttie (1935), Kline (1972) and Mitchell (1972)[65] have noted the distorting influence of patriarchial values upon Freudian interpretations of female behaviour.

To the advertiser, in particular, we can note here, that as much as female psychology is not circumscribed entirely by the exigencies of Freudianism, so the woman is not untiringly attracted to phallicism. The use of phallic packaging in recent years has been a naïve attempt by advertisers to de-contextualise Freud and throw part of a complex, sophisticated, psycho-analytic theory into popular marketing. It is as much an indication of fantasy, community-flashing, wishful thinking and exhibitionism on the part of the male marketer as anything to do with female psychology. For the affect it has on women and the satisfaction it gives to him he might as well manufacture packs shaped like buttocks and claim he is appealing to the anal stage.

CONCLUSION TO PART V

We have shown that the female consumer does not confront a total image of herself in advertising media: that there is often a gap between image and reality and the gap is widening. A narrowing of the gap will take place when we see advertisements which show, for example:

1. A woman coming in from work and helping her children and/or husband to prepare the family meal.
2. A couple leaving for work together, leaving the dishes in the sink to soak in that washing-up liquid.
3. A woman taking the analgesic to cure her headache while sitting next to a production line or by her desk, and not next to baby.
4. A man feeding, cleaning, holding, and hugging his baby or preparing the meal for the children while his wife either comes through the front door on her return from work, or is doing other work in the house.
5. The woman driving the family in her, or the family's car, and driving competently.
6. Women shown fixing, mending, constructing household equipment; taking a break to prepare a convenience meal while decorating a room; changing the plugs on the car; unstopping the sink.

7. Women shopping together, gathering in groups, laughing at or helping each other; combining housework, cleaning, washing, driving; sharing time, activities, worries and pleasures.

8. Women encouraged to finish their housework quickly and efficiently for the reason that it *is* boring, so that they can walk, work, go to the cinema, study for academic or professional qualifications, go to meetings, libraries, take the children to the zoo, drive into the country, or just simply sit down and read.

9. A woman doctor, a woman scientist, a female supervisor, engineer, manager, architect, executive, policewoman, traffic warden, factory worker, shop manager, office cleaner using the product during, after or before they go out to these occupations.

10. A woman explaining the product to a woman; a housewife to a housewife whether it is a soap powder, investment, a cleaning appliance, a car; or a mother explaining homework to her daughter or son.

11. Small girls building cranes, dressing as doctors and scientists, creating buildings, pictures, making chemicals and looking through microscopes; laughing, running, shouting, fighting with each other and with little boys.

The gap will also narrow when an advertiser or marketer stops, thinks, then reverses every stereotypical situation so that, for example:

1. The woman waits impatiently downstairs while her boy-friend rushes furiously through a pile of after-shave, hair lotion, lather, trousers, shirts and socks in an effort to get ready in a hurry, because he is late, she is on time. They drive away in her car.

2. The female counter clerk explains carefully to the male investor how his money will be invested; how safe his finances will be.

3. A queue of women wait impatiently outside a 'phone booth, while a talkative young man goes on and on.

4. A female scientist explains to the motorist how his oil works and why it will be good for his car. Or, better still, a woman researcher puts the stamp and initial on the pack of analgesics 'passed' by the laboratory.

5. The man sheltering under an umbrella in the storm is appreciatively appraised by a group of young women who then offer him a drink.

When one starts to think along these lines, it is amazing how many new ideas are there for the taking. Nevertheless, at this point it is easy for the advertiser and for the marketer to make the observation that they are only doing what everyone else has done and is doing; that they are only as assumptive as the rest of society; that sexism in advertising will automatically disappear with a corresponding disappearance in general culture. This argument has been well expressed by an American feminist (1970)[65] who said:

The confusion between cause and effect is particularly apparent in the consumerist analysis of women's oppression. Women are not manipulated by the media into being domestic servants and mindless sexual decorations, the better to sell soap and hair spray. Rather, the image reflects women as men in a sexist society force them to behave. Male supremacy is the oldest and most basic form of class exploitation; it was not invented by a smart ad man. The real evil of the media image of women is that it supports the sexist *status quo*. In a sense, the fashion, cosmetics, and 'feminine hygiene' ads are aimed more at men than women. They encourage men to expect women to sport all the latest trappings of sexual slavery—expectations women must then fulfil if they are to survive.

Sexism in advertising will right itself, she argues, when society sorts out its sexual priorities and: 'when we create a political alternative to sexism, the consumer problem, if it is a problem, will take care of itself.'

This attitude, however, provides the perfect cop-out for the advertiser and marketer who cannot cope with the fact that existing advertising imagery could be improved. It also ignores the contributory influence of advertising as part of general media in the process of social change. Advertisers are not merely the innocent recipients of mass culture, they help in its formulation, a point we shall develop in the next chapter.

REFERENCES

1. Adam Knowles, 'The Theory of Residual Imagery', *Advertising Quarterly* (Autumn 1971), pp. 17–20.
2. Carl I. Hovland, Arthur A. Lumsdaine and Fred D. Sheffield, *Experiments in Mass Communications*, John Wiley and Sons (New York 1949).
3. Carl I. Hovland and W. Weiss, 'The Influence of Source Credibility on Communication Effectiveness', *Public Opinion Quarterly*, Vol. 15 (1952), pp. 635–50.
   Carl I. Hovland, Irving L. Janis and Harold H. Kelly, *Communication and Persuasion*, Yale University Press (New Haven, Conn. 1973).
   William R. Catton Jr., 'Changing Cognitive Structure as a Basis for Sleeper Effect', *Social Forces*, Vol. 38 (1959) (60), pp. 348–54.
4. Herbert E. Krugman and Eugene L. Hartley, 'Passive Learning from Television', *Public Opinion Quarterly* (1970–1) (34), pp. 184–90.
5. Andre Cadet, 'Advertising and Self Image', *Advertising Quarterly* (Summer 1967), pp. 43–51.
6. Noted in Cadet op. cit.
7. Trevor Millum, *Images of Woman: Advertising in women's magazines*, Chatto and Windus (1974).
8. Alice E. Courtney and Sarah Wernick Lockeretz, 'A Woman's Place: An analysis of the roles portrayed by women in magazine advertisements, *Journal of Marketing Research*, Vol. VIII (February 1971), pp. 92–5.
9. Lawrence A. Wortzel and John M. Frisbie, 'Women's Role Portrayal Preferences in Advertisements: An Empirical Study', *Journal of Marketing*, Vol. 38 (October 1974), pp. 41–6.
10. Louis C. Wagner, and Janis B. Banos, 'A Woman's Place: A follow up analysis of the roles portrayed by women in magazine advertisements', *Journal of Marketing Research*, Vol. X (May 1973), pp. 213–4.
11. Judith M. Bardwick and Suzanne I. Schumann, 'Portrait of American Men and Women in T.V. Commercials', *Psychology* (1967) (4), pp. 18–23.
12. Alice Embree. 'Mental Images 1: Madison Avenue Brainwashing—The Facts' in *Sisterhood is powerful*, Robin Morgan (ed.), Vintage Books (1970).

13. Florika, 'Media Images 2: Body Order and Social Order' in *Sisterhood is Powerful*, op. cit. 12, (1970), p. 191.
14. Betty Friedan. *The Feminine Mystique*, Penguin Books (1963).
15. Don Grant, 'Women's Libs Fume at Insulting Ads: Ad gals unruffled', *Advertising Age* (44) (27 June 1970), p. 1.
16. Natan Katzman, 'Television Soap Operas: What's been going on anyway?', *Public Opinion Quarterly*, (136) (1972–3) pp. 200–12.
17. Nora Scott Kinzer, 'Soapy Sin in the Afternoon', *Psychology Today* (August 1973).
18. Michele L. Long and Rita J. Simon, 'The Roles and Statuses of Women on Children and Family T.V. Programmes', *Journalism Quarterly* (Spring 1974). pp. 107–10.
19. Sarah H. Sternglanz and Lisa H. Serbin, 'Sex Role Stereotyping in Children's Television Programmes'. *Developmental Psychology,* Vol. 10(5) (1974), pp. 710–15.
20. Ann Oakley, *Housewife*, Allen Lane: Penguin Books (1974).
21. Pamela Ferguson, 'Advertising to Women: is it a man's myth?', *Adweek*, Supplement 'Woman's World' (2 November 1973).
22. Study noted in 17.
23. Lucy Komisar, 'The Image of Woman in Advertising'. in Vivian Gornick and Barbara K. Moran (eds.). *Women in Sexist Society: Studies in power and powerlessness*, Basic Books (1971).
24. Cadwell noted in Komisar op. cit., 23.
25. Robin Wight. *The Day the Pigs Refused to be Driven to Market*, Hart-Davis. MacGibbon (1972).
26. L. A. Serbin, D. K. O'Leary, R. N. Kent and I. J. A. Tonik. 'A Comparison of Teacher Response to the Problems and Pre-academic Behaviour of Boys and Girls'. *Child Development*. Vol. 44 (1973), pp.796–804.
27. Jane Trahey noted in Komisar op. cit.
28. Phillip Purser. 'The Half-World of the TV Commercials', *Advertising Quarterly*, Vol. 4 (Summer 1965), pp. 52–7.
29. Ralph A. Luce Jr., 'From Hero to Robot: Masculinity in America-stereotype and reality'. *Pschoanalytic Review*, Vol. 54(4) (1967).
30. Mary J. Collier and Eugene L. Gaier, 'Preferred Childhood Stories of College Women'. *American Imago* (1958). pp. 401–9.
    Mary J. Collier and Eugene L. Gaier, 'The Hero in the Preferred Childhood Stories of College Men'. *American Imago* (1959), pp. 177–94.
31. L. M. Chiu. 'Reading Preferences of 4th Grade Children Related to Sex and Reading Ability', *Journal of Educational Research* (April 1973).
32. *I'm Glad I'm a Boy, I'm Glad I'm a Girl*. Simon and Schuster (1970).
33. Ann Oakley, *Sex, Gender and Society*, Maurice Temple Smith (1972).
34. Ron Goulart. *The Assault on Childhood*. Gollancz (London 1970).
35. Mary Beard. *Woman as Force in History*. Macmillan (1971).
    Julia O'Faolain and Lauro Martines, *Not in God's Image*. Maurice Temple Smith (1973).
    Sheila Rowbotham. *Hidden from History*. Pluto Press (1973).
    Elizabeth Gould-Davis, *The First Sex*, Dent (1971).
    Alice S. Rossi (ed.), *The Feminist Papers*. Bantam Books (1974).
36. Ann Oakley, op. cit.. 33.
    Corinne Hutt. *Males and Females*. Penguin Books (1972).
    Our Bodies Ourselves, The Boston Women's Health Book Collective. Simon and Schuster (1973).
37. *Women and Madness*, Phyllis Chesler, Allen Lane (1974).
    Janice Porter Gump. 'Sex Role Attitudes and Psychological Well-Being'. *Journal of Social Issues*. Vol. 28(2) (1972), pp. 79–92.
    Walter Gove and Jeannette F. Tudor, 'Adult Sex Roles and Mental Illness', *American Journal of Sociology*, Vol. 7(4) (1972–3). pp. 812–35.

Jean Baker Miller M.D., (ed.), *Psychoanalysis and Women,* Penguin Books (1974).
Juliet Mitchell, *Psychoanalysis and Feminism*, Allen Lane: Penguin Books (1972).
38. Corrine Hutt, op. cit., 36.
Ann Oakley, op. cit., 33.
J. S. King, 'Women and Work: Sex Differences and Society', Department of Employment Manpower Paper, No. 10.
Nona Glazer Malbin and Helen Youngelson Waehrer (eds.), *Women in a Man-Made Society*, Rand McNally Sociology Series (1972).
Joan Huber (ed.), *'Changing Women in a Changing Society'*, University of Chicago Press (Chicago 1973).
39. Hannah Gavron, *The Captive Wife*, Penguin Books (1966).
Editorial Article in *Social Trends,* HMSO (1974).
Lee Comer, *Wedlocked Women*, Feminist Books (1974).
Alva Myrdal and Viola Klein, *Women's Two Roles*, Routledge & Kegan Paul (1956).
Leon Trotsky, *Women and the Family*, Pathfinder Press (New York 1970).
Ann Oakley, *The Sociology of Housework*, Martin Robertson (1974).
Ann Oakley, *Housewife*, Allen Lane: Penguin Books (1974).
Eli Ginzberg and Alice M. Yohalem (eds.) *Corporate Lib: Women's challenge to management*, John Hopkins University Press (London 1973).
Ellen Peck, *The Baby Trap*, Heinrich Hanau Publications (1973).
40. Elizabeth Gould-Davis, op. cit., 35.
Elaine Morgan, *The Descent of Woman*, Souvenir Press (1972).
Margaret Mead, *Male and Female*, Penguin Books (1950).
Margaret Mead, *Sex and Temperament in Three Primitve Societies*, Morrow (1963).
41. Hans Peter Dreitzel (ed.), *Family, Marriage and the Struggle of the Sexes*, Macmillan (1972).
Sheila Rowbotham, *Women's Consciousness: Man's world*, Penguin Books (1974).
Kenneth Hudson, *The Place of Women in Society*, Ginn (1971).
Micheline Waldor (ed.), *The Body Politic: Writings from the women's liberation movement 1969–1972*, Stage One (1972).
Linda Jenness (ed.), *Feminism and Socialism*, Pathfinder Press (1972).
Juliet Mitchell, *Women's Estate*, Penguin Books (1971).
Shulamith Firestone, *The Dialectic of Sex*, Paladin (1973).
Michele Hoffnung Garsnoff (ed.), *Roles Women Play: readings towards women's liberation*, Wadsworth Publishing Company Inc. (1971).
Simone de Beauvoir, *The Second Sex*, New English Library (1949).
42. Inge Broverman *et al*, 'Sex Role Stereotypes: A Current Appraisal'. *Journal of Social Issues,* Vol. XXV(1) (1969). pp. 59–79.
Shirley S. Angrist, 'The Study of Sex Roles', *Journal of Social Issues,* Vol. XXV(1) (1969), p. 215.
43. *See,* for example, the refutation of the vaginal orgasm by Masters and Johnson discussed in texts noted in 37 and the history of matriarchy by Gould-Davis op. cit., 35.
44. Zoe Moss, 'It Hurts to be Alive and Obsolete: The Ageing Woman', in *Sisterhood is Powerful, see* ref. 12, op. cit.
45. Ellen Berscheid and Elaine Walster, 'Beauty and the Beast', *Psychology Today* (November 1973).
Ellen Berscheid, Elaine Walster and George Bohrnstedt, 'The Happy American Body: A survey report', *Psychology Today* (November 1973).
Robert Seidenberg, 'Psycho Sexual Adjustment of the Unattractive Woman', *Medical Aspects of Human Sexuality* (May 1973). pp. 60–6.
46. *See,* for example. Rosie Parker and Sarah Mauger, 'Self Starvation', *Spare Rib*, No. 28.

47. Sigmund Freud, 'Wit and its Relation to the Unconscious', in A. A. Brill (ed.), *The Basic Writings of Sigmund Freud*, (New York 1938), pp. 689–93.

48. William F. Fry M.D., 'Psychodynamics of Humour: Man's view of sex', *Medical Aspects of Human Sexuality* (May 1972), pp. 128–34.
    Martin Grotjahn, 'Sexuality and Humour: Don't laugh', *Psychology Today* (July 1972), pp. 51–3.

49. John H. Burma, 'Humour as a Technique in Race Conflict', *American Sociological Review*, Vol. II (December 1946), pp.710–15.

50. *See* Roz Carne, 'On the Bench', *Spare Rib*, No. 29, p. 15.

51. 'Women Working', *Retail Business*, 141 (November 1969); 'Labour in Retailing: The Equal Pay Act and other issues', *Retail Business*, 187 (September 1973).

52. Crawford and Hooper, 'Menopause, Ageing and Family', *Social Science and Medicine* (June 1973).

53. Joan Curlee, 'Alcoholism and the Empty Nest', *Bulletin of the Menninger Clinic* (1969).

54. Sharon C. Wilsnack, 'Feminism by the Bottle', *Psychology Today* (April 1973), pp. 39–96.

55. *See* chapter 18, refs. 58–63.

56. Barbara Harrell-Bond, 'Conjugal Role Behaviour', *Human Relations*, Vol. 22(1), pp. 77–91.
    Rhona Rapoport and Robert N. Rapoport, 'The Dual Career Family', *Human Relations* Vol. 22(1), (1969) pp. 3–30; 'Further Considerations on the Dual Career Family', *Human Relations*, Vol. 24(6), pp. 519–33.

57. Henry B. Biller, *Father, Child and Sex Role*, D. C. Heath, (1971). Mavis Hetherington, 'Girls Without Fathers', *Psychology Today* (February 1973).

58. Barbara Wallston, 'The Effects of Maternal Employment on Children', *Journal of Child Psychology and Psychiatry*, Vol. 14 (1973), pp. 81–95.
    Alberta Engrall Siegal and Miriam Bushkoff Haas, 'The Working Mother: A review of research', *Child Development*, Vol. 34 (1963), pp. 513–42.

59. *See* Robin Wight, chapter 6: *see* chapter 16(40).

60. *See*, for example, Portugues and Feschbach, 'The Influence of Sex and Socio-economic Factors upon Imitation of Teachers by Elementary School Children', *Journal of Child Development* (1972).
    L. Postman, 'Short Term Memory and Incidental Learning', in A. Melton (ed.), *Categories of Human Learning*, New York Academic Press (1964).

61. J. Deese, 'Behavioural Effects of the Instruction to Learn', in A. Melton, op. cit.
    See, for example, Susanna Millar, *The Psychology of Play*, Penguin Books (1968). Seagoe, 'A Comparison of Children's Play in six modern Cultures', *Journal of School Psychology* (1971).
    B. Sutton-Smith, 'Child's Play: A very serious business', *Psychology Today* (December 1971).

62. E. Maccoby and W. Wilson, 'Identification and Observational Learning from Films', *Journal of Abnormal and Social Psychology*, Vol. 55 (1957), pp. 76–8.
    Melvin L. Defleur, 'Children's Knowledge of Occupational Roles and Prestige: A preliminary report', *Psychological Reports*, Vol. 13 (1962), p. 760.
    Melvin L. Defleur and Lois B. Defleur, 'The Relative Contribution of Television as a Learning Source For Children's Occupational Knowledge', *American Sociological Review* (1967).

63. Thomas S. Szasz M.D. 'The Negro in Psychiatry', *American Journal of Psychotherapy* (1971–2), pp. 409–71.

64. Dr. Naomi Weisstein 'Kinde Kuche Kirche as Scientific Law: Psychology constructs the female', p. 205 in *Sisterhood is Powerful, see* ref. 12, op. cit. (1970).
    Mary Jane Sherfey M.D., 'A Theory of Female Sexuality', p. 220 in *Sisterhood is Powerful, see* ref. 12, op. cit. (1970).

Natalie Shainess M.D., 'A Psychiatrist's View: Images of women—past and present, overt and assumed', p. 230 in *Sisterhood is Powerful, see* ref. 12, op. cit. (1970).
Betty Friedan, *see* ref. 14, op. cit.
Phyllis Chesler, *see* ref. 37, op. cit.
65. Ian Suttie, *The Origins of Love and Hate* (London 1935), p. 221.
Juliet Mitchell, *see* ref. 37, op. cit.
Paul Kline, *Fact and Fantasy in Freudian Theory,* Methuen (London 1972).
66. 'Consumerism and Women: A red-stockinged sister', in *Woman in Sexist Society,* p. 658, ref. 23, op. cit.

PART VI

The Advertising and Marketing Industry and Women

There is a peculiarly mutual relationship between the advertiser/marketer and the female consumer on whom he depends, a relationship which we should be able to describe as symbiotic, but is perhaps more parasitic on the part of the advertiser. The advertiser feeds off the female consuming capacity, driving, manipulating, needing and at the same time defining his hostess's style of life. The relationship is not an honest one; it cannot be when neither side has a real idea of the truth and extent of the interaction. The female consumer is unaware of the slow, cumulative, build-up of advertising images lobbed at her since she was a child which combine with and reinforce all the other stereotypes which she receives from her parents, teachers and peers. In turn, the advertiser is doing a job, selling a product, pushing a line. He is not involved in anything so conscious as 'manipulation'. This concept is too strong to describe a process which is as much an unconscious perpetration on the female as she is an unconscious victim. No one would seriously suggest that the advertising and marketing industry is at work on some gigantic conspiracy to maintain women in their traditional role as befits them in a patriarchal society, or subdue them in roles which are neither 'natural' nor 'unnatural', merely age-old and accepted, in the same way that we once accepted the 'place' of the Negro, the status of the Victorian poor, the bondage of the serf.

The relationship between the marketer, the advertiser and the female consumer is safe and complacent: gentle and repetitive. It has none of the acerbity that exists between two political parties nor the suspicion that exists in the simple man-woman relationship. Yet it is 'political' in the sense that interests are often in opposition, and it is principally between men (the advertisers and marketers) and women (the consumers).

The relationship undulates quietly; receiver and transmitter, and the advertisements, the images, and the contentions are like pebbles thrown into a stagnant pond. The waves wander on outwards, never re-defined, never really different but always quietly attacking, quietly eroding the structure of the shore. There is no malice here, no great plan or conspiracy. Yet, each advertising agent, each account director, each product manager, photographer, copywriter, designer and artist send their undulations onto the shore, each seemingly unaware of the cumulative and erosive effect of their little short-sighted, over-stated, under-estimating, stereotypical messages to the female consumer.

So how can we structure this relationship?

Since it rests on a fundamental of deceit it seems appropriate that we should see it as a variation of the eternal triangle. The marketer lies on one corner, the advertiser or media at the other and the female consumer on the third. The relationship has several permutations but the most common one is a movement of information from marketer to advertiser who will engulf it and eject a campaign where the original ideas are turned into images, messages and designs. The female consumer will take the proffered offering and either accept or reject the invitation to buy. She will relate only to the marketer, if to anyone. Either way, a little of the imagery in that campaign will rub off on to her.

Here in this tight structure, bristling with self-interests and yet almost a vacuum within itself, for it is punctured rarely by outside interests, do we find the seeds of all the invidious sex-role sterotyping that we have noted in the last chapter. The triangle cannot allow one side to imbalance because the relationship would come unstuck. Should the advertiser seek to make drastic changes in female imagery for even simple reasons of social morality, then his relationship with his client, who may not share his views, may deteriorate. So it is with the marketer, for should he wish to make some changes he has to arrive at this awareness first, and then rely on it passing through the hands of the advertiser, who, through prejudices of his own, may subtly present the old images in a new form.

Both sides may seek advice and information from the female consumer herself but, as we shall see from the next section, the historical, social and individual personality of the women, the interview situation, the stratification system, the prejudices of the marketers themselves will militate against a truthful picture of female ideology, and encourage a mere reformulation and repetition of the old, old, stereotypical story.

In fact, looking at the triangle again, perhaps what we have is not so much a vacuum contained therein, as a cloudy atmosphere full of the prejudicial smog which emanates from the outside socio-cultural norms. Any potential truth of the condition of women, or of men, which lands from the clear air of outside is pushed through the murky atmosphere in the centre of the triangle and is somehow contaminated. Putting it simply, to what extent do the marketing and advertising industries contain the seeds of their own bias against women? This concept can be examined from four angles:

1. Is there something in the maleness of the advertising/marketing industry which will tend to produce prejudicial responses from women? How might advertisers project their own fantasies about women through the media they control?
2. What evidence is there from formal works on advertising and marketing that women are underestimated by advertisers and marketers?
3. What have women said about advertising imagery directed at them?
4. What can the advertising and marketing industries learn from similar problems that faced the black cultural minority?

16. *Industrial and Academic Masculinity*

The marketing and advertising industry is represented on one side by the practicalists and consultants, and on the other by the academics and advisers who teach potential marketers and research the more erudite peripheries of the marketing discipline. What, if nothing else, these two areas have in common is a hefty proportion of the 'Y' chromosome. The female consumer may be their mutual *raison d'être* but women have very little to do with the actual workings of the marketing enterprise. An examination of the implications of this masculine bias for the female consumer and her media portrayal in particular, is what this chapter is all about.

DISCRIMINATION ON THE INDUSTRIAL SIDE

The advertising/marketing industry is predominantly male. A spokesman for the Institute of Practitioners in Advertising estimated that at least two-thirds of their members were of masculine gender, and of the females who made up the remainder, the majority were women secretaries with little administrative responsibilities. There are obviously a few women who have swum to the top but they are still sufficiently exceptional for people to write articles about them, *see* Scott (1974), and Cedar (1973)[2].

Cedar, writing as creative group head of McCann Erikson points out that boards of directors in agencies are predominantly male and this was 'A traditional state of affairs which will be slow in changing'. In her case, half of her accounts were directed at men and she quoted a director of a high-powered employment agency who told her that, as a rule, it is stressed by agencies that they would prefer male rather than female staff; in fact, only one major agency had specified that the writer should be female and that was for a fairly middle-weight job. Unisex floats easily in and out of the results of agency work but within the structure of the organisation it is only men who seem to get off and on the advertising industry merry-go-round. A woman who wants a seat has to do some pretty fast, and often dirty, footwork and, once on, has to hold on that much tighter than the man next to her. In recognition of the dubious representation of the female advertiser. Mann, an agency creative planner, as noted in *Campaign* (1973)[3], put a resolution to the meeting of the Creative Circle in that year that:

> This meeting recommends to agency heads through the IPA that they consider whether they are using to the best advantage the female talents available in the advertising business and whether they are keeping pace with the increasing acceptance of women in management on the client side.

Nevertheless, despite this incidental accolade by Mann to the emancipated thinking of the 'clients', there is little evidence that they are much more radical in their employment policies than the advertising sector. The marketing department still resembles a gentleman's club which fosters and welcomes a chiefly 'gentleman' clientele and a quick flick through the membership figures of the Institute of Marketing will reveal very few women's names.

Women figure in the marketing industry in much the same way as they do in the great outside, as supporters, moppers of fevered brows and in service capacities such as market research, which many men regard in marketing now as 'women's work'. It is significant that, in an advertisement for the *Observer Magazine* on the back of the November 1974 issue of *Personnel Manager*, in a montage of business executives reading the *Observer*, only two women are featured, one as a market researcher and the other as a systems analyst, both service occupations.

There are, of course, even more women who occupy secretarial and clerk/fetch-and-carry roles who never get a look-in at the larger marketing projects, and many women who get on the sales-force teams are often there more for their legs and their charm than for pre-marketing training. The vast majority of field interviewers are women and they occupy about as much status as the women in the factory who produce many of the products that the marketers market and usually market back to them. We have, therefore, in the marketing and advertising industrial scenario a predominantly male army with female minions confronting a large female consuming population. Is it not beyond the bounds of possibility, therefore, that we might find in this mass male-female confrontation some of the same features of prejudice and manipulation that we find in the more narrow cultural interaction of a single man and a single woman?

Patterns of Discrimination

Is the businessman prejudiced against women? And how may the advertiser/ marketer, particularly, express this prejudice?

Kalen (1971)[4] in a study of professional married men found that these men had a far more negative attitude toward holding two roles, home and a job, than married professional business women, and that 'negative attitudes towards this dual role both in and out of the professional community may indicate why few women prepare for, and pursue professional careers'.

Prather (1971)[5] isolated three socio-psychological factors in American society which were concentrated in the business situation and thereby acted as barriers to women's advancement in the professions. These were the image of women as sex symbols, the perception of women as servants and the definition of work in masculine terms. Prather suggests that equality in the employment markets will follow equality in social situations and only after 'an exposé of the myths and beliefs that limit women's personalities'. Fabian (1972)[6] notes that women in industry are seen as women first and employees second, while with men the reverse is true. Consequently, men in business will view a woman's actions as principally 'female', and work-related, second. Furthermore, her male colleagues will put extreme interpretations on her behaviour to somehow dilute her influence and deny her effectiveness since she is contravening her 'place' and thereby providing a threat. For example, a short skirt becomes 'seductiveness', whereas a man's tight trousers are merely 'fashion'; her long skirt implies 'a lack of femininity' which is 'concealed beneath a professional role', while a man dressed effeminately becomes 'a fond eccentricity'.

Rosen and Jerdee (1974)[7] in their recent and detailed examination of the American businessman's attitude toward women noted two general patterns of discrimination. First, there was a greater organisational concern for the career of men than there was for women and second, there was a degree of scepticism about women's abilities to balance work and family demands. Generally, these managers, despite the vocalisation of anti-sexist attitudes, when confronted by case-study situations about women workers resolved them by falling back on traditional concepts of male and female roles.

This attitude to women is also found among embryo businessmen as Bass, Krussel and Alexander (1971)[8] found in a study of graduate management students in full-time staff or management positions. Strongest agreement among these businessmen was expressed for 'traditional mores about women deferring to men's ability and initiative and men deferring to the needs of the "weaker sex"'. The data also showed that the men who were most likely to give the most unfavourable responses about women were those who worked with women as subordinates; those with women working as peers gave favourable responses. Bass *et al* noted that since research on minority groups indicates that, in order for reduction in prejudice to take place, interaction between two groups must be on an equal basis[9], it is unlikely that male managers with women subordinates would change their attitudes toward women in work, and may even use this situation to make them even more convinced of female inferiority and the 'incongruity' of women in the work as opposed to the home situation.

Another problem which Bass *et al* found was the tendency for male businessmen to have a wide range of inaccurate ideas about women's biological and physical potential and how this affected women's dependability. This is despite the fact that a large body of research shows that sex bears less relationship to dependability than age, level and length of time on the job[8,9,10]. Jourdan (1973)[11] notes a similar misconception by the CBI who 'are still pressing the stereotyped objection that women are too emotional, not strong enough and not prepared to do dirty work'. This is despite, apparently, the obvious fact that the most emotional, backbreaking and dirty job of all, that of nursing, is dominated by women, and also despite the recent contention by the *Harvard Business Review*[12] that:

> Any organisation which ignores the potential of women will be making a fatal mistake since this largest minority (40% of the work force) represents an almost untapped resource of talent and skill. The women's movement is not a fad or aberration but a major social force with great and growing impact on business and other social, political and economic institutions.

The concept of male chauvinism in the business situation has recently found a strong challenger in the person of Korda whose book provides an intelligent and compassionate analysis of how the businessman as 'man' can have the power to affect the lives of women at work and beyond[13]. Korda elucidates on what the studies touch on: that men are men, in home or out, and prejudices do not stop in front of a drawing board or a campaign brief.

> It is not necessary to be an expert on marriage to know that domestic considerations influence office life to an extraordinary degree, sometimes in simple ways, sometimes very subtly . . . The main thing that men bring from home is the attitude that women are to be bullied or humoured or charmed or ignored. Like the hedgehog in the Russian fable, they know one thing and know it so well that they cannot unlearn it. In marriage men learn that the surest way to protect their own freedom is to restrict the freedom of someone else.

Korda makes a point that we must look at again and again, the difference between reality and imagery. Just as there is a break between the advertisers'/ marketers' perception of women in advertisements and the reality of female potential, so may there be a break in the truth of their own reality to which they are almost as blind.

> So strong is the male chauvinist's image of what the relationship between men and women should be that it doesn't matter to him that the reality may be at variance with the image; his wife may dominate him, he may be afraid of his secretary, . . . it matters not at all . . ., he simply cannot accept women as equal human beings or deal with them on their own merits.

There are visions of women in every businessman that reflect his own best interests but the visions are, by definition, contradictory. He lives with one vision and sells to another. That the two visions should coincide requires mental gymnastics and cognitive discomfort. Korda notes:

The price of male chauvinism is terrible confusion. The male chauvinist trying to combine in one person so many contradictory attitudes toward women can only end by fearing and hating them.

If, as Korda suggests, men must try to cram into one ill-shaped container all the different definitions of women that they feel, know of and see, work with and work for, it is in the huge male/female confrontation of the consumer advertising and marketing industry that the set-up reaches an intoxicating dilemma. If anything, we have here both the potential for enormous change or no change at all. The men involved can choose to throw away their cultural comforts and look hard and long for some objective truths about women, or sit back and use women to reflect all they want to know.

Virginia Woolf[13] wrote: 'women have served all these centuries as a looking-glass possessing the power of reflecting the figure of man at twice its natural size', but in the marketing/advertising industry don't we have a *distorted* image rather than an exaggerated one? Korda also considered this when he wrote:

Men use women as mirrors; but the worst of this is not just that it has reduced women to 'looking glasses' but it has reduced men to creatures who can only define themselves by means of women, and, unfortunately for men, the mirror is like the ones in an amusement park that distort and split up the image.

To cope with or, in effect, deny this distortion of image, marketers and advertisers seem to have two defences.

The Male Defences of Discrimination

First of all, they can vehemently defend their good intentions. Achenbaum, for example, (1972)[14] writes:

Advertisers and their agencies seek to satisfy consumers, not manipulate them. By their use of market research, they seek to know what the consumers want; to provide them with the products which satisfy those wants and to communicate with them in an acceptable, persuasive manner. If they appeal to emotion, it is because people do not live by fact alone. But to call what national advertisers do 'manipulation' is to do wrong both to the good sense of the American housewife and to the facts.

Greyser, meanwhile, assures us:

. . . every advertiser concerned with the success of his advertising has developed a very healthy regard for the consumer. He does a great deal of consumer research. He knows his advertising must reflect the realities of the consumer's life or the consumers will pay no attention to it.[15]

Self-congratulation, however, does tend to eliminate the potential for re-examination of basic assumptions.

The second defence of female media-stereotypes lies in an argument for the maintenance of the *status quo;* the housewife is a housewife. that is all we're here to say about her. Kirkwood (1973)[16], for example, recently contended that:

> ... you will find women are portrayed in many different ways, but, for the most part, in the role that any married woman with a family has to act out in real life.
> The emphasis is on the married woman with a family. because it is she rather than the single girl or the career woman who is the highest purchaser of the products advertised on the television.

The basic role of a woman, he suggested, was:

> ... as a wife taking care of her husband and satisfying his (may I say basic) |*sic*| needs ... She is a mother, housekeeper, marriage partner and friend.

Kirkwood omitted to mention that two-thirds of these husband-satisfiers were also workers, making a significant macro-economic contribution in their own right, and that this role was as important and possibly as significant a contribution to the woman's life-style as being a mother and a friend. Nevertheless he does concede:

> There is, of course. another role that some |*sic*| women perform in real life and that is as members of society in their own right: a person with interests outside the rather narrow sphere of looking after her husband and running her home—and this must be conspicuous from my list of examples |examples of advertisements he brought with him| ... I must confess that this particular role of women is not a noticeable feature of television advertising.

American advertisers have often been recorded for being considerably more honest about their attitudes toward the female consumer than the British ones. Komisar[17] in a review of such statements says:

> Men's reactions to charges of sexism in advertising vary from defensive—'we don't think that it is degrading' ... 'It's a woman's role to care for the home'—to the coldly. consciously contemptuous, 'all women are masochists'.

She also quotes the results of a survey which Haug Associates, Los Angeles, made on the housewife and printed in *Ad Age* as a true representation of the 'average' female consumer, which surely reveals more about the advertiser than the woman.

> She likes to watch television and she does not enjoy reading a great deal. She is most easily reached through television and the simple. down-to-earth magazines. She finds her satisfaction within a rather small world and the centre of this world is her home.
> She has little interest or skill to explore. to probe into things for herself. Her energy is largely consumed in day-to-day living. She is very much open to suggestion and amenable to guidance that is presented in terms that fit in with her needs and with her view of the world.

> She tends to have a negative or anti-conceptual way of thinking. Mental activity is
> arduous for her. Her ability for inference particularly in unfamiliar areas is limited.
> And she tends to experience discomfort and confusion when faced with ambiguity or
> too many alternatives . . .
>
> She is a person who wants to have things she can believe in with certainty, rather
> than things she has to think about.

Criticisms about the male advertiser's views of the female consumer have, surprisingly, come as often from their women colleagues as anyone else. Franchielli Cadwell [18], for example, President of the Cadwell-Compton advertising agency says of the men in the advertising profession:

> Most men in advertising think of women as having low intelligence. They believe that
> across the country women are really children. You can't say anything too fancy to
> them. Conversations with doves in kitchens, giants coming out of washing machines,
> crowns magically appearing on heads when a certain margarine is used. Even the calibre
> of daytime television soap-operas doesn't approach the idiocy of commercials. I think
> it's a security thing—they want to think of women as having very few interests—that
> her life really does begin and end with clean floors. You could substitute 'women' for
> 'mentally-retarded' and they say, 'It sells, doesn't it?' That is their principle argument.
> That this low level fantasy sells. They always show a woman in the kitchen so they
> always show a woman in the kitchen. They want the same old stuff because it worked
> the last time.

Gartner (1971) [19], vice president for research at Daniel and Charles notes the advertiser's justification of 'do it if it works, the consequences are not our concern'. She suggests that advertising men actually avoid the notion that the current images may be stereotyping and demeaning, and that other approaches *could work as well or better,* because the current approach is ultimately a reinforcement of their own prejudices. To change the method would need a counter-change, a reformulation of their own attitudes which would be cognitively discomforting.

Caroline Bird who spoke at the International Congress of the American Marketing Association in April 1970 found resistance to her talk on the implications of the changing role of women to be astonishing. The men, who were representatives of manufacturers and advertising agencies made fun of what she said and proclaimed it ridiculous. To attempt to combat the resistance of advertisers and marketers to suggestions about change in women's advertisements, Cadwell inserted an advertisement in *Advertising Age* which represented views both of her agency and her women colleagues about contemporary advertising imagery. It read:

> The notion that women are hysterical creatures with inferior intellects that respond
> best to tales of Aladdin—like giants and magical clowns—is horrendously insulting.
> When over 55% of the women in the country are high school graduates and 25%
> have attended colleges . . . aren't they beyond house-i-tosis? At the very least women
> deserve recognition as being in full possession of their faculties.

Komisar (1971)[17] puts particular stress on the fact that the advertisers' imagery addressed to women is patently a reflection of their own fantasies; these copywriters and designers. and the marketers who approve them are seeking re-affirmation of their own subconscious fantasies about women, not women's fantasies about men. She says:

> Advertising also reinforces men's concepts about women's place and women's role—and about their own roles. It makes masculine dominance legitimate—and conversely questions the manhood of men who do not want to go along with the stereotypes.

We have already noted how the use of phallicism in advertising could just as equally be interpreted as the male advertiser subconsciously acting out a demonstration of masculinity to a captive female audience. Ferguson (1973)[20] makes a similar observation. that most advertising directed at women, particularly that with a sexual content was as. if not more likely to be for male titillation as for selling female products. She states curtly: 'as most of women's advertising is done by men this is hardly surprising'. Seebohm (1969)[21] also took this point head-on when she directly examined the role of the advertiser's perceptions of women and how this would necessarily affect his advertising imagery. She cites the observation by Margaret Mead that there is 'the rise of a new and subtle form of anti-feminism in which men under the guise of exalting the importance of maternity are tying women even more tightly to their children'. Seebohm is not surprised by this. She draws attention to the vast numbers of commercials and advertisements which glorify the 'sacred role' of motherhood and notes that, since it is a male advertiser who is likely to have created these advertisements, is it likely that he will promote something which is against his own self-interest, stereotypy. insult and sales notwithstanding?

> ... obviously your male copywriter prefers the idea of his wife at home with the children than out at work—it's perfectly natural. Hence his fantasies are reflected in the copy he writes and in the client's acceptance. It is also perfectly natural that he should like the idea of woman as sexual object. and that he should produce advertising to support it.

Thus, can a man ever seriously disentangle his own fantasies about women from his work?

Gregory (1966)[22] encapsulates this problem for the designer. the copywriter, the photographer and the artist in the agency when he explains in his study on illusion that we do not draw or design or photograph simply 'what we see' *but do so according to rules which are culturally learned.* Similarly. we do not 'see' what is drawn. but what that image is interpreted as meaning and what the context indicates; that is, the camera, the pen and the brush code the world in front of them.

Men have always had images of women and there has never been a reason for this imagery to concede to women's reality, when women. as the inferior sex, have been effectively taught to conform with it. Woman is mother or whore, succouring or sexy, respected or reviled, and the advertiser, more than any man, has the chance to re-affirm these images continually through his work; see the well-taught housewife, like the original Uncle Tom, trustingly respond in the way she now knows; in fact, only knows.

Millum[23], in his empirical studies on the image of women in advertising media explains:

> . . . advertising . . . acts as a moulder of female outlook and does serve as a legitimisation of those roles in which so many women find themselves. The role, the life patterns indicated, the stances adopted, are all consistent in their occurrence and their form and are, it must be remembered, cumulative . . .
>
> The reification of the female, loss of individual independence, introversion, the retreat into the womb of the home, woman as the natural half of humanity, guardian of the past and the future, the emphasis on sexual attraction, competitiveness, all these occur again and again . . .
>
> . . . although the woman as man's foil, his servant and subordinate, seems to be the opposite of woman as a self-sufficient, inward-looking being, these are but two sides of the same coin. The alternative word coin shows woman as man's equal and woman as an independent spirit *and this is the missing image.*

THE TEXT BOOK

Given the enormous financial importance of women in the world of consumer marketing, it follows that each marketing text book issued for consumption by students of marketing and advertising, as well as practitioners, should contain a good section, or at least a chapter, on the behaviour, role or contribution of women to the operation of marketing business. In a chapter on retailing, for example, it should perhaps be noted that the majority of shoppers are women, and there should be an examination of female shopping frequency, how and when women work and how they shop with the family. In a review of marketing research, we should find an acknowledgement of the fact that most research studies in consumer-marketing are on female respondents, and find a good look at sex differences in interview interaction, and perceptual bases in female psychology. The consumer should be referred to as 'she' more than 'he' and if we look at the function of the household we should see it through the eyes of the woman, since she is both envoy and gatekeeper for the family purchasing behaviour. This is what we *should* find.

Unfortunately, from a random survey amongst the most used marketing and advertising texts it seems that a curious blindness seems to affect the authors so that they can accurately see and describe every aspect of the marketing process except the sex of the person who buys. There is an alarming coyness which prevents them from noticing the fact that the consumer is most frequently, most commonly and most importantly, a woman. Perhaps we have here the industrial textual equivalent of the Victorian tendency to cover up piano legs and the knees of chairs lest we be forced to recognise that they exist.

While the survey was essentially informal and did not intend to take the form of a technically and statistically accurate content analysis, the general trend and indications did not require such elegant methods. The absence of the female consumer was patently obvious.

These books were divided into three arbitrary sections which related to the level at which they are used.

SAMPLE

Marketing

1. Introductory texts.   Smallbone (1968)[24]; Giles (1966) and (1969)[25]; Watts (1972)[26]; Elvy (1972)[27]; Baker (1971)[28]. These are simple and descriptive texts which aim to give the bare bones and basic priorities of marketing to the student.

2. More advanced texts. Ehrenberg and Pyatt (eds.) (1972)[29]; James (1972)[30]; Field, Douglas and Tarpey (1966)[31]; Mathews, *et al* (1964)[32]; McIver (1969)[33]; Wills (1971)[34]. These are more complex texts which view marketing from a more integrated and technical aspect. They often deal with psychological and sociological concepts of consumer behaviour.

3. Basic texts.   Kotler (1972)[35]; Engel, Kollat and Blackwell (1968)[36]. These were included because they are popular and essential texts for students above the introductory stage. Kotler is used on a variety of courses from first degrees to master's courses and is the recognised 'major' work on marketing theory. Engel, Kollat and Blackwell is regarded as the most composite and definitive work on consumer behaviour theory, to date.

Advertising

The books used here were: Jefkins (1971)[37]; Adams (1971)[38]; Nicholls (1973)[39]. There are few books devoted exclusively to advertising theory and these three are used by students on advertising and marketing courses which specialise in advertising as a separate subject, such as the HNC and HND courses in Business Studies.

All the books were examined from three approaches:

1. A simple index search was made for terms which would refer the reader to information on the female consumer. Those chosen were 'female', 'woman', 'wife', 'housewife', 'consumer/customer (female)', 'sex' or 'sex differences'. At the same time a search was made for chapter headings or section headings of a similar ilk.

2. If there were references in the index these were followed up and the accuracy and quality of the text to which they related were examined.
3. A cursory search was made from beginning to end of the book to attempt to determine both the frequency of incidental references to the female consumer; the use of 'he' or 'she' in references to consumer behaviour; the extent of associated references such as to 'household', 'family' and 'housewife purchases' which were not referred to in the index.

Table 16:1   The Female Consumer in the Text Book

INTRODUCTORY TEXTS

	Index references	*Main observations in index references*	*Chapter/sections devoted to female*
Baker	none	n/a	none
Elvy	none	n/a	none
Giles (1)	none	n/a	none
Giles (2)	3	'female labour' 'influence of women' (@ 1.000 words)	'The Influence of Women' (page 81) @ 350 words
Smallbone	none	n/a	none
Watts	no index	n/a	none

MORE ADVANCED TEXTS

Ehrenberg	none	n/a	none
James	1	'women at work' (@ 60 words)	none
Field Douglas Tarpey	none	n/a	none
Mathews *et al*	5	'women as purchasers' 'women working' (@ 1.000 words)	'Distribution by sex' 'Sex and Buying Decisions' 'The Role of Working Women'.
McIver	none	n/a	none
Wills	none	n/a	none

TWO BASIC TEXTS

Kotler	none	n/a	none
Engel Kollat and Blackwell	none	n/a	none

ADVERTISING TEXTS

Jefkins	22	'women's footwear' 'advertising' 'women's press' 'women's institutes' 'sex in advertising'	none
Adams	2	'women's monthlies' 'women's weeklies'	'Women's Weeklies' 'Women's Monthlies'
Nichols	none	n/a	none

Introductory Texts

Taking the books, section by section, in the introductory texts we find
that of the five that had an index, four made no reference in any form
to the female consumer. Out of all six only one devoted a section heading
to the topic. The one text which did make reference to the woman buyer
was the larger work by Giles which referred once to 'female labour' and
twice to the 'influence of women'. The second reference was a sector in
its own right. He makes some observations on the emancipation of women
from their traditional roles and that 'Increases in educational opportunities
and widened horizons have made women, especially those of the middle
class, less content than their forbears with a dull domestic routine.' He
concludes that this trend would stimulate interest in 'anything which saves
time and labour in the kitchen or in the way of domestic goods'. He
does not mention that women are the main consumers of food and clothing
and domestic goods although this could be implied by his devoting over 500
continuous words to the woman as buyer. He states:

> The growing importance of women in society over the present century is an undeniable
> fact and the influence of the women's attitudes is extending to an ever wider range
> of products. No longer is the housewife's influence limited to the selection of food;
> she has a dominant part in deciding on the purchase of almost every article in the
> house and in a large number of cases on the selection of the house itself. Her view
> on the colour and styling of the car may carry equal weight with her husband's
> view on engine performance ... and the introduction of televisions and many
> home-comforts has helped wives to condition the habits of their husbands.

Compared to the total absence of reference to women in other texts, this
is generous and radical stuff indeed. Nevertheless, Giles falls into the trap
of over-generalisation by reference to the good old 'cake-mix' finding which
must take top prize among marketers for consistent textual reference. This
ancient research result was recorded by a motivational researcher who
found that women's purchases of a certain cake-mix increased when the
women were told to 'add one egg' and thereby, the explanation goes,
were convinced they were doing their role-fulfilling bit for the family. Using
this single, old and unsupported finding, Giles concludes that modern woman
still has 'underlying traditional states of mind'.

Making a trek through these six introductory texts again, this time from
front to back, it was found that women made slightly more of an appearance
than the indices would indicate. Nevertheless, Smallbone made no mention
that could be found of the female consumer, or even the *femaleness* of
the consumer, since he persistently referred to the consumer in masculine
terms. For example, on depth research (wherein most respondents are female):
'The technique consists of opening up a subject with a respondent and
allowing him time to expose what he knows or thinks about it.' (What—
buying cheese and bread or selecting clothes and detergents for the family?)

In the smaller work by Giles there were a few concessions that women shop (page 14) but this appeared to be all while in Elvy, a whole chapter on 'Marketing and the Consumer' only managed to mention, or at least imply, the sex of the consumer once and that was in relation to the 'housewife' panel. As far as could be seen, this priestly reticence persisted throughout the rest of the book since no more references to the consumer by sex occurred again.

Baker notes that 'markets are people' but omits to note which sex in particular, although it was gratifying to find women so honoured. He does, however, make an observation on page 44 that socio-economic classifications 'which are based on the household head and ignore the impact of the working wife on lower class incomes' are unsatisfactory. He makes a handful of mentions of the housewife, usually in connection with purchase choice. For example, on page 38 he refers to housewives and dishwashers, and on page 65 to housewives and detergents. He does, however, slip into the wrong sexual pronoun from time to time; for example, on page 56 he refers to goods for use by the ultimate household consumer and 'in such form as they can be used by *him* without further commercial processing' despite the fact that most household goods are ultimately and almost exclusively used by the woman of the house. Baker, nevertheless, makes some of the most fair and well-distributed references to the female consumer, in this section of texts.

This, however, one cannot say about Watts. In by far the most amusing book, he makes no concessions to the female shopper and implies that the male shopper is the norm with statements such as (page 91): 'but subconsciously many of them [advertisments] leave an impression that motivates him next time he visits a shop even if he does not realise it'. Most advertisments in the consumer market, to which he is referring, are aimed at women as are most of the shops, so why does he use this masculine reference? Generally, however, Watts leaves the consumer's sex carefully unspecified even in the notes on housewife panels (page 91), so much so that one would come away with the impression that the respondents were sexually neutral.

More Advanced Marketing Texts

The six more advanced marketing texts do not offer much better pickings than the previous 'introductory' six. Of the texts noted, four made no index reference to women except James who made one reference which related to 60 words on 'women at work', and Mathews. Mathews, in fact, was the honourable and only exception to the denial of the existence of the female consumer in this section. This text, an American one, made five references to women mainly under the two headings of 'women as purchasers' and 'women working'. Here were also three section headings devoted to the female consumer: 'Distribution by Sex', which noted the importance of sex segmentation as an arbiter of cultural differences, 'Sex and the Buying Decisions', which noted the greater role of the woman in the buying process and 'The Role of Working Women', isolating female labour as one of the major influences of change in marketing in the next decade. The references by Mathews are similar to those by Giles, noted above. They are enthusiastic and generous in their recognition of the relevance of the woman buyer.

> Women make or influence the buying decisions on a tremendous range of products ... Wives also purchase most of the deodorants for their husbands and most of the school supplies for the children ... often much of the furniture and many of the appliances for the home, and even the fertiliser for the lawn.
> Women also buy the so-called male luxury products such as home-workshop equipment and glass fishing-rods, and give them as gifts. Even before marriage, single girls buy many clothing accessories, such as leather goods and sports shirts for men.

As if these comments are not unusual enough, the authors then suggest that many marketing strategies could be more tailored to women, for example, life insurance and cars. They note the importance of *men* in *women's* purchasing decisions, that men shop more, buy some women's products for women, buy groceries and children's clothing and, in an interesting reversal of the usual attitude to consumer behaviour descriptions of the consumer durable market, note (page 82) that: 'Men participate with *or influence their wives* in the purchase of large appliances.'

James was the only text, apart from the one by Mathews *et al*, in this section to index a reference to women and this was to 'female labour'. His reference makes fairly feeble reading after the concessions by the American authors when, in a short reference to women at work, he makes some connection between this and the purchase of goods. He makes the somewhat subjective comment that:

> Even the desire to acquire a stock of goods and services in class-conscious, affluent societies may not be enough to offset the social opprobrium of a wife working.

This statement by Mr. James implies that the two-thirds of married women who currently work are doing so at the expense of some social acceptance. What is perhaps being referred to is the social unacceptance that some men feel *should* be aimed at women who work, a sentiment that we have found particularly prevalent among sections of the marketing industry. Looking through these texts again in greater detail, we find nothing of great importance to add.

Field, Douglas and Tarpey do make note of women and girls in relation to innovation (page 131) adolescent girls (page 128) and some other isolated but cursory references while, in the book by Wills, reference is made to the housewife panel but this is called 'household panel', which effectively neutralises the reference. In the book edited by Ehrenberg and Pyatt we find frequent descriptive references to the woman buyer in the context of research studies.

McIver also makes a few passing remarks about women but somewhat patronisingly:

> The objective of Point-of-Sale advertising is that the new idea which enters the house-wife's head at one of these opportunities should be the idea of buying your product.

> Consumer panels, like the Attwood Panel record the housewife's statements on the type of shops in which she makes her purchases. but the housewife may not be very expert in the classification of shop types.

Two Basic Marketing Texts

In the two basic marketing texts, those by Kotler, and Engel, Kollat and Blackwell, we find the similarly depressing pattern of omission of reference to the woman buyer from the indices, and no section or chapter references devoted to her behaviour. Strangely enough, Kotler and Engel *et al* make index references to the Negro markets which bears out an observation, which we will explore in more detail in the next few sections, that the Negro is in a more advanced state of media and marketing acceptance than women. Kotler has written a long book, so the examination was principally on the chapter on 'buyer behaviour' in which one would expect, more than any other, to find reference to the woman buyer. Nonetheless, only about ten small references were made, in isolated patches, to the female consumer and these only represented about 500 words at the outside. Although one recognised an implication of the importance of the woman buyer, this was never as honestly and directly stated as, for example, by Mathews. Kotler refers to women in passing. such as on housewives and brand selection (page 177, housewife brand-choice sequences) but with little enthusiasm.

With Engel *et al*, the bulk of research studies which they quote on consumer behaviour experiments are made on female subjects, principally the housewife. Frequent references, therefore, are made to women but throughout. there is a blurring of the sex differences in consumer markets and nowhere is all that data on the female consumer summated into some homogenous whole on the woman buyer. The largest section directly concerning the woman is one on the 'influence of the family' on buying behaviour which represents a greater proportion of print than any other book, about 10 pages in 600. Yet, this is approached from the nebulous angle of the total family rather than from the perspective of the housewife so the opportunity to understand the female family buying influence is lost.

Advertising Texts

With the advertising books, however. we find that of all the sample they make the most honest and representative survey of women in the marketing field. There is still a lot missing and while Jefkins makes 22 separate references in the index and Adams two, only Adams devotes sections specifically to the woman and these are on magazine types, the women's monthlies and the women's weeklies. Still, going through the texts again in more detail, there are obviously more concessions to the woman as buyer than in the marketing texts. Adams makes frequent sample breaks by sex for each of the main media and Jefkins refers to the advantages and the disadvantages of certain media in the light of whether they reach women buyers or not, and how they measure female readership. For example, in relation to newspapers as a vehicle for media, Jefkins notes that 'The housewife readership of morning newspapers is of dubious merit and suggests a very serious defect in readership surveying.' Nicholls also makes a fair and interesting appraisal of media in relation to women, and often quotes women and women-related products to illustrate his points so that, for example, on page 85 he berates some advertisements in women's magazines because 'these do not communicate because few women identify with them'.

It may seem rather nit-picking to grope one's way through these long marketing texts for evidence of the existence of the female consumer, but the fact that one has to search and worry through mountains of prose for the odd mention that woman is the most important buyer in the consumer market, is testimony to some lack of emphasis somewhere. Should one find among 17 standard marketing texts for students and general reference that only five of them make any index reference to the woman-buyer, or that out of a total of hundreds of thousands of words on marketing and advertising theory only about 3,000 words in these 17 books even mentions the woman buyer, and often only in the context of women's media or the description of female labour? We cannot expect students of marketing and advertising to respect and observe the behaviour of the female consumer, let alone understand the truth of her social, psychological and political/ economic role, if the very texts from which this fact could be gleaned manage to ignore her very existence.

I have had some experience of teaching young male students in marketing and advertising classes to recognise the relevance of women in consumer economics and the reaction has ranged from sheer disbelief that women do have this important contribution, to patronising and insulting remarks about women being incapable of working out simple money problems 'let alone buying responsibly'. The fact that the majority of housewives in this country carry out, every day, problems of income maximisation and purchase and household management which, rated objectively, would put them well above these students in terms of management responsibility and ingenuity, seems to be remote from their comprehension. I have also had no experience of any examination question ever touching the relevance of the women buyer, a topic that most male marketing lecturers find amusing and irrelevant, though no practical advertiser and some practical marketers would not dare to do so. Furthermore, students who write dissertations and essays on such things as food buying, shopping, consumer psychology and 'the family' manage to chase their way through anything from 1,000 to 30,000 words referring to the consumer constantly as 'he' and never once mentioning anything to do with female consuming behaviour, the influence of the housewife in her family and the relevance of female influence in all consumer goods. Women, it seems, are relevant so long as they may appear in media as simple-minded housewives and amiable, sexual objects, but once out of this capacity, they change their structure in the marketing concept and trickle away like sand in a timer.

Nevertheless, to conclude this section on a note of optimism, one must note a recent book by an advertising creative director, Robin Wight, who bravely breached the wall of traditional marketing masculinity and came out with a fair and emphathetic chapter on the 'new housewife' in his study of advertising and consumerism [40]. The refreshing quality of this chapter is the way it pictures the woman buyer as some multi-dimensional entity; not a two-dimensional, flat, predictable cardboard replica. He reports, for example, surveys which demonstrate the futility that some women feel about housewifery, observes the greater propensity for women to work and the increase of this trend in the future. He notes the growing domestic participation of the husband and the decreasing status of shopping. He sees women in a critical state of social flux not continuations of an eternal stereotype. Furthermore, in his last paragraph of this chapter he says more in one sentence than all the other marketing books put together. He notes a fact that they were unwise to ignore because it contains the seeds of all dynamism in consumer marketing. He says: 'if the consumer changes, so will her consumption.'

A simple statement? An obvious little remark? Think about it—because very few marketers have. How, for a starter, will most marketers know if the consumer has changed if they have never 'seen' the consumer in the first place?

In their recent study of the content of gynaecology textbooks, Scully and Bart [41] found that even among recent and respected texts, fundamental inaccuracies were perpetrated about the female sex drive and potential. Contrary to the extensive research and findings by Kinsey, and Masters and Johnson, at least half of the texts stated that the male sex drive was stronger than the female's (the reverse would be truer); she was interested in sex for procreation more than for recreation (it is the clitoris and not the penis which is constructed for no other function than pleasure) and that the vaginal orgasm was the 'mature' response (a finding completely refuted by Masters and Johnson who in fact found that the vaginal orgasm simply did not exist).

The authors concluded that the blame for this epidemic of misleading teaching in respected texts came evidently from the fact that the gynaecological sector was predominantly male, that the books were written from a male viewpoint and that 'Gynaecology appears to be another of the forces committed to maintaining traditional sex role stereotypes, in the interest of men and from a male perspective.'

As with gynaecologists, so it is with the advertising and marketing industry. Here we have it all: the predominance of males; the masculine attitudes towards the female potential unsullied by recourse to contemporary and accurate data; the control by men of a largely female population/clientele and the absence from text books of accurate or, in fact, any data on the importance or potential of the female consumer.

The only real difference between the two groups seems to centre on emphasis. At least the gynaecologists restrict themselves to one part of woman; the marketers feel they have a right to all of her. To paraphrase Scully and Bart: '|advertisers and marketers|, our society's official experts on women, think of themselves as the woman's friend. With friends like that, who needs enemies?'

REFERENCES

1. Rosemary Scott, 'Women in Marketing', *Marketing* (April 1974).
2. Sally Cedar, 'Women Don't Get Such a Bad Deal After All', *Adweek* Supplement, 'Women's World', (2 November 1973).
3. Pat Mann, President of the Women's Advertising Club, *Campaign*, (18 May 1973).
4. M. Kalen, 'Attitudes Toward the dual role of the Married Professional Woman', *American Psychologist* 26 (3) (1971), pp. 301–7.
5. Jane Prather, 'Why Can't Women be more like Men', *American Behavioral Scientist* (November 1971).
6. J. Fabian, 'The Hazards of Being a Professional Woman', *Professional Psychologist* (Fall 1972).
7. Benson Rosen and Thomas H. Jerdee, 'Sex Stereotyping in the Executive Suite', *Harvard Business Review* (March-April 1974), pp. 45–58.
8. Bernard M. Bass, Judith Krusell and Ralph A. Alexander, 'Male Managers' Attitudes Toward Working Women', *American Behavioral Scientist* (1971), pp. 221–36.
9. G. W. Allport, *'The Nature of Prejudice*, Doubleday (New York 1958).
10. E. Peterson, 'Working Women', in R. J. Lifton (ed.), *The Woman in America*, Riverside (Cambridge, Mass. 1965).
11. Philip Jourdan in the *Guardian* (14 February 1973).
12. *Harvard Business Review* (July 1973), Noted in ref. 11.
13. Michael Korda, *Male Chauvinism: How it works*, Barrie and Jenkins (1972).
14. Alvin A. Achenbaum, 'Advertising Doesn't Manipulate Consumers', *Journal of Advertising Research*, Vol. 12(2) (April 1972), pp. 3–13.
15. Stephen Greyser, 'What do Americans Think About Advertising?', *Advertising Quarterly* (Summer 1965), pp. 33–42.
16. Ronnie Kirkwood at the Convention of the National Council of Women, (March 1973).
17. Lucy Komisar, 'The Image of Women in Advertising', in Vivian Gornick and Barbara K. Moran (eds.), *Women in a Sexist Society: Studies in power and powerlessness*, Basic Books (1971), p. 304.
18. Franchielli Cadwell, noted in 17.
19. Diana Gartner, *see* chapter 18, ref. 65 (1971).
20. Ferguson, *see* chapter 15, ref. 21.

21. Caroline Seebohm, 'Sexual Appeals in Advertising: A feminine view', *Advertising Quarterly* (Autumn 1969), pp. 23–7.
22. R. L. Gregory, *Eye and Brain,* Weidenfeld and Nicholson (London 1966).
23. Trevor Millum, *Images of Women: Advertising in women's magazines,* Chatto and Windus (1974).
24. Douglas Smallbone, *An Introduction to Marketing,* Granada Publishing (1968).
25. G. B. Giles, *Marketing,* M & E Handbooks, Macdonald and Evans (1969).
    G. B. Giles, 'Marketing Management', (2nd ed.) MacDonald and Evans (1966).
26. Reginald Watts, *The Businessman's Guide to Marketing,* Business Books (1972).
27. B. Howard Elvy, *Marketing Made Simple,* W. H. Allen (1972).
28. M. J. Baker, *Marketing: An introductory course,* Macmillan Student Edition (1971).
29. A. S. C. Ehrenberg and F. G. Pyatt (eds.), *Consumer Behaviour,* Penguin Books (1972).
30. B. G. S. James, *Integrated Marketing,* Penguin Books (1972).
31. George A. Field, John Douglas and Lawrence X. Tarpey, *Marketing Management: A behavioral systems approach,* Charles E. Merrill Books (1966).
32. John B. Mathews Jnr., Robert D. Buzzell, Theodore Levitt and Ronald E. Frank, *Marketing: An introductory analysis,* McGraw-Hill (1964).
33. Colin McIver, *Marketing,* Pan Books (1969), published for the Institute of Practitioners in Advertising.
34. Gordon Wills, *Contemporary Marketing,* Pitman Publishing (1971).
35. Philip Kotler, *Marketing Management: Analysis, planning and control,* Prentice-Hall (Englewood Cliffs, N.J. 1972).
36. James F. Engel, David T. Kollat and Roger D. Blackwell, *Consumer Behaviour,* Holt Rinehart and Winston (1968).
37. Frank Jefkins, *Advertising Today,* International Textbook Company (1971).
38. James R. Adams, *Media Planning,* Business Books (1971), published for the Institute of Practitioners in Advertising.
39. David Shelley Nicholls, *Advertising: Its purpose, principles and practice,* MacDonald and Evans (1973).
40. Robin Wight, *The Day the Pigs Refused to be Driven to Market,* Hart-Davis MacGibbon (1972).
41. Diana Scully and Pauline Bart, 'A Funny Thing Happened on the Way to the Orifice: Women in gynaecology text books', in Joan Huber (ed.) *Changing Women in a Changing Society,* University of Chicago Press (1973).

17. The Woman and the Negro

We have suggested and demonstrated in chapter 16 that one major effect of the masculine nature of the advertising and marketing industry might be to effectively abort any enlightened attitudes or original imagery connected with the female consumer. This, however, puts considerable stress on a fatalistic indulgence of the opinions and prejudices of the men in the industry. Social evidence, unhappily, indicates that the industry has not really the time available for such indulgence.

If change is on the way, in the marketing to and the portrayal of the female consumer, then it is indicated by two areas. Both these areas are external to the industry, may well put pressure on it and the marketer and advertiser would be wiser to learn from them, rather than to ignore them. These two areas are the expressed opinion from women themselves about advertising and marketing strategy directed at them, and the evidence from America concerning marketing policy towards the Negro sector, a group which has faced many of the problems that now confront the female consumer.

EXPRESSED ATTITUDES OF WOMEN TOWARDS ADVERTISING IMAGERY

What we have looked at so far have been the attitudes of the advertiser and marketer to the female consumer, vocalised, implied and expressed through formal texts. Nevertheless, to balance the conceptual triangle of the three participants in consumer marketing, what have women said, and what reactions have they made to existing advertising imagery?

Until a very recent article by Wortzel and Frisbie (1974)[1] women had not expressly been asked their opinion of the images of the woman in mass and advertising media. Where studies have made an examination of consumers' attitudes towards advertising *and* made a sample break by sex there have usually been some other catches, such as categorisation of 'complaints' categories in such a way as to exclude all mention of the tone or quality of the image.

278

For example, one of the most recent published studies on the consumer's attitude to advertising by Jobber (1974)[2] makes an equal sample split of 480 respondents by sex; but none of the categories which measure the consumer response to advertising would measure attitude to imagery even if the consumer wanted to express something about it. Nevertheless, we can make some interpretations of the results as they stand. In the category of 'exaggerated and annoying advertising' it is interesting to note that women cite washing powder advertisements as by far the worst example, and while this could be attributed to the repetitiousness of this group of advertisements it could also be attributed to the fact that they have a tendency, more so than other advertisements, to both stereotype the housewife and to patronise her intelligence (the careful repetition by women of every word of more than three syllables—'bi-o-lo-gi-cal'—the patient instruction by the actor-demonstrator, the necessity to hire lecture halls to teach women how washing powder works). This contention is also supported by Jobber's finding that when women were asked generally why they found advertisements annoying they replied with particular emphasis on the fact that they were 'an insult to the intelligence'.

A second area where the women expressed some displeasure was with the use of gratuitous sex, woman as a sex object, in advertisments, which tends to support our earlier suggestion that these advertisements are as much an extension of the advertiser's fantasies about women as a means to sell a product. Women also ranked 'homely' and 'romantic' advertisements as third and fourth in their 'worst types of advertisements' categories, which take in most styles of imagery directed at women.

Isn't there something in this type of research result which should discomfort the advertiser?

A study by Greyser (1965)[3] also noted that 43% of a sample of 1,846 adults in America felt that 'most advertising insults the consumer' and that only 41% of people were favourably disposed towards advertising, but disappointingly did not make sample breaks or analyses for sex. Nevertheless, a more recent study by Haller (1974)[4] did make analyses by sex for advertisement approval/disapproval and his results are important since they come from students, that is, the up-and-coming generation of consumers. It is also interesting that it is among students, and American students in particular, that we find the most immediate effects of the Women's Movement.

The sample consisted of 249 women and 251 men from 62 fields of study, from five major metropolitan connurbations. Again we find 'insult to intelligence' creeping into the responses and particularly among the female respondents. Nearly 82% of students felt that about half of the advertising addressed to consumers insulted their intelligence but of the female students, 85% felt that *more than half* of all types of advertising insults their intelligence. Furthermore, while most men believed that less than half of all advertising was in bad taste, the majority of women felt that *more* than half was.

The rest of the responses were fairly consistent by socio-economic status, age and sex categories so that both men and women agreed with the notions discussed. For example, only one third of the students agreed with the statement that 'advertising is necessary' while 45% disagreed with the statement that advertising is a good information source. More than 60% believed that more than half of all advertising makes invalid advertising claims and/or misleading statements; 75% felt that the advertisements contained too little information and 66% felt that more than half of all advertisements were irritating; 80% of them gave television advertising the highest scores for 'annoying' advertising while magazine and newspaper advertisements were viewed as slightly less annoying. Nevertheless, for attacking the problem of women and advertising imagery, the best study, using some formal techniques, is the one published in 1974 by Wortzel and Frisbie, which is described in more detail because it looks at the very problem which this chapter is examining.

Wortzel and Frisbie make the perspicacious observation that while content analyses, such as those by Courtney and Lockeretz, and Wagner and Banos, (noted in chapter 15 [8,10]), have measured the incidence and type of advertising imagery directed at women, they do not measure its effectiveness. Intending to fill the theoretical gap, the authors submitted two hypotheses for examination:

1. When a woman appears in an advertisement, the desirability of the product advertised to women exposed to the advertisement will be enhanced if that women is portrayed in a career or neutral (less than traditional) role, rather than in a sex-object, family or fashion-object (more traditional) role.
2. Those women who most strongly agree with the tenets of the Women's Liberation Movement will most strongly consider a product's desirability enhanced when a woman appearing in the advertisement is portrayed in a career or neutral (less traditional) role.

The subjects were a hundred 21–35 year old women drawn non-randomly from a good distribution of demographic characteristics. Each subject was asked to 'make' an advertisement from two portfolios of pictures, the one containing a wide range of products and the other pictures of women in each of five roles—'neutral', 'family', 'career', 'sex object' and 'fashion object'—which were categorised before the experiment by a jury of women similar to the sample of subjects. After each woman built her advertisements she was given a self-administered paper and pencil test which had been previously validated on a similar sample of women and designed to measure attitudes toward several facets of women's liberation. The findings were very interesting:

1. Preferred role depiction in advertisements seemed to vary considerably by the product group. Where a product group had a certain use in the woman's life, the role portrayals associated with it tended to match this use. For example, products associated with 'women's grooming' were the most frequent choice for a career background, while food, household, and small appliances most often figured in a 'family background'. The 'neutral' background was most often chosen for the women's personal products (*see* Table 17:1).

Table 17:1 Per cent of Responses Selecting Each Type of Role-background by Type of Role-background

Product	ROLE BACKGROUND						
	Neutral	Career	Family	Fashion	Sex Object	No Preference	(n)
	(%)	(%)	(%)	(%)	(%)	(%)	
Small appliances	20	9	38	8	7	18	(300)
Large appliances	7	11	50	13	3	16	(300)
Women's grooming	20	23	6	30	17	4	(300)
Women's personal	32	19	16	18	10	5	(300)
Household	13	19	45	7	3	13	(300)
Food	7	8	56	4	4	21	(300)
Men's grooming and personal	3	21	9	25	17	25	(300)

Source: Wortzel and Frisbie (1974)[1].

The authors remark:

If these data support any conclusion beyond the original hypothesis it is that women react primarily to the product situation with which they are confronted and do not wish to be stereotyped into any particular role, cutting across situations in advertisements: they recognise and prefer to see themselves in a variety of roles, not excluding the more traditional one.

2. The product data, when controlled for subject's attitudes towards women's liberation, showed little consistent preference for neutral or career roles across all product lines. Feeling that this rejection of the second hypothesis might be the result of an insensitive measuring instrument for attitudes to women's liberation, the authors then constructed another instrument, 'a repression scale' based on the supposition that 'if there was any sub-group among women that would be concerned about the portrayal of women in advertisements, it would be the group that most strongly considered itself repressed by men'. This new sub-scale threw up some sharper differences:

(a) While women who scored high in positive attitudes to women's liberation sharpened their choice of roles compared to low scorers and negative scorers, high scorers on the 'repression by men' scale rejected *all* the roles presented and made 'no preference' scores.

(b) While these high 'repression by men' scorers still associated women with traditional roles for household and food products, and large and small appliances, they preferred this role less frequently than did those who scored low on this sub-scale. Nevertheless, the second hypothesis was still rejected and 'Even among women who have positive attitudes toward the Women's Liberation Movement, the product seems to be more important than the movement in determining which role portrayal will most enhance the product's desirability.'

These results provoke two observations (which the authors also note):

1. Although women agree that products for household use should be shown in a household setting, it should be interpreted as agreement with the *ways* in which these products are advertised. This finding does not allow for any criticism of tone of the advertisement. For example, a housewife will use a household product and no woman, liberationist or traditionalist, would disagree with this. What is important is not to show that household product in such a way as to imply that housewives who use it are idiots; that she has nothing to do except housework; or that her 'natural' role is that of housewife and she should feel guilty if she does anything else.

Women in this experiment by Wortzel and Frisbie were not given the opportunity to influence the tone, as opposed to the simple structure, of the advertisements. On this basis the authors concluded that advertisers should only interpret the results as general product positions in general role-types. They are to serve as 'broad guide lines for the *initial creative concept'.*

2. Socialisation will play some role in advertisement structure. Wortzel and Frisbie note: 'the reason why the women studied here prefer the role portrayals they chose is that advertising (not to mention other facets of society) have socialised women to expect and accept traditional role portrayals in ads.' They also note that there was a significant minority among the subjects who expressed 'no preference', and some of these may have preferred a man in the household role to any of the choices offered.

Nevertheless, given these qualifications to this interesting study, the authors conclude that 'women are both reasonable and reasonably rational in their preferences with respect to role portrayal in advertising. The data are most consistent with an interpretation that the perceived desirability of a product is *primarily a function of the product's own usage and end-benefits.'*

Thus, what do women feel about advertising imagery?

The answer is that we do not yet entirely know because no study has asked all the questions.

There is some evidence that women do not like advertising which is insulting to their intelligence, homely, romantic or non-informative, and when given the opportunity to define their own roles and associate them with products, their choice is catholic; they do not view these roles in less than five dimensions, often have no preference at all, and certainly do not perceive role homogeneity over all product categories.

Data, however, are lacking on any role alternatives other than those presented in the study by Wortzel and Frisbie and particularly roles which, while common in real life, have been ignored as viable alternatives in advertising media. These would include, for example, the working woman at her job, husbands helping in domestic work, the women preparing a meal with her children after a day's work or the woman in active work such as driving, gardening, and manual work such as decorating and household repairs. Future research into women's roles as portrayed by advertising media should develop this area.

THE NEGRO AND THE WOMAN

The advertiser can learn a lot from the fact that the woman today is facing the same problems of advertising and media representation that faced the black a few years ago. The stereotyping, the incidence of representation in general media, all follow a similar pattern. Nevertheless, while the image of blacks as a cultural minority has tended to become more accurate and realistic in line with their social emancipation, for women this has only just started.

Portrayal of the Black in Films and on Television

Colle (1968)[5], for example, notes that in early motion picture films blacks were lampooned and their inferior position in white society was accentuated. One which did not, a film in 1910 showing a black, Jack Johnson, knocking out white, Jim Jeffries, ran into official bans because it was so 'disturbing' to white audiences *and to blacks as well.* Colle also notes that three of the major landmarks in the development of the motion picture portrayed the black in negative, stereotypical fashion. In Griffiths' 'Birth of a Nation' the black was 'docile, happy, laughing', while the bad black was an 'arrogant, revengeful, conniving power seeker'. Al Jolson's 'The Jazz Singer' rekindled the stereotype of the black as a 'happy, laughing, dancing imbecile with permanently rolling eyes and a widespread, empty grin', while in Selznick's 'Gone With the Wind' blacks were pictured as 'liars, would-be rapists, mammies and devoted field-hands'.

A survey by Reddick (1944)[6] of the 100 motion pictures which had black themes or black characters of more than passing significance showed that more than 75% would have to be classified as anti-black, 13% as neutral and 12% definitely pro-black.

Colle notes that the radio had a somewhat better record in the depiction of black 'types' although the *Radio Reader's Digest* was regularly criticised by the black press for portraying the black as a chicken thief or coward. He also notes that reactions against the unfavourable presentation of blacks came first in the 1930s and 1940s, in particular, with the growth of the war effort and the NAACP. The movement was also supported by the black press, prominent show-business people and, finally, the federal government. One factor which they were all concerned about is interesting to us now in our examination of the imagery of women because a similar problem is faced by women in general media today; that was the black's invisibility. The black literally did not appear in many programmes and when he did, it was definitely not in proportion to his incidence in the general population.

This black invisibility was documented by a racial analysis of television programming on three major networks in 1962 by Plotkin who discovered that the blacks appeared on the screen about once every $2\frac{1}{4}$ hours and that half of these appearances were for less than three minutes. For half of this time they played traditional black roles, most often as singer, dancer or musician[7]. To increase representation of the black, however, meant trouble from those firms and people whose prejudices could not cope with accurate racial representation in the media. Philco sponsored a programme in 1955 with Sidney Poitier as the star, the first black to have a major role in a television drama, and was promptly beseiged with demands to boycott its products and the cancellation of its distributorships by Philco franchise holders. Similarly, when the Nat King Cole Show was launched by NBC some years later, advertising support could not be found, and the show was cancelled before the season was half over.

Colle notes that by the mid-1960s, owing to public and legal pressures, there was a self-conscious integration of models and subjects in motion pictures, advertisements, television programmes and magazines. For example, in a preview night of television network programmes for the 1966–7 season, a black performer could be seen in all but one half-hour of prime time. Some called it 'tokenism' but it still represented a recognition of a problem and a significant change in previous patterns of black depiction.

Comparison of Attitudes towards the Negro and Women

So how does this slow parallel development of the black's social and media emancipation compare with that for the woman?

1. The blacks received recognition of the fact of social and media stereotypy in the late 1930s and early 1940s, while women have achieved this stage only since the late 1960s when feminism became a recognised social movement. Recognition of stereotypy and the gulf between it and reality must precede anger and, ultimately, action.

2. Like the blacks who found it 'disturbing' that a black boxer should defeat a white opponent, so do many women find it disturbing to conceive of social equality and success in careers other than housewifery and motherhood. Like refugees who find all their old understandings and abilities to be misrepresented they are appalled, frightened and then aggressively conservative in their holding onto what is safe and known.

3. Both stereotypes seem to have depended on the portrayal of enjoyment in the traditional cultural role as presented by media. The black slave, servant and lackey was a 'happy laughing . . . imbecile' while the housewife today is, as we have noted, permanently cheerful in her domestic labour. The 'widespread empty grin' of the black compares to the table-hugging vaccuity of the housewife of today. In both media stereotypes we find a tendency to deny alternatives; while there was no black who was confident and capable so there is no confident and capable woman today.

4. The blacks were largely invisible in general media and were not represented in numbers equivalent to their incidence in the actual population. We have already noted studies by Kinzer (1973), Sternglanz and Serbin (1974) and Long and Simon (1974)[8], which have measured a similar invisibility of women in general media. It is also interesting to note an observation by Colle that the recent trend to portray blacks in cowboy films is the first attempt to use a situation which must have been a norm in the Mid-West of the 1800s. Up until recently, cowboy films were predominantly 'white'.

In comparison, we can note the denial in current media of the fact that two-thirds of married women now work outside the home.

5. There was an interest by strategically powerful groups in maintaining the blacks' imagery as it was. The blacks provided cheap labour in business, commerce and agriculture. It was in the interest of business and the white majority to curtail any opportunities for the blacks to recognise identity and the potential of social organisation. With women, it is similarly in the interests of men to maintain them in their dependent, economically powerless condition because they also provide cheap labour both in the factory as production workers and in the home as unpaid housekeepers, cooks and cleaners. Women, too, are discouraged from organising by a common belief that women cannot relate to women and by the continuous media-image of a woman isolated in the home.

Applying the Negro Experience to Women

Given this brief resumé of the comparable positions of the black and the woman in the field of media imagery, it is evident that if the woman is to stimulate the enthusiasm for reality that blacks now invite, she still has some way to go.

What, however, is there in data on the black in advertising media in particular which the advertiser/marketer would find useful in understanding problems associated with women? To begin with, we should note that content-analyses of the image of the black in advertising media have revealed similar traits to those found in analyses of the woman's image. For example:

1. The image of the black has been a fragmented one, relying entirely on small particles of stereotype which are expanded to create not a whole but a caricature of a whole. Compare, for instance, the description of 'Media Woman'[10] that Komisar built up from advertising imagery with a similar description of 'Media Black'[9] formulated by Colfax and Sternberg (1972):

> ...woman is a combination sex object, wife and mother, who achieves fulfilment by looking beautiful and alluring for her boy friends and lovers, and cooking, cleaning, washing, or polishing for her husband and family. She is not very bright; she is submissive and subservient to men; if she has a job, it is probably that of a secretary or air-line hostess. What she does is not very important, anyway, since the chief interest in her life is the 'male reward'...

> ...the black is a record star; an entertainer; a celebrity; if not one of these, he is a child, a woman or a foreigner. As a male he is in need of public or private charity, and he seldom, if ever, enjoys the occupational status of the white with whom he is depicted. Missing from these ads are black families and black males, at work and leisure—in short, the black American, rather than the black stereotype.

2. The image of the black in advertisements has been forced to change in line with more favourable social opinion and in comparison the study by Wagner and Banos, which re-tested earlier findings by Courtney and Lockeretz[11], found some small changes in the presentation of women in professional posts in American advertising which could also be attributed to small changes in public opinion about women. Nevertheless, one should note that the content analyses on black emancipation in advertising have been over much longer periods. For example, Kassarjian's classic study in 1969[12] looked at blacks in advertisements over a 20-year period (1946–65) when he traced reduction in depiction of blacks in service capacities in advertisements from 78% to 13%, while Cox's similar content analysis (1970)[13] based on a study over 25 years old, that of Shuez, King and Griffith (1953)[14], traced a reduction of depictions of blacks in menial roles from 75% to 8%. Overall, however, there is an indication that it has been social pressure which has led to this change in content of advertising media for the black and we could expect a similar change if pressure for social emancipation of women reaches a similar pitch.

In addition, the advertiser is faced with the same apprehensions about economic backlash in developing a new image of women, as once faced the advertiser who dabbled with a new social image for the black. Showing a strong and capable woman is the sexual equivalent of showing a strong and capable black. Many men and women, the argument could go, would be discomforted by a new, if truthful, ideal and may react by boycotting the product and company associated with such an image.

Stafford, Birdwell and Van Tassell (1970)[15], for example, noted that many marketers in America supported the notion of segregated advertising because of the fear of a white backlash. The white market was, after all, ten times the size of the black market, and their tendency to retain the *status quo* was often based on fear of the consequences of change, let alone prejudice against change that they may also intuitively have felt. This risk has to be taken where legalities and social regulations intrude but as long as the argument remains a moral one, the demands of the accountant will come first. Stafford, Birdwell and Van Tassell say (of the black market):

> You must integrate your advertising because it is morally reprehensible to do otherwise, the argument goes. But the advertiser is a businessman first and foremost, and although his final decision may be moral, he must evaluate objectively the economic consequences of alternative strategies.

Showing integrated advertisements with blacks and whites, or showing women in responsible and non-traditional, but more accurate roles, are two sides to the same problem. Will change produce economic results which are greater than the benefits in moral, social and political terms?

One way of finding out is, of course, to look at what happened when integrated advertising was produced and the reactions of consumers to it.

Integrated Advertising: a Model for Sexual Equality in Media?

Reactions to integrated advertising in America have ranged from the neutral to the favourable, certainly nothing worse. Stafford, Birdwell and Van Tassell (1970)[15], for example, in their study of integrated advertisements on 200 white consumers, found that the reaction fell into the neutral zone.

> ... no generalisable negative response — either verbal or perceptual was found among whites toward the two integrated ads under question ... Apparently the answer is a function of several components — race, product, individual differences, and the appeal of the ad itself. *From the practical standpoint, it might be concluded that whites are generally indifferent to well-conceived integrated advertising.*

In a similar experiment by Cagley and Cardozo (1970)[16] the sampling was loaded by using subjects who scored high or low on measures of racial prejudice. The results, as one might have predicted, related largely to the degree of prejudice. Subjects who were highly prejudiced rated advertisements which contained only white principals more favourably than advertisements which showed both white and black principals. In contrast, low-prejudiced subjects evaluated all three types of advertisements, (all-white, all-black and integrated) equally. Nevertheless, did these evaluations by subjects with high prejudice have any *economic* effect? Evaluation of products and companies associated with the advertisements were similar to evaluation of the advertisements alone—but minimally so. Although evaluations of identical products, when pictured in integrated or black advertisements, were somewhat higher for low-prejudiced subjects, these differences were not statistically significant. Again, the overall conclusion from the experiment was one of neutrality of response.

Guest (1970)[17] however, actually recorded a more favourable response to the integrated advertisements in a study which relied on depictions of three social power roles. Advertisements pictured an executive seated behind a large desk with a female secretary seated beside the desk in the customary position for taking dictation. In one version both models were white (WW), in another there were two Negro models (NN), another showed a white secretary and a Negro executive (WN), and the final one, a Negro secretary and a white executive (NW). (Interestingly, the woman never got a chance to be executive.) In assessments of these four variations, Guest found that one of the main results was 'that highest company regard was shown with the integrated advertisements (NW) and (WN)'.

Generally, the *remarks* about all the interactions in integrated settings were neutral. Like Cagley and Cardozo, Guest found that most of the comments of a non-neutral nature, (one could not use a stronger term), were expressed by older and more conservative people whom one would expect to show most resistance to change. The most favourable responses came from younger and student respondents. Overall he concluded:

> ... it appears that advertisers need not be fearful of the adverse effects of the use of Negro models, whether by themselves or integrated with whites, especially in view of the expanding market of young and educated consumers.

Muse (1971)[18] investigated student subjects particularly and came to the same conclusion as Guest, that 'white college students tend to rate ads using only black models as favourably as they rate ads using only white models'. What Guest also found, as was similarly noted by Stafford, Birdwell and Van Tassell, was the degree to which acceptance of integrated ads might also be product-related. Slight variation in the generally consistently favourable response to integrated advertising from a product standpoint was also noted by Barban (1969)[21]. This point is interesting since it compares to the product-related variability of response noted by Wortzel and Frisbie in their studies on women's reaction to advertising imagery. It seems that responses to role-depictions of any cultural group are not homogenous over all products.

Reactions to integrated advertising so far, however, have been measured by studies which have concentrated on the white consumer. What does the black consumer think of integrated advertising? This is important in considering the position of women in new advertising techniques since one would expect some resistance to a new image from women themselves.

Schlinger and Plummer (1972)[19] tested the reactions of white and black consumers to all-black and all-white versions of a television commercial, which were otherwise identical. It was found that the commercial which used black models was more 'meaningful' to black viewers than the all-white commercial, and black respondents clearly favoured the black-cast commercial, empathised more with the characters and reacted positively to the advertised brand. These differences were most pronounced and accentuated among low-income and non-college educated blacks. There was no evidence that black consumers might react negatively to black actors or that substitution of black for white models had much, if any, influence on the responses of white consumers. Schlinger and Plummer concluded:

> ... the available data suggest that featuring blacks in an advertisement can enhance its effectiveness among black consumers and that the mere presence or absence of prominently shown blacks may not make much difference to whites.

Almost identical conclusions were reached by Tolley and Goett (1971)[20] in their interviews of middle- and lower-class blacks and whites in New York in February 1970. They concluded that:

> ... the data suggest that the use of black models in ads represents an advantage for the retailer and this, in turn, suggests that retailers would benefit from a *greatly increased use of black models.*

Other studies[21] support the results we have noted so far on the neutrality or favourability of the response to integrated advertising, the support by black respondents of the greater depictions of blacks, the identification of the black consumer with white, middle-class consumer standards rather than the stereotypical black standard and the economic gain to the advertiser of persisting in the use of integrated advertising. In fact, Gould, Zigband and Zoerner (1970)[22] in a study which took the unique step of investigating not only blacks about their attitudes to integrated advertising but also the advertisers who had made up the advertisements, concluded amiably that:

> It seems reasonable that advertisers today are in a unique position to influence significantly the future relationships of blacks and whites in America.

Thus, to conclude this section on the Negro and the Woman, we can note that:

1. Observation and empirical data from content analyses have demonstrated that both historically and socially, the media-image stereotype of the woman and the black has shown marked similarities. Change in the image tends to be preceded by change in social attitude.
2. When confronted by the possibility of gambling with new media images for women, advertisers can rest assured that the potential for economic

rebound is minimal, if we use evidence from a wide body of research on integrated advertising.

3. Black consumers have expressed both relief and empathy with the non-traditional depiction of blacks in advertisements. This would suggest that women, far from being hostile to fresh perceptions of their roles, might actually welcome them. This contention may be supported by indications from consumer studies that women often dislike existing advertising imagery, and do not perceive their roles as homogenous across all products, as advertisers seem to.

4. If there is any variation in role-imagery, then a sensitive variable might be the perceived use of the product. It is likely that women have several role perceptions in their life-style but these are multi-variate by products and brands. Sympathetic research is needed to elucidate this point.

THE ADVERTISER AND RESPONSIBILITY: A CONCLUSION

On 22 January 1975, BBC 2 showed a brief examination of the image of women in advertising media. Two factions from the advertising industry expressed their different views on the image of women in advertisements. No one denied that media woman was either mother/wife/housewife or the whore/mistress/lover. Several spokesmen agreed that these images denigrated women.

What was particularly disturbing in this discussion, however, was the principal argument that some advertisers advanced for the maintenance of these media stereotypes. This argument basically assumed that if the housewife did not like her current media-image, she would inform the advertiser of the fact or simply react by not buying the product.

An argument like this is so logical and practical and self-evident that it is difficult to see where one intuitively knows a break in the logic should come. Nevertheless, it must come from two areas:

1. The argument denies any understanding of cumulative media effects on the woman which have both defined her and continually reinforced this definition, so that she can no longer see that the image is an abrogation of her reality.

2. The argument also denies the fact that, for the most part, women do not have sufficient mass consciousness to either see that their discomfort is a mass phenomenon or that boycotting a product will affect anyone except themselves.

The advertiser or the marketer who presents arguments which rest on maintenance of the *status quo*, or the 'If she only protested, we would change' variety, is attempting to absolve himself of any responsibility for the images and the stereotypes that he projects, which, in the absence of legal measures, is not difficult to do, and to imply lack of understanding of the power of mass media to mould the individual consciousness.

Society is not only the product of man in the Weberian sense but man is also the product of the society. The relationship of man and the society is a dialectic one whereby each is a function of the other. Durkheim, for example, suggested that to understand the process of society we must understand three fundamental stages or activities. First, there is externalisation, the collective creation by man of his own culture, which may be in the form of products, material and non-material. Second, there is objectivation, the emergence of a reality external to and other than the creators, and this may be material (tools, ploughs) or non-material (social institutions and values etc.). Finally, there is internalisation, the re-absorption into consciousness of the objectivated world so that it determines the subjective structure of the consciousness itself. Berger (1969)[23] encapsulates the principle thus:

> Man invents a language and then finds both his thinking and speaking are dominated by its grammar. Man produces values and discovers that he feels guilt when he contravenes them.

Man thus reappropriates his own, including values and cultural patterns, but also Portnoy's Complaint, Heinz beans, 'Guinness is good for you' and the whole consumer culture. Values, overt or assumed, can become accepted unthinkingly and be thought to be what they are because that is what is 'right' or 'natural' in some absolute way. Society transmits these values, which are of its own creation but which have power to influence. Yet the power to create these values is not equally distributed. Obviously, there is an imbalance and those with a proportion of power disproportionate to their numbers are the professional communicators. Those in the mass media business are both the product and the producers of the ideas and actions which form our concept of society. Mass media are one of the tools which define our concept of culture.

It is easy to forget that the mass media do not have an amorphous autonomy of their own: *the media exist not in spite of mass culture, but mass culture exists, to a large extent, because of mass media.*

Any study of social environment in relation to mass media must make this obvious and essential point. Gerbner (1972)[24] carefully underlined the fact that the significance of the mass media lay in their ability to mass-produce messages that create mass publics whose members have nothing in common except shared messages. Shekovin (1972)[25], in his discussion of the use of mass communications to solve social problems, underlined its power to convey knowledge, provoke attitudes, shape evaluations and opinions, and stimulate emotional reliving of actual events, that is, create and reflect mass cultural conceptions. Lifton (1971)[26] ascribed to the media revolution responsibility for cultural changes in man to a 'Protean' or 'constricted psychological type', while Klapper (1957)[27] suggests a new orientation to mass media, the 'phenomenistic' approach which 'is, in essence, a shift away from the tendency to regard mass communication as a necessary and sufficient cause of audience effects, towards a view of the media as influences, in a *total situation'*. He notes that mass communication (which by itself does not act as a necessary and sufficient cause by audience effect) must typically reinforce existing conditions as well as change them. Marchais (1972)[28] suggests that man has a different ecology from animals whereby media plays the important difference. Questions of survival for the human concern his psychic life, as well as the biologic which he shares with other animals. Media are an element in his psychic life, in his ecology and his mental health, a point which is also made by Ruesch (1962)[29] who draws the conclusion that mental health can no longer be limited to an individual approach but has to include the conditions which affect the mental health of all people in society, including the mass media.

There are numerous works on the effectiveness of the mass media in achieving any of a number of aims. Do they reflect popular culture or change it? Do they act as a uniform leveller or an arbiter of individual tastes? What are the ethics and morals of individual compared to mass communication? The arguments nevertheless invariably rest on a general hypothesis, that culture and mass media are mutually creative and to some extent, given a variety of variables, are mutually supportive. Stevens (1973)[30] sums it up succinctly when he says that both living and non-living media of communication can be considered as 'mediators of culture both in the enculturative and the acculturative processes'.

We must, nevertheless, underline that mass communication is not simply a synonym for mass culture. Media is both a mirror to and an artifact of mass culture. It has a peculiarly hermaphroditic function, which may be understood by differentiating between types and situations of mass media.

Certain sorts of mass media at certain times and in certain contexts are reflective of mass culture; at other times they are manipulative of it. A domestic comedy, Hedda Gabler, a *Guardian* leader and Jimmy Young are children of the same genus, mass medium, but perform different functions in relation to the wider culture.

The *Guardian* leader and Jimmy Young have more in common than they realise, for they both seek in their different ways to reflect, but also to manipulate a change in popular conceptions by a rearrangement, a re-explanation of existing facts. There is a didactic quality to the message. Hedda Gabler is a reflection of a cultural type, but not stereotype. The play is a reflection of a non-popular but nonetheless real, human, female personality. No doubt, Hedda Gabler exists in many permutations across human types but certainly has no place in the popular cultural stereotype of womanhood.

The domestic comedy ('And Mother Makes Five', 'Love Thy Neighbour') is perhaps the most pure reflection of mass culture in its popular sense. Is womankind reflected in a stereotypical sense—didacticism present in the sense of over-simplified example, actions always tightly confined to the popular image, adding nothing, reflecting something—a reality or a caricature of reality?

And where would one fit advertising and marketing media?

As a medium it can scarcely be said to offer something new, a didactic addition to mass cultural consciousness. It cannot equate with the clear reality, the human roundness, the total personality of Hedda Gabler. It can only fall into the final category, the sterile reflection of mass culture at its most uncontroversial. It can possibly be typified as reductionism since it concentrates women and men to their blandest, most blanket level.

By definition, a minority ideal cannot exist within a mass market framework. The popular cannot reflect the non-popular even if the non-popular is the reality. Whitehead (1973)[31] says of communicators in this category:

> The need to approach us all as units in a mass involves inevitably a levelling down in the general standard of taste—a studied avoidance of the areas of experience in which we live most fully, either as individuals or as members of a group sharing a common passion or enthusiasm; a drift towards the inertly conventional triviality which is utterly without character but for that very reason, antagonises no-one.

So what do advertisers and marketers think of this aspect to their social role? D. J. Sweeney (1972)[32] suggests that marketing, as a discipline, is presently experiencing an identity crisis, and that it is seriously questioning its fundamental nature and relationship to the society within which it thrives. Marketing, he suggests, is a social process, and as such marketing cannot be limited only to the technology employed by marketing organisations. An implication of this is that marketing becomes a social responsibility.

> Stated alternatively, if marketing is recognised as an effective instrument of society, then there would be no perceived difference between the goals and values of the marketing system and those of society in general. Marketing activity would not be considered exploitive behaviour, but as a medium through which society's values are fulfilled. The marketing organisation, considering its social responsibility from this perspective, would not ask itself 'what kinds of marketing activities can I get away with?' but 'what kinds of marketing activities will have the greatest positive effect on fulfilling society's goals, values and needs?'

Purser (1965)[33] suggests that the television commercials miss a very real opportunity for the realistic portrayal of human problems. He says drama in commercials is 'being milked of all pain, all hurt, all real joy, all relevance. This is why the television critic remains suspicious of all the commercials and why their glittering leadership *is never accompanied by any cultural leadership.*'

There is a strong belief among marketing critics and exponents alike that marketing and advertising philosophy, while fulfilling efficiently its functional goals in social life is, nonetheless, forgetting its wider function as an arbiter and reflector of social values and images.

Enough has been written and much argued in the ethics of materialistic philosophy, consumerist rights, obligations in violent and potentially child-harming advertising drama.

What, however, has been widely neglected in the constructive and critical evaluation of the marketing/advertising role is the dynamic concept of social and cultural values in the reflection of human types in advertisements. The Advertising Authority and the Code of Advertising Practice Committee certainly do little to help. By no means is the female consumer protected from media exploitation by existing provisions in the various media codes. The benign powers of the ASA seem to be far more concerned with the misrepresentation of objects than of people.

We may not, for example, claim that a product performs better or differently than it is capable. We may not mislead by the use of certain emotive terms, or harass by the depiction of fearful or embarrassing situations. Yet the advertiser/marketer is still almost totally free to depict women and men in roles and actions that may or may not reflect truthfully their potential or ability.

We cannot say that a product is 'rainproof' if it lets in water at the first smell of a shower, but we can suggest that men are incapable of cooking or caring for themselves or their children, despite the obvious ability of them to do so. We cannot claim that a cold-medicine 'cures', but we can imply that a woman who uses a certain soap or detergent or perfume will have instant success as a lover/housewife/mother; be a 'better' woman than the next.

We would be prosecuted under the Trades Description Act if we say that a cosmetic is harmless although, in fact, it contains several known harmful ingredients; but we can with impunity suggest that the average woman cannot do the simplest calculation, or has intelligence limited to the preparation of a pre-packed pie, or that little girls do not play with little scientist-sets, only dolly tea-sets, that none of these claims or subtle depictions of distorted reality are harmful either to individual women or to society as a whole.

All advertising, says the CAP Code, should be 'legal, decent, honest and truthful', yet most advertising which depicts women is in direct contra-vention of any standard of honesty and even the marketers standards of truth. Yet the ASA (chiefly a male board) has cheerfully passed all these demeaning media images of women for years, despite the fact that the cumulative effect has probably been far more damaging to female morale and expectations than any number of 'woollen' blankets made of nylon or renegade nipples in cigar advertisements. It is time that the ASA widened its eyes and its horizons and saw advertisements as total statements to and about people instead of sterile fragments of an arbitrary morality. Woman are the principal subjects in and audiences of the advertisements that the ASA review. These advertisements demean, insult and misrepresent the female potential.

What are they going to do about it?

The question is, of course, does the ASA really care? Or rather, will they choose to care before the sex-image issue, like the race/colour issue, becomes more fashionable and their caring can be interpreted as 'radical'?

The ASA should remember, along with marketers and advertisers, that mass media images are part of the 'internalisation' of our cultural values. We create them as a reflection of our own cultural artifacts and reabsorb them with very little thought as to their origin or their harm, their usefulness or their truth.

The obvious is often the easiest to ignore but may be the root of cultural immorality, and the person who seeks to ignore the potential of the obvious, whether advertiser, marketer or committee member, is a party to this immorality.

The advertiser, the marketer and their representatives are directly responsible for a significant sector in the mass depiction of human potential. If this depiction is inaccurate and untruthful, but easy and profitable, a reflection of their own prejudices as much as the prejudices of all men, then will they simply avert their eyes and just refuse to examine what they are doing?

REFERENCES

1. Lawrence A. Wortzel and John M. Frisbie, 'Women's Role Portrayal Preferences in Advertisements: An empirical study'. *Journal of Marketing,* Vol. 38 (October 1974), pp. 41–6.
2. D. Jobber, 'Television Advertising: A consumer viewpoint', *European Journal of Marketing,* Vol. 8 (2) (1974), pp. 158–67.
3. *See* chapter 16, ref. 15.
4. Thomas F. Haller, 'What Students Think of Advertising'. *Journal of Advertising Research,* Vol. 14 (1) (February 1974). pp. 33–8.
5. Royal D. Colle, 'Negro Image in the Mass Media: A case study in social change', *Journalism Quarterly* (Spring 1968), pp. 55–60.
6. C. D. Reddick, 'Educational Programmes of the Improvement of Race Relations: Motion pictures, the press and libraries'. *Journal of Negro Education,* 13 (Summer 1944), p. 369.
7. Noted in Colle, op. cit.
8. Nora Scott Kinzer, *see* chapter 15, ref. 17.
   Sternglanz and Serbin, *see* chapter 15, ref. 19.
   Long and Simon, *see* chapter 15, ref. 18.
9. J. David Colfax and Susan Frankel Sternberg, 'The Perpetuation of Racial Stereotypes: Blacks in mass circulation magazine advertisements', *Public Opinion Quarterly* (1972–3), Vol. 36.
10. Lucy Komisar, 'The Image of Women in Advertising', in Vivian Gornick and Barbara K. Moran (eds.), *Women in a Sexist Society,* Basic Books (1971).
11. Courtney and Lockeretz, *see* chapter 15, ref. 8.
    Wagner and Banos, *see* chapter 15. ref. 10.

12. Harold H. Kassarjian, 'The Negro and American Advertising 1946–1965', *Journal of Marketing Research*, Vol. VI (February 1969), pp. 29–39.
13. Keith K. Cox, 'Social Effects of Integrated Advertising', *Journal of Advertising Research*, Vol. 10 (2) (April 1970), pp. 41–4.
    Keith K. Cox, 'Changes in Stereotyping of Negroes and Whites in Magazine Advertisements', *Public Opinion Quarterly* (1969–70) (33), pp. 603–6.
14. Audrey M. Shuez, Nancy King and Barbara Griffith, 'Stereotyping of Negroes and Whites: An analysis of magazine pictures', *Public Opinion Quarterly*, Vol. 17 (Summer 1953), pp. 281–7.
15. James E. Stafford, A. I. E. Birdwell and Charles E. Van Tassell, 'Integrated Advertising: White backlash?', *Journal of Advertising Research*, Vol. 10 (2) (April 1970).
16. James W. Cagley and Richard N. Cardozo, 'White Response to Integrated Advertising', *Journal of Advertising Research*, Vol. 10 (2) (April 1970), pp. 35–9.
17. Lester Guest, 'How Negro Models Affect Company Image', *Journal of Advertising Research*, Vol. 10 (2) (April 1970), pp. 29–33.
18. William V. Muse, 'Product-Related Response to Use of Black Models in Advertising', *Journal of Marketing Research*, Vol. VIII (February 1971), pp. 107–9.
19. Mary Jane Schlinger and Joseph T. Plummer, 'Advertising in Black and White', *Journal of Marketing Research*, Vol. IX (May 1972), pp. 149–53.
20. B. Stuart Tolley and John J. Goett, 'Reactions to Blacks in Newspaper Ads', *Journal of Advertising Research*, Vol. II (2) (April 1971), pp. 11–17.
21. Henry Allen Bullock, 'Consumer Motivations in Black and White', Part 1, *Harvard Business Review* (1961), pp. 89–104; Part 2 (July-August 1961), p. 110.
    Arnold Barban and Edward W. Cundiff, 'Negro and White Response to Advertising Stimuli', *Journal of Marketing Research* (November 1964), pp. 53–6.
    Arnold Barban, 'The Dilemma of Integrated Advertising', *The Journal of Business of the University of Chicago*, Vol. 42 (October 1969), pp. 477–96.
    Raymond A. Bauer and Scott M. Cunningham, 'The Negro Market', *Journal of Advertising Research*, Vol. 10 (2) (April 1970), pp. 3–13.
    Ronald F. Bush, Robert F. Gwinner and Paul J. Solomon, 'White Consumer Sales Response to Black Models', *Journal of Marketing*, Vol. 38 (April 1974), pp. 25–9.
22. John W. Gould, Norman B. Zigband and Cyril E. Zoerner Jr., 'Black Consumer Reactions to "Integrated" Advertising: An exploratory study', *Journal of Marketing*, Vol. 34 (July 1970), pp. 20–6.
23. P. Berger, *The Social Reality of Religion*, Faber and Faber (1969).
24. G. Gerbner, 'Communication and Social Environment', *Scientific American* (Sept. 1972).
25. Yu. A. Sherkovin, 'The Mass Media and their Role in Social Life', *Soviet Psychology* (Autumn 1972).
26. J. R. Lifton, 'Protean Man', *Archives of General Psychiatry* (April 1971).
27. Klapper, 'What we know about the Effects of Mass Communication: The brink of hope', *Public Opinion Quarterly*, Vol. 21 (4) (Winter 1957–8), pp. 453–74.
28. P. Marchais, 'Psychiatry and the Media', *Annales Medico-Psychologiques* (June 1972).
29. J. Ruesch, 'Mass Communication and Mass Motivation', *American Journal of Psychotherapy*, Vol. 14 (1960) and 'Human Communication and Psychiatry', *American Journal of Psychiatry* (1962).
30. W. Stevens, 'Educational Media in Social Continuity and Social Change', *Carnet de l'Enfance* (April 1973).
31. Frank Whitehead, 'Advertising', in Denys Thompson (ed.), *Discrimination and Popular Culture*, Heinemann Educational Books (1973) and Penguin Books Ltd. (1964).
32. Daniel T. Sweeney, 'Marketing Management: Technology or social process?', *Journal of Marketing*, Vol. 36 (October 1972), pp. 1–3.
33. Phillip Purser, 'The Half-World of the TV Commercials', *Advertising Quarterly*, Vol. 4 (Summer 1965), pp. 52–7.

PART VII

Marketing Research and Women

We have seen that, in many ways, the image of women in advertising media is a travesty of the reality of woman in everyday life. We have also noted that the marketing and advertising industry hold views about women which are more in line with the expectations of masculine culture than much that is reality for women. Combining the two concepts we could suppose that all prejudice and inaccuracy in advertising imagery is entirely a result of false expectations and ignorance on the part of the marketer or the advertiser. but this would be to oversimplify the connection. While assumptions about women will affect certain basic marketing actions, to what extent is this fundamental prejudice also arising from marketing research in the form of bias, so that expectations of the marketer are being artificially reinforced by spurious research results?

Extending this concept, if we can show that marketing research is capable of presenting research results about women which reinforce the cultural stereotype, then could not these methods also be responsible for other forms of bias? For example, if women react towards marketers in stereotypical fashion because of biased expectations of women by those marketers. could not these women also feed back to marketing researchers expectations about more mechanical marketing factors, such as product design, names and brands, or package structure?

To what extent and in what way can bias intrude into the research intercourse between the marketing researcher and the female consumer? This section will examine this question in detail, from the more overt bias characteristics noted particularly in social psychological and marketing research to occur in interview situations involving women, through to the more marketing-orientated bias found in the stratification systems. Finally, it will examine two research methods which have been more realistic in their attempts to find adequate research methodology for the female consumer and in the process, birth pangs apart. come up with something considerably fresher than the existing systems.

18. Sources of Bias in Researching the Female Consumer

Marketing research has become an essential prerequisite to any marketing and advertising campaign and we have grown so cautious that even the tiniest decision, whether on a colour choice or a nuance in a phrase, is tested carefully on its prospective audience to ensure the minimisation of risk.

Yet, as much as we trust research to extinguish ambiguity and reduce inaccuracy, we have, at the same time, been afraid to look too closely at the research environment. Like a magic spell that might lose its potency if we examine it too closely, we have tended to ignore the possibility that we might find in research itself the cause of our bad decisions, our assumptive inaccuracies, our inaccurate generalisations. The methods and the statistics may be elegant and complex but what of the human links in the research chain?

Human bias must be a fundamental of research. One must always interview, choose a sample, assume an hypothesis, analyse and then act on the data; the processing of data by mechanical means must always rest on this human foundation.

Research is essentially an interpersonal situation and provokes all the misunderstanding and misinterpretation that that will imply. Even our greatest psychologists and philosophers suffered from this effect. Volicer (1973)[1] discussed the work of Sherrington and Pavlov in the context of their personal and philosophical biases and how it affected their physiological orientation, and contended that it was Pavlov's orientation towards dogmatism that strengthened his unidimensional belief in the sufficiency of conditioned reflexes in learning theory. Suttie in his analysis of Freudian psychology (1935)[2] and the parallel work by Kline (1972)[3] demonstrated the influence of patriarchial values and the rigidly father-dominated Jewish nature of Freud's childhood in his interpretation of female behaviour.

THE BIAS

Bias is pervasive and finds its roots in the individual unconscious. We cannot syphon off fundamental beliefs and attitudes merely because the activity we are currently engaged in is 'research' as opposed to cooking breakfast or making love. In fact, the worst kind of bias may be that of which we are consciously totally unaware and bias towards women may well fall into this category.

Page and Yates (1973)[4] noted that of 120 professional American psychologists most felt bias potential was of considerable importance and that many facets of research appeared to lack adequate experimenter controls. Innes and Fraser (1971)[5] suggested that those who research will always be biased by their environment and particularly the anticipated audience for the research findings, while Mills (1939)[6] noted that:

> For a scientist the audience may not be highly generalised but may be circumscribed by the theories and methodologies of the time. It may be that the ideas that occur to the scientist may well be only those which are 'in tune' with the expectations of the time.

As it is with psychologists, sociologists and scientists so it is with marketers and marketing researchers. Rosenthal pointed out in a letter to the editor of *Behavioural Science,* 9 July 1964 (pages 256–7):

> Whether we will ever be able to nail down all the sources of variance in the transactional data collection system is one of the philosophical questions.

Certainly, recognising bias potential in research is a depressing prospect, especially as in the case of marketing research such vast financial investment may often hinge on an outcome. It can only help to try to understand potential bias and to constantly challenge our assumptions. Venkatesen (1967)[7] in one of his classic studies on laboratory effect in marketing research suggests:

> It is important that the Market Researcher assume the attitudes and practices of the clinicians to become aware of experimenter bias in laboratory experimentation and try to reduce this bias. Only by improved methodology can the Market Researchers hope to advance experimental method and thus the science of marketing.

Finally, Kover (1967)[8] speculates on

> ... how much the marketing model of man has defined the kinds of research that are acceptable and how much research methodology has defined the model of man for marketing people.

He suggests that marketers have become too engrossed in method, that they should take a step back in order to redefine their basic terms. What are consumers like and how do they behave as opposed to how they are *expected* to behave?

> In short, Marketing Research should let explicit ideas about consumers define the methodology *rather than let the methodology define the consumer.*

In the context of the marketing researcher and the female consumer, this is what we shall examine here. To what extent do marketing and advertising researchers allow female consumers to define their methodology as opposed to allowing their methodology, and the researchers' prejudices, assumptions and biases about women working in all manner of ways through the methodology, define the consumer?

If Freud could so alter the course of psycho-analytic thinking while at the same time feed patriarchial bias into his findings, and yet remain undetected for years because this bias was in line with contemporary cultural prejudice, could there not also be the possibility that the marketing researcher also working within a masculine culture could introduce bias into *his* interpretation of female behaviour?

Bias emanating from researchers is not an area that is over-discussed in advertising-marketing circles. Two recent and respected texts on marketing research method either gloss over the subject or fail to mention it at all [9]. Nevertheless, there is no doubt that many researchers in the marketing field are extremely suspicious of the results they obtain from existing research on women. Trevor Millum in his study on advertising imagery and women (1974) [10] quotes representatives from the advertising profession on this topic, each one distinguished and experienced in his field. One notes that:

> Research is a bug-bear and a problem. There are group discussions for housewife information. We have a resident psychologist who takes group discussions and things . . . but what the ladies actually say is not necessarily what they are feeling; we are all suspicious of it, but it gives you clues. Most direct changes in advertisement themes or campaigns arise from research. But it is unreliable and only tells you vast generalisations.

Other comments noted by Millum were:

> It's a terrific problem | being an Art Director in London trying to picture a suburban housewife | although there is some help from research: things that most housewives react to, certain types of situation, you can get quite a bit of research to help you in relation to the product you are selling — shopping habits, what they give their kids for tea, what they feel about vitamins etc. . . . In a national campaign you have to produce the epitome of a housewife which is difficult and certainly changing . . .

> A lot of it is your own pure and simple common sense, experience etc. . . .

> The admen are using science — research etc. It's no good. They average out. You use what you know, your own intuition, feel . . . There's a terrible thing in advertising. They all seem to assume that the man in the street is a — well I don't know. They don't know what he looks like, they don't know what he does, because he's an average and averages don't exist . . .

'Averages don't exist', yet what else does one call the women in British and American magazine and television commercials? Are they, furthermore, the averages of women or the averages of 'women as perceived by marketing research'. Following from this, are the women in the marketing research situation just women or 'women in the marketing research situation', that is, artifacts of their environment?

How, and why is the marketing research situation capable of producing biased results from its female consumer sample?

The Interview as an Interpersonal Situation

Most marketing research situations ultimately involve face-to-face interaction. Whatever care goes into the structuring of a questionnaire, all must ultimately rest on at least two people communicating with each other. In the 'depth interview' situation where several subjects may confront the group leader, even more complex interactions arise when the subjects relate to each other and to the experimenter. Epstein, Sudefeld and Silverstein (1973)[11] note that an 'experimental contract' exists in the research situation so that subjects, when asked, can even articulate at least some of the implicit contract between themselves and the experimenters, and also have a repertoire of negative sanctions for violation of these agreements. When violation of these 'unwritten' rules is perceived, as with any other interpersonal situation, subtle performance changes take place without any deliberate retaliatory action on the part of the subject. Stebbins (1972)[12] posited that in an unstructured interview, particularly, there is reason to believe that the modern interviewer is for many people an 'opening person' and that the unstructured interview has characteristics of a 'pleasing sociable conversation'. Awareness by the two that they are being scrutinised by one another causes certain interpersonal variables to come into play. The same effect is also noted to a reduced extent in structured interviews.

Thus, one situation which will encourage biased response by the female interviewee lies in the fact that she sees herself pulled into an interpersonal relationship with the interviewer and, as with any such situation, she will tend to respond in such a way as to maintain the balance of the relationship in her favour. Also, as with any interpersonal interaction she will be pushed hither and thither, in cognitive terms, by subtle variables against which she will constantly attempt to maintain her psychological equilibrium. Attractiveness of the interviewer may be one of these variables and although interview interaction can depend to an alarming degree on overt characteristics such as clothing and voice quality, (Hoult (1954)[13], Lerner (1965)[14]) it can also depend simply on whether the interviewee finds the interviewer pleasing to look at.

Byrne, London and Reeves (1968)[15] found that interpersonal attraction was far greater towards physically attractive strangers, regardless of sex, than towards unattractive ones, and that physical attractiveness accounted for a significant source of variance in interpersonal perception. Bruner, Shapiro and Taguiri (1958)[16] found that once this attractiveness has constituted the initial stimulus input about another person, then a set of expectancies about that person are activated by a process of trait inference. One of the side-effects of this phenomenon is that the recipient (interviewee) may also try to please the attractive person (Sigall and Aronson (1967)[17]) and enters into a parallel state of anxiety and desire to demonstrate efficacy and willingness. The smart agency interviewer and the pleasant, gregarious female field interviewer are not likely to be seen as unattractive by the housewife interviewee, and it is quite likely that perception of smartness and attractiveness by women respondents of their interviewers is likely to be a factor which will encourage them to make positive and socially 'correct' answers. Certainly, anyone who has seen the interview of a housewife sample by a professional interviewer cannot help but note that many of the respondents are totally fascinated by their questioners.

Nevertheless, it should be remembered that none of this interviewer-interviewee response is necessarily overt. Relationships like these often occur on a subliminal plane and may be only slightly, if at all, available to the interviewee. Maintaining the pleasantness of this social interaction is operating on a non-conscious level and the female respondent works by subtle cues from the interviewer of mood, movement, body posture and eye contact. This is a common phenomenon.

Ekman and Friesen (1967)[18] working with patients undergoing psycho-therapy, identified relationships between body acts, body position, facial expressions and head orientations, and the nature and intensity of emotion. He found that occurrence of specific body acts enabled observers to identify the emotional states of patients at different stages in therapy treatment. He summarises empirical evidence which showed that 'information about effect, the on-going interpersonal relationship, and psycho-dynamics and ego-defences are provided by *non-verbal behaviour*'.

A variation of this phenomenon was recorded by Phillips and Clancy (1972)[19] who described an interaction called the 'modelling effect'. This is a bias which emanates from the investigator who consciously or un-consciously projects his views onto the respondent who receives these cues and uses them to modify her/his responses in line with the investigator's expectations. 'Modelling effects' are said to take place when there is a relationship between the behaviour or responses of the investigator and the behaviour or responses of those being investigated. Rosenthal (1966)[20] said of this important and dangerous effect:

> From the evidence considered, it seems plausible to conclude that modelling effects occur at least sometimes in psychological research conducted in field or laboratory. We find it difficult to predict the direction and magnitude of modelling effects. In survey research they tend to be positive but variable as to magnitude. In laboratory studies, modelling effects are variable not only in magnitude but in direction as well.

Modelling effects, according to Phillips and Clancy, may come about through various kinesic and paralinguistic cues, that is, shifts in posture, gestures and tone of voice, and most of the time words express only a tiny portion of our meaning when we interact with other persons. Birdwhistell (1970)[21] estimates that: 'no more than 30–35% of the social meaning of a conversation or an interaction is carried by words'. The interviewer is, furthermore, totally unaware for the most part of what he is doing: 'Obviously the interviewer does not tell the respondent his own views, but he may unknowingly and inadvertently communicate his views through paralinguistic, kinesic and other cues.'

Some interesting results concerning the sex of interviewees were noted by Rosenthal (1966)[20] who was able to show that male experimenters offered significantly more positive cues to women interviewees for 'right' responses than male interviewees; for example, they smiled and nodded more to the women subjects than to the male ones. It was shown, furthermore, that there were distinct interaction patterns for female–female and male–male dyads, and that women were more comfortable in maintaining response and a positive balance in the interaction when they could see the other participant. This was possibly because their skill in maintaining interpersonal cognitive balance depended more than men upon being able to see and act on paralinguistic cues. As we shall show later, women have a highly developed ability to 'pick up' subtle cues from other persons, more so than men, and rely on these to cue them to the 'correct' response as perceived in terms of what the other party expects from the interaction.

Female Personality Characteristics

Closely linked to the interpersonal factors of the interview situation are the personality variables of the respondents. Of particular interest are those personality characteristics of women which are a function of cultural expectations of female behaviour, and which tend to encourage women to conform or respond to bias in the interview situation. These personality traits and related behaviour depend on perception of the interview as a 'demand' situation. Orne (1962)[22] noted these 'demand characteristics' and concluded that the subject is not a passive respondent but has a demonstrable interest in the successful outcome of the experiment or interview. 'Demand characteristics' exist when the experimenter and subject are within the same social context, the experimental or interview situation. The subject will concede that the experimenter is competent and tries to be a 'good subject' and may behave quite differently if he/she must perform a task in the experimenter's presence. This particular aspect of Orne's observations was used by Musante and Anker (1972)[23] when they investigated the effect of experimenter's presence on the subject's performance in a simple task of 'not responding to a tone'. The simple presence of the experimenter heightened the success of the experiment and facilitated the subject's ability not to respond.

The fact of a subject's special response to the experimenter may be due to increased anxiety in the experimental situation and also 'acquiescence response set', in colloquial terms, a 'desire to please by positive response'. 'Acquiesence response set' is an accepted source of bias in psychological research, but what is particularly interesting in the context of our female consumer is the extent to which this factor is essentially a 'female' pheno-menon and relates to certain personality characteristics associated with a 'desire to conform'.

Sistrunk and McDavid (1971)[24] investigated sex differences in conforming behaviour and criticised previous research such as that by Nord (1962)[25] and Kretch, Crutchfield and Ballachey (1962)[26] which purported to show that this 'desire to conform' in women was simply 'conditioned consequence of differences between prescribed roles for males and females in our culture'.

It is true that while in several experiments women have been shown to conform more than men to group and individual pressure (Patel and Gordon (1960)[27] and Nakamura (1958)[28]), in others they have not reacted in this way (B. Vaughan and White (1966)[29] and Allen and Levine (1969)[30]).

Sistrunk and McDavid studied the effect in more detail and found that sex differences in conformity could be more adequately explained by personality variables other than simple conformity. Particularly important among these variables was the 'need for affiliation', which was noted particularly in the female sample and which, Sistrunk and McDavid suggested, was a basic factor in the greater tendency of women to conform in certain interpersonal situations. Thus, 'need for affiliation', 'acquiesence response set', 'conformity' and 'desire to please' are all subtly differentiated aspects of the same phenomenon and this phenomenon tends, possibly because of culturally prescribed elements of passivity and ingratiation in women, to be a female trait.

The vulnerability of women to this effect in the research environment was noted by Rosenthal (1966)[20] who felt that research supported the contention that: 'where a sex difference does occur it is the female subjects who show the greatest susceptibility.'

Data from Simons and Christie (1962)[31] on thematic apperception tests strongly corroborate this statement and Epstein, Sudefeld and Silverstein (1973)[11] also note the effect in work on the experimental contract. In the latter case, subjects of experiments were asked what they felt they owed to the experimenters as part of the experimental situation. In the section on 'subject's obligation to the experimenter' it was found that significantly more females than males (68·2% compared to 49·7%) reported the obligation of co-operation. This included such behaviour as answering all questions, trying to perform as well as possible, being obedient and paying attention. Females were also more concerned with the obligation to complete the experiment.

Another personality trait which is particularly relevant to women in the interview situation is the need for self and social approval. The sex difference in this trait was noted by Becker and Dileo (1967)[32] who found that males score higher on self-approval and females on social approval, and was based on earlier work by Becker (1968)[33] which also demonstrated that self approval and social approval are sex-related.

What is particularly interesting is a finding by Crowne and Marlowe (1964)[34] who went on to note that need for social approval was also related to high susceptibility to personal influence. Subjects high in 'need for approval' were found to be most sensitive to both direct and vicarious social reinforcement and to comply more with experimentally-varied situation demands. Thus, women will not only look for social approval but this need will also make them particularly sensitive to demands of the experimental situation. That this sensitivity will make women respond to even the most subtle of biased cues on the part of the experimenter was noted by Smith and Fleming (1971)[35] in an experiment which should be a dreadful warning to the marketing researcher.

In the Smith and Fleming study, subjects had to rate 10 photographs into successes ($+5$) and failures (-5) in living. The experimenters, who would confront the subjects with the photographs, were deliberately biased beforehand by informing three of them (six in all) that the photographs were of business tycoons, and the other three that they were of mental defectives in a state hospital. The photographs were then assessed in the experimenters' presence by 48 females divided previously by test results into high 'need for approval' and low 'need for approval'. As predicted the high 'need for approval' groups differed significantly in their mean ratings *in the direction of the experimenters' expectancy*, while the low 'need for approval' motivated groups showed no significant difference in mean ratings. Smith and Fleming conclude that:

> These results indicate that the need for approval is related to even this very subtle form of interpersonal influence |and that| research seeking to assess functional relationships between psychological motive states and classes of behaviours need to evaluate and take into account *the arousal properties of experimental situations.*

Thus, to review the evidence so far women, by virtue of personality characteristics related to their culturally acquired 'female' behaviour, are susceptible to high need for affiliation, social approval and may be particularly sensitive to personal influence. This extreme sensitivity has been shown in experimental situations to make them respond positively and accurately to very subtle biasing effects generated by the experimenter.

Sex of Experimenter

Within the framework of personality variables and interpersonal aspects of the interview situation that we have already noted, an additional source of bias, which may be relevant to interviews involving the female consumer, is that of experimenter's sex. Two common situations in marketing research involve opposite types of sex interaction. In the 'depth interview' situation the psychologist employed by the agency is usually male, so there is a male–female interactive norm, but in research field-work the majority of interviewers are women, producing a female–female interaction. Sex effects will operate in both these contexts and may render results of the two types of research, incomparable. Different attitudes might be expressed in each situation and, as a cultural effect, this has also been well documented in relation to, for example, white interviewers confronting black interviewees. Athey *et al* (1960)[36], for example, reported that blacks are reluctant to express accurately their attitudes to white interviewers who thus obtain a higher proportion of 'acceptable' answers and Lenski and Leggett (1960)[37] noted that:

> The data gathering interview brings into existence a social relationship and the respondent is affected by the various norms governing such relationships. Thus the answers that he gives to the interviewers' questions reflect his perceptions of the interviewer, his interpretation of the nature of the relationship created, his judgement of what social norms are relevant and also his peculiar personality traits . . .

Sex differences are cultural variables, as we shall note in more detail later, and should, therefore, be considered by the marketing researcher as mediating influences in the interview interaction. Sex, as with race, can affect the outcome of an experiment. Allen (1964)[38] showed motor performance in a marbles test to be a function of the interaction between the sex of experimenter and the sex of the subject, and that subjects performed better for the opposite sex. When investigating the influence of sex of the experimenter on the production of sex responses of subjects on the Rorschach, Curtis and Wolf (1951)[39] noted a significant difference between the subjects' sex responses associated with sex of the experimenter. Binder, McConnell and Sjoholm (1957)[40] found that a female experimenter had a greater positive influence on a subject's learning and verbal tasks than did a male experimenter.

The sex variable can mediate to produce a variety of reactions, and the effect is difficult to predict. Rosenthal[20] notes that reviews of literature concerning sex of the experimenter and its effects on the subject's performance, such as by Kintz *et al* (1965)[41] and Masling (1960)[42] tended to favour the notion that: 'at least sometimes, the sex of the experimenter can determine in part the response made by the experimental subjects.'

These are established findings in psychological research, and derive mainly from work done by Rosenthal, but the same effects have also been noted in marketing research experiments. Herkommer (1966)[43] suggests that 'there should be a systematic investigation of the interviewer role in the field situation' and that one should seek to introduce some value to this effect. Other marketers have been more explicit. Thumin (1962)[44] notes:

> Another potentially important variable, largely neglected by the marketing researchers, has to do with the sex of the interviewer. When dealing with topics of a personal or

psychological nature, are respondents more likely to speak truthfully to members of their own sex or the members of the opposite sex, or does the sex factor matter at all? For reasons of cost or convenience female interviewers are used in the great majority of marketing surveys and the possibility that different results might be obtained with male interviewers is generally ignored.

Thumin then went on to investigate 'sex of interviewer' effects in a study on insomnia and found that sex of the interviewer had a significant effect on respondents' answers. With male interviewers, 22% of the respondents admitted insomnia, while the corresponding percentage for female interviewers was 13·7% (significant at the 0·5% level of confidence). Both male and female respondents showed a greater tendency to admit having insomnia to *male interviewers* than to female interviewers.

This finding indicates that the sex of the interviewer can be a critical variable in consumer research. When female interviewers collect the data, it cannot be safely assumed that similar results would have been obtained by male interviewers. Nor can it be assumed that validity is automatically maximised by employing females to ask the questions.

A similar observation on women interviewers was made by Brandsma (1969)[45] when he pointed out that women are over-represented in the interview teams in the main research organisations, such as Gallup, NORC and Roper, but the potential for bias in this over-representation had not been investigated and was probably ignored.

Hyman *et al* (1954)[46] found that distinct effects, however, could be found in cross-sexed interview combinations so that male interviewers influenced female respondents to give 'male' answers and, conversely, female interviewers influenced male respondents to give 'female' answers. Kenkel, on the other hand, found that wives report differential responses for female–female interactions so that they admit exerting more influence on family decisions when they report to female interviewers than when they report to male interviewers.

It would be extremely difficult to control an experiment for effects of sex interaction but, in the context of evidence that women respondents are peculiarly liable to reflect and respond to bias from their interviewers, it is just one more variable that the researcher should be wary of. This will be particularly so in the context of a male interviewer and a female respondent where the male party has prior and prejudiced expectations about women. The woman, true to tendencies we have noted above, is more than likely to pick up and return to him all the expectations about feminine response that he holds, not only because of the interpersonal nature of the situation but also because the woman is maintaining a power balance between herself and the man which is an extension of male–female response that she would maintain anywhere else. In everyday male–female interaction, it is not unknown for a woman to tell a man exactly what he wants to hear.

Finally, we move onto a form of bias which is considerably more overt and widespread than any of those we have mentioned so far, yet which. in many ways, is the bias which the marketer will be least aware of and is most likely to resist. This is, of course, cultural bias against women.

Woman as a Cultural 'Minority'

With black minorities, it has often been shown that cultural expectations of their ability and behaviour have tended to bias research results in a negative direction. Crawl and MacGinchie (1970)[47], for example, found that teachers rated tape-recorded responses of blacks significantly lower when they learnt they were blacks than in the comparable situation with white children. Similar effects with psychologists in the rating of black patients was noted by Thomas (1970)[48] and Innes and Fraser (1971)[49].

Biased expectations have also been noted in examination of lower-class samples; Levy and Kahn found that interpretation of the Rorschach indicated more pathological factors for patients with lower-class than middle-class histories (1970)[50] and Levy (1970)[51] found that lower-class children were significantly underestimated as to their 'true intellectual capacities'. Levy, in a review of literature on biased research on lower-class respondents, found that:

1. Biased test measures discriminate against lower-class people.
2. Different personality structures and configurations within social classes cause different responses to test stimuli.
3. Higher interpersonal anxiety in lower-class people in psychological test situations produce different responses to test stimuli.
4. Examiner bias operates against lower-class subjects during testing and interpreting results.

We will return to these four points later.

Bias has also been noted in interviewer response to lower-class groups by Carter. Trodahl and Schumann (1963)[52] who found that interviewers tended to select houses that they 'liked' in random sampling and which were usually perceived as having high income, while Dohrenwend, Colomboton and Dohrenwend (1968)[53] found that middle-class interviewers with a negative attitude to lower status persons bias the answers of black and white lower-class respondents more than do counterpart interviewers without this attitude.

In terms of social discrimination, women are also a cultural 'minority' but the largest one of all. Hacker (1951)[54] in her classic article on this subject, notes a definition by Louis Wirth that a minority group is:

A group who because of their physical or cultural characteristics, are singled out from others in the society for differential and unequal treatment and who regard themselves as objects of collective discrimination.

If women are a 'cultural minority', then it is in relation to men that they are 'minor'. Simone de Beauvoir notes:

Just as in America there is no Negro problem but rather a white problem, just as 'anti-semitism is not a Jewish problem: it is our problem', so the woman problem has been a man's problem.

To illustrate the similarities in the social positions of the woman and the Negro, Hacker drew up a table of behavioural and personality attributes which they share (*see* Table 18:1).

Table 18:1   Castelike Status of Women and Negroes

Negroes	*Women*
1. HIGH SOCIAL VISIBILITY	
(a) Skin color, other 'racial' characteristics.	(a) Secondary sex characteristics.
(b) (Sometimes) distinctive dress— bandana, flashy clothes.	(b) Distinctive dress, skirts etc.
2. ASCRIBED ATTRIBUTES	
(a) Inferior intelligence, smaller brain, less convoluted, scarcity of geniuses.	(a) ditto
(b) More free in instinctual gratifications. More emotional, 'primitive' and childlike. Imagined sexual prowess envied.	(b) Irresponsible, inconsistent, emotionally unstable. Lack strong super-ego. Women as 'temptresses'.
(c) Common stereotype 'inferior'.	(c) 'Weaker'.
3. RATIONALISATIONS OF STATUS	
(a) Thought all right in his place.	(a) Woman's place is in the home.
(b) Myth of contented Negro.	(b) Myth of contented woman—'feminine' woman is happy in subordinate role.
4. ACCOMMODATION ATTRIBUTES	
(a) Supplicatory whining intonation of voice.	(a) Rising inflection, smiles, laughs, downward glances.
(b) Deferential manner.	(b) Flattering manner.
(c) Concealment of real feelings.	(c) 'Feminine wiles'.
(d) Outwit 'white folks'.	(d) Outwit 'menfolk'.
(e) Careful study of points at which dominant group is susceptible to influence.	(e) ditto.
(f) Fake appeals for directives; show of ignorance.	(f) Appearance of helplessness.
5. DISCRIMINATIONS	
(a) Limitations on education—should fit 'place' in society.	(a) ditto.
(b) Confined to traditional jobs—barred from supervisory positions.	(b) ditto.
(c) Their competition feared, no family precedents for new aspirations. Deprived of political importance.	(c) ditto.
(d) Social and professional segregation.	(d) ditto.
(e) More vulnerable to criticism.	(e) For example, conduct in bars.
6. SIMILAR PROBLEMS	
(a) Roles not clearly defined, but in flux as result of social change. Conflict between achieved status and ascribed status.	

Source: Hacker (1951)[55].

Levy's Four Bias Characteristics

If women are a 'cultural minority' then we should expect them to share some of the prejudiced research expectations that we have noted for other minorities. If we look once more at the four bias characteristics that Levy associated with research on lower-class minorities then we can make some direct comparisons with research biases that have been associated with women.

Biased test measures discriminate against lower-class people.   Biased test measures have also been shown to discriminate against women. For example, Harmon (1972)[55] in a paper on masculinity—femininity testing reviewed tests for women interviewees and concluded that: 'Inventories can be biased in a number of ways. The bias inherent in different item pools and different scales for men and women is clear-cut.' She noted that almost all interest inventories have separate norms by sex, and the effect of the biases was to reduce the occupational choices open to women who took these tests. The very construction of the tests ensured that women could not do as well in them as men. (Similar effects were noted by the AMEG special commission on sex bias in measurement[55].)

Different personality structures and configurations within social classes cause different responses to test stimuli.   We have already shown that women perform quite differently to men in measures of conformity and 'need for affiliation'. Women have also, for example, been shown to react differentially to tests on 'need for achievement'. Cultural prescriptions that the 'feminine' woman is not successful will tend to encourage women, in achievement and competitive tests, to deliberately 'fail' in order to maintain equilibrium with cultural norms of femininity. This is known as the 'need to avoid success', and has been remarked by Horner (1969)[56] and McClelland (1953)[57]. Thus, men and women will, on tests of achievement motivation. demonstrate 'different configurations' within the same test stimuli.

Higher interpersonal anxiety in lower class people in psychological test situations produce different responses to test stimuli.   It was higher levels of anxiety in the female sample that contributed to their higher conformity rates in the experiments by Sistrunk and McDavid (*op. cit.*). This anxiety was a function of the greater 'need for affiliation' among the female subjects compared to the male ones.

Examiner bias operates against lower-class subjects during testing and interpreting results.   Psychologists and other researchers have been shown to operate negative bias towards women in interpretation of their behaviour. This is illustrated at length in the recent work by Chesler (1974)[58] on women and mental illness. For example, she notes an experiment by Broverman *et al* (1972)[59] wherein psychiatrists rated attributes of 'healthy men' as equating with attributes of a 'healthy adult' but rated attributes of a 'healthy woman' did not relate to either of the other two concepts and, in fact, were those which objectively would be rated as belonging to a person who was psychologically unstable. The expectations of these psychiatrists indicated that a woman, to be a 'healthy adult', would have to demonstrate 'masculine' characteristics and thereby be 'non-feminine' and so 'unhealthy'. If she demonstrated the attributes of a 'healthy woman' she was thereby considered to display 'neurotic' tendencies. In other words, she could not win. Other examples of instances where examiner interpretation has been biased against women were demonstrated by Goldberg (1968)[60] who showed that an article written supposedly by a woman was rated significantly lower by examiners than one written supposedly by a man. Both articles were identical. Similar effects were noted by Pheterson, Kiesler and Goldberg (1971)[61] in the rating of a professional painting, and Pheterson (1969)[62] in the assessment of an essay on child education. There is also evidence that academic articles written by women are negatively received by academics compared to ones written by men[60].

We thus have good grounds for assuming that women, in a research situation, are open to all the biases that are faced by any social 'minority group' and these biases are likely to be negative ones. If there is a cultural stereotype of woman, as there is of the black or the 'poor man', then her stereotype, as with theirs, will pervade interpretation and operations of research on her behaviour. Cultural expectation is the last and the biggest source of bias facing any one who attempts to research the woman, whether as worker, wife or consumer. Naomi Weisstein (1971)[63] in her article on psychological research bias on women says:

> ... even in carefully controlled experiments and with no outward or conscious difference in behaviour, the hypotheses we start with will influence the behaviour of the subject enormously ... Since it is beyond doubt that most of us start with notions about the nature of men and women, the validity of a number of observations ... is questionable, even when these observations have been made under carefully controlled conditions.

She notes experiments by Rosenthal concerning expectations by interviewers of the behaviour of women and the contentions by Bruno Bettelheim that all women basically need to be are wives and mothers (which is not far from the expectations of the average marketer or advertiser) and concludes that:

> ... the Rosenthal experiments point quite clearly to the influence of social expectation. In some extremely important ways, people are what you expect them to be, or at least they behave as you expect them to behave. Thus, if women, according to Bettelheim, want first and foremost to be good wives and mothers, it is extremely likely that this is what Bruno Bettelheim and the rest of society want them to be.

Advertisers, marketers and marketing researchers are also 'the rest of society' and in their expectations of the behaviour of women it is quite likely that they are receiving back through their research these expectations from women themselves. The irony of this situation is that, in the case of the marketing industry, they are, as we showed in the chapters on mass media and on advertising imagery, one of the forces which suggests to women who and what they are. They portray these ideas through the mass media and then receive this information back through their research programmes as part of a huge and complex circle which they have not yet realised how or when to break. Weisstein says, in a review of experiments where subjects have reacted totally in the way that experimenters have told them to react:

> ... if subjects under quite innocuous and non-coercive conditions can be made to kill other subjects and under other types of social conditions will positively refuse to do so: if subjects can react to a state of psychological fear by becoming euphoric, or angry, because somebody else around is angry: if students become intelligent and rats run mazes better because experimenters are told the rats are bright, then it is obvious that a study on human behaviour requires, first and foremost, a study of social contexts within which people move, of the expectations about how they will behave, and *of the authority that tells them who they are and what they are supposed to do.*

And what evidence, what documented investigation is there of this very real possibility of cultural biasing of female response by the marketing researchers?

Very little exists at present. The whole area of sex differences, sex roles and biased sexual expectations has only percolated relatively recently into social psychology, while marketing, which perhaps has more to lose by investigating this area, has paid little attention to it as yet. Nevertheless, one set of observations by Diana Gartner[64] has helped to show that the theory of sexual pressure in the marketing research situation is not so much a question of existence as one of willingness to document it or even the sensitivity to observe it.

In her note on market research techniques (copy-testing specifically), she makes some interesting comments on marketing researchers:

> They assume that anything showing a woman getting a man's praise or attention is automatically motivating. It is a firmly established principle.

Of some 'Focus group sessions' she writes:

> ... it was clear that the women wanted to say that they wanted products that would save time and energy. There was only a mention of doing something creative, but the man who conducted the session played on this theme more than the other.

Again, of market researchers (in the same context), she says:

Instead of giving them 'conveniences to save time', they try to funnel the creative urge back into the household scene. The motivation is 'You can fulfill your duties and responsibilities to your family'. They won't play on a woman's own needs, they play on her guilt. And there's a lot of guilt around.

Gartner also recalls another 'Focus group' session that looked at a pre-packaged meal. In answer to prodding from the questioner, one woman, finally stung to a response over the use of these meals, laughed and said 'OK, maybe I *should* feel guilty', a response which probably encapsulates this whole problem of sexual bias in marketing research. Gartner concludes:

When men do the interviews, they are more likely to want women to live up to |their| expectations. And it's such an emotional area, a woman's identity is so tied up with this that women are almost afraid to admit to themselves, much less to an interviewer, that the sex role stereotypes bother them.

Certainly, it's time that sex-role stereotypes started to bother the marketing researchers but until that time we can safely conclude that they are likely to:

1. Receive results which confirm existing cultural prejudices about women because they are, in many ways, a discriminate cultural minority group with all the negative expectations that that implies.
2. Never receive a totally accurate picture of women, as buyers or anything else, unless they can isolate their prejudices about women, or research in a non-expectational environment.

In fact, until that time, marketers, advertisers and researchers alike will receive from research on women results which are mere mirrors of existing marketing and advertising imagery and reflections of their own cultural expectations of women. What they will *not* receive is accurate research on the female consumer, how she thinks, functions, works, conceptualises or behaves. That will be her truth, not theirs.

OTHER SOURCES OF BIAS

We have seen that in the interviewing of the female consumer there exists a potential for bias in response. Moving beyond this area to the actual collection of data there are three related points worth noting which concern sampling in the female consumer market:

The Wife as Representative of the Family

Discrepancies in reported information have been noted across a wide variety of areas. Consumer mis-reportings of what they spent were noted by Kildegaard (1965)[65], and the inability of children to rank or describe their father's occupational status was noted by Wallin and Waldo (1964)[66]. Discrepancies between parents and children were further noted by Cohen and Orum (1972)[62] in the reporting of socio-economic data, such as occupational and educational status.

Similar discrepancies have, however, been found in the sociological and marketing literature in the reporting of actions and decisions of one spouse by another[69, 70]. There is evidence that the research responses of husbands and wives are very similar when compared on an aggregate basis but dissimilar when compared on a within-family basis. Various studies have found no significant differences between husbands' and wives' responses using a variety of questions for comparison, but studies which compared husband and wife responses on topics such as, amount of family income, what subjects they discuss, who initiates conversation and how much time they spend in conversation, and the frequency of coitus, have found considerable disagreement. To what extent, therefore, can a wife represent actions or decisions of her husband and family? Can we be safe in just interviewing the wife or should we obtain data from the husband as well?

Davis, in two recent studies (1970 and 1971)[68] investigated this point specifically. He notes that marketers and sociologists have often been content to obtain information on husbands' and wives' influence within families in the most convenient and direct way, which is to rely on the wife as the family's sole respondent. This is a logical method because, as the main representative of the family's buying tastes, the female consumer is probably the best informed. It is also convenient, since the wives are easily located at home and make a reasonably large sample available to costing constraints. From his two studies he concluded that:

1. If the investigation is of a simple factual nature, for example, researching the level of purchase of certain products, simple family preferences for brands or an investigation of aggregate trends, where individual subtleties are unnecessary, the wife alone is adequate for research purposes.

2. If more complex matters in the family purchasing are being investigated it would be wiser to also interview the husband or other relevant family members. For example, when investigating the total decision-process the opinions of these members might be equally valid. Many people can quite honestly interpret different events in different ways and each may see their part in the decision as the crucial one. In relation to this second point, Davis quotes a sociologist who notes that: 'Each spouse perceives facts and situations differently according to his own needs, values, attitudes and belief. An "objective" reality could possibly exist in the trained observer's evaluation if it does exist at all.'

3. The member of family, be it wife, husband or child who makes the final decision is not always the one who made the main decision. Thus, it can be seen that the wife's data alone would tend to disguise this factor since she may finally decide to buy but be merely instrumental to the main decision maker.

Another factor that Davis noted, as we have noted throughout this chapter, is the distortion that may be produced in family research data by the research environment. We have already shown that constraints of the research situation, sex differences between interviewer and interviewee, demand characteristics of the research confrontation, the specific tendency towards positive, interviewer-biased response on the part of women as a function of certain female personality characteristics, will tend to create results which are a function of the being-interviewed phenomenon rather than much reality. Additionally, Kenkel (1961)[69] found that the presence of a male or female interviewer significantly altered the roles husbands and wives played in the contrived decision situation. O'Rourke (1963)[70] showed that families interacting in a laboratory situation differed from those observed at home in terms of amount of disagreement, and the ratio of instrumental to expressive activities and roles played. Davis (1970)[68] also showed self-reports about specific decisions and activities to be uncorrelated between different family members.

It seems that the research situation involving the family, as it does with the individual female consumer, encourages stereotypical, cultural role-playing. A family may vocalise to the marketer patterns of decisions and activities which are socially accepted, such as the dominance of the husband and the subordination of the children, while the real family power structure may be completely different. Most respondents have good ideas about cultural norms for family behaviour and, in the research interview situation, they stick to them.

Before leaving this topic, there is one other point to be noted in relation to the female consumer, the family and data accuracy, and this is in relation to the mechanics of filling in the questionnaire itself. There is a danger that research questionnaires sent by post, specifically, and left to be filled in and returned, do not always carry the responses of those persons to whom they are sent. This vicarious questionnaire response was noted by Nuckolls and Mayer (1970)[71]. They remark that it is not uncommon for mail panel operators to claim that they can reach any member in a co-operating household. This claim is made despite some evidence that it is only the housewife who has agreed to participate. Through the housewife, completed questionnaires are then obtained from any designated household member, but it is a moot question as to whether these designated members have actually done the filling in themselves.

In their investigation of this problem, Nuckolls and Mayer found that despite clear instructions not to discuss the questionnaire almost a third of the wives (31%) and almost as many husbands (27%) did so. These are probably minimum estimates. Further direct questions revealed that the discussion was mainly on factual items such as dates and income.

With indirect questioning, other examples of lapses appeared. Two experienced coders rated the questionnaires as valid or suspect and some of the more obvious indications of duplication were identical handwriting and identical wording of responses to open-ended questions. There were also common errors in the completing of the forms: for example, the same page left blank or both of the respondents giving the year of the car when it was not asked for. There were also distinct characteristics of valid and suspect households. Response accuracy was, for example, related to education of the wife and even more strongly to that of her husband. Of the questionnaires received from families in which the husband did not reach ninth grade, 77% were judged as suspect. This compares with 20% judged suspect from families where the husbands were college graduates.

Nuckolls and Mayer conclude:

> This study has proved that mail panels cannot produce independent responses from the homemaker and her family ... the study also raises doubts about the ability of an investigator to reach members of the family other than the homemaker through a mail panel survey.

The Absence of Men

Few men are included in samples which investigate family consumer behaviour. Oddly enough, this is also one aspect of bias that marketers do *not* share with psychological and sociological research where it has been vehemently noted by Holmes and Jorgensen (1971) and Carlson and Carlson (1960)[72] that social science research is dominated by male subjects and females are under-represented. While it is easy to argue that it would be illogical to introduce male response into female consuming research, the marketer should also be aware that sex-role norms for men and women are moving closer and it may be a practical step to find out what men are up to in this field. How much involvement by men in domestic and child-care routines is being missed simply because we do not include sample controls for male respondents?

The Over-representation by Students

Male students are often used by academic marketers in research on buying behaviour which is normally demonstrated by housewives. To say the least, this may render the results a little dubious. Ennis, Cox, and Stafford note on this sampling carelessness (1972)[73]:

> Few would deny that students are consumers, but they are typically, psychologically, socially and demographically different from other segments of the population. The consumer of interest in many marketing studies is the housewife but the respondents most convenient to marketing professors are, largely, male undergraduate business students. Are conclusions based on their response valid when applied to housewives?

Men students who shop and care for themselves are probably more likely than other men to display regular shopping behaviour but it is still unrealistic to expect data on their behaviour to apply to experienced housewives.

REFERENCES

1. L. Volicer, 'Relationship Between Physiological Research and Philosophy on the work of Pavlov and Sherrington', *Perspectives in Biology and Medicine* (Spring 1973).
2. Ian Suttie, *The Origins of Love and Hate* (London 1935).
3. Paul Kline, *Fact and Fantasy in Freudian Theory,* Methuen (London 1972).
4. Page and Yates, 'Attitudes of Psychologists Toward Experimental Controls in Research', *Canadian Psychologist,* Vol. 14 (2) (April 1973).
5. Innes and Fraser, 'Experimenter Bias and other Possible Biases in Psychological Research', *European Journal of Psychology,* 1(3) (1971).
6. Mills, 'Language, Logic and Culture', *American Sociological Review* (4) (1939).
7. M. Venkatesen, 'Laboratory Experiments in Marketing: The experimenter effect', *Journal of Marketing Research,* Vol. IV (May 1967), pp. 142–6.
8. Arthur J. Kover 'Models of Man as Defined by Marketing Research', *Journal of Marketing Research,* Vol. IV (May 1967), pp. 129–32.
9. Robert M. Worcester (ed.), *Consumer Market Research Handbook,* McGraw-Hill (1972). Joseph Seibert and Gordon Wills, (eds.), *Marketing Research,* Penguin Books (1972).
10. Trevor Millum, *Images of Women: advertising in women's magazines,* Chatto and Windus (1974).
11. Yakov M. Epstein, Peter Sudefeld and Stanley J. Silverstein, 'The Experimental Contract: Subjects' expectations of and reactions to some behaviours of experimenters', *American Psychiatrist* (March 1973), pp. 212–21.
12. Robert A. Stebbins, 'The Unstructured Research Interview as Incipient Interpersonal Relationship', *Sociology and Social Research* (January 1972).
13. T. F. Hoult, 'Experimental Measurement of clothing as a factor in some social rating of selected American Men', *American Sociological Review* (19) (1954), pp. 324–8.
14. M. J. Lerner, 'Evaluation of Performance as a Function of Performer's reward and attractiveness', *Journal of Personality and Social Psychology* (1) (1965), pp. 355–60.
15. Don Byrne, Oliver London and Keith Reeves, 'The Effects of Physical Attractiveness, Sex and Attitude Similarity on Interpersonal Attraction', *The Journal of Psychology,* Vol. 36 (1968), pp. 259–71.
16. J. S. Bruner, D. Shapiro and R. Taguiri, 'The Meaning of Traits in isolation and in Combination', in R. Taguiri and L. Petrullo (eds.), *Person Perception and Interpersonal Behaviour,* Stanford University Press (Stanford 1958), pp. 276–88.
17. Harold Sigall and Elliott Aronson, 'Liking For an Evaluator as a Function of her Physical Attractiveness and Nature of the Evaluations', *Journal of Experimental Social Psychology,* (5) (1967), pp. 93–100.
18. Paul Ekman and Wallace V. Friesen, 'Head and Body Cues in the Judgement of Emotion: A reformulation', *Perceptual and Motor Skills* (24) (June 1967), pp. 711–24.
19. Derek L. Phillips and Kevin J. Clancy, 'Modelling Effects in Survey Research', *Public Opinion Quarterly* (36) (1972–3), pp. 246–53.
20. Robert Rosenthal, *Experimenter Effects in Behavioural Research,* Appleton Century Crofts (New York 1966).
21. Birdwhistell, *Kinetics and Contexts: Essays on body motion communication,* University of Philadelphia Press (1970).
22. M. T. Orne, 'On the Social Psychology of the Psychological Experiment: With particular reference to demand characteristics and their implications', *American Psychiatrist* (17) (1962), pp. 776–83.
23. Gerald Musante and James H. Anker, 'Experimenter's Presence: Effect on subject's performance', *Psychological Reports* (30) (1972), pp. 903–4.
24. Frank Sistrunk and John McDavid, 'Sex Variable in Conforming Behaviour', *Journal of Personality and Social Psychology,* Vol. 17 (2) (1971), pp. 200–7.
25. W. R. Nord, 'Social Exchange Theory: An integrative approach to social conformity', *Psychological Bulletin,* Vol. 71 (1962), pp. 174–208.

26. D. Kretch, R. S. Crutchfield and E. L. Ballachey, *Individual in Society*, McGraw-Hill (New York 1962).
27. A. Patel and J. E. Gordon, 'Some Personal and Situational Determinants of Yielding to Influence', *Journal of Abnormal and Social Psychology* (61) (1960), pp. 411–18.
28. C. Y. Nakamura, 'Conformity and Problem Solving', *Journal of Abnormal and Social Psychology* (56) (1958), pp. 315–20.
29. G. M. Vaughan and K. D. White, 'Conformity and Authoritarianism Re-examined', *Journal of Personality and Social Psychology* (3) (1966). pp. 363–6.
30. V. L. Allen and J. M. Levine, 'Consensus and Conformity', *Journal of Experimental and Social Psychology* (5) (1969), pp. 389–99.
31. Simons and Christie, 'Verbal Reinforcement of a TAT Theme', *Journal of Projective Techniques*, Vol. 26 (1962).
32. G. Becker and D. T. Dileo, 'Scores on Rokeach's Dogmatism Scale and the Response Set to Present a Positive Social and Personal Image', *Journal of Social Psychology* (71) (1967), pp. 287–93.
33. Gilbert Becker, 'Sex-Role Identification and the Needs for Self and Social Approval', *Journal of Psychology* (69) (1968), pp. 11–15.
34. Douglas Crowne and David Marlowe, *The Approval Motive*, John Wiley and Sons (New York 1964).
35. Ronald E. Smith and Frank Fleming, 'Need for Approval and Susceptibility to Unintended Social Influence', *Journal of Consulting and Clinical Psychology* (36) (1971), pp. 383–5.
36. K. R. Athey, Joan E. Coleman, Audrey P. Restman and Jenny Tang. 'Two Experiments Showing the Effect of the Interviewers Racial Background on Responses to Questionnaires Concerning Racial Issues', *Journal of Applied Psychology* (44) (August 1960). pp. 224–6.
37. Gerhard E. Lenski and John C. Leggett, 'Caste, Class and Deference in the Research Interview', *The American Journal of Sociology*, (March 1960), p. 407.
38. Robert N. Singer, Jack H. Llewellyn and Sara Allen, 'Adult Performance as a Function of Sex of Experimenter and Sex of Subject'. *Journal of Abnormal and Social Psychology*, Vol. 68 (1964), pp. 216–26.
39. Henry S. Curtis and Elizabeth B. Wolf, 'The Influence of the Sex of the Examiner on the Production of Sex Responses on the Rorschach', Cleveland V. A. Mental Hygiene Unit (1951).
40. Arnold Binder, David McConnell and Nancy A. Sjoholm, 'Verbal Conditioning as a Function of Experimenter Characteristics', *Journal of Abnormal and Social Psychology*, Vol. 55 (1957), pp. 309–14.
41. B. L. Kinz *et al*, 'The Experimenter Effect', *Psychological Bulletin*, Vol. 63 (April 1965), pp. 223–43.
42. Joseph Masling 'The Influences of Situational and Interpersonal Variables in Projective Testing', *Psychological Bulletin*, Vol. 57 (1960), pp. 65–85.
43. Sebastian Herkommer, 'The Interview—Weakest Link in the Survey Chain', *European Market Research Review*, Vol. 1 (1966), pp. 69–75.
44. Frederick K. J. Thumin, 'Watch for Those Unseen Variables', *Journal of Marketing* (July 1962), p. 58.
45. P. Brandsma, 'The Role and Influence of the Interviewer', *European Market Research Review*, Vol. 4 (1969), pp. 26–35.
46. H. H. Hyman *et al* 'Interviewing in Social Research', University of Chicago Press (Chicago 1954).
47. Crawl and MacGinchie, 'White Teachers' Evaluations of Oral Responses given by White and Negro 9th Grade Males', Proceedings of the Annual Convention of the American Psychological Association, Vol. 5, Part 2 (1970).
48. C. W. Thomas, 'Psychologists, psychology and the black community', in Karlen, Cook and Lacey (eds.), *Psychology and the Problems of Society*.

49. John M. Innes and Colin Fraser, 'Experimenter Bias and other Possible Biases in Psychological Research', *European Journal of Social Psychology*, Vol. 1 (3) (1971), pp. 297–310.

50. M. R. Levy and M. W. Kahn, 'Interpreter Bias on the Rorschach Test as a Function of Patients's Socioeconomic Status', *Journal of Projective Techniques and Personality Assessment*, Vol. 34 (2) (1970).

51. M. R. Levy, 'Issues in the Personality Assessment of Lower-Class Patients', *Journal of Projective Techniques and Personality Assessment*, Vol. 34 (1) (1970).

52. Roy E. Carter, Verling C. Trodahl and R. Smith Schumann, 'Interviewer Bias in Selecting Households', *Journal of Marketing* (April 1963), pp. 27–34.

53. Barbara Snell Dohrenwend, John Colombton and Bruce P. Dohrenwend, 'Social Distance and Interviewer Effects', *Public Opinion Quarterly*, Vol. 32 (1968), pp. 287–94.

54. Helen Mayer Hacker, 'Women as a Minority Group', *Social Forces*, Vol. 30 (October 1951) pp. 60–9.

55. Lenore W. Harmon, 'Sexual Bias in Interest Measurement', *Measurement and Evaluation in Guidance*, Vol. 5 (4) (January 1973), pp. 496–501, and 'AMEG Commission Report on Sex Bias in Attitude Measurement', in *Measurement and Evaluation in Guidance*, Vol. 6 (3) (October 1973), pp. 171–7.

56. Matina S. Horner, 'Toward an Understanding of Achievement-Related Conflicts in Women', *Journal of Social Issues*, Vol. 28 (2) (1972) and 'Fail: Bright women', *Psychology Today* (November 1969), pp. 36–8, 62.

57. D. C. McClelland, *The Achieving Society*, Van Nostrand (New York 1961).

58. Phyllis Chesler, *Women and Madness*, Allen Lane: Penguin Books (1972).

59. Broverman, *et al*, *see* chapter 15, ref. 42.

60. P. A. Goldberg, 'Are Women Prejudiced Against Women?', *Transaction* (April 1968), pp. 28–30.

61. G. I. Pheterson, S. B. Kiesler, and P. A. Goldberg, 'Evaluations of the Performance of Women as a Function of their Sex, Achievement and Personal History', *Journal of Personality and Social Psychology* (19) (1971), pp. 114–8.

62. G. I. Pheterson, 'Female Prejudice Against Men', unpublished manuscript, Connecticut College, New London (Connecticut 1969).

63. Naomi Weisstein, 'Psychology Constructs the Female' in (eds.) Vivian Gornick and Barbara K. Moran, *Woman in a Sexist Society: Studies in power and powerlessness*, Basic Books (1971), p. 207.

64. Diana Gartner, Vice-President for Research for Daniel and Charles, noted by Komisar, *see* chapter 17, ref. 10.

65. Ingrid C. Kildegaard, 'How Consumers Misreport What They Spent', *Journal of Advertising Research*, (1965), pp. 51–5.

66. Paul Wallin and Leslie C. Waldo, 'Indeterminacies in Ranking of Fathers' Occupations', *Public Opinion Quarterly* (1964), (28), pp. 287–92.

67. Roberta S. Cohen and Anthony H. Orum, 'Parent-Child Consensus on Socioeconomic Data obtained from Sample Surveys', *Public Opinion Quarterly* (1972–3) (36), pp. 95–8.

68. Harry L. Davis, 'Dimensions of Marital Roles in Consumer Decision Making', *Journal of Marketing Research*, Vol. VII (May 1970), pp. 168–71.
    Harry L. Davis, 'Measurement of Husband-Wife Influence on Consumer Purchase Decisions', *Journal of Marketing Research*, Vol. VIII (August 1971), pp. 105–312.

69. W. F. Kenkel, 'Sex of Observer and Spousal Roles in Decision-Making', *Marriage and Family Living*, 23 (May 1961), pp. 185–6.

70. John F. O'Rourke, 'Field and Laboratory: The decision-making behaviour of family groups in two experimental conditions', *Sociometry* (27) (December 1963), pp. 422–35.

71. Robert C. Nuckolls and Charles S. Mayer, 'Can Independent Responses be obtained from Various Members in a Mail Panel Household?', *Journal of Marketing Research*, Vol. VII (February 1970), pp. 90–4.

72. Holmes and Jorgensen, 'Do Personality and Social Psychologists study Men more than Women?', HUMRRO Professional Paper (June 1971), and *Representative Research in Social Psychology* (January 1971).

73. Earl R. Carlson and Rae Carlson, 'Male and Female Subjects in Personality Research', *Journal of Abnormal and Social Psychology*, Vol. 61 (3) (1960), pp. 482–3.

74. Ben M. Ennis, Keith K. Cox and James E. Stafford, 'Students as Subjects in Consumer Behaviour Experiments', *Journal of Marketing Research*, Vol. IX (February 1972), pp. 72–4.

19. Stratification of the Female Consumer Market

We do not reach the end of bias towards women in marketing research when we have isolated the bias of the research situation. There is another system of bias which warps the perception of female behaviour and consuming patterns, which originates much further back in the system and a bias which is, again, shared by the marketer with other social sciences. This is the bias which is inherent in the stratification system—a bias which is so tied up with cultural prejudice as to be an extension of it.

STRATIFICATION METHODS

Most markets will exhibit some general homogeneity but it is often small segments that any one marketer or manufacturer will be interested in at any one time. The principle of stratification is ultimately one of profitable convenience but it also reflects a tendency of interpersonal relationships to classify people, to extract certain cues from which certain traits will automatically, to our simplisitic minds, be connected. There are very few people who are sufficiently aware of their own cognitive processes that they can recognise and curtail this classificatory tendency we all have. It is not a fair or even a logical process and it finds its roots in stereotypy, but it is a system which on a mass level can be used to simplify our conceptions of large groups of people.

Nevertheless, just as we can make inaccurate and harmful inferences from categorisation on a micro or interpersonal level, so may we make harmful and inaccurate inferences on a macro or mass level. Market segmentation and social stratification are only the extensions of interpersonal trait inference to a wider audience, but because they are established and respectable and much used we often forget to criticise their basic function, that is, to what extent do they accurately reflect the portions of the population which they claim to represent. and to what extent are they merely reflections of a tendency to stereotype?

Few in marketing research or even sociological and psychological research are happy with our present systems of social stratification. Class, income

322

and occupation have provided the bases for our existing stratification systems, although these are continually coming under criticism, and each of the three perspectives on social strata swings in and out of favour by various combinations with remarkable regularity. What is surprising, however, is the way that people will naturally tend to group themselves into very few 'classes' while academic stratification systems will use anything up to seven groupings. Kahan, Butler and Stokes (1967)[1] report on a study where the overwhelming proportion of people interviewed classified themselves simply into 'middle class' (20%) or 'working class' (67%).

Class is the most difficult concept to pin down yet there have been frequent attempts to do just that, dating from the original class index by Stephenson which 50 years ago was based on five hierarchial grades. Stephenson's system was used in the decennial census classification of occupation up to 1961, but by that time its 'class 3' sector for 'skilled' occupations contained a ragbag of inhomogeneous professions ranging from pilots to manual tradesmen. So, in 1950, Hall and Jones[2] introduced seven hierarchial grades which by the late 1950s were used in a slightly collapsed form by the market research organisations. This had six categories designated as A, B, C1, C2, D and E which were first employed by Research Services Limited when that firm had responsibility for the National Readership Survey of the Institute of Practitioners in Advertising (IPA). And there, with many not-quite-happy rumblings, it has remained till now and is still the most widely used classification system for marketing and advertising research. The system is based primarily on occupation and uses income as a modifier.

There have been many discussions on the topics of income, occupation and other cultural variables appertaining to stratification. Lewis (1963)[3] makes some neat observations on why we think of class in so few categories and Wasson (1969)[4] suggests that since consumer spending is not particularly well related to income levels, we should dispense with the income criterion forthwith and revert to the old class concepts on cultural bases such as education and prestige. Rich and Jain (1968)[5] maintain that recent changes, for example in education, income and leisure, have rendered social class obsolete and Martin (1954)[6] raises questions about whether vertical or non-vertical methods of status grouping are important. The subject of social class is multi-faceted and students of the problem could plough through marketing and sociology books for hours and still come up with variations on the theme.

Nonetheless, there is one important aspect of social stratification which is of considerable relevance to the female consumer and which none of these worthy studies has ever noted as being a particular weakness in the marketing stratification system. With very few exceptions, such systems make one big assumption whether they are dealing with income, occupation or status: that the status of a woman is directly and only related to the social status of her husband. The only exceptions to this occur when a woman is unmarried and her own income and occupation may be taken into account (even then she will often receive the social status of her father) or when certain new methods of stratification are used, such as the 'life style' or 'psychographic' methods which use personality data on the women themselves. These will be examined later. Otherwise, the social groupings of women that are used at present by marketing research are based on status by proxy and not direct status of the woman. That there should exist a potential for bias in this system is hardly open to dispute, and this is leaving aside arguments concerned with the social attitudes assumed by such an approach.

Steinmetz in a very recent article on discrimination in the social ranking of women (1974)[7] made an interesting appraisal of the history behind invisible woman in social systems. She notes that the present system of social stratification is ultimately an extension of a principle of law on the status of women promulgated by an eighteenth century lawyer, Blackstone[8] who asserted that:

> By marriage, the husband and wife are one person in law; that is the very being or legal existence of the woman is superceded during the marriage, or at least is incorporated and consolidated into that of the husband: under whose wing, protection and cover, she performs everything . . . A man cannot grant any thing to his wife, or enter into a covenant with her, for the grant would be to suppose her separate existence.

It seems that even as woman was assumed to have leapt out of the person of Adam to gain her separate existence, so when she married was she assumed to leap back in and bury her personality and self once more in his.

More than a century after Blackstone and a couple of thousand years after the creators of the Adam and Eve doctrine made their particular contribution, it seems that woman is still considered to be incapable of having a social status separate from her husband, and if her social status is indistinct then so, it seems, is she. With the tying of the nuptial knot an entire human personality sinks from view. While one can understand, if not support, this levelling process in aggregate studies of income and expenditure it is extremely difficult to justify its use in smaller samples. It is particularly irrational in the case of marketing research where women are the principal parties and their husbands only of secondary importance. To be sure, the husbands usually supply some income so we ought to be aware of this fact, but in consumer marketing income supply is subordinate to its expenditure. By measuring the socio-economic variables of the husband we are looking at the purchasing behaviour of the female consumer one step removed and are clouding, if not ignoring, the more sensitive variables of her personality.

These variables may be related to those of her husband, in that, for example, a man of higher socio-economic status is likely to marry a woman of similar status with attendant aspects of above-average education and occupational levels, but why thresh around in the twilight? Given the money to spend, *how* the wife spends it is then going to be a function of her personality, her age, her social class (which was determined long before she met her husband), her occupation (she may not always have been a house-wife), the number of children she cares for every day and, most important, her family of origin wherein the nurturing behaviour of her mother and father will be primary indicators of her attitudes and general expectations. The woman's husband is an interloper who looms into her life after around twenty years of living; how did we ever assume that he was the primary effect on her behaviour? The most we may attribute to him is a supply of money.

Consumer behaviour is only one aspect of total human behaviour and any text on psychology will devote considerable attention to the vital importance of family and early environment on all determinants of later adult behaviour. A woman, say, from the age of majority will be the sum total of experiences she has known before that age, so that her education, occupation, parental income and status are among the factors which will decide her patterns of dressing, eating, ambition, income disposal, budgeting and, of course, consuming. They are also highly likely to decide her choice of future husband. In fact, it would be instructive for us to note that the socio-economic status of the husband is probably only relevant to the female consumer *because* of her own prior social and psychological experiences.

In short, the stratification of the female consuming market by recourse to socio-economic variables of the husband alone is at best illogical and at worst, practically useless. Intuitively, we can see that this should be so, yet many marketers will assert that they have used this system of stratifying women for many years and found it eminently 'workable'. In answer to this we can only say that any system of categorisation will be workable some of the time. If we used Swift's contention in *Gulliver's Travels* that a nation should be split into 'big-enders' and 'little-enders' (after which end they cracked their boiled eggs) and then worked this into a six-point system we should still find this 'workable'. People will fit into whichever categories you choose to put them in. In the case of women, however, we should look for the system which best predicts their behaviour. Social class of the husband will 'work' as a system of classification but only because it subsumes the real variables. For example, we have already suggested that the husband's socio-economic status may be related to the woman's education, occupation and former family status in the sense that people with similar attributes are likely to be attracted to one another. Class AB women are those with a husband in upper professional strata, such as doctors or barristers, yet these men are likely to have married women with higher than average educational and occupational levels and be from families with similar attributes. Thus, Class AB women have educational variable X, occupational variable Y, income disposal priorities Z and so on. Yet, because we are only looking at the husband's status we have no value to put on these associated variables of their wives despite the fact that it is these variables which are likely to be the ones which will best predict her purchasing behaviour.

In a careful study on the decision-making by housewives in two social classes, Fry and Siller (1970)[9] noted that social class was a good predictor of differential responses to variables such as price deal sensitivity and search duration among women. This finding could be taken as a possible vindication of the social class system but this study nonetheless justified many of the social class 'differences' by detailed explanations of the personality variables of the two groups of women so that·differences in social class were explained by differences in confidence, perceived threat, intelligence and education of these women. That these 'class' effects could have been explained by the women's personality variables without recourse to social status of their husbands was not explored by Fry and Siller despite the fact that overt behaviour between the two classes was so close that it was often *only* the personality differences which could help to differentiate them.

Linked social class and psychological information is rarely available as it is in Fry and Siller study, but it would be instructive to re-examine many of the studies on social class and women to find out if these differences are not also related to underlying personality factors and, if so, whether these variables or those of the husbands' social rating are the best indicators of female consuming behaviour.

Obviously, the time is ripe for a new system of female consumer stratification although the enthusiasm and intensity of the search will depend a great deal on the recognition by the marketer that there is something unfair and socially destructive about the present system, quite apart from its potential for biasing consumer behaviour data. A social stratification system which assumes that women are extensions of their husbands and not worthies in their own right is only one more factor in a cultural attitude toward women that regards them as possessions. The marketer who unquestioningly supports such a system must also by definition support the cultural contention. Furthermore, if the marketer wants to aid the re-birth of a new stratification system for women he should first understand some of the assumptions that led to the creation of the existing system and understand some of the evidence that indicates its impracticability.

THE MECHANICS OF STRATIFICATION

It is now ten years since some studies on the status of women have been available and while these have discussed the irrationality of the invisibility of women, they have tended to deal with women in professions rather than women *in toto*. Oppenheimer (1968)[10] looked at how the existing stratification system affected assessment of female occupations, and Hughes (1949)[11], while supporting the need for a new approach, is notable for his contention that in such an approach the non-traditional career woman should be placed in the role of 'marginal man', a theory which seems to bear uncomfortable comparisons with the 'honourable white' of apartheid.

Lenski (1966)[12] is one of the few who recognised the problem of sex in stratification theory and observes that: 'in analyses of advanced industrial societies it is impossible to ignore or treat as obvious the role of sex (differences).'

Acker (1973)[13] in a challenging analysis of sexism in social stratification notes that: 'Very few sociologists have even recognised that we have, with the exceptions of the study of the family, constructed a sociology that tends to deal with only the male half of humanity.'

Steinmetz (*op.cit.*) notes that the social invisibility of women often conceals their real status in relation to their husbands and fathers. In many segments of the population, notably among black Americans and the working classes of most western cultures, women have traditionally had greater education and occupational opportunities and as a result have a higher position in society than that which is assigned to their husbands, as male 'heads' of the house. In fact, Watson and Barth (1964)[14] in an American study found that of employed women 22% had occupations equal to their husbands and 42% had occupations ranked above those of their husbands. This trend may be expected to continue, if it has not already since the study by Watson and Barth, because many women have been returning to school to complete their career plans and more women are returning to work after the birth of their most recent child.

Acker, Steinmetz and others in their examinations of the weaknesses in the existing stratification systems established certain basic examples of illogic and irrationality in the assumptions on which the systems are built. When these assumptions are broken down and re-examined it is easier to see where the old methods cloud important information on female behaviour and where we can also look for bases for a new and more sensitive system.

The Man is Head of the Family

This contention is always at the bottom of social stratification yet it may be that this is an over-generalisation that we should learn to modify.

'Family head' is usually defined in terms of income and since it is the norm for men to earn more than women they, usually, are the designated heads. While this is the norm it is by no means the rule. Steinmetz notes of the American situation that in 1960, 42% of employed women held higher-ranking occupations than their husbands and in 1973, in a 5%

sample of the census, 263,573 women were employed during that year while their husbands were not. Watson and Barth, in relation to the American market, note that in 1964 [14] two-fifths of the households in the USA did not have a male head in the sense we have implied. These were: 'Females or female headed households of the husband-wife families in which the husband is retired or otherwise not in the labour force. is unemployed or is only working part-time.'

In Britain, there is no standard definition of 'head of the household' but those used still relate to income. For example, the Family Expenditure Survey of 1973 defines a household 'head' as

he /she is the person, or the husband | *sic* | of the person who:—

a. owns the household accommodation
b. has the household accommodation as an emolument
c. is legally responsible for the rent of the accommodation
d. has the household accommodation by virtue of some relationship to the owner who is not a member of the household

When two members of different sex have equal claim the male is taken as head of the household.

This report does not tell us how many women constitute the 'head of the household' under this definition but does give the number of working married women as just under 40% of the sample. Among this group of women there may be many who are 'household heads' but this is not made available to us.

In *Social Trends* (1973), 'household head' appears to relate to chief wage-earner but this term is not specifically defined although consistent reference is made to it. Nevertheless, since the Family Expenditure Survey assures us that women contribute just under 13% of average weekly income to the household, we can unfailingly conclude that, on grounds of income, men are normally the 'household head'.

Yet, it is at this point that the marketer should stop and think. The logic from here follows:

1. We want data from households on consuming behaviour.
2. The household head is usually the man.
3. Data from the household head can form the basis of household consuming behaviour data.

We have shown that the 'household head' is usually designated on income contribution, while in consuming behaviour we are principally concerned with income disposal and it is the wife and not the husband who is responsible for this. The man may be head of the household in terms of income contribution but the woman is undoubtedly head of the household in terms of consumer spending. Points relevant to the marketer can be made here:

1. Is the 'head of the household' the one who supplies the income or the one who disposes of it in terms of consumption? Women dominate

consuming behaviour of families and in this situation the provision of income is the secondary and related factor. Should we see the male as 'head' in terms of income and the woman as 'head' in terms of consumption?

2. In a family where both husband and wife contribute to the income but where we are investigating consuming behaviour which is dominated by the wife, do we then establish consuming behaviour of the family by her income level and socio-economic characteristics and then adjust this by the income contribution to consumption of the husband?

Either way, viewing stratification from this angle opens up a new range of possibilities which the marketer should consider.

The Status of a Woman is that of her Man

In marketing research the status of a woman is designated by questions relating to income and occupation of her husband. To all intents and purposes his status is her status and his behaviour is her behaviour.

An assumption like this throws up various problems:

1. Education and occupation characteristics of the female consumers are levelled so that interesting nuances about a market may be lost. Larger and more important aspects to female social behaviour may also be extinguished. When the marketer is accused of rarely depicting housewives employed outside the home although, as we have shown, up to 60% of them do just that, we could well relate this aberration of the truth to data collection which would not show a woman's employment if she had one. It is rather like classifying all children as male 'for ease of tabulation' and then concluding that there are no female children in the country.

This factor was examined by Steinmetz in a review of major American social studies. Of 180 questions which formed the bases for seven major social investigations of the family, she found that only 31 dealt with the occupation of the female member. In addition, although 14 questions were asked about the educational level or occupation of the father-in-law, in none of the studies was any question asked about the respondent's mother or mother-in-law (1974)[7]. In a particular survey by Blau and Duncan (1967)[15] on American occupations, the sample was entirely male and in investigating information about the respondent's background only his father's occupation and education were looked at.

In Lenski's study (1961)[12], the respondents' fathers' party preferences were asked but not the mothers'. In the Kinsey study of 1948[16], a 9-way breakdown of education was used for males but a 4-way breakdown was used for females, and the social class of the females was designated to be that of the parental home rather than individual occupations of the women. Steinmetz notes that in the Kinsey study the correlations were not even noted with the female occupational status ratings.

Data gathering of this type will automatically underestimate educational and occupational ability of women and understate their social contribution.

2. Intergenerational patterns of female consuming behaviour are lost. Since data on mothers are ignored then we have no reliable basis for comparing behavioural changes throughout generations; for example, how different educational opportunities have changed perception of purchase decisions or the influence of the family. As it is. we have already lost much valuable information on female intergenerational social mobility. Blau and Duncan (1967)[15] note that social mobility patterns are based primarily on studies of white males and the social mobility of women is assumed to be attached to this like ivy on an oak tree. For example, Lopata (1971)[17] notes in a study on a sample of housewives: 'the occupational ranking of husbands of the women interviewed is generally higher than that of their fathers, thus the *women* had achieved upward social mobility.'

It is interesting that Lopata did not assume that the women might have achieved this mobility in their own right if, for example, mother to daughter mobility patterns had been used. How, furthermore, should one classify a situation where the daughter of a sales manager becomes a doctor and marries a clerk? In the existing system she has achieved downward mobility. The situation is further complicated if we include her mother's occupation who may be a housewife now but used to be, say, a nurse. In terms of her mother she has moved up. in terms of her father she has moved across. in terms of her husband she has also moved up. Yet. under the existing system she has undoubtedly moved down. With more and more women working, and not only in the more menial areas, this sort of farcical anomaly will become more prevalent until we find a way of assessing a woman's intergenerational patterns. whether of consumption or mobility, on grounds which relate to her own ability and that of both of her parents.

3. Domestic data about men are lost. As much as women are not asked for 'male' data on income. occupation and education. so men are not asked for 'female' data on domestic and child care. This ommision can only reinforce existing cultural prejudice on the 'domestic' orientation of women and will never accurately represent the changing contributions of men to household matters. Marketers are particularly guilty of this. To what extent in investigations of family behaviour do they ever ask about the contribution that men make to the housework and the care of their children? We have already shown that men are rarely depicted in advertisements as involving themselves in these areas so to what extent is this bias introduced at the data collection stage? Furthermore. to what extent is it a fault of the rigidity of stratification methods?

Steinmetz notes that in a classic study by Bloode and Wolfe (1960)[18] on the family, women were asked eighteen questions on their feelings about their children: one question was aimed jointly at the husband and wife but the husband, specifically. was asked nothing. She also notes that even where both partners were found to go out to work, there was still a tendency to ask only the mother about domestic and child-related matters.

4. Information on a woman as a buying unit suddenly dries up the moment she marries. The illogic of the present stratification system is that it assumes a woman ceases to exist only and when she ties the nuptial knot. From the moment she says 'I do' she disappears automatically from individual social view. Acker notes of this strange phenomenon:

> If |single| women do have such resources why do we assume that they are inoperative if the woman is married? It is inconsistent to rank an unmarried woman on the basis of her occupation and then maintain that these factors are of no importance to her social status or class placement after she gets married the next day.

If all women were rated according to their personal behavioural variables then this could not happen.

The Status of the Married Woman is Equal to that of her Husband

This final assumption is the one where the illogic plumbs new depths. For the sake of administrative convenience, the married woman, even though she works and especially when she is a housewife, is given a status equal to that of her husband. Outside of this system no one in their right mind would claim that a housewife had equal social status with her husband, no matter what he did, unless the status of his work was so low that comparison was inevitable, such as cleaning lavatories or sweeping roads. Even then, since this work is done by a man, it would still be perceived as somehow 'better' than housewifery which is 'woman's work'. Ennis (1974)[25], in a pamphlet on women's work (page 12). notes an unemployed man interviewed on Radio 1: 'I sometimes fill in time doing housework. But it's not man's work, is it? I mean, it's so boring, isn't it?'

It seems that lack of employment has greater status than housework employment. Thus, how can we assume that a woman's status is equal to that of her husband? Would it not be more useful to find a way of assessing housework in such a way as to give it a status of its own? Assumed homogeneous status is convenient, but contradictory. Acker notes:

> Equality can be assumed on numerous dimensions; style of life, privilege, oppor-tunities. income, education. Occupation, equated by the functionalists with full-time, functionally important social roles. is often used as an indicator of position for men. However, the full-time occupation of many women. that of housewife, is never considered as a ranking criterion in stratification studies.

Acker then asks a question which could be directed straight at the marketing and advertising industry:

> Are we to conclude that this role. |of housewife| is either not functionally important or not a full-time activity, or are we to conclude that only those activities which are directly rewarded financially can bestow status upon the individual or the family?

The marketer and the advertiser direct disproportionate attention to the housewife sector but do they, by their denial of her place in the stratification system, regard this role as not 'functionally important' in the sense that it is not 'financially important', or that it does not 'bestow status on the individual and the family'? If they agree with this, and it is difficult to see how they cannot, then is not their whole assertion through their advertising imagery and philosophy that 'the housewife is queen' totally hypocritical?

If they do regard the housewife as financially and functionally relevant, then they should start as soon as possible to look at some stratification systems which reflect this view more honestly than the systems that they use at present.

With the working, married woman and the professional woman, married or single, can we assume, however, that the status of the woman might have a greater chance of estimation in its own right or some greater approximation to husband's status? A study by Haavio-Mannila (1969)[19] suggested that we cannot. She tested the assumption that wives share the same status ranking as their husbands by comparing the ranks of men and women employed in certain occupations with the ranks assigned by a sample of respondents to the wives of men in these occupations. The data suggested that gender role *is* influential and women would be ranked lower than men and wives lowest of all. Thus, one can say that wives are not perceived as equal with their husbands even when they are *not* solely housewives and actually hold a professional status in their own right

Table 19:1   Mean Ranks of Male and Female Representatives of Modern Occupational Groups and Wives of Men in these Groups (Ranks Ordered on an 18-point Scale)

		Male	*Female*	*Wife*
2·4	Male architect	1		
2·8	Male psychologist	2		
3·7	Female architect		1	
4·2	Female psychologist		2	
6·6	Male advertising agency secretary	3		
7·2	Female advertising agency secretary		3	
8·9	Male student	4		
8·9	Wife of architect			1
9·3	Wife of psychologist			2
9·4	Female student		4	
10·6	Male furniture salesman	5		
11·6	Female furniture saleswoman		5	
12·8	Wife of advertising agency secretary			3
13·1	Male office messenger	6		
13·5	Wife of student		6	
13·9	Female office messenger			4
15·1	Wife of furniture salesman		6	
13·3	Office messenger's wife			6

Source: Haavio-Mannila (1969)[19].

(*see* Table 19:1). Oakley (1974)[20] also notes that this assumption is congruent with other parts of the social system such as the fact that 'reflected status' was not adequate for the married woman who wanted to fill in a hire-purchase agreement or who is treated as 'dependent' by the income tax system, whatever her own economic and social situation.

Finally, Oakley (1974)[20], using an ascribed status for the housewife, social status by occupation for the married woman and adaptations from the 1971 census, was able to draw up a table which put a numerical value to the percentages of wives whose social class was different from their husbands', thus making a direct challenge to the stratification systems which assume such equality.

She showed, for example, that women in the class (2) 'manual' grouping were most likely to have a social class similar to their husbands and those in class (1) least likely (*see* Table 19:2).

Table 19:2 Married Couples with Both Partners Economically Active, by Social Class of Husband and Wife (1971)

Husband's social class		Percentage of wives whose social class is different from husbands
1		93·8
2		66·2
3	non-manual	48·7
3	manual	87·8
4		63·5
5		77·6

Source: Oakley (1974)[20], adapted from 1971 census, 1% sample, summary tables, Great Britain, Table 36.

In conclusion, there are basic inequalities and absurdities in the existing social stratification system for women. In order to eradicate them, we should look at more personal variables associated with the woman's own life style and less at variables associated with her husband. In short, married women should be treated in a way which compares to the existing social stratification of single women and men. Factors which are worth examining are:

1. Her education level, type, aspirations and quality (including orientation: science, art, practical, etc.).
2. Any training, occupation or employment at the time of the interview.
3. Occupation before marriage. Time and conditions for returning to employment, if at all.
4. Age.
5. Number of children, ages, stage in their life cycle.
6. Attitudes toward work—housewife and full-time industrial etc.
7. Masculinity–femininity orientation.
8. Income before and after marriage. Differential by marrying.

9. Income, occupation and education of parents—particularly mother for behavioural factors, and father and mother for life-style habits.
10. Disposable income available for consumption behaviour by her.
11. Combined income of her and her husband, where applicable.
12. Combined or dominant occupational status.
13. Perceived real and observed actual household head on combined variables of above factors.

Until a system is introduced which takes advantage of these variables, information from existing data is wide open to bias and will tend to reflect the cultural assumptions about woman's place that the system subsumes.

At this point, it is particularly interesting to look at those new systems of marketing stratification which have been developed and it will be seen that already they have started to generate data which, since it is based directly on female response, is more colourful and sensitive in its portrayal of female consumer personality and behaviour than anything the present system has to offer.

LIFE STYLE AND PSYCHOGRAPHIC MARKET SEGMENTATION

These two areas of research are still in relative infancy as useful tools for segmenting and predicting female consumer behaviour. Nevertheless, their principle value lies in the fact that they measure the purchasing behaviour of women by measuring female variables.

Much of the pioneer work on 'life-style' research has been sponsored and developed by the Leo Burnett Advertising Agency. It has been available for many years in the United States but only really arrived in UK marketing as an alternative concept for segmenting the female market in the early 1970s. Basically, the idea is to measure the opinions, interests, occupations, income, education, and so forth, of the individual respondents, and then group these respondents into categories on the basis of life-style patterns which they share. These categories are then used to analyse, segment and predict purchasing behaviour in the same way that socio-economic variables of the female consumer's spouse attempt to do now.

The proponent of this system developed it from a recognition of the insensitivity of existing methods. *Retail Business* in a small note on the new system comments somewhat acidly that [21]:

> Certainly anyone who tries to build up a reliable picture of the British life-style of today from statistics such as the National Food Survey, national income data, advertising data and television audits, will agree that there is room for some realistic way of reflecting the social changes which have taken place within various groups in our society.

That this style of research should also change the resulting image of women projected by advertising media, simply because it reflects their profile more accurately, had been noted by Anthony Thorncroft in *Marketing* (November 1972). He said:

> For some time now mums in television commercials have been soppy, sentimental creatures locked in a cosy domestic cocoon. If the research boys can influence the creative teams in agencies this could soon change. For the passion now is for studies into life-styles rather than consumer wage packets, and as far as housewives are concerned, the research maintains that they are much tougher and more practical than the commercials suggest. They are also contemptuous of much advertising.

Dr. Simon Broadbent who pioneers this research in the UK and who works for Leo Burnett has always come out strongly against the class categories as accurate predictors of consumer behaviour. What was good enough for the sociologist could not be dragged wholesale into the marketing arena and told to work. The Leo Burnett Agency, as a result of this method, had already decided that housewives would not be patronised so much in television commercials, and that older people may get more attention as buyers of new brands.

The life-style method has already found seven clusters of women after interviews with over 3,400 women (they have them for men, too) and these are characterised by names such as 'Kathleen' and 'Joan' instead of the old C2 and DE grades. For example, there is 'Joan' who, among other things, is 'uncommitted and depressed, a grey woman without many enthusiasms; liable to headaches'. As many as 21% of British women are placed in this category, whose average age is 46. This obviously, as a starter, throws up the discrepancy between this method and the old one which allowed for no profile of the women in the class group and relied alarmingly on an image of the 'average housewife'. As Joseph Plummer notes in his review, (1974)[23] the value of life style research rests in its perspective:

> It begins with the people, their life styles and motivations—and then determines how various marketing factors fit into their lives. This perspective oftens provides fresh insights into the market and gives a more three-dimensional view of target consumers.

In a paper presented at the 55th International Marketing Congress in April 1973 Dr. Broadbent noted that one of the main values which originated from life-style research was that it did not assume anything about the female role. It asked women for their attitudes about being a housewife, (which many advertisers assume is an absolute scale of acceptance), their work and whether they enjoy it (advertisers assume they do), and what other work and income they have. It also assumes that women have widely differing scales of attitudes, beliefs and interests and a personality which is not homogeneous to the entire housewife population or to her husband. But do life-style criteria segment behaviour like the old methods did?

Broadbent was able to show in his paper that two or three segments can account for 60% or more of the total business in that market where the method is used, which relates to the old idea of 'heavy' and 'light' users and style of those users. It can also throw up differences between women consumers where none existed before. He cites one case where the market consisted of three closely allied product categories when analysed on traditional husband-based data. When the consumers were looked at on their own terms, however, three quite different categories were thrown up which has re-orientated the entire product positioning of that market. Obviously, seeing a market accurately, but differently, may mean whole new product, promotional, advertising and copy strategies as well as opportunities for new product and market segments.

The information on which life-style segments are based is set out in Table 19:3. Broadbent[22] justifies the more detailed investigation of markets on these factors with the observation that: 'The basic premise of life-style research is that the more you know and understand about your customer the more effectively you can communicate to them.'

Table 19:3   Table of Life Style Dimensions

ATTITUDES	INTERESTS	OPINIONS	DEMOGRAPHICS
*Work	*Family*	*Themselves	*Age
Hobbies	*Home*	*Social issues	Demographics
Social events	*Job	Politics	*Income*
Vacation	Community	Business	*Occupation*
Entertainment	Recreation	Economics	*Family size*
Club membership	Fashion	*Education	Dwelling
Community	Food	Products	Geographic
Shopping spots	*Media*	Future	City size
	*Achievements	*Culture	*Stage in life cycle*

Source: Broadbent (1968)[22].

Note: Those in italics indicate those variables which a marketer *might* have looked at before and those with asterisks are the variables which have been established in psychological theory as affecting individual behaviour patterns but which have been largely ignored by the marketer in his studies of the female consumer.

It is important to distinguish here between research methods based on the life-cycle theory and those based on 'psychographic data'. Psychographic stratification and segmentation uses various psychological variables to cluster different groups of people. Instead of Class C1, for example, there would be a group of people who shared positions on dimensions of, say, neuroticism, femininity, affiliation and aggression. There are many different measures of psychological personality variables and the tests for measuring them are of common usage in psychology. This is, however, an area much in its infancy and with many special problems. For example, psychological characteristics are often rich, but lack reliability when applied to a mass audience, and there are problems of large-scale measurement.

Ruth Ziff (1971)[24] made one of the few published analyses of this method in recent years when she reported a study by Benton and Bowles which classified housewives into six 'psychographic' categories which were very similar to those in life-style segmentation. These were the 'outgoing optimists', the 'conscientious vigilants', the 'apathetic indifferents', the 'self indulgents', the 'contented cows' and the 'worriers'. For example, the 'apathetic indifferents' were 'not outgoing, involved with family, irritable, had a negative grooming orientation, were lazy, especially in terms of cooking pride'. The 'outgoing optimists' were 'outgoing, innovative, community-orientated, positive towards grooming, not bothered by delicate health or digestive problems or especially concerned about germs or cleanliness'. The links between this segmentation and purchase rates of certain products were that, for example, 'worriers' were the biggest purchasers of 'liquid cold remedies', and 'contented cows' were least likely to buy 'hangover remedies'.

(There are two criticisms, however, which can be levelled at these results. The first is that these are not 'pure' psychographic categories because they do not relate to established psychological variables. The second is that they do tend to fall into somewhat stereotyped appraisals of female behaviour so that 'vigilants' are categorised by 'high cooking pride'.)

In conclusion, we have shown that the existing system of stratifying the female consumer market, which is based principally on socio-economic data from the respondent's husband, is ambiguous, inaccurate and generates special absurdities. Since it is based on certain prejudicial and patriarchial assumptions about women's place, we have shown that it is also capable of producing data which reinforces negative cultural stereotypes of women.

If the marketer wishes to generate data on a stratification system which avoids these sources of bias he should investigate systems which rely on more direct data from the woman herself, and we have seen that one such system which may offer scope in the future is that of life-style segmentation.

As a postscript to this chapter, however, it is interesting to note a remark on female market segmentation by Franchielli Cadwell, President of the Cadwell Compton Advertising Agency, who has consistently championed the cause of more enlightened market stratification systems for women. She predicts that:

> Free to express themselves, women are veering off in dozens of new ways. Neither will the old standbys, age and income, any longer tip off how she will act ...

> With new money and self-confidence women discriminate among the products on a new basis, there is a more intellectual buying process.

Which is perhaps how it has always been, except that we are just learning how to spot it now.

CONCLUSION TO PART VII

Marketing research, the good friend, the innocuous partner of marketing has been too smug for too long. If marketers are going to rely on this sector for accurate reporting of female consumer behaviour in the future then they, very quickly, must take a long hard look at the methods that the researchers employ, the expectations they hold and the enviroment in which women are interviewed.

No-one would question the sophistication of the marketing researchers methods and few would argue with the elegance of their statistics. Yet, the same people are demonstrating a myopic and indulgent naïvety about the context of their research to an extent that they would not, in relative terms, tolerate in their numerology. Any changes in the marketing research enviroment is, however, to a large extent in the hands of the marketers. If they want the female consumer to reflect a creation of the researchers then they can go ahead. It is their money and their waste.

The question is, of course, do the marketers, any more than the researchers, really want to know the truth about the female consumer?

Or do they all feel considerably more comfortable in a twilight world which is only truthful to a point and beyond that point supports everything they would rather hear?

Is that marketing contentment merely the result of blissful but chosen ignorance?

REFERENCES

1. Michael Kahan, David Butler and Donald Stokes, 'On the Analytical Division of Social Class', *European Market Research Review*, Vol. 2 (1967).
2. John Hall and D. Caradog Jones, 'Social Grading of Occupations', *British Journal of Sociology*, Vol. 1 (1) (March 1950), pp. 31–49.
3. Lionel S. Lewis, 'A Note on the Problem of Class', *Public Opinion Quarterly*, Vol. 27 (1963), pp. 599–603.
4. Chester R. Wasson, 'Is it Time to Quit Thinking of Income Classes?', *Journal of Marketing*, Vol. 33 (April 1969), pp. 54–69.
5. Stuart U. Rich and Subash Jain, 'Social Class and Life Cycle as Predictors of Shopping Behaviour', *Journal of Marketing Research*, Vol. V (February 1968), pp. 41–9.
6. F. M. Martin, 'Some Subjective Aspects of Social Stratification', in D. V. Glass (ed.), *Social Mobility in Britain*, Routledge & Kegan Paul (London 1954), p. 55.
7. Suzanne K. Steinmetz, 'The Sexual Context of Social Research', *The American Sociologist*, Vol. 9 (August 1974), pp. 111–16.
8. Sir William Blackstone, *Commentaries on the Laws of England* (1765), chapter headed 'Of Husband and Wife'.
9. Joseph N. Fry and Frederick H. Siller, 'A Comparison of Housewife Decision Making in Two Social Classes', *Journal of Marketing Research*, Vol. VII (August 1970), pp. 333–7.
10. Valerie Kincade Oppenheimer, 'The Sex-Labelling of Jobs', *Industrial Relations*, 7 (May 1968), pp. 219–34.
11. Everett C. Hughes, 'Social Change and Status Protest: An essay on the marginal man', *Phylon* (10) (first Quarter 1949), pp. 58–65.

12. Gerhard Lenski, *Power and Privilege*, McGraw-Hill (New York 1966).
13. Joan Acker, 'Women and Social Stratification: A case of intellectual sexism', in Joan Huber (ed.) *Changing Women in a Changing Society*, The University of Chicago Press (London 1973), and in *American Journal of Sociology*, Vol. 78(4) (January 1973).
14. Walter B. Watson and Ernest A. Barth. 'Questionable Assumptions in the Theory of Social Stratification'. *Pacific Sociological Review* (7) (Spring 1964), pp. 10–16.
15. Peter M. Blau and Otis Dudley Duncan. *The American Occupational Structure*, John Wiley and Sons (New York 1967).
16. Alfred C. Kinsey, Wardell B. Pomeroy and Clyde E. Martin. *Sexual Behaviour in the Human Male*, W. B. Saunders (Philadelphia 1948), and Kinsey, Pomeroy. Martin and Paul H. Gebbhard, *Sexual Behaviour in the Human Female*, W. B. Saunders (Philadelphia 1953).
17. Helen Z. Lopata, *Occupation: Housewife*. Oxford University Press (New York 1971).
18. Robert O. Bloode Jr. and Donald M. Wolfe. *Husbands and Wives*, Free Press (New York 1960).
19. E. Haavio-Mannila. 'Some Consequences of Women's Emancipation'. *Journal of Marriage and the Family* (31) (February 1969), pp. 123–34.
20. Ann Oakley. *The Sociology of Housework*, Martin Robertson (1974), p. 10.
21. *Retail Business*, 175 (September 1972), Marketing Review, p. 3.
22. Dr. Simon Broadbent. *Life-Style and Psychographics* (uses of Leo Burnett life-style segmentation). Leo Burnett (London, June 1972).
23. Joseph T. Plummer. 'The Concept and Application of Life-Style Segmentation', *Journal of Marketing*, Vol. 38 (January 1974), pp. 33–7.
24. Ruth Ziff, 'Psychographics for Market Segmentation'. *Journal of Advertising Research*, Vol. I (2) (April 1971), pp. 3–9.
25. Kath Ennis. 'Women Fight Back', (Women's Voice and the International Socialists) (1973–4).

The Female Consumer—a Final Note

It is a moot point whether a book on the female consumer could be definitive at a time when women generally, let alone women as buyers, are undergoing what is only the tip of a major change which few fully comprehend and the final effects of which we can only begin to speculate on.

Nothing is certain. It is even possible that we should find in 1985 an edition of 'The Male Consumer' which subsumes for men everything we now attribute to women in this edition.

Thus, while this investigation of woman as buyer has been relatively catholic, it is by no means exhaustive. It would have been possible to cover the same proportion of ground again but with other data, other angles, other facts. What have been covered have been those areas which the author considered to be ripe for summary or crying out for criticism.

Nevertheless, no matter how we observe the women buyer, we must note that the relationship between her and the marketing industry is certain to undergo some fundamental and exciting changes. We must also note, unfortunately, that the timing of these changes will probably depend to a larger extent on the resistance of the marketing industry than the potential for change in women which, on political and historical analyses, is largely inexorable.

If, however, the marketing industry can accept the fact of this change, then perhaps the observations and suggestions made in this book will be perceived as useful to some future policy. If, in addition, it challenges the assumptions of one reader, whether in or out of the industry, forces a different image of the female consumer into the set of variables with which the reader is working, then, it will, to some extent, have achieved its purpose.

To conclude, however, we must note that the female consumer is an enigma we have known 'not wisely, but too well'. The problem is, the time has run out when we could get away with doing so.

Author Index

Achenbaum, A. A., 263
Acker, J., 327, 331
Adams, J. R., 268, 269, 273
Alexander, J., 173
Alexander, R. A., 261
Allen, S., 307
Allen, V. C., 305
Anderson, W. T., 103
Anker, J. H., 304
Appel, D. L., 62, 65
Appel, V., 84
Arndt, J., 101
Aronson, E., 303
Athey, K. R., 307
Attenborough, B., 175

Back, K., 119, 120
Baker, M. J., 268, 269, 271
Bales, R. F., 120, 121
Ballachey, E. L., 305
Banos, J. B., 224, 225, 228, 230, 233, 234, 280, 286
Barban, A., 288
Bardwick, J. M., 224, 233, 237, 239
Barron, N., 82
Bart, P., 275, 276
Barth, E. A., 327, 328
Bass, B. M., 261
Bauer, R. A., 104
Becker, G., 306
Behnke, A. R., 185
Berey, L. A., 145, 146, 147, 148
Berger, P., 291
Bettelheim, B., 312
Biller, H. B., 247
Billson, A. 92
Binder, A., 307
Birdwell, A. E., 97, 287, 288
Birdwhistell, 304

Blackstone, Sir W., 324
Blackwell, R., 77, 91, 95, 99, 101, 102, 151, 268, 269, 273
Blau, P. M., 329, 330
Bloode, R. O., 121, 330
Blum, M. L., 84
Boyd, H. W., 94
Brandsma, P., 308
Britt, S. H., 95
Broadbent, Dr. S., 335, 336
Broverman, I. K., 95, 312
Brown, R., 160
Bruner, J. S., 302
Bucklin, L. P., 7
Burdus, A., 229, 230
Butler, D., 323
Byrne, D., 302

Cadet, A., 224
Cadwell, F., 265
Cagley, J. W., 287, 288
Caldwell, F., 337
Cardozo, R. N., 287, 288
Carlson, E. R., 317
Carlson, R., 317
Carman, J. M., 98
Carter, R. E., 309
Catton, W. R., 224
Cedar, S., 259
Charlton, P., 64, 66, 67
Cheskin, L., 83
Chesler, P., 249, 311
Chiu, L. M., 241
Christie, 305
Christopher, M., 70, 72, 73, 75
Clancy, K. J., 303
Cohen, R. S., 315
Coleman, J., 101
Coleman, R., 91

341

Subject Index

347